XEROX

AMERICAN SAMURAI

Dantotsu is a Japanese word for striving to be the "best of the best." We Americans have no such word, perhaps because we've always assumed we were the best. As Xerox has discovered, we can't assume that anymore.

XEROX
AMERICAN SAMURAI

Gary Jacobson

John Hillkirk

COLLIER BOOKS

MACMILLAN   PUBLISHING   COMPANY

New York

Macmillan Publishing Company
866 Third Avenue, New York, N.Y. 10022
Collier Macmillan Canada, Inc.

Library of Congress Cataloging-in-Publication Data

Jacobson, Gary.
Xerox, American samurai.

Includes index.
1. Xerox Corporation.   2. Copying machine industry—
United States.   3. Competition, International.
I. Hillkirk, John.   II. Title.
[HD9802.3.U64X475   1987b]   338.7′68644   86-31009
ISBN 0-02-033830-9 (pbk.)

Macmillan books are available at special discounts for bulk purchases
for sales promotions, premiums, fund-raising, or educational use.
For details, contact:

Special Sales Director
Macmillan Publishing Company
866 Third Avenue
New York, N.Y. 10022

10 9 8 7 6 5 4 3 2 1

First Collier Books Edition 1987

Printed in the United States of America

Contents

v

PART FOUR · RECOGNITION

PART FIVE · THE NEW XEROX

Preface

It was quite a sight. Five grown men—two six-foot-tall American writers and three short Japanese businessmen—squeezing into a Japanese taxi. But it was late and only a short ride to our destination, the Toride train station about thirty-five miles outside Tokyo. Reiji Shirahase, a Canon director and Ami plant manager, wanted us to see something special: the home of a Japanese factory manager. Shirahase's home turned out to be a 780-square-foot, three-room apartment in a brick highrise next to the train station. Shirahase lives there weekdays. Every Monday morning he takes an hour and a half train ride from his family home on the west side of Tokyo to Toride, leaving his wife and two daughters behind. Friday evenings he returns to his family. The apartment cost 27 million yen (about $130,000) but by American standards it was cold and somewhat bleak with bright white fluorescent lights and a heater under a living room table to keep the feet warm. Shirahase amused us with his putting green, a long strip of green artificial turf with a hole in the end. He offered Jack Daniels and White Horse Scotch, American peanuts, and canned Alaskan king crab meat. He played a tape, "Only the Lonely" by Bobby Vinton, he had picked up in the United States in the 1960s and showed vacation pictures from Canada. He obviously enjoyed having company, but he missed his family. Like us, he felt as if he were a long way from home.

We'd come 7,000 miles to see things relatively few Americans have ever seen before. "Generally speaking, we keep things classified," said Canon's Keizo Yamaji, chief executive for copiers. "For you, we disclose everything. You are very unusual visitors. And you were shown many places we don't show."

We spent nearly a month in Japan, conducting more than a hundred interviews and touring the factories of Canon, Ricoh, Fuji Xerox, Toshiba, Sharp, Fuji Photo, Minolta, and Konishiroku. We also conducted another 180 interviews and toured Xerox and Kodak factories in Europe and the United States. Xerox was especially cooperative. Wayland Hicks, head of copier development and manufacturing, allowed co-author Gary Jacobson to travel with him on a review of Xerox's European facilities. Xerox had never done anything like that before. It was a rare opportunity for an outsider to get an insider's view of how one of the largest corporations in the world works. Jacobson was also granted a series of three long interviews with Xerox patriarch C. Peter McColough and several sessions with chairman and chief executive David Kearns. Altogether, we interviewed twelve of the thirty-six executive officers of Xerox and most of the top managers at Fuji Xerox, including the president, Yotaro "Tony" Kobayashi.

Why was Xerox, with no control over the form or content of this book, so cooperative? Basically because the company thinks it has a good story to tell. Having been effectively gagged for ten years by antimonopoly actions, Xerox workers at all levels seemed to welcome the chance to talk about the New Xerox and its renewed attacks on IBM, Kodak, and "Japan Incorporated." Their objective has become an obsession: Beat the Japanese at their own game.

We first became interested in Xerox during its massive job-cutting program in 1981. We were both covering the company for the Rochester *Times-Union*. That's when we started to see the painful transformation a company and its people have to go through to regain a competitive edge. In 1983, when Xerox regained market share for the first time in more than a decade, we knew it was onto something, not only for itself, but for other companies as well. Xerox's strategy could serve as a blueprint for corporations everywhere that were trying to survive in a highly competitive world. It was clear that if Xerox couldn't make it, the prospects were bleak for all of American industry.

Neither Xerox nor its fierce Japanese rivals had asked for government subsidies, trade barriers, or voluntary import quotas. For this reason we see the battle as a paradigm, an excellent example of the competitive struggle between the United States and Japan today. Xerox, perhaps more than any other American company, is involved in pure competition against the Japanese. The plain paper copier industry pits three of the finest American companies—Xerox, Kodak, and IBM—against each other and against six of Japan's most successful—Canon, Sharp, Toshiba, Minolta, Ricoh, and Matsushita (Panasonic). The prize: Worldwide control of a $25-billion industry.

The factory tours were a rare treat. At one time, years ago, Japanese and American copier plants were relatively open to visitors.

"Japanese used to come through here with their cameras all the time," says Xerox's Paul Regensburger. "They'd say, 'Oh, look, we have to get one of those, one of these.' A year or two later, they'd come through again. One would be about to take a picture and another would say, 'No, you don't have to. We already have one of those.' "

So Xerox closed its doors and so did the Japanese. Rarely do outsiders get a glimpse of a Canon or Fuji Xerox factory.

Copier companies closely guard their information. No one releases machine sales reports every ten days, as they do in the auto industry. The Japanese companies release annual production information to the Japanese government, but that's as detailed as it gets. There is no precise breakdown for copier models, and you can't tell from the reports whether the machines are on a boat, in a warehouse, in a dealer's showroom, or at the customer's site. Not even Dataquest, the top number-crunching research firm for the copier industry, has been able to pin down market shares for plain paper copiers in Japan. "Everybody is guessing about the numbers," says Dale Kredatus, an analyst for Data Decisions, a New Jersey research firm. "Nobody knows for sure except the vendor, and he's not telling anyone."

Xerox is usually even more secretive. It rarely discusses its production numbers publicly, and never talks about its copier placements or market share. Although we were able to break through that secrecy while preparing this book, we still met some resistance. For example, Fuji Xerox would not disclose how many of its landmark model 3500 copiers had been produced, even though the machine was introduced in 1978 and is no longer in production.

We have tried to make clear in this book whether our information comes from the companies themselves, officially or unofficially, or other industry sources, such as analysts and vendors.

The competition in copiers is so fierce, and the detective work so sophisticated, that Ricoh doesn't even field test its machines anymore, such is the fear that they will be discovered by competitors. Even photocopies made on new machines are treated like trade secrets. Xerox destroyed millions of test copies it ran on the 1075.

Not to miss a trick, Japanese and American managers and engineers frequently pumped us about their competitor's factories: How many copiers are they producing? How does our factory compare to theirs? Our answer: Read the book.

Authors' Note

One of the risks of writing a contemporary industrial history in book form is the possibility of its quickly becoming outdated. Change is a fact of business life, especially in today's global marketplace. But as more and more of America's corporate and political leaders take up the battle cry of competitiveness, the story of how Xerox continues to regain its dominance in a mature industry like photocopiers becomes even more significant as a trail marker for all of American industry. The fundamental process of change that the company began in 1980 continues, with success, today.

"The quality process is working," Xerox chairman and chief executive Dave Kearns said during an interview in early 1987. "In fact, the tougher or dirtier a problem is, the more politics involved, the better the process works. Our managers can't make arbitrary decisions anymore."

Other companies have since embarked on the same tough course toward quality and competitiveness: IBM, General Motors, Eastman Kodak, and AT&T. Kimberly-Clark, the maker of Kleenex tissue and Huggies diapers, started a quality process at its factories in 1982 and is now taking that same process into its offices. In a unique approach to corporate education, the company even closed down its world headquarters in Dallas one day in early 1987 and put all 115 employees on buses to its Paris, Texas, diaper plant. "When people think of quality, they normally just think of the factory," said Kimberly-Clark chief Darwin Smith, who led the tour. "But the people at Paris have demonstrated that quality extends to every facet of everyday work life."

How well these companies and others succeed in streamlining their organizations, so they can develop and deliver new and higher-quality products faster and more efficiently, will ultimately determine the future economic health and prosperity of the United States.

xi

A few pertinent updates need to be made since the hardcover edition of this book was published in May 1986:

- Xerox gained overall market share in copiers during 1986, a tough year for nearly all manufacturers of office equipment. Company executives also expect market share increases in 1987.
- Wayland Hicks, who heads worldwide copier development and manufacturing, has taken on the same additional duties for most of Xerox's office systems business. He is now an executive vice president of the company and lives in Connecticut.
- Dwight Ryan, who headed the U.S. marketing group in Rochester, New York, now lives in California and heads a new special-markets group, which will focus on improving, among other areas, the company's sales through independent dealers and other alternate channels.
- Paul Allaire, a former managing director of Rank Xerox and chief staff officer in the Stamford headquarters, became president of Xerox in September 1986.

—GARY JACOBSON
JOHN HILLKIRK

February 1987

PART ONE
XEROX TODAY

1

An American
Strategy

RAMSEY, N.J.—Minolta vice president Atseo Kusada was remembering, with a great deal of pride, how he and his Japanese competitors (Canon, Ricoh, Konishiroku) came to rule the world's 35mm camera industry. At one time, he said, "It appeared that we could kill Xerox, too. Now I don't think so . . . now I don't think so. Japanese people don't talk about it, but Xerox is taking more and more market share back."

XEROX CHAIRMAN and CEO David Kearns used to say ours would be the first generation of Americans not to pass on a better life to its children. The United States had, quite simply, forgotten how to compete, especially against the Japanese.

Now Kearns has changed his mind. "I think we *will* pass on a better life," he says. He wants Xerox to be remembered as the first company to beat the Japanese at their own game. He and his company are doing just that by becoming the first American company to regain market share against the Japanese. Chrysler wants government protection. Motorola wants a 20 percent tariff on Japanese products. Xerox doesn't want help from anybody.

"We don't believe in protectionism," says Peter McColough, former Xerox chairman who now chairs the company's executive committee.

From 1976 to 1982, Xerox's share of worldwide copier revenues dropped by half, from 82 to 41 percent. Japanese companies, led by Canon, Minolta, Ricoh, and Sharp, were mostly responsible. The 10 Series of Xerox copiers, introduced in 1982, stopped this decline. Using plants in Japan, Europe, and the United States, but relying primarily upon a strategy made in America, Xerox stopped its slide and increased its market share by two or three points in 1983. Those gains continued in

3

1984 and 1985. In 1984 alone, Xerox regained more than a dozen points in the key middle range where it makes most of its money, climbing to more than 30 percent.

The 10 Series, first shipped in volume in late 1983, is the most successful new copier line in history. By the end of 1985, more than 750,000 machines had been rented or sold and accounted for nearly 38 percent of the world's 2 million-plus Xerox machines in use. The 1075, built in Webster, New York, was the first Xerox copier "Made in America" and shipped into Japan. And it was the first American-made product to win the Japanese Grand Prize for Good Design. Benny Landa, technical wizard for Savin, a Xerox competitor, said, "The 1075 really set the standard for quality. We gave it a 10."

The 10 Series revitalized the company's financial outlook and its battered morale. When the machines were introduced, employees at Webster chartered a plane trailing a huge illuminated banner that said, "We did it!" Union members asked for a new label on the 1075: "Made in the United States. Made by union people."

"That's how proud they are," said Tony Costanza, union manager. United States Marines accompanying President Reagan on a trip to China cheered when 10 Series copiers, packed in cartons painted red, white, and blue, were unloaded from air force planes.

"We Americans are the kind of people that you can leave us, you can slap us, you can kick us around until you get us to the point where we're going to fight back," said Paul Charlap, former chairman of Savin, who was responsible for developing and introducing the first quality Japanese-made plain paper copiers to the United States. "And, man, you better watch out. Xerox is going to shock the hell out of everybody. Can we compete with Japan? You betcha we can. You betcha we can. And Xerox is proving it."

TOKYO—The rays of the afternoon sun, pleasantly warm on a cool day in January, shone through a picture window at Canon's headquarters, illuminating half of Hiroshi Tanaka's impassive face.

"Your counterpart at Xerox, Wayland Hicks, is traveling through Europe trying to wake Xerox people up, make them understand the competitive battle they're in," Tanaka was told. "Do you do that?"

For the first time in two hours Tanaka grinned. "No, I don't, because we Japanese, we are always awake."

But word of Hicks's crusade worried him.

"Who is this Mr. Wayland? For if they [Xerox] are now awake, then tremendous things will happen."

It's difficult to believe these days, in a world dominated by multinational conglomerates, that individuals or small groups held together by personal friendships, make any difference. Yet that's what the copier industry is all about. Individuals from all corners of the globe—some virtual unknowns, others drawing six-figure salaries—were directly responsible for the rise, the fall, and eventual resurrection of Xerox:

- **Chester Carlson,** an American who hated the inconvenience and inaccuracies caused by retyping patent applications, came up with a method to make plain paper copies; a technology no one else wanted, not even IBM.
- **Joe Wilson,** president of a tiny Rochester, New York, firm took a risk, changed his firm's name to Xerox, built the 914 copier, and made fortunes for himself and Carlson, much of it given away. The 914 eventually became the single most profitable product in American history.
- **Robert Metcalfe,** an Australian, came up with a cheaper, more energy-efficient way to make photocopies. **Paul Charlap** took Metcalfe's work and personally orchestrated an effort by 250 people on four continents to unseat Xerox with Japanese-made machines.
- **Haruo Murase,** a native of Japan, postponed a move home in 1978 to take over Canon's sagging American copier business. By 1982, Canon was placing more copiers in the United States than any other company.

Despite the hundreds of millions of dollars spent on research and product development in the industry today, individual effort still makes a difference.

HANOVER, West Germany—On a perfect spring day, 400,000 Europeans, Americans, and Japanese maneuvered 60,000 cars into the site of the Hanover Fair, the world's largest trade show. Their primary mission: Buy and sell copiers. Inside, seventy-four companies, from the world's most dominant (IBM and Kodak of the United States; Sharp, Toshiba, and Matsushita of Japan; Hoechst of Germany; and Olivetti of Italy) to its most obscure (Iberica De Reprograafia, Tomoegawa, Transimex) clamored for international attention. Every fifteen minutes, Toshiba ran a magic show, handing out free binoculars to anyone stopping to watch. A curtain, roped off and surrounded by security guards, concealed the prototype of their digital color copier. Ricoh baited passersby with 3-D holograms and a one-act play. Canon boasted that it was the "best of the best" in ads stripped on the doors of hundreds of Mercedes taxis. Meanwhile, professional snoops from Xerox and the other copier companies went about their scouting missions, collecting sample copies and eavesdropping on the latest product pitches.

It's easy to look at the copier sitting in the corner of your office or library and think, "Uggh! What a boring machine." Plunk the paper down and most of the time it spits out a fairly decent copy. But tucked inside that machine is, arguably, some of the world's most sophisticated technology: chemical, electronic, optical, and mechanical science wrapped in one box.

"You have to think of a copier as a small chemical plant running inside a box," says John Shoch, a Ph.D. in computer science who was president of Xerox's Office Systems Division and is now a partner in a venture capital firm. "Because of the heat it generates and the speed you want it to run at, you are always working with a process that is overconstrained. For engineers, it's a tremendous technical and intellectual challenge."

Complex, "like the human body," says Zene Kumagai, a director of Konishiroku.

The Xerox 9900, for example, contains ten microprocessors, each one as powerful as a small personal computer. Developing a high-speed copier can cost nearly as much as a new jet fighter and take even longer—it took Eastman Kodak more than a dozen years to go from a working engineer's model to its first commercial Ektaprint copier—and yet a copier has to be simple to understand so that anyone in a modern office can use it.

"A copier can't be something that you have to have a triple E to operate," says IBM's Proctor Houston. "The challenge is not only how to capture this technology but also how to express it in a way that is going to be friendly for the user."

That humdrum box, and others like it, make 2.5 billion copies a day—that's nearly ten copies per day for every U.S. resident. And that's just the beginning. In the near future, the digital copier/printer will be the heart of office communications. Not only will it print on paper, but it will convert images to computer form, then transmit the information to computers and other printers upstairs, downstairs, across the United States, or around the world.

WASHINGTON, D.C.—W. Edwards Deming, the most important American behind Japan's success, is understandably cynical about America's future. "Were it not for agriculture, we'd be in major trouble right now. We need a total change in style, but it's not taking place. The Japanese, meanwhile, are continuing to go faster and faster. If we don't change, we'll be an agrarian society."

The U.S. trade deficit in 1985 surpassed $140 billion; larger than the federal budget twenty years ago. A third, or $50 billion, of the deficit was the result of our trade with Japan.

Electronics is now the United States's biggest manufacturing employer; more Americans are building computers, telephones, copiers, and electronic equipment than are making cars. Yet in 1984, for the first time ever, the United States imported more electronics products than it exported. On the whole, the country lost market share in seven out of ten high-technology markets. At one time there were twenty-five companies manufacturing television sets in the U.S. Now there's only two: RCA and Zenith. No American company makes VCRs, videocameras, digital audio disc players, 35mm cameras, or car stereos. IBM's Personal Computer is a great success, but only the case and some computer chips are American-made.

Detroit's big comeback is partly an illusion. Until April 1985, American carmakers were protected by voluntary import restraints that boosted sticker prices both for Japanese-made cars, and American cars. Those voluntary quotas have since been eased, but they still exist. Auto analyst John Hammond says that, without quotas, it would take the Japanese three years to knock Ford, GM, and Chrysler out of the small car business.

ROCHESTER, N.Y.—In 1981, Xerox president David Kearns called in twenty-four of his top people, mostly a new wave of vice presidents, from all parts of the company, even Fuji Xerox in Japan. In the first of two week-long sessions, Kearns told them that he wanted to know, no holds barred, what Xerox had to do—reorganize, restructure, or whatever—to turn the company around.

"He felt we were stagnant, that we took too long to do almost everything," recalls Wayland Hicks. "And he was determined that if we didn't change that, we would not survive."

Hicks was asked whether the situation was that serious.

"I absolutely think so. Could we have hung on longer? Yes. Six months wouldn't have killed us. Even a year wouldn't have killed us. But each day we would have been weaker."

The 1960s were the boom years for Xerox and the rest of American industry. At that time, Xerox held the record for reaching $1 billion in sales faster than any company in American history. "We were able to sell almost everything we made at whatever price we wanted to charge for it," Kearns said. Riding that wave, Xerox privately considered buying Control Data, Burroughs, and Digital Equipment Corporation.

However, sometime around 1969, the Golden Era of American industry died. And Xerox, as America's Cinderella business story, died, too. McColough believes you learn in life mostly by making mistakes, and during the 1970s Xerox made plenty of them. The company ignored the Japanese threat, concentrating instead on besting Kodak and IBM. It built huge layers of bureaucracy, and wasted millions developing products, such as the world's first personal computer, that never reached the marketplace. The old American strategy of throwing people at problems, and raising prices as costs went up, just couldn't compete against the Japanese. But it took Xerox almost ten years to recognize that.

The company was like a sick old man too proud to see a doctor. Occasionally, its health improved, creating a false sense of security. People weren't worried. Profits were jumping $100 million a year. Xerox needed a crisis to shake it out of its dream world.

"Hell, it's simple to issue an order, but I can tell you, in a company of 100,000 people, things don't work that way," said McColough. "Only when they saw it was necessary, that their jobs were on the line, other people's jobs were on the line, did they respond."

It wasn't until 1980 that Xerox finally realized just how good its Japanese competitors were. "We were horrified to find that the Japanese were selling their small machines for what it cost us to make ours," Kearns said. "Our costs were not only way out in left field, they weren't even in the ballpark. Let me tell you, that was scary, and it woke us up in a hurry."

Xerox, at that point and during a subsequent job-cutting program, could have blamed the Japanese government, the strong dollar, or a conspiracy by its Japanese competitors. McColough and Kearns could have asked for government protection. They never even considered it.

"American business," said Kearns, "has got to stop blaming government for its problems. There are other reasons why we're falling behind."

The basic fact is that the Japanese are taking over American industries, "because they are damn good," McColough said. "No real excuses. They have done a helluva job."

Since those crucial 1981 meetings, Xerox has done thousands of little things to improve the company. But these ten factors have been the main driving forces behind the turnaround:

1. **Competitive Benchmarking.** Xerox swallowed its pride, admitting that others (especially the Japanese) might have a better way of doing things, and sent investigative teams on worldwide scouting missions to find out. Benchmarking can help determine not only the cheapest sources for quality parts, but the best manufacturing and service methods. Xerox even examined L. L. Bean's distribution methods to see what it could adapt. "Before 1981, I guess we thought we always had it right," said Paul Regensburger, Xerox's benchmarking manager.

2. **Pushing Responsibility Down.** Small teams of product designers and engineers are now almost completely responsible for conceiving products, developing them, and following them through to the manufacturing stage and into the market. No more endless layers of bureaucracy leading to endless product reviews that do nothing but slow projects down interminably and raise their cost.

3. **More Emphasis on Market Research.** Xerox uses such sophisticated techniques as surveys, videotapes, and observation through one-way mirrors to find out what customers really want and need so they can provide it.

4. **A Rallying Point.** For Xerox, it was the 10 Series. The new line of copiers helped re-create some of the fighting spirit the company had during the days of the 914.

5. **Driving Technology.** According to Dataquest analyst Monica Camahort, Xerox's 10 Series is so sophisticated, it's difficult for the Japanese to mass-produce. "So technology stops the Japanese from taking advantage with their automated plants." The electronics on the 1075, for example, were designed to remain state of the art for a decade.

6. **Internationalization.** Xerox's marketing presence in a hundred countries, and manufacturing presence on four continents, especially Fuji Xerox in Japan, gives it a major advantage over smaller Japanese competitors. Xerox can design products on a worldwide basis right from the start and introduce those products quicker. Says Michael Porter, a Harvard Business School professor and member of Presi-

dent Reagan's Commission on Industrial Competitiveness, "Before, Xerox had a country-centered strategy. Now they're doing world-wide sourcing, they've split up the product line and they're manufacturing in different parts of the world. Now they have a global strategy."

7. **Just-in-Time Manufacturing.** Xerox reduced its parts vendors from 5,000 to 400. It balances the advantages of lower-cost sources overseas with the timely deliveries of local vendors. Defect-free parts are now the rule. The company reduced copier parts inventory levels by $240 million and automated its parts warehouses. Its efforts in this area earned *Purchasing* magazine's Medal of Excellence in 1985.

8. **Automation and Computerization.** Wherever possible and cost-effective, Xerox has modernized its operation. It even has some vendors tied to its own CAD systems so that Xerox engineers can make a design change, push a button, and transmit the change right to the vendor's computer.

9. **Moving Faster.** Xerox has to step up the pace because the industry is. Product lives are becoming shorter so product development must accelerate, as well as product launches and introductions. That means Xerox has taken control of its manufacturing processes to assure that the first machines of any new model are of the highest reliability and quality.

10. **Emphasis on Quality.** For Xerox, this is synonymous with focusing on the customer. The company defines quality as conformance to customer requirements, whether those customers are external, a *Fortune* 500 company leasing 1,000 copiers, or internal, a secretary typing a report for a manager. Xerox no longer inspects quality into its products, it designs quality in. By 1987, all 100,000 Xerox employees around the world will have gone through up to forty-eight hours of training in Leadership Through Quality, a program that emphasizes the prevention of defects and meeting customer expectations. Kearns thinks this is the single most important effort the company has ever made. By emphasizing quality, Xerox thinks it can grow to be a $30-billion-a-year company by 1992.

NEW YORK—April 30, 1985. It was a million-dollar show to herald the introduction of ten new office systems products, including laser printers, personal computers, and workstations. Xerox rented the Vivian Beaumont Theater at Lincoln Center. The curtain went up on a stage set up in a series of offices filled with Xerox equipment. In the morning, more than 150 reporters, including one from *Reader's Digest*, showed up for a press conference that was also televised live to 15,000 Xerox employees and another 2,000 customers in nine U.S. cities and Toronto. Dave Kearns was there with vice chairman Bill Glavin, marketing head Dwight Ryan, and systems chief Bob Adams. In the afternoon, Wall Street analysts saw the same show, and that night, more Xerox employees. The rest of the week, customers. Glavin said: "Today is to our systems business what the introduction of the 10 Series was to our copier/duplicator business." At lunch, Ryan was ebullient. He had just received the April sales report from his office in Rochester and he liked the numbers. His sales force was now responsible for selling all of the company's systems products as well as its copiers. "You know, it's exciting being in competition," he said. "That may sound odd coming from a guy with my background in a monopoly, but it is. And you know why? Because we will be able to see it all played out in the next four or five years. We'll be able to see if our strategy was right. If it was any good. That's exciting." Ryan was asked if, despite Xerox's new success, the days of 20 percent-plus profit margins were gone for good? Was the world getting so competitive that everyone would be sliding toward Japanese-style returns of 5 to 6 percent? Would Xerox ever again earn an operating profit (before taxes, interest, and general corporate charges) on its copier business of almost $1.4 billion, as it did in 1981? Ryan paused. "Those are tough questions that deserve some thought. I'm not going to talk specific numbers, but we have some advantages now that we never had before. If we do our job right. . . ." Ryan didn't finish the sentence but his meaning was clear. Always the optimistic salesman. Why not?

"There's a new spirit in the United States today," said Harvard's Porter. "Xerox is the example of a threatened company that really pulled up their pants and responded. We've lost a lot of industries. Not copiers."
   Some other American companies with American manufacturing bases are showing the new spirit, too:

· Apple Computer's $20-million plant in Fremont, California, is as automated and cost-effective as most Japanese factories. It can produce up to 500,000 Macintosh computers a year. Labor accounts for less than 1 percent of production costs.
· General Motors is creating the $5-billion Saturn Corporation to make as many as 450,000 subcompact cars a year, starting in 1988, in the United States.

Major Photocopying Machines

	Copies/Minute	Xerox	Canon	Ricoh	Kodak	IBM	Minolta	Sharp
Low End	8		PC ($700–$1,200)	M5 ($300)				Z-60 ($1,100)
	10	1020 ($1,700)		M10 ($1,200)				SF 7200 ($1,700)
	15		NP 150 ($1,800)				EP 350 Z ($2,500)	
	20	1025 ($2,600)						SF 8200 ($3,200)
	25			FT 4085 ($4,000)			EP 450 Z ($4,500)	
Mid-Range	30		NP 350 ($4,300)					
	35	1040 ($6,000)		FT 5070 ($6,500)			EP 550 Z ($5,400)	
	40	1045 ($6,500) 1048 ($8,000)	NP 400 ($6,000)					
	50	1055 ($15,000)	NP 7550 ($11,000)	FT 6080 ($10,000)	EK 85 ($16,000)		EP 650 Z ($6,500)	SF 9500 ($5,800)
	70	1075 ($60,000)			EK 200 ($55,000) EK 225 ($65,000)	III-Model 60 ($29,000)		
High End	90	1090 ($80,000)			EK 250 ($100,000)			
	120	9900 ($129,000)						

· IBM spent $350 million automating its Lexington, Kentucky, electronic typewriter plant. Its personal computer printer plant in Charlotte, North Carolina, is even more advanced.

With faster product development, automation, strict quality control, and technology, American companies are eliminating Japan's labor-cost advantage. And Xerox is moving faster than anybody. The company's first Memorywriter plant, opened in Dallas in 1981, epitomized the new Xerox way of manufacturing. It produced up to 1,000 electronic typewriters a day with just a hundred workers per shift. The Memorywriter was designed by seven people in just three years. Now the copier division and the rest of Xerox are following the same pattern.

"We can get our production costs down to anyone's," said Joseph Sanchez, president of Xerox's Printing Systems Division. "The keys are to cut the number of parts in half with every new product and getting labor down to 5 percent of product cost."

PITTSFORD, N.Y.—Horace Becker, a Xerox veteran who worked on the 914, was relaxing in his backyard explaining the group mentality of the "Warriors of Japan," often considered that country's biggest strength. "But that's the way we're going to beat them," Becker said. "Every one of us is an individual. Every one of us can think. They're in a mold. They have lived on this same island. It's closed in. They all think the same. Here in the United States, we have all different kinds of people. We all think intelligently and separately."

To understand the plain paper copier industry you have to understand one concept: Xerox doesn't sell copiers, it sells copies. In fact, economists would do well to add the growth rate of Xerox's copy volume to their list of economic indicators. It rises and falls with the health of the economy. Before the 1981 recession, Xerox copy volume grew at a 15 percent annual rate. During the worst of the recession, the rate declined to 7 percent. During all of 1984 and 1985, it was a stable 11 to 12 percent.

Let's look at a few numbers: Each Xerox 1075 or 1090, or Kodak Ektaprint 200 or 225 for that matter, leased to a customer means more than $20,000 in annual revenue for the manufacturer, sometimes much more depending upon the copy volume. That revenue will keep coming in throughout the life of the contract, which is generally three or four years, sometimes longer. Even if the customer purchases the machine outright, it comes with a service and maintenance contract that can mean

The World's Largest Copier Companies
(ranked by revenues)

	1985 (in millions)	1984 (in millions)	1983 (in millions)
Xerox*	$ 8,900	$ 8,500	$ 8,000
Canon	2,178	1,400	1,200
Ricoh	1,926	1,300	1,200
Kodak	900	790	660
IBM	700	720	690
3M	400	590	540
Minolta	743	516	500
Océ	600	498	538
Savin	448	409	397
Konishiroku	470	337	346

*Includes Xerox U.S., Canada, Latin America, Rank Xerox, and Fuji Xerox.
SOURCE: The Office Products Analyst.

Copier Placements in United States
(in thousands of units)
(outright sales and net rental additions)

	1985	1984	1983
Canon*	326.5	233.5	145.3
Sharp*	124.3	115.8	95.6
Xerox	106.2	98.9	75.6
Mita	87.4	60.1	39.3
Minolta	72.8	64.2	57.0
Ricoh	68.0	47.0	24.5
Toshiba	58.0	45.8	23.3
3M	54.0	49.2	33.3
Savin	48.3	41.0	36.1
Royal	43.6	35.3	33.0
Pitney Bowes	38.6	29.6	19.3
Panasonic	35.0	29.5	25.0
IBM	8.1	11.1	10.5
Kodak	5.2	4.9	5.2

*Canon totals include 190,000 personal copiers in 1985; 119,000 in 1984; 66,000 in 1983. Sharp totals include 24,000 personal copiers in 1985; 15,000 in 1984.
SOURCE: Dataquest.

thousands of dollars a year in revenue. Service revenues on sold Xerox equipment were $1.8 billion in 1985, a 20-percent increase over the previous year.

The Japanese companies, on the other hand, are in the business of selling machines. The smallest Canon personal copier lists for well under $1,000. Of that, about $400 goes to Canon, the rest goes to the dealer or retailer. That means Canon's total revenue from the estimated 120,000 personal copiers sold in the United States in 1984 was roughly $50 million. Total revenue from the 14,000 1075s Xerox placed in the United States in 1984 exceeds $300 million a year, most of that continuing for the life of the rental contracts.

You can begin to see why Xerox has always focused on the upper end of the copier market, always the most lucrative segment of the business. The low-volume market is a low-margin business. The high-volume market, primarily because of the high product development costs—hundreds of millions of dollars—has always been a high-margin business.

Of course, Xerox is afraid that low-volume products—whether Japanese- or Xerox-made—will pull business away from the crucial high-volume, high-margin end of the business. On top of that, the copier business is extremely competitive. IBM's Proctor Houston probably says it best: "There's no loyalty in the copier market today. A customer will sign a contract with IBM today. At the end of three years, if we don't continue to be the best-priced performer, we're going to be out. That's what happens. It's very tough, very demanding. Close your eyes for two seconds and you lose."

One of the great frustrations for Xerox is that despite the fact it is winning this competitive battle—Xerox is selling and leasing more copiers than ever—its revenues and earnings are growing more slowly than its machine placements. This is happening for a couple of reasons. First, the general price decline, about 10 percent a year, on low- and mid-volume machines, which shows up in the absolute decline in the prices of machines, and the fact that customers are able to get more copying features on the machines for the same money. Second, the strong dollar. In 1984, for instance, Xerox Corporation revenue from its copier business alone grew by $150 million over 1983 to reach $6.6 billion. Profits from copiers and systems products increased a respectable 8 percent to $354 million. However, Xerox estimates that if it had been able to raise prices by 2 or 3 percent, as did the American auto industry, profits would have increased 70 percent. And if the dollar had remained stable after

1982, overall company revenues in 1984 would have been $700 million higher than the $8.8 billion reported. In 1985, if it weren't for the strong dollar, Xerox revenues from reprographics and information systems ($8.7 billion) would have been 3 percent higher.

People tend to view the plain paper copier market as one huge continuum. It isn't. It is many smaller segments, each with a different set of customers and a different set of competitors. There is a market for fast machines, slow machines, console models, desktops, sold machines, and rentals. There are customers who expect the supplier to do all the servicing, and fast. And there are customers who want to take care of the machines themselves. Some major accounts take hundreds of machines while some small offices take only one. There are machines with fancy input and output devices that allow the customer to make and bind booklets. And machines that don't do much except make a lot of copies in a hurry. Xerox has to satisfy everyone from dedicated operators in company copy centers to casual operators who walk up to a machine in a hallway.

There is only one full-line supplier—Xerox—which can be an advantage because for some customers it is more convenient to deal with just one vendor for all of their machine's needs. But it can also be a disadvantage because, as IBM's Houston says, it's "one heck of a job to protect all your flanks." In general, Xerox has different strategies for different competitors, and those strategies vary from country to country. In Japan, Fuji Xerox prices its products 3 percent above similar Canon products, trading on the Xerox image for quality. In the United States, Xerox says it won't lead the price level down, but it is committed to remaining competitive against the Japanese, and that means matching the prices of similar Japanese machines and dropping those prices if necessary.

In the high-volume end of the business, the last thing either Xerox or Kodak wants is a price war. Xerox's strategy is to add more features to its machines so that it can price them above similar machines from Kodak. Both companies actually increased prices on some high-end products in recent years.

There is some overlap in the market segments, and the boundaries are always changing. The 914, for instance, made only seven copies a minute, but it was a heavy-duty console model and has always been considered the upper end. Dataquest, probably the foremost research firm covering the field, used to divide the PPC (plain paper copier) industry into six segments. Anywhere you go today—except Xerox, which has its own categories—you hear about the Dataquest segments. The research firm, however, has recently redefined its own system and divided

Dataquest Segments

	Copies/Minute	Cost
PC	1–12	up to $1,000
1A	1–15	up to $2,000
1B	15–20	up to $4,500
2	21–30	up to $5,000
3	31–45	up to $7,500
4	40–75	up to $20,000
5	70–90	up to $60,000
6	91 plus	up to $130,000

Xerox Segments

	Copies/Minute	Cost
Low-volume Classes A & B	less than 25	under $4,000
Mid-volume Classes C & D	25–90	$4,000–$60,000
High-volume Class E	90 plus	$80,000–$130,000

its Segment 1 into two, and added a separate category for personal copiers, making eight segments altogether.

Despite that market segmentation, there is some commonality among customers where you would least expect it. Xerox researcher Deborah Hall says the customer profile for someone using a Canon personal copier is much the same as for someone using a Xerox 9900, which costs $129,000. Both are usually used by a single operator who treats the machine as if he owns it. "Like a baby," Hall says. She compares mid-volume machines, which are usually located in a common hallway and shared by many people, to orphans. These machines get rougher treatment. The goal, then, is to design machines to meet the requirements of each customer—a herculean task.

Hall, by the way, has interesting advice for copier engineers. Her research indicates that the more approachable a machine looks, the better customers will like it. "In the old days, the thing was to make it look high-tech," she says. "But let's face it, a copier is dull. We tell the engineers the only way to hit a home run is to make it look dull and reliable. Don't worry about making it look sexy. Copiers are like toasters, they are considered just a convenience." Or, as the Japanese copier-maker Mita says in its advertisements: "Copiers are pretty boring till they go wrong, then they're very boring."

Hall says customers rate machine reliability as their first priority. There is nothing more frustrating than a copier that is down when you want to make a quick copy. She has not found a prevalent "buy American" attitude among customers. In fact, many people aren't aware which companies are Japanese. Some think Ricoh is an American company. Essentially, customers want the best copy quality at the lowest possible price. They might be willing to accept lower quality for a document that is going to be circulated internally, but not for a copy that is to be sent outside the company. If it comes to a trade-off, customers are not willing to sacrifice quality for low price.

The United States is the largest copier market in the world. Dataquest estimates that about 1.2 million machines were placed in the United States in 1985; about 3 million worldwide. The total number of annual placements is expected to exceed 5 million by the end of the decade. Dataquest counts only outright sales and net rental additions in its estimates. This method underestimates the placement activity of such companies as Xerox and Kodak that do a large rental business because a rental machine that replaces another machine rented from the same company does not count. Privately, Dataquest admits that Xerox's actual placements could be as much as two times greater than what Dataquest has estimated.

Generally, as you move up market, more machines will be leased and fewer sold outright. In the early 1980s, the lease/sale ratio for high-end Kodak and Xerox machines exceeded 90/10. It is declining steadily as more emphasis is put on sales.

Worldwide copier revenues for Xerox, including Rank Xerox and Fuji Xerox, supplies, paper, and service, totaled more than $8 billion in 1985; total operating profit was more than $1 billion. Industry sources estimate that about 40 percent of Xerox's revenues and profits come in the mid-volume range. Mid-volume console copiers, as opposed to desktop models, are generally perceived to be better constructed and capable of handling more copy volume each month, regardless of the speed of the machine. As the Japanese move into the mid-volume market, two major issues in the industry are: Can the Japanese build reliable console models? (Ricoh and Canon are the first serious threats with the 6080 and 7550.)

And, what is the customer's perception of the reliability of faster Japanese desktop models? Can they handle the work loads of the American-made consoles? Xerox is betting on the consoles.

Xerox thinks Canon is the greatest Japanese threat, followed by Ricoh. Both companies have a broad range of products and have indicated they want to continue to move up market. Xerox is also keeping a watchful eye on Sharp (the low-cost producer of small copiers with its cost-effective automated factory), Toshiba, and Matsushita. The latter two are giants of Japanese industry, specialists in mass-produced consumer goods. If the home copier market opens up and these two companies get serious, they could become major forces. Minolta was at one time seen by Xerox as a technological leader, but that has changed because Minolta has not proven to be adept at marketing its innovations. Mita, which still does a large coated-paper machine business, is gaining strength in the United States, but not with a market leadership strategy. Mita seems to be content as a secondary product for American dealers.

Here is a look at how Xerox views the market in each of the volume segments:

LOW-VOLUME

These machines retail for less than $4,000 and are designed to make fewer than 5,000 copies a month. Xerox has been getting kicked here but is regaining some market share with the help of Fuji Xerox, primarily the 1020, 1035, 2830, and 1025. (The 1035 and 2830 were discontinued in 1985 when the 1025 was introduced.) The Xerox goal is market leadership by the end of the decade. Xerox defines leadership pretty much the same as Japanese companies: at least 30 percent market share.

This is the segment where most of the unit placement and revenue growth will occur in the industry. By 1988, Dataquest estimates that 500,000 personal copiers a year will be sold in the United States; more than 1.3 million PC and Segment 1 and 2 machines. Xerox expects placements of low-volume machines to triple between 1984 and 1989. Virtually all of that growth will be in machines that cost less than $2,000. The challenge for Xerox is to produce a personal copier like Canon's. Several concepts have been considered, but none has yet made it to the market. The company is now talking about a "multifunction" device in the very low end to penetrate the home market. This machine would be a combination copier, facsimile machine, and even computer printer. Xerox introduced the first of these hybrid devices, the 4045, in early

1985. Priced at less than $5,000, the 4045 is the first machine to combine a laser printer with an optical copier.

Low-end machines, especially those that wind up in the home, must be reliable. The customer wants something that never breaks down, like a telephone. Canon has tried to meet that need with its cartridge concept on the PC. Virtually everything that can break is thrown away and replaced after 2,000 copies. This can be expensive. For the cartridge alone, a customer is paying about three cents a copy. On a 1075, by comparison, at the lowest lease rate, the customer pays less than one cent apiece. Because the manufacturer does not want the customer to think he is throwing something good away, some manufacturers are making their cartridges in several pieces, so that different parts can be replaced at different times. But that gets away from the original concept of ease of maintenance.

Within Xerox, some strategists argue that the company must produce a personal copier machine, even if the best it can do is break even. Advertising costs would be heavy to support such a machine, witness Canon, which devotes about $20 million in the United States and $50 million worldwide to support its copier line.

Everyone in the industry recognizes the need to develop new distribution channels—besides a direct sales force—for low-end machines. Most of the low-end placements will come from such diverse channels as Fuji Xerox's joint venture distributors and dealers, and Xerox's mass market retailers, direct mail firms, and office equipment or computer dealers.

Generally, the per unit manufacturing costs that Xerox has been benchmarking among the Japanese low-end manufacturers have been declining at the rate of 10 percent a year. The rate is expected to slow for the rest of the decade. For now, the Japanese still have an edge in the low end because they can deliver low-cost products with many features on short schedules. Profit margins on the machines are miniscule, further complicating Xerox's effort to design a competitive machine.

While Canon is the undisputed leader in the low end, Xerox has not ruled out selling a small machine made by a Japanese manufacturer other than Fuji Xerox, if it cannot successfully design and produce its own machine. The OEM (original equipment manufacturer) supplier would probably not be either Canon or Ricoh—that would be strengthening an already strong adversary.

MID-VOLUME

This is the heartland for Xerox, the area where it has always earned the most revenue and profit, the area IBM attacked with its Copier II. The area Xerox has been defending ever since.

Machines here cost up to $60,000 and make up to 100,000 copies a month. Xerox drew the line in 1982 with the 1045. The strategy succeeded. In 1984, the company regained more than twelve points of market share in the unit placements, all at the expense of the Japanese. Xerox says it controls about 35 percent of the mid-volume market worldwide, and that figure was less than 20 percent in 1982. As in the low end, there is tremendous price pressure, led by Canon. The strategy is well known: Increased market share and higher production volumes lead to more efficient production and lower prices.

Xerox has reached manufacturing parity with the Japanese in this segment, especially when you calculate freight, duty, and insurance penalties involved in shipping from Japan. Xerox, with its factories around the world, incurs less of a penalty. But the general price erosion, again about 10 percent a year, in this segment of the market continues to put pressure on profit margins. Dale Kredatus of Data Decisions estimates the manufacturing cost of the Ricoh 6080, as it leaves the factory, at $3,840; and the Canon 7550 at $3,500. He thinks Xerox's costs on the 1045, 1048, and 1050 are slightly less. All of these machines, fully loaded with features, sell for more than $10,000. (Kredatus offers two rules of thumb for estimating manufacturing costs of 50 copies per minute [cpm] and slower machines: $8 a pound, or list price equals 2.5 times the unit manufacturing cost or UMC.)

At the top of the mid-range Kodak is the premier competitor. The marketing strategy in this range is much different than at the bottom where the Japanese are cutting prices; Kodak and Xerox want to avoid that. Here, Xerox is the leader in machine features and copy quality; it is also producing machines for less than Kodak. The 1075, for instance, is estimated to cost less than $13,000 to manufacture. The Ektaprint 225, more than $17,000. The IBM Series III/Model 60, a 75-cpm machine, is estimated to cost $11,000, but it is not nearly as sophisticated as either the Xerox or Kodak machines. Xerox expects the Japanese to make a play for this market and has set its targets on future products accordingly. Kredatus looks for the landed cost in the U.S. of a comparable Japanese machine to be about $5,600, when and if they appear. If Xerox gets its costs that low and the Japanese don't show, the profit potential is immense.

Service is a very important factor in the mid- and high-volume segments. Customers expect a rapid response when they have a problem. Kodak has the best reputation for fast service, but Xerox is closing the gap with the increased reliability it is building into its 10 Series products. The Japanese still lag behind.

HIGH-VOLUME

This is the land of milk and honey for Xerox. The 9000 series, introduced in 1974, took a while to catch on, but it is now immensely profitable. Industry sources estimate that it accounts for more than $1 billion in annual revenues and $250 million in operating profit, much of which is from machines that have been fully depreciated.

Xerox's only competition is the Kodak Ektaprint 250. IBM doesn't appear interested in this segment and most of the Japanese companies publicly say they are not interested. Xerox has more than 75 percent of the market worldwide in this segment; a virtual monopoly in such areas as South America and Japan. Growth, however, will be limited by the impact of high-speed laser printers, also called electronic printers. IBM already has a high-speed electronic printer and Kodak is developing one.

SUPPLIES

A good and growing business; paper alone accounts for about $500 million in annual revenue and $25 million in profit for Xerox. Toner (the dry xerographic ink) and photoreceptors (the xerographic equivalent of film) have much higher profit margins. Xerox is the low-cost producer of xerographic supplies in the world. Its strategy is to remain in that commanding position by using the latest manufacturing technology and America's natural advantage of low-cost energy. Xerox has built a new, $30-million toner plant in Rochester that employs only twenty people. It has begun to OEM some items, such as photoreceptors, to distributors who in turn sell them for replacement use on competitive machines. It will continue its efforts to take as much of that business as it can away from the Japanese.

If there's one threat to Xerox maintaining its turnaround, it's compla- cency. It has often appeared as if Xerox was making a comeback, mag- azines and newspapers have written the story since the late 1970s. But Xerox's newfound success vanished when the Japanese cut prices or in- troduced a new generation of machines. This time, "I think they've learned," said Joe Castrianni, vice president of Sharp in the United States. "They aren't going to make the same mistakes again."

To make certain, Xerox management is fighting to keep people on their toes. No one, says Savin's Charlap, is better at doing that than Wayland Hicks. "The guy's a genius," Charlap says. "He's the best I've seen in this entire industry, and not by a little, by a lot. Xerox may have once been a stodgy and dead company. It's not with Wayland Hicks around."

2
Four Days of the Gospel

Rochester is called a seven-to-seven town because the people on the fast track at Xerox and Kodak work from seven in the morning to seven at night. Salesmen at the vendor companies supplying parts to these two giants can be found in bathrobes at home, sipping coffee, when they make their first telephone contacts of the day.

Wayland Hicks fits that seven-to-seven pattern. He rises every morning at five for a three-mile run. Then it's off to his office at Webster for a sunrise meeting with engineers or product planners. It's usually pushing 7:00 P.M. by the time he turns out the lights and heads home again. One round-the-world business tour took him from Rochester to Venray (Holland), Amsterdam, Frankfurt, Moscow, Tokyo, Seattle, Chicago, and back to Rochester in twelve days. "The flying time itself was forty hours, but I only missed one day of work," he recalls. "We did all of our traveling either at night or on weekends." Such total dedication does have its rewards: Hicks earns about $400,000 a year.

In 1983, at the age of forty, Hicks became head of copier development and production for Xerox Corporation. He oversees engineering facilities and copier plants in North America and Europe. He decides what products the company is going to manufacture and sets general sales targets and prices for the operating companies. As a chief architect and implementer of the company's copier strategy, he is the key man in Xerox's fight to reestablish undisputed dominance in the industry.

"IBM is obviously a good competitor. Kodak is a good competitor. I have a great deal of respect for both organizations," he said at the time of his appointment. "But when I think of our real enemy, it's Japan.

"If I were a company and heard that IBM was coming into my marketplace, that in itself would cause me a certain amount of consternation. Look at Apple. If I then woke up the next day and read that Eastman Kodak also intended to participate in that marketplace, that's double trouble. And then you say you got a Canon, a Ricoh, a Toshiba, a Minolta, a Matsushita; each one of them is very fine and very large—and, by the way, the string of companies goes on—in their own right. To have all of them come at you at the same time and stay healthy is some undertaking.''

To see exactly how Xerox is fighting back against the Japanese and staying healthy, co-author Gary Jacobson accompanied Hicks on a review of Xerox manufacturing facilities in Europe. For four days through four countries, Jacobson followed Hicks everywhere, attending every meeting and new product review, touring every plant. At each stop the message was the same: Beat the Japanese. The only subjects off the record were long-term future products.

W E MET in the lobby of the Portman, Hicks's favorite London hotel. He lived just outside London from 1976 to 1981 when he ran the UK operating company and then worked at Rank Xerox headquarters, so he knows the area well. He seemed intense, as usual, even a bit more so. We went to the bar to have a drink before dinner. Hicks rocked back and forth in his seat, one leg pumping up and down. I ordered a pint of bitter and he had a large vodka on the rocks.

"In England, a regular shot is about half the size it is back in the States,'' he said. "And a large is still only about three-quarters what it is back home.''

Soon, he was talking about his favorite subject: the Japanese. Hicks said Xerox research had determined that 60 to 70 percent of Canon's copier profits come from such supplies as toner and photoreceptors. "Xerox is the only company making money on paper and that is only because the volumes are so high,'' he said. "There is no margin in paper, but toner is like gold. The toner and photoreceptor business is very energy-intensive and one thing God gave the U.S. is cheap energy. We can make both much cheaper than they can.

"Canon sells a photoreceptor for about $135. Their cost is about $21 or $22. We could make the same photoreceptor for about $14. So you know they're making a lot of money at $135. We have about 30 percent of Royal's (Konishiroku-made machines) photoreceptor follow-on business in the U.S. and we have the same goal in Canon toner. We'll sell it cheaper, make money, and say it's Xerox, which means quality.''

He recalled a meeting with the project manager on the Canon-like toner project. Hicks said he wanted it available in June 1985. The engineer said there was no way it could be ready before January 1986.

"Are your people working seven days a week?'' Hicks asked.

"No."

"Why not? If you went back to those four or five people who are working on it and told them you would give them a million-dollar bonus if they did it by June, would they be able to?"

The manager was speechless, Hicks said. The point was made. The workers could be doing more.

"Guys at Xerox in the early days were working seven days a week and liking it when they were putting out the 914," Hicks continued. "Apple did it at the start and still seems to be doing it. Why can't we? I want to make this company even more entrepreneurial. Break it down into groups of four, five, and six. Give them bonuses. Give them incentives. Push stock options way down in the organization. Make everyone profit-oriented.

"Then, maybe I could get rid of this constant bickering between engineering and manufacturing. When a problem comes up, one side blames the other. The engineers say it's a manufacturing problem and the manufacturing guys say, 'Look at the designs we have to work with.' Everyone protects their own interests. I don't really give a damn about manufacturing or engineering. I just care about what's good for this company and I want those guys to think that way, too. We have to get people thinking about what's good for the whole company instead of just their little unit."

Hicks wore a black pinstripe suit with a white button-down shirt, his standard business uniform. His collar was buttoned. When you see him from a distance you don't get the impression of a big person. But up close he is. He stands just over six feet and walks with the slightest hunch forward, like the crest of a big wave.

Before we went upstairs to the restaurant for dinner, he gave me a preview of the week ahead. "It's going to give you a unique insight," he said. "The meetings haven't been planned for you. No dog and pony shows. You will hear everything as it happens. I will get mad. Other people will get mad. By the end of the week you will have a real insider's view of how this company operates. Most business books I have read are very naive. That's not how business operates. It's not that simple-minded."

I first met Hicks in New York on September 22, 1982, the day Xerox launched the 10 Series of copiers. He led the development teams for both the 1045, aimed directly at the Japanese, and the 1075, aimed at Kodak and IBM. I remember trying to get a diagram of the interior of a 1075 from him to publish in the Rochester afternoon newspaper. Hicks agreed, and then quickly reconsidered. "I don't want this thing getting across the river to Kodak any faster than it normally would. I'm not going to help my competition."

We talked more than a dozen times between our first meeting and this trip in October 1984. We talked about his business philosophy and the copier industry in general, the mistakes Xerox made and how its competitors were able to take advantage of them. "This is a business capable of cranking out hundreds of millions of dollars of profit at Xerox for a long, long time," he said. "But nobody is going to believe the good stuff if you don't have some bad stuff, too."

I once asked him if he was disappointed being in the copier division when all the so-called glamour businesses of Xerox were located on the West Coast.

"That's bullshit," he said. "This is where the glamour is."

"The money sure is," I said, referring to the fact that virtually all Xerox profits still come from copiers.

"That's glamour," he said.

In his office in the Rochester suburb of Webster, an enlarged, framed poster of a 1984 article from *Forbes* magazine hangs on the wall behind his desk. It's the first thing you notice. His predecessor had decorated the office with framed art prints. Hicks took them down. "I can't stand that stuff," he said. The *Forbes* story talks about Canon's imminent push into high-volume copying and is headlined with a quote from Canon president Ryuzaburo Kaku: "And then we will attack." Kaku said that Xerox is too concerned about its financial business and not concerned enough about its copier business, opening up a weak spot for attack. Hicks had a brass plate mounted next to the article. It says: ". . . And when they do they will lose."

"The next story I see about the Japanese and Xerox I'm going to put on that wall and I'm going to keep putting them up until I can paint black over them," Hicks said. "I'm not going to let those bastards beat us. I have studied them. I know how they operate. I feel like that scene from the movie *Patton* when the general is awakened in the middle of the night and told the Germans are on the move and his showdown with Rommel is coming. 'This is what I have been waiting for,' Patton says. 'I was born to do this. Rommel, I read your goddamn book!' "

Hicks likes war analogies. He often talks about the dangers of fighting a two-front war in business and avoiding it if at all possible. He says the introduction of the 10 Series was for Xerox what the battle of El Alamein was for the Allies in World War II: "The day after the battle, Churchill spoke to the House of Commons and said, 'This is not the end. It is not the beginning of the end. But, it is perhaps the end of the beginning.'

"We have overcome our greatest fear about the Japanese. It absolutely scares the holy hell right out of you when you first realize how good they are, how far behind you are, but you have to understand you have a problem before you can do anything about it. We can compete with the Japanese. We can compete with anyone."

Hicks joined Xerox in 1966 as a salesman selling the 914 and the 2400. He became a branch manager in Michigan, moving the operation from last place to second place in sales. The year after he left it hit first place. He set up the service support system for the 9200, moving $60 million worth of supplies and spare parts into the service pipeline before the product's announcement and introduction in 1974. Hicks went to England and became the first American to ever run a foreign Xerox operating company. He returned to the United States and took over the development of the 1045 and 1075. Both projects had started years earlier, but were slipping badly. By creating a new environment of urgency, he forced those two products into the market.

"He's a quick learner. He's decisive. He's tough. He's a workaholic," Hicks's boss, Bill Glavin, says of Hicks. "He drives people, including himself, too hard. He and I talk about that at least once a week."

Shelby Carter agrees that Hicks is a workaholic. "Hicks has the highest energy level of anyone I have ever seen." Carter should know about energy levels. When he ran the Xerox marketing organization in the United States it was common practice for him to leave his Rochester home on Monday morning and not return until Friday night. The rest of the week was a nonstop tour of Xerox branches around the country. Carter has since retired from Xerox and now runs a savings and loan in Texas.

Hicks's Bible is Alfred Sloan's *My Years with General Motors*. He refers to Sloan constantly.

"I think Alfred Sloan was the foremost strategist who reached chief executive officer of any modern corporation," Hicks says. "There are certain strategic plans that I think are very important to the reprographics business that I have stolen from General Motors. One of them is it doesn't matter if you are late to the market. If you are late, be better. Another one is that you want to have the cost of the volume leader and the features of the feature leader. When Chevrolet first came into the market, Sloan would say put some feature on it that Ford doesn't have and then price it above Ford, even though your costs are the same. That way, if anybody tried to get into a price war with you, you could kill them. He conceptualized this way back in the twenties when Ford dominated the market.''

Kodak's Ektaprint 250, a ninety-copy-a-minute (cpm) machine aimed at central reproduction departments of large corporations, is an example of how Sloan's pricing strategy works in the copier industry. The Xerox 1075, which makes only 70 cpm but is loaded with features that increase its productivity, nibbles away at the bottom of the 250's market and the Xerox 9900, at 120 cpm, squeezes the 250 from the top. "And then I hit them right in the eyeball, too,'' Hicks said, referring to the Xerox 1090, a 92-cpm machine introduced in February 1985.

Hicks pushed development of the 9900 when he heard that Kodak was coming out with its own 120-cpm machine. He would have preferred to take more time and base the 9900 on new technology so that it would be less costly to manufacture; but he was convinced he couldn't take that chance. He had to make sure Xerox had a superior product in the market. As it turns out, his information was wrong. Kodak's rumored 120-cpm machine was the 90-cpm Ektaprint 250.

"Another thing that I learned from Sloan is that I will hold market share,'' he said. "I'll hold market share up to the point of taking a loss. Particularly in a mature industry, when you start getting close to the point of saturation—we think we're five to seven years away from that—whoever owns market share today will own it for a long time. It's easy to pick up five to ten points a year if the market is growing like a weed. If you're in a stable industry, though, making five-, six-, seven-point gains is terrific. Ford and General Motors would kill each other for two points.''

If Sloan's book is Hicks's Bible on strategy, *Let's Call it Fiesta,* by Edouard Seidler, is his handbook on market research. He keeps extra copies in his office and distributes them to his managers. It chronicles the development of Ford's Project Bobcat, concentrating on Ford's extensive customer research. Hicks actually used the same research team that studied the Fiesta to decide whether to enclose protruding paper trays on an upcoming copier.

"It really looked hideous,'' Hicks said, drawing a sketch of the machine with trays sticking out the left side. "Some people said, 'This is customer requirements? The customer doesn't care about those things.' I said I think one of the requirements is that it be an attractive machine. So we set up the showrooms, brought the customers in, showed them the competitive machines and then put three different versions of this cardboard mock-up in the room. Nobody knows it's Xerox. We asked the customers which machine they preferred. Low and behold, all of the customers said just what I thought they would say: 'Close the machine in because the machine looks more robust. And if it looks more robust it must be more robust. And, by the way, if it is more robust we would even pay you more for it.'

"This was a beauty contest, but it made sense. When you go out and buy a car a lot of the decision is a beauty contest. This is part of customer requirements. Basically, the question for me was, am I going to spend $30 more apiece to make the machines look pretty? Intuitively, I think it's worth $30. And by the way, if it's a question between your intuition and my intuition I will always rely on mine because that is what the company pays me all the money for. But if it comes down to something you can resolve by asking your customers and not having to rely on intuition, don't be dumb. Spend the money. Ask your customer.''

Hicks thinks this is one area in which Xerox is far ahead of its Japanese competitors. "Look at the Japanese machines," he said. "They are getting better, but basically what you are looking at is aesthetically unattractive. They look like Rube Goldberg devices. Appendages sticking out on the side. When you talk to customers, they say, 'Those trays, you can run into them. You can hurt yourself.' They articulate what their concerns are. Don't get me wrong, we did market research before. We spent millions of dollars on it. But I don't think we went about it as well as we could. It was that Fiesta book that really gave me the idea of videotaping and looking in agonizing detail at what the customers were trying to tell us. We'll let customers actually build a machine.''

This was an important week for Hicks. He regularly visits European operations, but before this trip he had never made such an extensive tour. He would review every manufacturing facility except Mitcheldean, England. He would review new product development programs, two of which were in the key mid-volume range, and an existing product that was having severe quality problems in the field. The new copiers were part of the "brick wall" he was assembling to keep the Japanese from moving up market. The 1045 had been introduced first in September 1982. Then the 1048 was introduced in March 1984. The 1048, however, wasn't meeting customer expectations. And the schedules of the two new products, code-named Somerset and Andes, were in danger of slipping and missing their spring 1985 launches.

That was the old Xerox, the Xerox of the seventies. Would the company truly be able to consistently deliver products faster and cheaper to compete with Canon and the other Japanese companies? Or, would Xerox slip back into bureaucratic lethargy? Was the company really changing?

Or, was the original impact and momentum of the 10 Series going to be lost? Four days of plant reviews and tours by the boss certainly weren't going to solve the problems, but they would allow Hicks to prod, cajole, provoke, and generally spread the gospel of a new state of mind at Xerox, a new sense of urgency to keep the products on schedule. The company was engaged in a battle for survival, and Hicks wanted everyone to understand.

"Part of the mind-set we are trying to create around Xerox now is that we will do business fundamentally different than we have ever done it before," he once told me. "Don't be embarrassed to try something new. Don't be embarrassed to go to someone for help if you need it. I am competing against world-class competitors and to do that I need every trick in the book."

Between bites of broiled Dover sole in the Portman restaurant, Hicks described a special plaque he had brought with him for the Venray plant manager, Willi Sonneborn. Hicks had been forced to divert an entire shipment of more than a thousand new 1048s directly to the Xerox refurbishing center at Irvine, California, after a manufacturing problem was discovered. Usually, only used copiers were sent to Irvine for reconditioning before they could be leased again. The plaque had a color photograph of the Irvine center with the caption: "Irvine, Calif. . . . Venray West." It was a gentle prod at the pride of Venray's managers.

"When I present it to him, everyone will understand," Hicks said. "By the way, Venray has a very good reputation."

At one point during dinner, Hicks delighted in the fact that profits were slim in the very low end of the copier market where Xerox did not have a product. "Canon was forecasting 40,000 personal copiers a month," he said. "Ricoh, Sharp, the same. They all geared up for the big push and it didn't come. Sharp invested millions in its automated facilities and it's not paying off. This is one product I'm glad I'm not pioneering."

Earlier that year, Hicks had killed a personal copier project, code-named Gnome, because the manufacturing cost was too high and Gnome didn't bring anything new to the market. Xerox engineers had shifted their attention to several other concepts for low-end products.

"We're watching it very closely," he continued. "But no one is making any money. I told David Kearns we couldn't even break even with Gnome. I want to do things I can make money at. But I also want to do things that will make it tough for my competition. The very low end is important, but I don't have to worry about it right now because I know the troubles the other companies are having. They're keeping each other from making money.''

After dinner we went for a walk. We had talked about the number of Japanese cars in Britain. I thought the percentage was small. Hicks said it was the same as in the United States, about 20 percent. He suggested an impromptu field survey to see who was right. So we checked all the cars around Portman Square, walking in the middle of the street and ticking off the makes. "If anybody is watching us, they probably think we're crazy," Hicks said. But he was hooked on the test. There were Fords, Vauxalls, BMWs, a Honda, a Datsun, a Porsche, a Jaguar, thirty-six in all. Only five were Japanese, less than 14 percent.

"That's still too much," Hicks said as we walked back to the hotel.

I discovered later that Britain and Japan have an informal agreement allowing Japanese automakers no more than 11 percent of the market. Hicks, by the way, drives a Pontiac Fiero to work. He would rather drive a Jaguar. "But until America turns around the auto industry," he says, "I will drive an American car."

DAY ONE

The car to Heathrow was scheduled to leave at 6:30 A.M., and Hicks, who had already run his three miles through Hyde Park, came down to the lobby exactly on time. His precision is legendary in Rochester. The story goes that a janitor once came into a room where Hicks was about to convene a meeting. A light bulb needed changing. Hicks looked at his watch and said, "If it's going to take you longer than thirty seconds to screw that bulb in, leave now."

Maureen Jones, a secretary at Rank Xerox House in London, coordinated the itinerary for the week. It was a lesson in efficiency. She sent out a detailed memo to each person traveling with Hicks, at times there were as many as eight, outlining the arrangements for cars, flights, and hotels. If she wasn't personally responsible for making the arrangements, she listed who was. If there was a change, she sent out an updated itinerary. In London, they were hand-delivered directly from her office at Rank Xerox House. In Venray, they were sent by facsimile.

It was Tuesday and we were supposed to fly to Lille, France, on a private jet. Lille was fogged-in, so after sipping airport coffee for an hour and fifteen minutes, Hicks decided to go to Welwyn Garden City instead. "The fog may never lift," he said. "It's always foggy in Lille." Welwyn, which is about forty miles north of London, is home to one of

Xerox's engineering centers. Some quick calls by Andy Dougall, controller for the European manufacturing division who would accompany Hicks most of the week, set it up. Welwyn's people weren't expecting Hicks until the following day. Now they would have less than two hours to prepare.

Hicks's top aides from Rochester, strategist Lyndon Haddon and controller Raghunandan "Sach" Sachdev, would also be with him for most of the tour. Haddon, an Englishman, joined Rank Xerox in 1973 and moved to the United States in 1981. In 1978, he had helped Rank Xerox devise a strategy to compete directly against the Japanese for market share. Now Xerox was focusing on market share in the U.S. Sachdev, from India, joined Xerox in 1969 and had worked in both Rochester and Stamford. He managed the money for the copier engineering and manufacturing group. If one project is allowed to go over budget, then another one has to be cut.

Jack Fryer, the head engineer for the 1045 family of copiers, greeted Hicks in the lobby of the engineering building at Welwyn.

"Now I'm convinced you can do anything," Fryer said. "You've changed Wednesday into Tuesday."

The first product review concerned the problems of the 1048. Hicks met with the engineering group that designed the machine and was responsible for tracking its performance in the field. Their first slide was entitled "RBG President's Review," RBG stands for Reprographic Business Group, the official name of Hicks's organization. "The British are a lot like us except they are very class conscious," Hicks said, referring to the formality of the slide title. "You won't see that reference to president again the rest of the week." We didn't.

The 1048 was conceived as a follow-on to the 1045. At the time of the review, more than 100,000 1045s and more than 20,000 1048s had been sold or leased. Xerox had never before moved mid-volume machines in such large numbers, but the 1048 was coming back to haunt its maker. Except for its two-sided copying capacity, the 1048 was a lot like the 1045. About 60 percent of the 1,200 parts in the copier mainframe, or marking processor, were identical and 85 percent of the parts in the recirculating document handler were identical. But the electronic control system was completely different. Customers complained of noise problems, paper feeder problems, duplexing (two-sided copying) problems, too much background on copies, software problems, and just plain poor machine reliability.

"We have some machines that come off the end of the line that can't make five copies," Welwyn's Geoff Paton said. "How can that happen?" Paton had called in sick that day with a 102-degree fever, but came in on short notice to make his presentation when Hicks changed his itinerary.

The problems resulted in a high rate of service calls. These cost money and greatly influence a customer's perception of reliability. "In our surveys, the first month's reliability sets the tone for the customer's perception for the next year," Haddon explained. "That's why this is so critical."

The 1048 situation also questioned the reliability of Xerox's quality measuring methods. In essence, what was being perceived as a problem in the field was not necessarily being perceived as a problem at the end of the manufacturing line. The British operating company was shipping machines it never should have passed. Some of the problems were caused by faulty parts from vendors. Most of the noise complaints, for instance, came from the clutches used on the small motors that move such components as the optics housing. Another problem was excess background on copies, which occurred because the roller that released toner into the development chamber was leaking. Earlier, Xerox had complained to the vendor about excess glue on the rollers. So the vendor changed his manufacturing process, without telling Xerox, to cut back on the glue, but that led to shrinkage in the foam rubber material on the metal shaft, and that in turn led to the toner leakage and customer complaints.

Paton had spent several days in Washington, D.C., New York, Dallas, Chicago, and Toronto reviewing the 1048. "The salesmen love it," he said. "It's an easy sell. Customer expectations for the 1048 are high and we are not meeting them. It was designed as a machine that could make up to 12,500 copies a month, but customers are actually using it to make 40,000 to 50,000 copies a month and even 100,000. The general customer reaction is that the copy quality is excellent but the equipment and service are poor."

"It was never meant to go that high," Hicks said. "That's one of the reasons we're having these problems."

One of Paton's recommendations for improving the 1048 was a 1,000-copy burn-in, 300 copies minimum, at the end of the Venray manufacturing line. This would be in addition to the normal test copies (100 to 200) made during the production process. If a machine couldn't make 1,000 copies without a problem then it would be sent back. "Canada is doing a 5K burn-in and getting good month-one performance," Paton said.

"That's a stopgap, but a hell of a way to run a company," Hicks replied. "All burning them in at the end of the line will tell me is that I have a problem. I already know I have a problem. This is an illogical way to solve it. One thousand burn-in is okay, but to my mind it is incredibly dumb."

"We know Canon burns in," Fryer said.

"I don't think they do," Hicks said. "And I know Fuji Xerox doesn't and they build machines every bit as complicated as ours. Burning in is just an excuse for poor quality. We're not doing a good job of manufacturing quality."

The meeting, which involved a dozen people, lasted two hours. The same subject would be discussed again on Thursday with manufacturing personnel at Venray. At the end Hicks said, "I want to make sure this is the last one of these meetings we have. When did we launch the 1048?"

He waited for an answer. None came. He answered himself.

"March. What month is it now? October. That's eight months. I want to make fucking sure this never happens again. The next time we launch a product I want you to be crawling all over it from the start. If we have a problem I want us to find it before it finds us."

After the meeting, Hicks toured the Welwyn facility with plant manager Brian Weyman. The photoreceptor manufacturing process requires a clean room, just like for semiconductors. We put on blue oversuits and caps. Then, one by one, we went through a sealed chamber that automatically turned us around and blew off the dirt and dust. "Any piece of lint off your suit can ruin a belt," Weyman said. "It gets embedded in the selenium."

The photoreceptor for a 9000-family machine is a seamless, flexible aluminum belt coated with selenium (a rare metal imported mostly from South Africa). It is 16½ inches wide and 5½ feet in circumference. The selenium is baked on in giant crucibles that hold forty-five belts. At the time, normal practice at Welwyn was to test one of the belts to make sure the hardening process was complete. But that meant the yield could be no more than forty-four good belts from each batch. Hicks pointed out that Webster, which made photoreceptors for the United States, had discovered a way to save the forty-fifth belt. "That's an automatic two and a half percentage point improvement in yield," he said. "When you've struggled for years to get to 83 percent yield, that's a quantum leap." Weyman said he would contact Webster to see if the same technique could be employed at Welwyn.

We also toured the area where Xerox recycles selenium-based photoreceptor drums for its smaller machines. Hicks said the same methods could be used to recycle Japanese-made photoreceptors, which the Japanese don't recycle because of the long distances back to the homeland. "We're working that opportunity right now," he said. "Any place where we have a chance to go against their volume or their business, I want to exploit."

As we walked through the area where Xerox manufactures 6,000 PC (printed circuit) boards a day for 1045-family copiers, Weyman said the current trend in British industry is away from the forty-hour week and toward a thirty-five hour week.

"We're competing against guys who go the other way," Hicks said. "I want you to stress to the Welwyn managers what we're up against."

Later that day another engineering group, which included Bill Drawe, the head of the mid-volume business unit, reviewed the progress of a future product for Hicks. The group was struggling with issues as diverse as excess platten heat, ozone filtering, a shortage of software engineers, and a unit manufacturing cost (UMC) target that was about one-half that of the previous generation machine. One proposed solution to the platten heat problem, for instance, was a second blower fan, but that would add $30 to the UMC.

The product was slipping and the engineers were already building delays into a schedule that was still more than a year and a half from launch. As one of the engineers reviewed the new schedule, I was reminded of a discussion I had had with Hicks about personal accountability at Xerox. He said that, in the past, people at Xerox tended to sign off on problems once they pointed them out to their boss. If costs were too high, or a schedule was slipping, it was the boss's problem. "Coming to me for absolution just doesn't help at all," Hicks had said. "I would rather have the chief engineer wrestle with the problem himself."

I knew what was coming.

"May I remind you that slips start a day at a time," Hicks told the engineers. "You're talking about a thirty-day slip, but we have more than that in weekends and holidays before the launch and I hope you take every advantage of that you can."

The meeting ground on. In addition to starting right on time, Hicks doesn't like to conclude a meeting until all of the issues have been discussed. At 6:00 P.M., with darkness falling, someone said the cars for the return trip to London were ready. The cars waited. Finally, at 7:30, Hicks ended the meeting.

The driver must have had another appointment. He went 100 mph all the way back to London. In the backseat of the Mercedes 280, hurtling down M1 and weaving through the roundabouts, Hicks said: "Did you hear them say the car was here at six o'clock? That was a gentle hint. They thought that would get me out of there. But I wasn't about to end the meeting until we had finished."

At dinner with Sachdev that night at Trader Vic's in the London Hilton, Hicks again talked about reorganizing and making people more responsible for profit to end the self-interested infighting between engineering and manufacturing. "We have to revamp our incentive system," he said. "Japan gets that commitment and it's not even mercenary. We're mercenary and we can't get that commitment."

He talked about employment and corporate decisions that mean lost jobs.

"It costs $20 million more for us to make the United States the main manufacturing site for the 1075, but that's less than 5 percent on a $500 million manufacturing cost program. It just wasn't worth it to make the decision to move production elsewhere when it would have taken so many people out of Webster. Rank Xerox is now having a problem with its Mitcheldean plant. There are just too many people there. That's a good lesson for small companies. Don't make early plant decisions only on the basis of convenience because a site is available. Think twenty years down the road and try to get something that will have value then if you ever have to close it down. Don't put something out in the middle of the Forest of Dean."

DAY TWO

The car left the Portman for Heathrow at 6:30 in the morning. No fog. The plane, a private jet chartered by Xerox, took off on time—eight o'clock.

"What time is it in France?" Hicks asked.

"The same as us," answered Charlie Christ, who headed the manufacturing division that oversaw copier plants in the United States and Europe. Christ reported to Hicks. He had flown to London from New York the night before and would join the review for the next two days. "The continent is usually an hour ahead but for a couple of weeks a year they're on the same time."

"Good," Hicks said. "That means we'll get started by nine. I didn't think it would be until ten."

Christ turned to me. "You know, when you tell your neighbors you are going to Europe on business, they think it must be great and exciting and glamorous. But look at this. You spend most of your time in airplanes, airports, and inside cars going to and from hotels, airports, and plants. This is glamour?"

Lille is about 170 miles from London, across the channel. The plant, which is about fifteen miles from the city of Lille, produces electronic typewriters and sorters for 1045-family copiers. It also assembles other Xerox office equipment and, at the time of Hick's review, was gearing up to begin production of the 1075. Hicks, in response to the opening of a Canon factory in France, was shifting the European 1075 line from Venray to Lille. "All I want to tell Canon is if they want to play, join the big leagues," he said.

Local content and value added are big considerations in Europe, as in many other areas of the world that are trying to boost their own industries. When a government allows a foreign company to manufacture within its borders, it wants as much as possible of the factory's output to come from local parts and labor. Value added, generally a product's selling price minus its materials cost, is a measure of the value of a work force. The Memorywriter typewriter (called the 600 series in Europe) at Lille is 74 percent sourced by French vendors. That allows a "Made in France" label and preferred status with the Fench government, explained Lille plant manager Pierre van Coopernolle during a tour of his facility.

The 1075 would be assembled from parts shipped from the United States so it couldn't have a "Made in France" label. "Instead," van Coopernolle said, "it will have a name label with the address of the Lille plant." Van Coopernolle ran a small telecommunications company and then worked for IBM before joining Xerox in 1973.

In general, the French were much better dressed than the English. That day, van Coopernolle was wearing a blue double-breasted suit. There was not one sportcoat in the group of eight top French managers. The French also eat better. Lunch at Welwyn had been a stand-up, cold-cuts-and-salad buffet in a spare meeting room. Lunch at Lille was served sit-down style in the plant's dining room, complete with linen tablecloths and napkins, candles, four courses, and several wines—French, of course.

At lunch, Haddon joked about the differences among European, American, and Japanese attitudes toward profit. "The Europeans would be very happy with a three times mark up," he said. "Americans would try to figure out a way to make it four times. And the Japanese would cut their price in half and sell four times as much."

The typewriter assembly line at Lille is controlled by a Digital Equipment Corporation (DEC) computer. All of the incoming parts, subsystem kits, and outgoing machines are computer coded. At various stages in the manufacturing process the computer monitors all of the incoming and outgoing inventory levels and alerts the workers when it is necessary to resupply parts or kits to the line. The process is complicated by the fact that Lille makes six models of the Memorywriter for fourteen different languages, about a hundred variations in all. Xerox's copier manufacturing lines around the world are adopting a similar control method.

We walked through a warehouse area where some Xerox 3600s were waiting for shipment to Iran. The 3600, which makes sixty copies a minute, was introduced in 1968. It is a faster version of the 2400, which was introduced in 1964. Iran buys thirty or so a year for $12,000 apiece. It costs Xerox $4,000 to make each 3600. The Iranians specify "new" machines in their contracts; they won't take anything used or reconditioned. "The 3600 is built like a tank," Hicks said, "but why would anybody want twenty-year-old technology?"

No one had an answer.

Later, Hicks asked to see a 1048 going through preinstall, the final operation when the paper feeders and sorters are attached to the processor. "Tell the technician to make 300 copies on the machine," he said to van Coopernolle. "I want to check that recommendation from Welwyn." The copies were made without a problem.

Someone pointed to the complicated clusters of wires worming their way up the back of the machine. "That's why the Iranians want twenty-year-old technology," he said. "There aren't so many wires on the 3600."

Hicks laughed.

We finished an hour and a half ahead of schedule and headed back to the airport only to wait for the pilots and crew who were still in Lille. Christ, Sachdev, and Dougall were scattered around the waiting room. But everyone was listening to Hicks's conversation with Haddon.

"I think we should change the schedule tomorrow and talk about the 1048 first and then Somerset and Andes," Haddon said to Hicks. "A decision to go or not to go on them could depend on resolution of the 1048 question."

"If you decide to push ahead on Somerset and Andes you're going to stress the system," Christ said from across the room. "You're going to run into problems again."

"I can tell you exactly what you are going to hear tomorrow," Haddon said. "The engineers are going to say it's a big challenge, it's going to be tough, but let's go for the launch date. Manufacturing is going to say, if you do you're going to have the same problems as on the 1048. It's going to cost you money."

"I can decide to say okay and slip, but the problem is my competitors aren't," Hicks said. "They stress the system and don't have the problems we have. Why can't we do the same thing? Maybe it's worth it to spend the money up front and kick the product out."

"If you do, you're going to have the same quality problems," Christ said.

"What you really have is a credibility problem," Haddon said. "We can't keep saying the problems on the 1048 are fixed and then have new ones keep cropping up. And we can't keep promising new products on schedule and then keep slipping them. The operating companies aren't going to believe us. They don't now."

"I'm going to take a poll at Venray and ask how many people have worked weekends and holidays in the last month," Hicks said. "I'll bet no one has." Hicks was getting frustrated. After a pause, he continued.

"I have two choices. I accept this constant slipping or I tell Charlie Christ and Bill Drawe to start looking for new jobs. It's the same thing we were talking about at dinner last night—motivation. How do we drive motivation throughout this organization? Getting these products out on time is becoming my direct responsibility when really it should rest with the groups working right with them. The incentives should be there so that their compensation depends on delivering on schedule. I do have one other option," he continued. "If my own people can't deliver, I can move the work to Fuji Xerox. We'll just sell what they design and build."

The pilots and customs agents soon arrived to break the silence that had fallen.

On the plane to Eindhoven, Holland, Hicks asked Haddon: "Is there a strategic way to use value added? Put a plant in a country where you get some credit for it. Everyone counts it but it doesn't really help in the UK, Holland, and Germany. It helps more in France and really helps in Spain."

"The real question is how do you build a new plant one place and add employees when you're cutting elsewhere, especially in a country with 20 percent unemployment like Holland," Haddon said.

"But doesn't it make more sense to put a plant where it gives you some advantage against your competition. Couldn't we effectively block Canon out if we manufactured copiers in Spain?"

"We've got 5,000 manufacturing employees in Europe now, and that's already too many by a factor of two."

The exchange continued. Later, Hicks leaned over to me and said, "You see why I like Lyndon. He makes me think."

That night, Sonneborn hosted a dinner for about twenty Xerox managers at De Hosflaug restaurant in Helmond, near the Venray plant. Jack Fryer and Bill Drawe had flown in from London.

"We're British but we are in American company," Fryer said of his Welwyn group. "You could pick us up and plunk us down in Webster and we would operate quite nicely. The big difference is wage rates. They're slave rates in England. A project through me costs half as much as it would through the U.S. Then you add the currency movement on top of that."

After the drinks had been served, Hicks proposed a toast, "I want to congratulate Willi and his Venray management team on the production of their 100,000th 1045." Willi smiled. There was applause. "And Willi, I've got something else for you." Hicks reached under the table and brought out the Irvine plaque, wrapped in brown paper. Sonneborn opened it and smiled again, but this time his face was red.

"I'm going to hang it in my office," he said.

"Maybe you should rotate it among your top managers," Hicks said.

The table of managers laughed, politely.

DAY THREE

It was cold and windy when the cars arrived at 7:00 A.M. to pick us up at the Hotel Cocagne in Eindhoven for the hour-long drive to the Venray plant. For much of the way, no one spoke.

The conference room, with its wall of windows revealing the gloomy day, was crowded with twenty-five people. Everyone spoke English, but their accents told how truly international this gathering was. There were Yanks, Brits, Dutchmen, Frenchmen, and one German—Sonneborn.

Fryer began with an overview of the Somerset and Andes projects.

His conclusions: In regard to Somerset, an April 1 launch was still viable, but because of some problems, primarily with the paper loading cassette, a two-week slip was possible. He recommended a conservative launch that cut back on some of the planned initial volume. He said there could be some cost exposure on tooling for the cassettes, up to $1.2 million. The Andes project's five-week slip made a May 1 launch difficult. Although Andes was similar to Somerset, it had 200 unique parts, including a complex software operating system that could cause an additional four-week slip. Welwyn was having difficulty finding qualified software engineers, and some of its own engineers had left for other companies. "It's a volatile situation now," Fryer said. "Software engineers are in demand." He said June 1 was a safe launch target for Andes with two weeks earlier possible. The plan on both machines was to launch in the United Kingdom first and the United States one month later.

UMC targets were being met. Ninety-five percent of the parts on the current Somerset prototype had been quoted by suppliers. The only parts of significance still missing were the cassettes.

Mike Green from Welwyn then gave a manufacturing readiness report. He said his group had identified 1,200 problems on early Somerset prototypes. Most of those had been fixed, the remaining ones would be, and he didn't expect any new ones of significance to arise. About 160 machine tools were required for the Somerset/Andes line. In two months, by December 17, all but fifteen should be in place. The plan was to get "customers," people with Xerox who use copiers a lot, at the end of the pilot line reviewing machines, and to exit the pilot line by December 21. The main production line would then be retooled for Somerset/Andes during the Christmas holidays. Green forecast a per month rate of ten engineering parts changes where a new part is designed to improve or fix an old part. That was a significant number, considering that they had to be cut into the main line after start-up. But it wasn't nearly as high as for the 9900, built in Webster, which was averaging two parts changes a day.

The pilot line concept, where early models of a new machine are built under conditions that simulate mainline production, was adopted by Hicks to try to foster a closer working relationship between the engineering and manufacturing divisions. It is used both in the United States and Europe, where product designers are physically separated from the production site. At Fuji Xerox's main copier facility in Ebina, the engineers are separated from the manufacturing floor by only a short hallway. Fuji Xerox does not use a pilot line, but it does use mainline production workers to help build prototypes of new machines in a model shop.

One option to speed the mainline start-up on Somerset/Andes was using full manpower, which would allow for a faster build up but cost an additional $500,000. It takes time to learn how to build a machine right, so although Xerox had the manpower to potentially build 140 machines a day, it might only be making twenty-five a day during the learning process.

"What does Fuji Xerox do?" Hicks asked.

"I think they use full manpower," someone from the group said.

"Don't think, find out," Hicks said. "If Fuji Xerox does, let's spend the money and do it, too."

Haddon asked about a hedge to provide machines to Xerox's operating companies in case Somerset did not launch on time. "Do we order 1045 parts to backfill in case we don't make the Somerset launch? What do we tell the Opcos today?"

Drawe recommended ordering one month's worth of parts, 3,000 1045s, as a hedge. Venray would not be stuck with those unnecessary parts if Somerset did indeed make its schedule, because the 1045s could be diverted to other Xerox plants in Mexico and India.

It was past lunchtime. Hicks told Dougall to get on the phone and find out exactly how many sets of parts could be diverted to Mexico and India, if necessary. He then told everyone to leave the room except his top management team: Haddon, Sachdev, Christ, and Drawe.

"Did everybody hear enough?" he asked.

"Because of the timing involved in making the launch decision and ordering the backfill parts, I don't think we're talking 3,000 machines," Haddon said. "I think it's 6,000 machines."

"That's another $4 million to $6 million in inventory," Sachchev said.

"I really think it's a mistake to push the launch," Christ said. "I think this cassette problem is more serious than we realize. Cassettes were a problem on the 3300. We pushed ahead then and got burned."

"If we decide to slip Andes and hedge Somerset, what I don't want is a huge sigh of relief from these people," Hicks said. "We'll come back in a month and find out the programs have slipped even more."

The 1048 session in the afternoon went much as it had in Welwyn. This time, however, there were manufacturing people present and several people from the operating companies to reinforce the field rep's disappointment. The basic problem, the field reps said, was that machine defects they considered serious weren't being picked up on the line. Machines were being passed that shouldn't. Maybe the quality checks themselves were faulty. In response, one of the Venray manufacturing managers alluded to an engineering problem. "All I can speak of is manufacturing," he said.

Hicks had his opening.

"I don't want to hear that," he said. "We've got a real barnburner here and I don't understand why. And after listening to everything today and in Welwyn I don't think you do either. We've got a problem that affects the whole company. I want you to get on that machine like ugly on a monkey until we have it licked. Willi, I want you to make it a habit of going out personally to see your customers. If there's a problem I want you to find it instead of it coming to you. Go out once a month or so and see what they are saying."

Production of 1048s was running at 180 a day. The decision was made to cut back to ninety a day, with a 1,000-copy burn-in, until the quality was improved.

Dougall returned to the meeting after making his international telephone calls. "There should be no problem bleeding off 3,000 parts kits to Mexico," he said. The group decided to press on with the Somerset launch but hedge by ordering parts for 1,500 1045s. The Andes schedule was slipped.

"I'm certainly disappointed," Hicks said in closing. "We made the case a month ago to go 1,500 contingent and press on. The situation isn't any better now. I don't want anyone to let up. The Japanese aren't."

It was raining. Hicks had two hours to catch a flight from Amsterdam to Madrid, but Sonneborn wanted a photograph of him with the 100,000th 1045. They ran in the rain from the office building to the plant. After the photograph, Hicks wanted to see the pilot line for Somerset. Mike Green showed him the paper cassette and explained the loading problem. The paper wasn't feeding correctly into the copier because the snubbers on the cassette weren't snapping into place on top of the paper. Hicks tried to load the paper. It took several attempts before he was successful. "Boy, that really is a dog," he said. "Fix it."

Then it was off to Amsterdam, at 90 miles per hour, in the rain. Hicks and Sonneborn sat in the backseat of the Mercedes 280 SE. "I really mean that about seeing your customers, Willi," Hicks said. "Get out there and talk to them. Find out what they think." They talked again about the quality problems on the 1048. "We have to lick this problem,'' Hicks said. ''And we have to do it now. If you have to cut production back even further, go ahead.''

On the Iberia Airlines flight to Madrid, Hicks talked about the rapid launch concept. ''What I want to do is hit my competition with a blitzkrieg on product launches. The idea is to roll out quickly, flood the markets, and not give my competition a chance to respond. With product cycles getting shorter—anywhere from twenty-four to thirty-six months—why should I give my competition up to 25 percent or more of that time to respond just because I have a slow rollout. Launch in the United Kingdom one month and the United States the next—no one has ever done that before. I want to hit all the markets right away.''

Hicks confided that he didn't think the Somerset program would make the April launch date. ''I had the same contingency plan on the final launch of the 1075, but we made it,'' he said. ''Somerset might, too.''

He then picked up on the value added strategy discussion from the previous day.

''I want to get Lyndon and some other people together and just think about what we can do when that consent decree comes off. We have been playing a defensive game too long. I like offense much better. I think we can play a much better strategy game against the Japanese in Europe. I want to take all of the business I can away from them. Willi was telling me about Océ [a Dutch maker of copiers] in the car. I might go to Océ and say, 'Hey, we aren't the enemy. Let's cooperate.' Maybe I can sell him toner or photoreceptors and then he can do something for me.

''That's why it's so important to get this product development operation moving. In the past, people have always said they would do something, but they never followed through on schedule or cost. Everything ran late. The 1075 was two years late. I want to get a steady stream of copiers rolling out not only in the mid-range but in every part of the market.''

Luis Pastor Garrido, manager of the Xerox toner plant in Coslada, picked us up at the Madrid airport. We checked into the hotel Miguel Angel downtown and then went to a midnight dinner. ''Everyone eats late in Spain,'' Hicks said. He bought a vacation home in the mountains fifty miles west of Madrid when he worked in England, so he had been in Madrid often. His wife and daughter had spent a month in Spain that summer, and he had joined them for a week. ''Most vacation days would end with me out on the balcony just sitting and staring up at the stars,'' he said. "You can do a lot of thinking about strategy at two A.M."

He spoke Spanish much of the time with Pastor Garrido, whom he was meeting for the first time. Hicks had never been to the Coslada plant before. Although it was after midnight and the business day still had not ended, talk naturally turned to wives and family life.

"My wife and I often exchange letters at home," Sonneborn said. "I will get in late and she will already be in bed so I will write her a note, 'Dear wife . . .' In the morning, she has to leave by six and I don't have to go until seven so she writes, 'Dear husband.'"

"Salli and I do that, too," Hicks said. "Only I write the note at night and then again in the morning."

This was the furthest from business that the conversation strayed all week. In the hotel lobbies in the mornings, in the cars on the way to the plants, and in the airports and airplanes, the talk was always about Xerox or some competitor. The World Series was being played the week of the tour and no one mentioned it.

At dinner Hicks explained how he had once made a proposal to the top management at Xerox to sell the 1045 and the other low- and mid-range models through a separate Xerox dealer network. He admitted it was a controversial idea. The direct sales force is what made Xerox.

"We would set these dealerships up on a joint venture basis or fund them completely," he said. "I would sell them anything they wanted from service to billing help. I would invite 200 of the top dealers from around the country to spend a week in Bermuda on us. I would make the invitations real nice. 'Come on us, but come prepared to spend $100,000. If you don't have it, we will finance you.' It would be costly for a couple of years but we could expand our market share by fifteen points. It would be immensely profitable. And, it would all be at the expense of the Japanese.

"You know, I often have a dream of Japanese ships loaded with freight, presumably copiers, heading for the United States. Halfway there they turn back to Japan. Instead of sinking them with submarines we had learned to beat them at their own game of manufacturing."

DAY FOUR

Spain is different. Maybe it's because the mountains have kept the country isolated for so long. Everywhere else on this trip the day had started at 6:30, 7:00 at the latest. In Spain, the car came at 8:30, and then because of the traffic and one-way streets, it took a half hour just to go around the block. Madrid is a 4-million-person gridlock.

Sonneborn and I sat in the backseat of Pastor Garrido's Ford Ghia. Sonneborn told me that he started with Rank Xerox in 1973. He said there was some suspicion among his employees at first about his being German. "You know, the war and everything," he said. "But now it's different. Now my employees say, 'Willi, he's 150 percent Dutch.' "

Sonneborn, who runs the biggest plant in Rank Xerox, supervises Pastor Garrido, who runs the smallest. "Luis has the best job in all of Rank Xerox," Sonneborn said. "His plant is modern, efficient, profitable, and he is far away from all of the top management so that nobody bothers him. Wayland is the highest-ranking Xerox manager to ever review the Coslada plant, by a long ways."

Garrido's plant is about ten miles east of Madrid, near the American air base. It opened in 1974 and makes toner and the cleaning brushes that wipe excess toner from copier drums. We saw brushes being made for the 914, Xerox's very first automatic office copier, introduced in 1959. About sixty people work at Coslada, compared to about 2,000 at Venray.

Coslada provided the best example of the entire trip of how exchange rates can affect an operation's performance. Since 1981, the output of the Coslada plant had grown more than 250 percent in terms of pesetas. But in dollars, output had actually shrunk. "You can be growing like a weed and it doesn't show up," Hicks said. In 1981, it took about 70 pesetas to equal a dollar. For 1984, the Coslada plan forecast an exchange rate of 130, and 153 for 1985. At the time of Hicks's review it had risen to more than 170.

Hicks pressed the Spanish manufacture issue.

"What does it cost to import a machine here?" he asked.

"On machines from the EEC [European Economic Community], 18,000 pesetas plus 10 percent of the DIF [duty, insurance, freight] value," one of Pastor Garrido's managers answered.

"What about from Japan or the United States?"

"Twenty-five thousand pesetas plus 10 percent of DIF plus 10 percent of the price of the machine landed. On machines that cost less than £500, the duty is 15.6 percent of cost plus 10 percent of DIF. We have been importing 'complete machines' to get around the duty. Otherwise each unit—processor, sorter, etcetera—would be considered a separate machine."

"What if I manufacture a machine in Spain? How much has to be local content?"

"Sixty percent of the value of the machine has to be local content—that includes labor, overhead, and material. You can import 40 percent and there is no tax on the 40 percent if the machines are for export. All of this will begin to change, of course, when Spain joins the EEC in 1986."

The discussion shifted to toner. Sonneborn said Venray had a spare processor for toner. Pastor Garrido said there was vacant space to use it at Coslada.

"We cannot, of course, sell Canon toner," Pastor Garrido said. "But we can sell Xerox toner made for Canon."

"The capacity of the processor is 1.5 million kilos," Sonneborn said. "That's a lot of Canon toner."

Hicks turned to me. "You see why I go on these tours." He seemed to have found at least one new product he could make in Spain.

The toner manufacturing process starts with a white polymer to which is added carbon black. It is then heated and rolled out in one long continuous sheet, like saltwater taffy. The sheet is broken into chunks, and those chunks are broken up again and again until only a fine, black powder is left. No clean room here. Black dust covers everything, and the workers have to wear surgical masks to keep from breathing it.

When the plant tour was over, Pastor Garrido presented Hicks with a bound copy of the day's presentations. On the cover was a color photograph of the Coslada plant. "That's just for you, Wayland," Pastor Garrido said. He then asked the photographer, who had been following Hicks around the plant, to take a shot of both of them in front of the plant. It was raining, again. Hicks stood, smiling, with Pastor Garrido. Then it was off to lunch at a restaurant in a 450-year-old building—La Casa Grande. Then to the airport to catch an Iberia flight back to London.

On the plane, after a long week on the road, Hicks pulled a copy of Alan Drury's *Decision* out of his briefcase and settled back. The A-300 Airbus droned on. Sunset came and then darkenss. Hicks's chin rested on his chest. So did his book. He was napping. For the first time all week his tie was loosened and his collar undone.

Hicks awoke just before landing and buttoned his collar and cinched his tie. "I have to get back into uniform," he joked. He checked one of Maureen Jones's memos. "If all goes well, there should be a car waiting." It was. In the crowd at Heathrow a driver held up a sign: "Wayland Hicks, Rank Xerox."

That night Hicks would join his wife and friends in the English countryside. She had been antique hunting all week. Saturday they would fly back to Rochester. Sunday he would play tennis with Haddon in the morning and confer with Sachdev in the afternoon. Monday his crusade against the Japanese would continue.

Somerset, Xerox's 1040, was launched in May 1985, four weeks late, Andes (1050) was postponed until early 1986. The success of Xerox's midvolume line-up against Canon and Ricoh convinced Hicks he could wait that long to make sure all of Andes's software problems were solved. After his conversation with Hicks on the way to the Amsterdam airport, Sonneborn returned to Venray and the following week reduced the production rate on the 1048 even further: to seven a day. His managers instituted a customer compliance test at the end of the manufacturing line in which each machine had to make a total of 2,600 copies in several operating modes that stressed all of its capabilities. If a machine couldn't make the copies or had any other defect, it was returned to the beginning of the line. The idea was to keep repeating the testing process to force quality in. The same compliance test was used during the pilot-line production of Somerset and Andes. Venray also went to a second shift to increase production of Somerset to make the rapid launch.

"Boeing doesn't have its customers—its passengers—test its jets," Hicks said later. "We shouldn't either. If we make sure we have quality in the pilot line we won't need the compliance test after we start mainline production.

"I was a little upset that Venray had a solution and didn't institute it earlier. But once you have made it their responsibility and they have fixed the problem, you can't complain."

PART TWO
THE OLD XEROX

3
Legend of the
914

When prototypes of the Xerox 914, the world's first automatic plain paper copying machine, were being tested around the clock during the winter of 1959–60 in an old building on Lyell Avenue in Rochester, the landlord turned the heat off every night at 5:00 P.M.

Xerox didn't want to pay any more money to keep the heat on all night, so the engineers made tentlike canvas enclosures around the machines that threw off some heat of their own. At night, the workers wore hunting jackets and boots and stayed inside the enclosures to keep warm. By morning, their feet were freezing, their hands were cold, and they were dead tired. Yet they would still hang around after their shift ended to discuss with the next crew what they had learned during the night. They did this seven days a week.

THOUSANDS OF DOLLARS were spent for the study and the best names the consultant could suggest were "American Xerography Corporation" and "National Xerographic Inc."

Completely unsatisfactory, Joe Wilson thought. He wanted to change the name of his Haloid Co. to more closely identify it with the new technology it was developing, but the consultant's suggestions simply would not do.

Then, one Sunday morning, Wilson and Sol Linowitz were out for a walk. They walked together for a couple of hours every Sunday. Some mornings it would be around the Cobbs Hill Reservoir on the eastern edge of Rochester, sometimes around Wilson's neighborhood in Brighton, or in the woods at Mendon Ponds Park. They talked about the company, politics, their families. Their walks became famous within the company. In later years, co-workers would phone Linowitz and suggest items he should discuss with Wilson.

This particular Sunday, more than thirty-five years ago, they had been walking in the woods, when they came upon a clearing near a road.

"Look at that," Linowitz said, pointing at a large "Kodak" sign.

Wilson was thinking the same thing.

"Why doesn't that make sense?" he said. "Xerox, with an *x* on the end."

Thank you, George Eastman. The founder of the largest photographic company in the world created the name Kodak for his first roll film camera because it was short, easy to remember, and began and ended with his favorite letter. Can you imagine one of the great Cinderella stories of American business being named National Xerographic Inc.? Actually, Wilson never liked it when people referred to Xerox during its spectacular growth years as a Cinderella story. The company earned its success, he said. The only magic was the magic of hard work.

As a boy, Wilson grew up in the shadow of Kodak's largest manufacturing facility in Rochester—Kodak Park. His dream was to build a company as great as George Eastman's. He didn't want to make a quick killing and then retire with his riches, he wanted his company to have an impact on the world. He wanted to make his company his life's work, just as Eastman had done.

Chester Carlson and the 914 copier helped Wilson realize his dream. Carlson, the inventor of xerography, filed his first patent in 1937, calling his discovery electrophotography. His first successful image was made in 1938. Over the next nine years he tried to sell his idea to more than twenty companies, including RCA, Remington Rand, General Electric, Kodak, and IBM. They all turned him down, wondering why anyone would need a machine to do something you could do with carbon paper.

Although Carlson was often frustrated by the lack of interest in his invention, he never quit. Sometimes he put his idea and equipment on the shelf for a few months, but soon the enthusiasm would return. He scraped together a few hundred dollars in 1939, a large sum during the Depression, and had a prototype of an automatic copier built by a model shop in New York. It didn't work. Another model maker got it working, briefly, but soon the war diverted expert machinists to more urgent tasks. Carlson went back to demonstrating his process with manual plates. Finally, in 1944, Battelle Memorial Institute in Columbus, Ohio, signed a royalty-sharing agreement with him and began to develop the process. A short time later, John Dessauer, Haloid's director of research, showed Joe Wilson a technical article on Carlson's electrophotography in *Radio News*. Haloid made the initial contacts with Battelle, and in 1947, it signed an agreement with Battelle and began funding research. With the help of a professor from Ohio State University, the term "xerography," Greek for "dry writing," was coined.

The early manual copying process was excruciatingly slow, almost like developing a photographic print. An early Haloid brochure describes *Thirty-Nine Steps* for making good copies on its first commercial copier, the Model A Xerox, which was sometimes called the Ox Box. The best operators took two to three minutes to make a print, a long way from Carlson's vision of an automatic machine. Still, Wilson and Haloid pressed on. Over the next thirteen years, Wilson committed more money than his company made to developing the process.

Carlson and Wilson both made fortunes on xerography; Carlson earned more than $200 million, Wilson more than $100 million. Their backgrounds and personalities were different, but both of them were reflective men who were concerned with more than money and business. Carlson was a quiet, shy man from a poor family who struggled to put himself through college and never knew material comfort until late in life when the royalties from xerography finally started to arrive. During the early years at Haloid, Dessauer once asked him out to lunch. Carlson declined because he couldn't afford to reciprocate. When he made his great breakthrough in xerography he was working days in a patent office, going to law school at night, and doing his experiments on weekends. He always felt uncomfortable in large groups and avoided public involvement in causes, although he anonymously donated millions of dollars to many of them.

Carlson was never on the regular Xerox payroll, though Wilson made several offers. Instead, he preferred the independence of working as a consultant. He died in 1968, at the age of sixty-two, of a heart attack. A year before his death his wife asked him if he had any unfulfilled desires. "Just one," he said. "I would like to die a poor man." When he died, he had given away more than $150 million. U Thant, secretary-general of the United Nations, sent this tribute to Carlson's memorial service in honor of his substantial financial contributions: "His concern for the future of the human situation was genuine, and his dedication to the principles of the United Nations was profound."

Wilson was a graduate of the Harvard Business School. His father was president of Haloid before him and his grandfather had served as mayor of Rochester. Unlike Carlson, Wilson was an outgoing person. His speeches were as likely to contain quotes from Byron and Dostoyevski as they were to contain the latest earnings and revenue numbers. Even after the company became successful, he would frequently lunch on peanut butter and jelly sandwiches at his desk so he could catch up on his reading. He welcomed involvement in community affairs, often speaking about the obligation of successful enterprises to contribute to society. Wilson died in 1971, at the age of sixty-one, of a heart attack, while having lunch with the governor of New York, Nelson Rockefeller. A frayed, blue, index card that he had carried since the early days of his career was found in his wallet. It summarized his goals: "To be a whole man; to attain serenity through the creation of a family life of uncommon richness; through leadership of a business which brings happiness to its workers, serves well its customers and brings prosperity to its owners; by aiding a society threatened by fratricidal division to gain unity."

On September 16, 1959, twenty-one years after Carlson made his famous "10-22-38 Astoria" image, the Xerox 914 copier was announced. *Fortune* magazine would later call it "the most successful product ever marketed in America." Xerox's long-time chairman and chief executive Peter McColough goes even further. "It has to be one of the most successful, if not *the* most successful, product of all time in any industry," he said. One of the original 914s is now in the Smithsonian Museum.

The business world would never be the same. The 914 changed the course of history for graphic communications and Xerox. It was almost totally responsible for transforming Haloid, still dependent on manufacturing photograhic paper for much of its $31.7 million in sales in 1959, into today's $14 billion giant with its more than 100,000 employees in a hundred countries around the world.

"Xerography has become almost like the internal combustion engine as a permanent part of our lives," McColough says. Xerox, like Kleenex, is part of everyone's vocabulary. Suddenly, after the 914, people were saying, "Make me a Xerox of this." The company still takes out ads in journalism magazines cautioning reporters that Xerox should always be used with a capital *X*. "To xerox" is not a verb. Cartoons about this social phenomenon began appearing in popular magazines. One showed a guy in a cast from his neck down, saying, "Whatever you do, don't sell the Xerox stock!" Another shows a fellow walking into a room marked "Copying" with a beautiful woman. On the way out he is accompanied by two identical women. That cartoon is still a favorite of Chester Carlson's widow, Dorris. When it first appeared, she cut it out of the magazine, wrote on it "I'm ag'in it" and gave it to her husband.

Then there are the tales of fortune and misfortune that always accompany great American success stories. The cab driver and assembly-line foreman in Rochester who became millionaires owning Xerox stock.

The Xerox workers with the "million-dollar" houses who sold their stock in the early days, before the big run-up, so they could buy their homes. E. Kent Damon, who joined Haloid in 1949 for a salary of $100 a week, sold some stock in the early 1950s to redecorate his home. "That stock would be worth a good many million today," he says. It was Damon's job to raise the money Wilson needed to develop xerography. Damon still has an office at Xerox Tower in Rochester where he displays a photo of Joe Wilson and a large statue of a black bull, a gift from his wife during the heyday. "It was exciting then." he says. "One of my responsibilities was dealing with the financial guys; the bankers, the stock analysts, and guys like that. Everyday there were any number of them on the telephone. It was just unbelievable."

Apple Computer Corporation is commonly recognized as the fastest company to reach sales of a billion dollars, making the leap in just nine years from 1975 to 1984. Xerox cracked its first billion dollars eight years after the introduction of the 914 and a bit of a running start. And, because of inflation, a dollar in 1968 was worth about three times as much as it was in 1984. Even today, stockbrokers and financial advisers are always searching for "the next Xerox."

Carlson thought his invention would change the world. As his basic patents began running out, about the time of the 914, he sometimes wondered if he would see any reward for his work. But he always knew it was important. Wilson agreed. But the same can't be said for some of their co-workers.

"None of us really saw how big it would be," remembers Linowitz, who helped set up the company's patent protection, went on to become Xerox chairman and then a United States ambassador. "When Joe would make some of his prophecies about how it might be a billion-dollar company, people would wonder what he was smoking. Joe was always a man who saw things with great optimism. He wanted to believe what he said. But it used to cause some head shaking and eyebrow lifting among more pragmatic types, including some inside the company."

Today, the legacy of Carlson, Wilson, and the 914 lives on. The spectacular past acts as a sometimes haunting reminder of the spirit the company is trying to rekindle. No company has been so buoyed and yet so haunted by its past.

· In the lobby of Xerox Tower in Rochester sits a 914, with a small sign talking about its significance. Someone has scribbled on the sign: "The day the free lunch stopped," a reference to the more competitive recent years.

- At PARC, the Xerox Palo Alto Research Center in California, scientist Gary Starkweather has a photograph of Chester Carlson on the wall of his office. It's fun and respectable to work on copiers again. In the mid- and late-1970s, when Xerox had focused all of its attention on the office of the future, "real" scientists didn't work on copiers.
- In Tokyo, Fuji Xerox President Yotaro Kobayashi talks about the spirit of Joe Wilson, which Xerox had, lost, and is now trying to regain. Kobayashi admires Wilson's management style and patterns his own after it.
- Each of the six corporate jets in Xerox's domestic fleet is named after a Xerox product. The names change, depending upon what's new and hot. One name that will never change is the N914X.
- At Xerox's largest manufacturing site, the Joseph C. Wilson Center for Technology, in Webster, New York, new Xerox employees are shown a training video that includes a pep talk from Wilson. "It just raises everybody right out of their seats," says Hal Bogdonoff, who once was a special assistant to Carlson. "They can't believe it was made in 1964."

Among the items on the walls of Bogdonoff's office are a color photograph of Wilson and two photos of Carlson. Beneath them, in a locked cabinet, are copies of Carlson's voluminous personal scrapbooks. "You can see I still have a great admiration for the man," says Bogdonoff, whose job today is to monitor competitors' machines.

The people and stories from the early days seem larger than life today. Bogdonoff tells how Carlson was strangely protective of his expertise when he first started working directly with Haloid employees. Carlson would mix the coatings for toner carrier beads in the privacy of his basement at home and then bring them to the Haloid labs. "We used to joke that the recipe was two bottles of ginger ale and a bottle of 7-Up," Bogdonoff says. "That's how Chet would bring the stuff to us." Carlson loosened up as he developed a rapport with Haloid workers, but even today, Xerox considers those formulas a deep corporate secret. They have never been patented to keep the exact contents unknown.

Horace Becker is another of the early employees. Young Xerox workers have great respect for Becker and his accomplishments. He joined the company in 1958 and took the 914 all the way from the concept stage to the marketplace. Some call him the father of the 914. "They have it wrong," he says. "I was the midwife. I am not an inventor. I understand what is required to take a product that is a concept and help make that product a commercial reality.'' In time he became the director of manufacturing—training many of the people who now hold key positions in the company—a vice president for engineering, and a member of the Fuji Xerox board of directors. He is now semiretired, working on Xerox's joint-venture manufacturing facility in China. Becker regularly lunches with the mayor of Shanghai and carries business cards in three languages: English, Japanese, and Chinese. His recollections of the early days lay a good foundation for understanding the company then and now:

The reason the 914 became a success at the Haloid Company was that if it had gone anywhere else and that company had anything else to do, they would have lost interest in it. Joe Wilson was facing a shrinking marketplace with his products and it was xerography or nothing.

We built the beginnings of this business on a single device, the 914, that we tried to sell to lots of people. The two most important were IBM and Bell and Howell. We tried to sell it to them and they weren't interested. IBM said that ''it had no place to go, there really wasn't a need for it, it was a very specialized thing and maybe you'll build 5,000.''

We started to build the first building in Webster before we had shipped the first 914. It was the greatest gamble mankind has seen. Joe had vision and courage and enthusiasm. He didn't drive us, he led us.

What was the competition in copying, besides carbon paper? Verifax by Kodak, $350 per machine, a little box, several cents a copy. Thermofax by 3M; $350 for a Thermofax. We came along with something the size of a desk and we say to the customer, ''Don't worry, this is a new technology, nobody is practicing it, trust us.'' And you know what? We knew nobody would buy it because it would cost too much.

So Joe Wilson and company came up with the absolutely fantastic invention that was more important than xerography, the decision to rent the machines. We rented the 914 for $95 a month, for which you got 2,000 free copies and four cents for each additional copy.

Now, are you ready? . . . with a fifteen-day cancellation clause.

Can you imagine? You go out and you borrow the money to build a machine the size of a desk which costs several thousand dollars to manufacture and you put them out and you sit back very calmly and you don't worry. And you do all this with a fifteen-day cancellation clause that lets the customer kick it right back to you if he doesn't like it.

It's called madness.

Today, if someone walked in and made that recommendation to Dave Kearns, he would be destroyed.

Becker remembers seeing Carlson in a hallway struggling to get an early 914 to work. Becker couldn't make it work either.

"We better walk away from here right now," Carlson said. "You're the chief engineer on the machine and I'm the inventor. If people see even we can't get the thing working, they're going to think we're headed for disaster.''

To the contrary, a better name for the 914 might be the machine that never died. In the late 1970s, Xerox decided to scrap several 914s in California. Since they were all still in good shape, the company ordered them destroyed to keep them out of the hands of the competition. They weren't. Later, an enterprising businessman bought them from a junkyard, refurbished them, and put them back out on lease under his own plan.

About 200,000 914s, and simple variations, were made around the world between 1960 and the early 1970s when production of the 914 was stopped. Half were made at Webster, about 80,000 in Europe, and the rest in Japan. During 1985, more than twenty-five years after its introduction, there were still more than 6,000 in operation in the United States alone. About 200 were still on lease by Xerox, providing about $1 million in annual revenues. A milestone of sorts was reached at the end of 1985 when Xerox announced it would no longer renew service contracts on the 914. Repairs would still be made, but on a time and materials basis only.

"Do you know what it's like to put out a product that doesn't die?" says a Xerox engineer. "It's not like putting out a machine that has only a two- or three-year life span when you can stop making the parts. We've got to keep those 914 parts in stock forever.''

Business Week put Joe Wilson and the 914 on its cover in September 1959. Other important national publications played down the introduction or didn't mention it at all. *The Wall Street Journal* carried a five-paragraph announcement. *The New York Times* ignored it, even though the introduction (the same day Soviet leader Nikita Khrushchev arrived in New York during a tour of the United States) was at the Sherry-Netherland Hotel in New York. *Financial World* had a seven-paragraph story. The two hometown Rochester newspapers provided modest coverage. One carried an eight-inch story under the headline: "Haloid Unveils Device for Automatic Copying." The other carried an eleven-inch story, headline: "Haloid to Manufacture Office Copying Device." *Forbes* magazine interviewed Wilson in 1957 but didn't publish an article because Haloid had only $19 million in assets. The magazine corrected the oversight in a 1965 editorial.

Only *Business Week* recognized the 914 for what it was: a revolution in what was then *the* glamour industry—office copying. "The growth rate of all copying equipment has been more spectacular than that of even the electronics industry,'' the magazine said. ''Sales in 1950 were $60 million; this year they will hit an estimated $225 million, and the predictions for 1965 range from a conservative $371 million to $500 million.''

Even the optimistic projection would prove modest.

In 1959, about thirty-five companies made copying equipment, including Kodak, Minnesota Mining & Manufacturing Co. (3M), and American Photocopy Equipment Co. They used five different processes, including Diazo printing, which required one-sided, translucent originals. Though the prices per copy were competitive, ranging from four cents to nine cents, none of the other machines offered all the features and simplicity of the 914.

In Kodak's Verifax dye transfer method, for instance, a negative image of the original was made. Then it had to be passed through an activator solution and two sheets of special paper had to be peeled apart by hand. With the 914, which used ordinary paper, the operator just placed the original face down on the glass patent, dialed the desired number of copies from one to fifteen, pushed a button, and waited for the copies to start popping out in a tray. Copying suddenly became easy.

It sure beat carbon paper, which was the most common method of copying a document. Make a mistake and you had to plow through the whole stack of sheets and correct each one. Copies were often torn or smudged, sometimes barely legible.

With the 914 came the ''era of mass copying,'' as a 1965 Department of the Army bulletin called it. Since then, there have been countless other government and private studies commissioned to help control the costs of copying. During budget crunches, the office copying machine is often one of the first casualties. Some companies even put charts on top of each of their machines, showing employees exactly how much each punch of the print button costs. A 1985 study conducted by Burke Marketing Research estimated that 29 percent of all copies made were unnecessary, costing American companies $2.6 billion a year. Those 130 billion wasted copies, laid end to end, would stretch to the moon and back forty-seven times.

Oh, the 914 did have its bugs, such as paper jams that still plague copiers today. When the company staged a demonstration of the 914 at Grand Central Station in New York it had to have three machines on site to make sure one would be running every half hour. ''The engineering was never really completed,'' Becker says. ''After we shipped them, because we rented them, we would keep improving them until they became dependable enough. We had very little competition, so customers would accept us improving the machine after they received it because it would cost them nothing. They were leasing, we would improve it and we would get to where we had to be. Today, the minute it goes out the door it's got to be there. We no longer have the luxury of being the only company in the marketplace with the technology."

There was also a tendency for the copy paper to catch on fire when it came in contact with the 914's hot fuser rollers. In such cases, Xerox urged operators to do nothing and let the fire burn itself out. Each machine was equipped with a small fire extinguisher, which for public relations reasons the company called a "scorch eliminator." That precaution didn't placate consumer advocate Ralph Nader. Still riding the success of his book, *Unsafe at Any Speed*, Nader flew into Rochester in November 1969 and publicly assailed Xerox for the "shoddy design" of some of its copiers. He said the 914 in his Washington office had caught fire three times during the previous four months. A Xerox official said the company would help Nader resolve the problems.

Nader aside, the 914 had a special appeal that kept most customers satisfied. John Brooks, in his 1967 article in *The New Yorker*, "Xerox Xerox Xerox Xerox," wrote that he had never before observed such a close relationship between an office worker and a machine as he did with the 914. He wrote: "A 914 has distinct animal traits: it has to be fed and curried; it is intimidating but can be tamed; it is subject to unpredictable bursts of misbehavior; and, generally speaking, it responds in kind to its treatment."

A month after the 914 was first shown in New York, it was featured in a business equipment show in Washington, D.C. A short time later, the company received a letter from the White House ordering two machines. "You gotta get your kicks out of things like that," Becker says, proudly pulling a copy of the letter from his files. "How many engineers have a letter from the White House saying they want to buy something you helped deliver?"

The 914 cost $12.5 million to develop, a small sum in retrospect, but still more than Haloid's total earnings from 1950 through 1959. And that doesn't count other xerographic investments the company made. In 1959, Haloid Xerox spent $2.8 million on research and development. That was $700,000 more than it made. "We shipped our first 914 on March 1, 1960," recalls McColough, who joined the company in 1954. "About six months later, after we saw the customer acceptance, we knew we had a real winner."

Company revenues and profits exploded. It was the atomic decade of growth. Revenues first cracked a billion dollars in 1968, hitting $1.125 billion. Profits went from $2.6 million in 1960 to $134 million in 1968.

Wilson made the decision to grow the company as fast as possible, knowing there would be some inefficiency. He also had the foresight to set up international alliances, establishing Rank Xerox in 1956 and Fuji Xerox in 1962. Eric Steenburgh remembers the growth. He started on the production line in 1965 when Xerox had 7,000 employees. Later he switched to personnel. "I personally hired fifty to a hundred people a month during the boom," he recalls.

Most of that growth came from the 914. In 1965, for instance, the 914 accounted for about 62 percent of the company's $392.6 million in revenues, or about $243 million. "None of our other machines really started showing up on our income statements until late 1967," Becker says. The 813, a desktop copier introduced in 1963, sold well but never contributed much to earnings. That experience influenced, and is still influencing, Xerox strategy in the low end of the market. Since the 914, it has always been the big, console models that have made money. The 914 alone accounted for about $1.5 billion in revenue and $300 million in profit during its first eight years on the market. Total profit from the 914 has been more than $1 billion.

Just two years after the introduction of the 914, Xerox made the *Fortune* 500 for the first time, ranking 423rd in 1962. The next year it climbed to 294th and continued upward to reach 60th in 1970. Today, counting financial service revenues, Xerox ranks among the forty largest companies in America. "Joe's decision clearly was that there was no way we could put in all the controls and grow at the rate the opportunity presents itself," said Kent Damon, retired Xerox treasurer. "The decision was, we are going to grow and we are going to have some inefficiency. We'll someday catch up with that. And, of course, we did have a helluva lot of catching up to do in later years." In 1959, there were only five buildings on the Webster manufacturing site. By 1966, Xerox had invested $56 million in its Webster facilities, with twenty-nine buildings complete and three more under construction. Today, there are seventy buildings with more than 5.5 million square feet of space.

That rapid growth had to cause some consternation at IBM—the consternation of missed opportunity. Shortly before the 914 was introduced, IBM had had another chance to buy into Xerox's copying business. While IBM was considering a proposal, Wilson put McColough in charge of a group to draw up a recommendation on whether to accept an offer when and if it came. "The younger guys in the group didn't want to sell," says McColough, who was thirty-seven at the time. "Basically, we felt that we should not give that machine to IBM because it would kill our future. Before I got to give my recommendation to Joe Wilson and before he got a chance to voice an opinion, IBM turned us down. Joe Wilson never told me where he really stood on the issue. To the day he died, he never told me. I'm quite sure he would have turned them down."

Linowitz isn't so sure: "My sense is that had IBM said yes, Joe would have felt he had gone so far in urging them to do it that it would have been very difficult for him to say, 'No, we won't.' "

IBM based its decision in part on the recommendation of Arthur D. Little, Inc., a New York–based research firm, which said there was a nationwide market for no more than 5,000 Xerox 914s. Undoubtedly, both organizations would like a second chance. "The fundamental mistake A. D. Little made," McColough says, "was that they didn't consider our concept of pricing, the leasing of machines and metering of copies. We gave them a bundle of material—everything they asked for—on the technical aspects of the machine, but we didn't give them our concept of pricing and marketing. It wasn't as if we were trying to hide anything, they just never asked for it. It may have made a difference in their recommendation."

Later, after the 914 had been rolled out and Joe Wilson himself had demonstrated it at a New York television station, IBM's Tom Watson called and wanted to talk a deal. This time it was Wilson who said no.

The 914 was so named because it could reproduce documents up to 9 inches by 14 inches in size. It took about 15 seconds for the first copy to come out and then 7½ seconds for each additional copy from the same original. It was 42 inches high, 46 inches long, 45 inches wide, and weighed 648 pounds. "It was a God-awful big desk," Becker says.

A 914 cost roughly $2,000 in parts and labor to build. It originally was leased for $95 a month and four cents a copy for every copy over 2,000. The lease rate in early 1985 was $80 a month and six cents a copy. As with every Xerox copier since, the per copy charges are a more important revenue producer than the monthly rate. For instance, a research firm estimated that each of the 9,000 914s in use in 1967 brought in about $4,500 in revenue. That would mean that each 914 made an average of over 100,000 copies a year, well beyond the 2,000-a-month allowance in the lease agreement. It also meant Xerox could recoup most of the money it spent building, advertising, and marketing a 914 in the first year of rental. Except for servicing costs, everything else was pure profit.

Xerox actually made four versions of the same machine—914, 420, 720, and 1000. "We would bring back a 914 and change it into a 720," Becker recalls. "The only difference was the motor speed." The 914s could make seven copies a minute, while the 1000s could make almost seventeen. In 1973, Xerox introduced the world's first color copier, the 6500. A close look would reveal that it was basically the 914 frame and chassis with a multiple exposure filter set up for color reproduction.

"Our original plan was to build five 914s a day for twenty-five a week," Becker says. "Before we got going very far we switched the plan to twenty-five a day. At one point, we got up to ninety a day. That was a lot of hardware."

Getting the parts for that hardware, and getting vendors to meet strict tolerances required on a mass-produced product, was a constant problem. Many suppliers weren't used to such precision. Becker's favorite example is the fur brush that rotated against a selenium drum to clean it after the xerographic image had been transferred to the paper. The outer diameter of the fur layer could vary by no more than $\frac{1}{64}$ of an inch.

"We went to see the vendor who had made some of the brushes for one of our earlier machines called the Copyflo," Becker recalls. "He was a furrier. He made women's coats, mounted deer skins for hunters, and had a little shop where, with his wife and father, he would sew our rabbit skins together on hand sewing machines. He wore the typical yellow measuring tape around his neck, and after we told him the requirements he looked at the tape measure and asked, 'What is a sixty-fourth?' Here was a fellow used to working to plus or minus half an inch when he made a lady's coat, and we had him using sophisticated measuring equipment and, eventually, he was turning out fur brushes by the thousands."

Becker also recalls an emergency trip for fuser parts to keep the 914 assembly line running: "I remember taking an airplane to Chattanooga, Tennessee, getting caught in a snowstorm, ending up in Washington, D.C., without any money, borrowing some from an employee of the company in Washington because the railroad wouldn't take my airline ticket as a credit, going to Chattanooga, getting caught in an ice storm, driving a taxicab because the cab driver didn't know how to drive on ice, and getting the parts. Then we divided them in two packages because there was a fellow from purchasing with me, and each of us started back to Rochester in separate ways so that somebody would get back with parts in time to keep the assembly line from stopping. That was the wildest trip I've ever taken. It took three days. During that time we hadn't shaved and we lived on peanut butter and jelly. And yet we did it because we were fired up.''

Why was this machine so successful?

Two things contributed to the breakthrough, McColough says. First, the technical superiority of the machine. It was technologically complex yet easy to use. Just push a button and the copies came out. Second, and equally important, the marketing genius of the pricing concept of selling copies, not machines. "One aspect without the other wouldn't have worked," he said. "We had come to the conclusion in late 1959 that we couldn't sell the machines outright because they would have been too expensive." In fact, Xerox discouraged outright sales through its pricing.

"The purchase price will be such, I think, that people will rent it," Wilson said when the 914 was unveiled. Indeed, when the 914 was first offered for sale in January 1963, the price was $29,500.

The leasing and metering concept actually started in 1955 with the introduction of the Xerox Copyflo, a much larger machine that produced enlarged prints on a continuous roll from microfilm originals. "We copied IBM's system of leasing and even used the same contract," McColough says. "The contract said there would be a $1,250 fee each month for one work shift. Every regular second shift would be an additional $800. When the machines got out there we found that they were used around the clock, but we were only being paid for one shift. We told the companies this wasn't right. The contract said we were to be paid for the second shift. The companies said these were not regularly scheduled shifts. The people just happened to be working.

"There was a great debate within Haloid on how to solve this problem. We decided to base our rate on the number of feet of paper that ran through the Copyflo each month. This was the start of our metering. We had IBM cards for each machine that the user sent to us each month and then our bills went out, based on the cards. There was some skepticism within Haloid on the procedure, but it worked. So, based on our experience with the Copyflo, we decided to lease and go to copy metering. It has been so long since that happened and there are so few of the original people still around that very few people in the company today realize how that decision was arrived at.''

The 914 was a milestone in communications history. "I think it was the forerunner of making graphic communications possible," McColough says. "It broke through that big logjam. It allowed people to share information inexpensively and easily. The 914 killed carbon paper. And that was good because carbon paper was inefficient. The thing that surprised all of us on the 914 and gave us a lot more volume was what happened in making copies of copies," he continues. "No one anticipated that."

In the mid-1950s, 20 million copies were made annually in the United States on the crude equipment of the day. In 1965, largely because of xerography and the 914, 9.5 billion were made. In 1966, 14 billion. In 1985, more than 700 billion worldwide.

"In the early days there were some people who needed this capability so bad we had several customers who were running 2,000 copies a day on the 914," Becker recalls. "That's five hours a day steady and that doesn't count changing paper, or any other slowdowns. We had customers who were running the daylights out of them because there was a latent need for copies."

It's evident from reading the public statements of Xerox officials that even they didn't completely realize what they had in the 914. Sure, people in the company and some outsiders knew the 914 would have a great impact on Haloid Xerox. "It's like seeing the tip of an iceberg, while knowing that seven-eighths is out of sight below the surface," Wilson had said. But at the time Haloid was a $30-million company whose main ambition was to get to $40 million. No one was thinking about $14 billion.

Wilson predicted in 1959 that the 914 could double Haloid's sales volume to $60 million by 1965. Actual revenues in 1965 were $392.6 million. In 1962, when revenues would hit $115 million, a *Fortune* article on Xerox stated, "No one believes that the 914 is going to keep on going at its present rate forever." That same year Xerox made its first acquisition, University Microfilm.

By 1963, when plans for a twenty-six-story headquarters tower in downtown Rochester were first announced, acquisitions had become an accepted strategy to diversify the corporation's holdings. In 1965, when plans for the office tower had grown to thirty stories and doubled in size to 456,000 square feet, then–executive vice president McColough predicted that the copier industry would hit $1 billion in annual sales in five years. Xerox alone did it in four.

When ground was broken on the tower in early 1965, Wilson predicted that within a decade most of Xerox's profits would come from new-technology acquisitions such as Electro-Optical Systems. Two decades later, most Xerox revenues and profits continue to come from copiers.

In 1967, when Xerox moved into its new $28-million headquarters building, it retained some of its downtown office space because the new tower wasn't big enough; McColough said future growth on a large scale wasn't possible in xerography.

The predictions were always behind the fact. Xerography never slowed.

In Horace Becker's office are several momentos of the 914. On one wall is a collage made of 914 parts. Next to it is a framed version of the two-page ad introducing the 914 in *Fortune* and other magazines. "Which is the $2,800 Picasso? Which is the 5¢ Xerox 914 copy?" the ad asks. Xerox offered to send each reader who guessed correctly a genuine "xerocopy" of the original. Xerox received 16,000 replies to the ads. "After all these years I don't remember which one is the original," Becker says. Today, a single copy of the Picasso made on a 914 would cost about six cents. The original piece of art, which was given as a retirement gift to John Rutledge, who was then manager of field sales, is worth up to $25,000.

"An opportunity to work on something like the 914 only happens once in a lifetime," Becker says. "I remember when we first went over $100 million revenue [1963]. We had a big party. Joe Wilson took about twenty-five of us from Rochester to England during a joint meeting with Rank Xerox. We were guests in the House of Parliament. All of us got into tuxedos and went to dinner. It was quite an entourage. We all thought that was pretty good for a small company from Upstate New York."

Joe Wilson's dream did come true. His company became as large and as well known as George Eastman's and has had a great impact on the world. Kent Damon was asked what Joe Wilson would say if he saw the size of Xerox and the xerographic industry today.

"He would probably lick his chops," Damon answered.

4

The Lost Decade

We just didn't make anything happen. It
was all foreplay and no climax.
—ERIC STEENBURGH, Xerox

ON APRIL 22, 1970, the event Xerox had been anticipating, and
dreading, occurred.

IBM introduced its first office copying machine, the Copier
I. It wasn't very sophisticated. It made only ten copies a minute, used
roll instead of ordinary cut-sheet paper, and couldn't copy from books.
But it was made by IBM, the premier company in American industry.
Xerox was so concerned that it purchased one of the first machines
available and ran it two shifts a day for three months, making no more
than ten copies at a time, mimicking the use it would get in a typical
office. The verdict: Copier I was built like a tank, just like the 914 and
other Xerox machines. It was reliable enough to make 50,000 copies a
month.

The competition had finally arrived. The monopoly was over. Copier I would account for at least two customer cancellations of each
Xerox model then produced, including the 7000, which ran at sixty copies
a minute, could reduce the size of the original, and make copies on two
sides of a sheet of paper.

The same April day Xerox sued IBM, charging infringement on
twenty-two patents. It also charged IBM with misuse of trade secret information.

The tone was set for the rest of the decade—the lost decade for
Xerox—it was a period of increasing litigation, increasing competition
and stagnating product development. In fact, at one point during the
seventies, there was almost a complete breakdown in the company's

product delivery system. Hundreds of millions of dollars were going into product development and very little was coming out. Only three completely new copying machines were introduced in the U.S. market the entire time—the 4000, the 3100, and the 9200. The 3100 and 9200 were successes; the 4000 was not "We had nothing but refried beans in the marketplace," says Shelby Carter, who headed the U.S. sales division from 1975 to 1981. "I was out there with a rusty bayonnet and an empty rifle."

Xerox had come as close to Nirvana as you could in business. It had an immense technological advantage, plus patents. But it almost blew it all.

Instead of product announcements, you were more likely to read in the newspaper headlines such as: "Xerox Sued Again." In 1972, the FTC accused Xerox of illegally monopolizing the office copier business. In 1973, SCM, an office equipment manufacturer, sued Xerox for antitrust violations. In 1975, the Van Dyk Research Corporation sued Xerox for antitrust. IBM countersued Xerox. There were several other lawsuits by manufacturers, copying service firms, and even customers seeking the same antitrust relief sought by the FTC. The very existence of the company was threatened. "We *had* to win those lawsuits," Peter McColough says.

The plague of antitrust suits made this formerly courageous, glamorous company a much more conservative organization. "There is no question in my mind that the FTC and SCM cases did absolutely impact our pricing policies," Xerox chief executive David Kearns says. "We were not as aggressive as we should have been." Kearns thinks Xerox kept its prices up too long, creating a perfect opportunity for its competition to gain market share.

Some Xerox top executives went through a period when they were afraid to move because of the potentially catastrophic legal ramifications. Managers could not send memos without having lawyers review them. They were coached on what they could and could not say. Certain words, such as "annihilate," were stricken from their vocabularies. When they met with other companies to discuss possible cooperative deals, lawyers had to go along to make sure there was no hint of illegal collaboration. And then, right smack in the middle of the decade, Eastman Kodak entered the market with a copier that was technically sophisticated—the Kodak copier did everything Xerox was trying to do, and better. IBM by this time had introduced its Copier II, which made twenty-five copies a minute. The new Kodak machine did 70 cpm. Both attacked the mid-range where Xerox made most of its money. Kodak leapfrogged Xerox technology and reliability. The momentum switched. Now Xerox no longer set the tone for the industry. It was forced to play defense rather than offense. It reacted to the competition rather than making the competition react to it.

This was the environment into which the Japanese copier manufacturers launched their assault. Xerox was preoccupied with the wave of lawsuits and had come to consider IBM and Kodak the main competitive threats. IBM and Kodak were going after the same lucrative segments of the copier market as Xerox. They played by the same rules as Xerox. They focused on major accounts and leased most of their machines. The Japanese were much smaller and much different. They produced low-cost machines that they sold instead of leased. "It was a question of whether you concentrate on the potential elephants or the mosquitoes that were running around," Hal Bogdonoff says. "We focussed on the elephants."

"The focus on the low end wasn't there because we didn't see it as important," Kearns says.

The antitrust cases required an enormous amount of management attention. The FTC case wouldn't be settled until 1975, IBM 1978. The SCM case went to trial in 1977 and Van Dyk, in 1978, but the appeals lasted into the 1980s. McColough gave thirty days of depositions to his lawyers in preparation for the SCM trial and then spent ten days on the witness stand.

The FTC, in its formal complaint against Xerox in 1973, demanded that Xerox make all of its copier patents available for unrestricted, royalty-free licensing, along with any other patents it might obtain in the next twenty years. It also sought to make Xerox divest itself of its foreign partners, Rank Xerox and Fuji Xerox. It was a landmark monopoly case. First of all, the FTC was treading on what normally was considered the turf of the Justice Department. Second, no American company had ever been forced to sell its foreign holdings because of antitrust charges.

Xerox vowed to fight the divestiture. "We will not consent to any provision calling for the divestiture of Rank Xerox Limited or Fuji Xerox Limited," McColough said at the time. Xerox also felt the FTC assault against it was an assault against the very nature of the U.S. patent system. "It is clear that the commission feels we have been too successful," McColough said.

Xerox even had private discussions with the FTC, alerting them to the new competition coming into the market. "That was an environment where they couldn't see past the nose on their face," says Robert Banks,

Xerox general counsel. "We were telling them about the Japanese and what was coming with increased competition, but they wouldn't listen. They were purist. If you had market share you were evil."

Through negotiation, Xerox agreed in late 1974 to provide its competitors with written know-how, including drawings, specifications, and blueprints for existing and subsequent machines. It made an estimated 1,700 patents available to its competitors. One of the FTC's concerns was that Xerox was "fencing out" potential competition by patenting developments it never intended to pursue commercially. "I will be dissatisfied if Xerox's market share isn't significantly diminished in several years," James Halverson, director of the FTC's Bureau of Competition, said in November 1974. At the time, Xerox had an estimated 85 percent of the worldwide plain paper copier market. His hope would come true.

The competition wasn't satisfied. They didn't think the provisions were tough enough. The FTC, after hearing strong complaints from SCM and Kodak, among others, withdrew the agreement. Finally, in July 1975, a tougher consent decree was signed. It included the previous "know-how" provision, but in addition it banned the favorable pricing schedules Xerox gave to customers who leased several Xerox machines, making it difficult for a competitor to penetrate an account. "That provision did make it easier for us to get our one machine in at the time." acknowledges Kodak's Mike Murray. The FTC consent decree also said Xerox must license at least three patents to another company before it can require that company to cross-license any of its own patents. Most of the provisions of the decree remained in effect for ten years, expiring in July 1985.

"They went down to 40 percent market share so it went pretty well," Halverson, now a private attorney in New York, says about the Xerox case. "Next to AT&T it was the most successful antimonopoly case in history."

Xerox settled with the FTC, Banks says, because it couldn't fight the government and the private lawsuits at the same time. "The things the FTC wanted us to give up we were going to give up in the marketplace anyway," he says. "The patents were running out. The competition was coming in. It was basic economics. Suddenly, we had competitors come in and people were saying, 'Hey, they are in our market.' Well, it was our market. But not anymore." Banks and others at Xerox agree that the environment in Washington today is so different that in similar circumstances such a government action against Xerox, or any other company, would be unlikely.

The SCM trial, which lasted fourteen months in 1977 and 1978, was one of the longest and costliest courtroom battles ever between two private corporations. SCM claimed $500 million in damages because Xerox would not license its copier patents. The damages would have been trebled under federal antitrust provisions. In the years between the original complaints and the trials, Xerox had sued both SCM and Van Dyk for patent infringement. The trial was held in Hartford, Connecticut. Xerox moved twenty lawyers and nearly a hundred aides into most of one floor of a downtown high-rise office building three blocks from the federal courthouse. SCM, with fifteen lawyers and eighty-five aides, had two floors in a similar building across the street. Most of the people involved lived in two downtown hotels that came to be known as the Xerox Sheraton and the SCM Hilton. Xerox and SCM introduced ninety-six volumes of documents, a stack twenty feet high, and entered more than 60,000 exhibits. The official transcript of the trial ran 45,000 pages. Legal expenses were estimated at $500,000 a month for SCM and $750,000 a month for Xerox.

After thirty-eight days of deliberation, the jury awarded SCM $111.3 million in damages, three times the amount it determined SCM actually suffered. U.S. District Judge Jon Newman set aside the award, however, saying patent laws are meant to forbid financial liability for companies protecting their inventions. The 2nd U.S. Circuit Court of Appeals agreed in 1981, while saying Xerox enjoyed an "absolute monopoly" in plain paper copiers from 1960 to 1970. The U.S. Supreme Court upheld the appellate court ruling in March 1982.

Before the appeals process began, SCM estimated its legal expenses at nearly $20 million. Xerox spent $23.3 million on the case from 1975 through 1978, $9.2 million in 1977 alone. That's just the fees and expenses of the outside law firms involved in the case. It doesn't count the time and expenses of Xerox personnel. Combined litigation costs for both companies are estimated to have been more than $50 million.

"You really can't measure the cost," Banks says. "The biggest expense was taking Peter McColough out of his job for thirty or forty days a year. We had a lot of executives pulled out of their jobs. You can't replace your most precious resources—your people."

Sol Linowitz, the former Xerox chairman and U.S. ambassador, left the company in 1966, but gave three weeks' worth of depositions for the SCM trial and was later called to testify. "The thing that hasn't been emphasized enough, in my view, is how remarkable it is that with all the possibility for getting into trouble, Xerox has emerged with an absolutely clean bill of health," he says, reflecting on the litigation. "Xerox hasn't lost a single case. For years I was hoping that what I was about was really going to stand up and assure Haloid and Xerox of legal clearance if and when the challenge came. The kind of explosion that took place in the growth of the company and all the things that could have happened that might have caused trouble later, and have happened to other companies, did not happen to us. We escaped all that and came through absolutely clean."

Linowitz, by the way, provided a moment of levity at the trial. He, of course, negotiated the Panama Canal deal. In order to ensure an impartial judgment, the judge instructed the lawyers not to bring up anything to do with Linowitz's involvement with the canal. Some of the jurors may have disagreed with giving it away. Linowitz had agreed not to refer to his ambassadorial title.

The SCM lawyers asked him what he did for a living.

"I'm an attorney," Linowitz replied.

They asked what he specialized in.

"I'm in real estate," Linowitz deadpanned.

The Van Dyk case was similar to SCM. The company originally claimed $459 million in damages. By the time of the trial, that was reduced to $63 million. Van Dyk lost the trial and the subsequent appeals, including the U.S. Supreme Court in 1981.

Xerox and IBM settled their disputes, involving twelve lawsuits in the United States and Canada, in 1978 when IBM agreed to pay Xerox $25 million. The disputes involved IBM's Copier I, II, III, and the Xerox 4000 and 4500. Both companies agreed to share their copier knowhow for the next five years. The previous year, 1977, the Canadian Federal Court had ruled that IBM had indeed infringed upon Xerox patents in producing its Copier I.

Bob Gundlach testified at the IBM trial in Canada and helped with technical consulting at the SCM trial. He joined the company in 1952 and has 130 patents, the most of any Xerox inventor. "I've always felt good about Kodak," Gundlach says of the photo firm's entry into the copier business. "They earned their way. They did their research for two decades before they came to the marketplace. But IBM, and we proved that in Canada, just stole it. They copied our technology. They violated our patents."

Xerox had licensed some xerographic technology to IBM for computer applications, not the copier business. Xerox even provided IBM with selenium drums and developer materials and exchanged personnel to work on the project. That's one reason Xerox was able to file its patent infringement lawsuit the same day IBM announced its first copier. Xerox knew what IBM was working on.

Xerox's disastrous breakdown in the product delivery system is more puzzling. Xerox had a well-defined strategy: Hit IBM and Kodak hard. But it couldn't pull it off. The product development process got bogged down in bureaucracy and the disease of creeping elegance, the desire to make the biggest, fastest, and most sophisticated machines. The emphasis was on huge projects involving huge numbers of people. It took too long for decisions to be made. And when they were made and a product was getting close to launch, product planners and marketeers would sometimes change their minds. No one stood up and said, "Let's push this product out." "We wasted a lot of R and D money," Gundlach says. "More than 50 percent of our product programs during that span were aborted before marketing. What we missed in the seventies was the opportunity to maintain unquestioned, unchallenged leadership in xerography. Why did Kodak first come out with a copier that everybody perceived as the most reliable machine in the marketplace? There's no question we could have done that if that had been set as a goal."

The project code-named Moses is by far the most glaring example of waste and missed opportunity. "Moses was supposed to lead us into the promised land," Steenburgh says. "Instead, the Red Sea came crashing down on us."

Moses was a response to the Kodak Ektaprint. It was fast, a projected replacement for the 7000, and had an elaborate document handler that recycled originals. The product concept had been around for some time. Xerox stoked it up in 1975 after seeing the original Ektaprint and killed it suddenly in late 1976, just six months from launch according to reports from some people who worked on the project. At the time of its death, Moses had consumed $90 million in development costs, including $20 million in tooling. More than 1,000 people were working on it.

Moses had many problems. "We called it warmed over xerography," Gundlach says. But what finally killed Moses was a recirculating document handler introduced by Kodak in 1976. "That was a shocker," Kearns says. Xerox didn't think it could be done. The Xerox philosophy was that the worst thing a machine could do was damage a customer's original, so it was important to minimize manipulation. Recirculating handlers increased that risk because they shuffled originals through the machine. The Kodak method, for instance, could copy a looseleaf booklet in sequence by just setting it in the handler. The Xerox method on

Moses was different. Xerox was trying to build a document handler that could take onion skin, carbon paper, and card stock at the same time. The handler worked, but not at the high speed designed into Moses. Kodak wasn't as ambitious. In fact, Kodak recommended that if a customer had a potentially troublesome original, too thick or too thin, he should first make a single copy of it on regular paper and then use that copy as an original in the document handler.

Because of the failure of Moses and other projects in that market segment, Xerox didn't have a replacement for the 7000 until the 1979 introduction of the 8200, which was a rush-project Shelby Carter championed because the 1075 had slipped so badly. That's a ten-year void. Actually more, because the 7000 was based on the 3600, which was based on the 2400, which was introduced in 1964. "It was a crime," Steenburgh says of the product void. "When you run out that string, we perhaps spent hundreds of millions of dollars on projects that we killed. If we had done some of them they would have been acceptable in the marketplace. We were looking for the champagne, candlelight, and nice steak dinner and what we really needed was hamburger. We needed a good, solid meat-and-potatoes product in that market segment. We were screwing around trying for perfection and we weren't happy because we couldn't get it. The product planners were dreaming up things, but by the time the engineers were ready to deliver, the product planners would have a different dream."

At one point, in 1979, the problem got so bad that McColough went to Rochester and told the engineering community, "You're putting this company's future in jeopardy."

The company was organized so that the functions of product planning, engineering, and manufacturing didn't come together until you got to Stamford at the president's level. A lot of time was wasted in meetings and presentations. Many problems that should have been resolved in Rochester wound up going to Stamford for resolution. "There was a lot of conflict," Steenburgh says. "There were too many functional nits that became showstoppers. We had vice presidents yelling at vice presidents over nits."

Inside of its engineering organization, for instance, Xerox had a drafting function and a service engineering function. After a design engineer designed a part or subsystem, he would pass it to the drafting department. The drafting department would do a drawing. The draftsman would then pass it to a detailer who would put the critical dimensions on it. Then the drawing would go to service engineering. They would determine if it was practical for maintenance out in the field. Could the tech reps around the world make that product work? If the answer was yes, then the drawing would go to the manufacturing engineering organization. They would determine if they could manufacture the part. If anybody along the line sent it back to the engineers who designed it, then the design engineer would have to either redesign the part or try to convince the service or manufacturing engineers to see things his way. Each function had its own hierarchy. There was a vice president of service engineering and a vice president of advanced manufacturing engineering. The process chewed up a lot of time.

Unfortunately for Xerox, the groups were most interested in their own functional responsibility rather than meeting cost targets or getting the machines out the door on time.

Xerox marketing organizations around the world were the same. Rank Xerox had its own group of product planners as did the United States, Canada, and Latin America. The idea was to be as close to customers in the various markets as possible and then bring all that information together in one place, a reprographics strategy office in Rochester reporting to Stamford. "All of that sounded beautiful, but what happened was you couldn't get that group to agree on what time of day it was if they were all looking at the same clock," Wayland Hicks says. "I can remember one argument over what the color of the paper tray should be."

One group would want reduction on a machine. Another would want eleven by seventeen capability. While the strategy office had responsibility for pulling everything together, it didn't have the same clout as the other groups, so it tried to compromise.

To make sure that things didn't get hopelessly bogged down, Xerox put a program manager on each product. He was accountable for delivering the product and pulling all the functions together—such as getting the sales and service forces trained and preparing the literature for sales promotions. He had these functional people reporting to him, but he didn't have any leverage if they were dropping the ball.

It was a cumbersome system designed to prevent Xerox from making mistakes; designed to put more controls in the company and eliminate some of the inefficiencies that were created when Joe Wilson and Peter McColough decided to grow the company as quickly as possible. However, what the system actually did was prevent the company from getting products out. And when they did come out, they came out at higher cost and behind schedule.

More and more during this period, Xerox management was turning its attention away from the business of copiers and toward the office of the future. Xerox acquired a computer company, Scientific Data Systems, in 1969 for almost $1 billion in stock. It failed and was closed down in 1975. Xerox also acquired several computer peripheral companies in the seventies—Diablo Systems, Versatec, and Shugart Associates. They fared well for a time, but even though management was focusing more on office systems, Xerox didn't pay enough attention to its new subsidiaries. "When I was president of Shugart, I recommended it be sold because the Japanese were going to take the industry over," says James Campbell, founder of Xerox Computer Systems and former vice president of Xerox's Information Products Group. "It should have been sold in 1981 or 1982." Xerox wound up closing Shugart's disk drive business in 1984.

Communications broke down as well. The Office Products Division (OPD) in Dallas didn't talk to the systems guys in El Segundo because they had competing technologies. People at Xerox's Palo Alto Research Center saw products coming out of OPD that they had never seen before. In many ways, the people of Xerox were working in two different worlds—a copier world and a computer world—separated by thousands of miles and layers of bureaucracy. "People in headquarters are like willows, moving whatever way the wind is blowing," Campbell said. "And the wind in El Segundo is a long damn ways from Stamford."

At one point in the mid-seventies, the xerographic experts in the research department at Webster, sixty out of a total staff of 200, were transferred to the engineering department. "The real frustration in the seventies came when research management decided that xerography was a mature technology and the best thing research could do is explore new opportunities like ink jets, magnetography, thermal printing, and alternative imaging systems," Gundlach says. "That was a real blow to me. Finally, the corporation realized it had been a big mistake." Gundlach says that at one point a top Xerox manager told the research organization that the technological cupboard was bare. "It was our impression that the cupboard was locked," he said.

Kearns agrees that producing a replacement for the 7000—he considers the 1075 the replacement—was a failure, but he adds one caution: "I do think that we carried some projects farther than necessary," he says. "But it's not the number of projects. One of the ways you get good projects out is that you have a lot in development. By the way, anytime you kill a project, it's a problem. It causes a lot of trauma."

In the end, Xerox was fortunate on two counts. First, Kodak took advantage of the outmoded machines in the Xerox lineup, but moved very slowly and deliberately in developing markets for its Ektaprint line.

Second, the IBM Copier III initially was a flop. Thomas Holmes, of Datapro Research Corporation, who covered the copier industry when IBM's 75-cpm Copier III was first announced in 1976, says his phone started ringing from angry customers within the first two weeks of the launch. "Paper jams were the worst problem," he says. "The paper path was so long and complicated that if you had one piece of paper jammed you probably had three or four."

One flustered customer, waiting for an IBM service call, pushed his machine outside. When the serviceman was late and it started raining, the machine stayed out there.

Dale Kredatus of Data Decisions says the Copier III was doomed from the start. He tells of a special preintroduction demonstration of the machine for the company's board of directors that never took place because the machine fell off a forklift.

"Datapro had a Copier III," Holmes said. "I always felt sorry for the poor serviceman. It seemed like he lived here."

In January 1978, after it had placed 10,000 Copier IIIs in the field, IBM announced that the machine had some problems and was going to limited shipments. IBM started a new development effort to reengineer the copier. Machines that had been placed were either taken back or retrofitted. Some were practically torn down to the frame and rebuilt right at the customer's site, taking three technicians an entire week. In November 1978, IBM reannounced the Copier III. IBM won't say how much it spent to fix the problems, but others in the industry estimate the cost at more than $400 million. "The cost was substantial, but I don't think it was unusual," says Proctor Houston, a former director of IBM's copier operations. "To quote a number is missing the point. The point I want to make is our commitment to quality. We will leave no stone unturned in our effort to satisfy the customer. When we came back in November, we had a much improved product."

But IBM's reputation and copier momentum had been damaged. While today's Copier III, now called the Series III Model 60, is very successful—some industry experts estimate that about 10,000 are placed a year—IBM never became the major full-line force in the industry that Xerox feared. The Copier III experience caused IBM to reassess its copier strategy. Originally, it had flirted with the idea of having a full range of products, but later IBM backed off. It never replaced its Copier I or II. After spending a considerable amount of money trying to develop its own machine for the very low end of the market, IBM dropped that project and took a small machine from Minolta in 1981. That OEM (original equipment manufacturer) effort failed. IBM found it couldn't compete efficiently against dealers with its high-priced direct sales force. Minolta salesmen are said to have actually followed IBM salesmen on their rounds and then made the same calls the next day with Minolta's version of the same machine. Rumors persist even today of a new high-speed, light lens copier coming from IBM, but both Xerox and Kodak analysts doubt anything will ever come of it. IBM's copier business, by the way, was aided tremendously by Dr. Roland M. Schaffert, who joined the company in 1956. Before then he worked at Battelle Institute directing many of the experiments that helped commercialize Chester Carlson's invention for Haloid.

"If IBM had had Kodak's product, we would really have been hurting," Steenburgh says. McColough agrees. "We were competing in a marketplace in that period with what we considered very inferior products." We were still using 3600s and 7000s. That was old hardware. It was reliable because we had worked the bugs out of it, but it wasn't what we wanted. If IBM with its superior marketing skills and their size had the Kodak machine it would have been a much different story. Frankly, I've never understood why Kodak was so slow in launching that machine around the world, not only in the United States."

After the 914, and until the 10 Series, the only machine McColough considers to have been developed satisfactorily was the 2400. Work on that 40-cpm copier began in 1960. Five years and $40 million later, it was finally introduced. The 2400 became the 3600, which later became the 7000.

"The 9200 was a good program in terms of coming out with a good machine," McColough says. "But it was done with massive amounts of money and massive manpower. It took too long. Now it has paid off, but that is not the way to do it. The 4000, incidentally, was not a good machine. And its successors were not good." The fact that Xerox was still able to grow despite an inferior product lineup is a testament to the power of McColough's direct sales force. Revenues grew from $1.6 billion in 1970 to $8 billion in 1980. Profits went from $190 million to $565 million. Of course, Xerox also adopted a strategy that only a lease-based company can use; in the late seventies it started selling off the rental base, in effect keeping profits higher than they normally would be.

The same sort of developmental stagnation was hurting the low end of the market and it continues even today for the designers in the United States. The last successful low-volume machine Xerox designed and produced in the United States was the 3100, introduced in 1973. There have been many product concepts and projects started—SAM (Simply Amazing Machine), Mohawk, Elf, Yankee, Rebel, Gnome, Nothing—but all have been killed. By 1979, Xerox had decided to import low-end machines to the United States from Japan, taking the 2300 from Fuji Xerox. Designers in Webster are still working on low-end concepts, but the designs from Fuji—for the 1020, 1025, and 1035—have been the ones to reach market.

"In our classes," says Michael Porter of the Harvard Business School, "we tell our students, 'Okay, you're running Xerox in the mid-seventies and you see this Japanese threat in small copiers. What are you going to do?' Well, look at the negatives. You're going to obsolete the rental base, accelerate replacement of your large copiers with small copiers, [and] anger the FTC. And what about the sales force? If you get dealers, you're going to piss off your sales force. Those problems caused Xerox to go in a different direction—office automation, supervolume copiers. For them, that was a logical thing to do."

The logic would change, though, as the Japanese grew stronger and replaced IBM and Kodak as the primary threat to Xerox. That recognition, however, wouldn't occur until 1980.

5
Kodak: The Rival Across the River

There were just enough customers who
were turned off by Xerox's dominance. That's
the American spirit. We were viewed as an
underdog.

—MIKE MURRAY, Kodak

IKE MURRAY lives in Pittsford, the nicest suburb of Rochester. He jokes that it is a Xerox ghetto. Dwight Ryan and Dave Myerscough, the top two Xerox marketing executives in the United States, live nearby, as do a couple of Xerox patent lawyers.

Murray, a vice president in charge of copiers, sometimes flies a gigantic Kodak flag on wage dividend day, when Kodak gives bonuses to all its workers. A typical factory worker with five years experience can receive a bonus of $3,000 or more a year. "My Xerox neighbors used to say, 'Murray, if you fly that flag again we're going to come out at night and burn a big *X* on your lawn.' You ought to see it whenever I go to a cocktail party," he says. "The conversation stops dead across the room. I can always tell when something is going on because I'll see a few Xerox guys over in the corner buzzing away. I'll just walk over and they all get red in the face."

That concern for security hasn't always been the case. Before they were copier competitors, Xerox people talked freely to Kodak people about their projects. "We used to send nondrinkers to cocktail parties," laughs Joe Quickel, who headed the team that prepared the first Kodak Ektaprint copier for production.

"Often times we knew they were going to take a certain action before their own general people did just because they didn't understand security," Murray says. "They openly talked about it and the information got out, at least to us, before it got into their own field organization. They were so prideful of what they were doing. They really didn't think anybody could compete against them. They'd tell you almost anything you wanted to know."

All that has changed.

"It was almost ridiculous," Murray says. "Now they have slammed a lid on it."

By the time Xerox made its first run for fame with the 914, Eastman Kodak was already an industrial powerhouse. In 1907, it employed 5,000 workers in Rochester alone. By 1927, that number exceeded 20,000. Today, more than 50,000. Over the years, Kodak has surrendered some of its camera-making to foreign competition, but it has never retreated on its mainline business of photographic film. Even today, with Fuji Film getting more aggressive, Kodak controls 85 percent of the film market in the United States and 50 percent in Europe. That dominance makes it one of the most profitable companies in the world, with earnings each year of about $1 billion.

Ever since Eastman introduced his Kodak roll-film camera in 1888, Rochester has been a Kodak town. When little Haloid made photographic paper, Joe Wilson used to say that Haloid was in business by the grace of God and Eastman Kodak. But as plain paper copying became big business, all of a sudden this upstart Xerox thrust itself into the Rochester and national spotlight, taking some attention away from Kodak. The most visible manifestation of the battle for recognition is the companys' office towers. Kodak's tower is located on the west side of the Genesee River, near downtown Rochester. George Eastman had it built in 1914. At nineteen stories, it used to be the tallest building in town. Now that distinction belongs to the thirty-story Xerox Tower, located on the east side of the Genesee, right in the heart of downtown. When Xerox was constructing its tower in the late 1960s, the talk around town was that Kodak was actually lobbying to keep the Xerox tower shorter than the Kodak tower.

Kodak was and still is a paternalistic company, almost Japanese in character. It is sometimes called the Old Yellow Father, after its film boxes. Eastman introduced the worker bonuses in 1912, one of the first American companies to have such a program. Kodak has no unions in the United States; in fact, when one group of workers wanted to organize in the early days, Eastman changed their minds by giving them the capital to start their own business and act as a vendor. Kodak workers can save and borrow money from Eastman Savings & Loan. They can practice their putting during lunchtime on the artificial greens outside Kodak Park. They can learn photography in Kodak camera clubs and play softball or bowl in Kodak recreation leagues.

The company and its people are conservative, although they are becoming more aggressive in pursuing acquisitions and new business opportunities. No flashy dressers, no outspoken personnel, modest offices. Kodak is secretive and closed to public view. It has commissioned three biographies of George Eastman, but they are all locked away in company vaults. None of them met with approval. Thousands of people worked on the Instamatic camera in the 1970s and the Disc camera in the 1980s. Many even tested prototypes at home, but until they were introduced, no one outside the company really knew what Kodak had coming. Kodak workers are unusually loyal. It's common for them to join the company when they are young and stay for life. Top executives work their way up from the bottom. When the company was forced to begin eliminating thousands of jobs and actually terminate workers in 1983, the community was shocked. This wasn't the Old Yellow Father it knew.

When Kodak introduced its first plain paper copier in 1975, the rivals for hometown attention became direct competitors in a billion-dollar industry, and that competition has extended around the world. Kodak has teamed with Canon to directly challenge Xerox across a broad range of copiers. Xerox, of course, is linked with Fuji Photo Film, Kodak's number one film rival, through its partnership in Fuji Xerox.

Kodak's efforts in xerography illustrate the difficulty of mastering the technology and bringing it to market. The company didn't announce its first plain paper copier until more than two decades after it first began experimenting with xerography in the early 1950s. In the late 1940s and early 1950s, xerography was seen as a potential threat to silver halide photography. Carlson had big ambitions, he was experimenting with continuous tone xerographic portraits of people to expand the use of the technology. Those ambitions received support from the Army Signal Corps, which funded research into the uses of xerography for combat and intelligence photography. Edwin Land introduced his Polaroid process about this time, but it was much more expensive and limited at extreme temperatures. Conventional photography was slow and unreliable when radiation from nuclear weapons was present. "We would like to turn a photograph into something approaching a true signal," E. K. Kaprelian, chief of the Photographic Branch of the Signal Corps Engineering Laboratories, said in 1949 in reference to xerography. His statement was prophetic, both photography and xerography have been digitized today.

Kodak built an engineering model of a high-speed plain paper copier in 1963, but it wasn't until 1969 that it made a corporate commitment to enter the field. It took another six years before it launched its first machine, the Ektaprint 100.

"We kept asking ourselves, isn't there an easier way of doing it," says Joe Quickel, who once headed Kodak's Atex Computer subsidiary and has since retired. "And by God, it's hard to find another way of doing it. If you want to use a reusable photoconductor you have to go through the whole process of taking the photoconductor back to normalcy, charging, exposing, toning, transferring, fusing. You have to go through all of those excruciating processes in order to produce a copy. It is complicated. The copier, the xerographic process, involves a lot of skills and expertise—electronics, optics, chemistry, mechanical—which I don't see in the computer industry where you are dealing particularly with electronics and software."

During the 1950s, Kodak was a major force in the emerging office copier field with Verifax, the first successful commercial copier. "When Xerox came with 914 it literally cleaned everybody's clock," Murray says. "I mean Verifax went down the tubes within a three- or four-year period. It just about wiped out our entire business. I can remember Xerox recruiting people to market their product. They attracted really first-class people. They had such a unique product, a unique position. In the 1960s, I think it was just as prestigious to work for Xerox as it was to work for IBM. They were going after the same kinds of people, very aggressive. And they did attract very talented people."

Murray first became involved in the Ektaprint project in 1967 when he was asked to develop the strategic marketing and service plan. He was brought to Kodak headquarters and told that top management had a project they would like him to accept. However, if he accepted, he could not tell his wife or anyone else what he was doing. This is a common caveat at Kodak; even today, workers are sworn to secrecy on projects.

Murray's copier revenue and profit projections were big compared to Kodak's total revenue, then about $2.5 billion, but not as big as they turned out to be. "The copier business is much, much larger than we expected," he said. "We were pretty close on the number of placements we thought we could get, but the number of copies made on each unit were much higher."

Kodak doesn't release specific data on copiers, but its revenues from copiers are estimated at just under $1 billion a year, about 8 percent of the company's total revenues. In the late 1970s, while IBM was retrenching and Xerox was shifting its focus from copiers to the office of the future, Kodak zeroed in on plain paper copiers, concentrating on the high-volume segment of the market. It has introduced two basic machines designed by Kodak engineers; one runs at 70 cpm (Ektaprint 100, 150, 200, 225) and the other at 90 cpm (Ektaprint 250). In mid-1985, Kodak introduced two machines from Canon, a 30-cpm laser copier (IM 40) and a 50-cpm conventional copier (Ektaprint 85). Kodak may not have expanded its business as rapidly as possible, but it has grown steadily. Even today, Kodak still refers to copiers in its annual reports and earnings statements as one of its fastest growing businesses.

"We really did see it as a fantastic opportunity for Kodak," Murray says. "But we were very respectful of Xerox. We did not underestimate in any way their marketing clout. We felt their sales force was a substantial obstacle, but they were really the only player at that point. We felt that if we did bring something to the market, image quality, we had a fairly good chance. We weren't looking at 50 percent market share. People tend to view the industry as one, but it's really the individual market segments that are very critical. By segmenting the market in that way, we gained a respectable market share at the high end. The need to have a full range of products wasn't there. Today, it is."

The first Kodak copier project, Model A, was scheduled to be introduced in 1970 or 1971. Model A was strong on copy quality, concentrating on solid area development while Xerox was still focusing on fringe development. The Xerox method outlined a character nicely, but it was terrible on solid areas. They washed out. Kodak engineers also came up with the concept of cartridges, popular today, to quickly change the photoconductor. Model A was essentially a me-too product. And, as is true of many of the first copiers from companies just entering the business, it had reliability problems. Kodak felt that to be successful against Xerox it had to have a better product, it had to bring something new to the market. So Model A was abandoned in 1968 and the researchers went to work on Model B, which became Ektaprint.

Kodak was the first company to use microprocessors in copying machines, even before the Japanese. Model A was designed around electromechanical devices. Electrical signals opened or closed relays. When Kodak moved on to Model B, it decided to abandon electromechanical control and use transistor-to-transistor logic. This involved big boards with many transistors, many components. It was proven technology, but the boards could get complicated. Most of the designs for Model B were in place in 1973 when someone from Kodak attended a seminar and heard Intel talk about its 8008 chip. "We thought wouldn't it be nice to have that little thing in there and get rid of all those discrete components," Quickel says. "The chip increases reliability and gives a lot more flexibility." Kodak got some of the first samples from Intel and started to design a new control circuit. It also continued to work on transistor logic. In 1974, Quickel decided to go with the microprocessors exclusively.

"From a marketing standpoint, we really capitalized on that," Murray says. "We were able to point to this as representing a quantum technological leap. 'Microprocessor' has always been a buzzword and still is any time you talk about electronics. It did give us a very significant advantage. It also permitted the utilization of the accessories, the finisher. Without the microprocessor we would not have been able to hang on all those other very productive accessories."

Many industry insiders criticize Kodak for moving too slowly in copiers, thereby missing opportunities to get the most out of its technological advances. Analyst Dale Kredatus knows the company's conservative nature well: "Kodak sticks to its plans and that has proved to be one of the company's strengths over the years. Let's say the plan was to place 5,000 Ektaprints a year, plus an x-percent increase each year. Everybody else could go out of business and Kodak would still place its 5,000-a-year-plus-x-percent."

That "too slow" knock irritates Murray. "You have to look at who was there, IBM and Xerox," he says. "This was an untested product for Kodak and here we were going up against two of the blue chip companies in the United States. The level of respect from the corporate standpoint was significant. Perhaps we weren't quite sure that we could do as well as we did. Kodak at that time was very dealer-oriented except for the micrographics business. Everything was on a sold-basis. Make it and sell it. Get your money back. That wasn't true of the copier/duplicator business back in the seventies when 90 percent was rented and 10 percent was sold. The front-end cost was staggering to enter this business, just in depreciation on the equipment you were placing. We felt the risk was very substantial even though we knew we had a technological advantage."

Going from an engineering model to full-scale production is complicated. Just ask Savin, which has been working on its 8000 series since 1977. In late 1985 it abandoned any hope of ever making the machine in its own factory. Kodak had to build a service organization, a marketing organization, as well as a manufacturing group before it could enter the market.

Murray especially remembers a 1978 *Fortune* article about Xerox. It said if IBM had Ektaprint it would have handed Xerox it's head on a platter. "I have never forgotten that piece because it bothered me," Murray said. "People failed to recognize the fact that IBM already had in place a gigantic organization. Sure, if you took Ektaprint and just handed it to a company that already had a large servicing organization, a large sales force, they certainly could have done it. It's different when you are starting from scratch. You can't add resources fast enough."

Kodak probably wouldn't have been able to build a good reputation for copy quality and machine reliability—in surveys by Datapro, users have consistently ranked the Ektaprint models at the top of their class—if it had rushed the machines out. It took Kodak a year and a half to remedy the problems with the recirculating document feeder. In the meantime, customers stopped buying multiple units. The real proof of the wisdom of Kodak's strategy is its market strength today. "There aren't too many companies around capable of generating that kind of business in that short a time," Murray says. "We felt that to compete against IBM and Xerox we had to lay a very strong foundation. We couldn't afford to stumble. I think in the long term our approach paid off. There wasn't a helluva lot of money left on the table if we had moved faster." He estimates the lost opportunity at maybe just 3,000 to 4,000 units over the years. According to industry estimates, Kodak has a population base of about 45,000 machines around the world.

Kodak knew it had an opportunity to place fast, reliable machines, but was surprised to find out just how far behind Xerox was in product development. "From a technology point of view, we were somewhat puzzled," Quickel says. "It was quite visible that they were spending a lot of dollars on research and development. You could pick up the annual report and see that. They certainly were active, at least in filing for patents, which says that there was some basic, fundamental research going on. But we were really puzzled that there wasn't much coming out in regard to hard, commercialization of that technology, whatever they had been doing. They left themselves vulnerable."

Kodak sees the light lens or optical copying industry growing at 5 to 6 percent a year through the eighties. It is such a large industry that the replacement business itself is significant. "Any company that would not continue to develop stand-alone copiers would be making a mistake," Murray says. In the high end of the market, Murray sees a two-player game between Xerox and Kodak for the rest of the eighties. He doesn't see IBM making a big effort, and he doesn't see the Japanese coming on strong. It's not their style. The volumes are lower and the development costs are high. "The upper end never becomes a commodity," he says. "If you accept that premise then it will always have a limited number of players. The front-end cost of developing a high-end copier/duplicator ranks right up there with developing a new fighter plane," he said, referring to the $500-million-plus Northrup invested in the F-20.

Kodak became involved with Canon because it saw a movement toward decentralization of copying. It needed to broaden its product line. "Customers were pressing us hard," Murray says. "They liked our high-volume copiers but they wanted mid-volume units, too."

By acquiring the capability instead of developing it internally, Kodak did not have to build additional manufacturing facilities. The risk was less, especially in a market segment where product lives are only two to three years. Kodak's main copier building at its Elmgrove plant in Rochester, for instance, cost $50 million. It sells its machines only in the United States and Europe, where it has a plant in West Germany, although there is some speculation that Kodak will begin marketing in Japan, with the help of Canon.

Kodak considers Canon the best Japanese copier company. Murray said it was interesting to read about the alliance in the press in both the United States and Japan. "In Japan it was considered a super deal, a coup for Canon and Kodak," Murray says. "Here, it was viewed as a sign of weakness for Kodak: They can't do it themselves. I thought I was reading about two different happenings."

Why was Kodak initially successful in copiers and how has it continued to be successful? "First of all, technology," Murray says. "Second, staying power. We had the financial resources. Xerox and IBM knew that by price erosion we had as much staying power as they did. Third, there was window. We wanted the upper end, but we didn't realize Xerox was as far behind on technology as it was; that it would take them as long to respond as it did. Fourth, the industry, quite frankly, wanted a viable alternative to Xerox. Kodak had the reputation. We were quite welcomed. . . . The rest of it is all in execution. We had management skills. We had a solid service organization. We had a good marketing organization. We had a very strong manufacturing capability."

PART THREE
THE JAPANESE

6
Myths About Japan's Success

"I've been gone from Japan five years," Ricoh's Masami Takieri was saying as the taxicab whizzed along a superhighway outside Tokyo. "Things have really changed. There's so much English here now, on signs, on TV. . . ."

Takieri, a Ricoh marketing rep, was taking us to Ricoh's Atsugi factory. "I was in Brazil," he continued. "We've been having a tough time because of languages. Only one guy in the entire company knew Spanish, no one knew Portuguese. Now learning English and at least one other language is a requirement of all international staff."

It was January 1985, and marketing in Europe and the United States was Ricoh's biggest concern. One thing no one was worried about was manufacturing: In Atsugi, Ricoh supposedly had one of the finest plants in the world. As we arrived we noted a long line of buses parked outside what otherwise looked like any other high-tech plant, American or Japanese. Inside, we met Koichi Endo, general factory manager, who chuckled as he greeted us: "Because we cannot see our competitors' factories, we'd appreciate hearing from you about any bad points here." We'd been told that wouldn't be easy. And one floor down, in 600,000 square feet of floor space, we saw why:

Seven conveyors three miles long, each carrying parts or copiers, snake their way through a sea of 450 white suits, 65 percent of them women, standing motionless as their fingers dance about the circuitry. There's no need to bend over, even to throw out trash: Waist-level cardboard chutes take it away. That's where the buses come in, too. They pick line workers up and, after each "455-minute" shift, take them home at night. Only green plants and three gold-painted model 4060s—the 100,000th, 200,000th, and 300,000th produced—break the long, uncluttered view down the assembly lines. You don't see clipboards, or supply personnel ordering parts. That's all done by computers tracking what's produced (and therefore what's needed) with scan-

ning laser beams. There are no jitneys or forklifts either: At the Hitachi computer's command, parts go from the warehouse to workstations on 3-mph
unmanned robots that blare out the workers' favorite rock music to keep people out of the way. The result? Workers and the robots assemble six completely different models, containing 550 to 3,020 parts each, on the same
assembly line. The day's production: 2,000 copiers. Number of copies made
to check quality: zero. Down time per month: less than a hundred minutes.
Manufacturing cost advantage versus Fuji Xerox (according to Endo): 25 to
30 percent. Dozens of companies are trying to buy the secret Ricoh software
that runs the system. Ricoh won't sell.

J IM ABEGGLEN, a professor at Japan's Sophia University and former
vice president of the prestigious Boston Consulting Group, is the
envy of Japan watchers everywhere. He has weaved his way in and
out of Japan's top companies for nearly thirty years, longer than any
other American consultant. One sunny afternoon, in his plush
nineteenth-floor office on the outskirts of Tokyo's financial district, just
north of the Ginza strip, he remembered when it wasn't so easy: "Building
a career on Japan in the 1950s was literally impossible. In the early sixties, you could give a talk on Japan here and there, and there was vague
curiosity about this exotic place. By the late sixties, you could get a
business audience made up of semiconductor people . . . there was some
real interest starting. But it wasn't until the seventies that people really
understood what the hell happened. By then, the truck was effectively
running over them."

Company after American company was crushed by that truck, and
Abegglen got a big kick out of watching American pundits and scholars
try to explain why. First, he says, came the "happy horseshit" period.
"If you look at that first wave of books—*Theory Z, Japan as No. 1,
Miracle by Design, The Art of Japanese Management*—all this happy
horseshit was around in 1981–82. It said Japan's one big happy family,
they all work together, cooperate like hell because of the culture, they
all love one another.

"Next came the 1982–83 books—*The Japanese Conspiracy, MITI
and the Japanese Miracle*—that said it's a sinister fucking Japanese plot
and they're going to kill us. So we had the happy horseshit period, then
the sinister conspiracy . . . what next?"

Of course, neither group of analysts was wrong. To say Japan's culture, work style, and government prodding have had little to do with
Japan's success would be ludicrous. But a lot of what has been written,
according to Paul Regensburger, Xerox's manager of competitive

benchmarking, "tends to be superficial and somewhat mythological. There's a lot attributed to them that is not unique."

Japan's camera and copier companies illustrate why many supposed truths about Japan's success have serious flaws:

When You Join a Japanese Company, It's For Life.

For men, yes. For women, no. In the mid-seventies, when Canon was having severe financial and managerial problems, four or five men left the company. Since then, says Hiroshi Tanaka, director of Canon's reprographics group, "None have left. Not one."

But in the factories of Canon, Ricoh, Minolta, Konishiroku, and Fuji Xerox, it's a different story. About 80 percent of the 400 assembly-line workers at Canon's Toride factory are young women, usually ages twenty-one to twenty-five. At Ricoh's Atsugi plant, it's the same story: 65 percent of 450 line workers are women. For cheap labor, American firms use Hispanics, Europeans hire Mediterraneans. Chalmers Johnson, a Berkeley professor, and author of *MITI and the Japanese Miracle*, said, "Japan's answer to their labor shortage was robots and women."

When you look up and down the assembly lines at these plants, all you see are women, uniformly dressed in Minolta blue, Ricoh white, Konishiroku gray, or Canon lime green, working at a frenzied pace—wielding electric screwdrivers, power wrenches, and the like. They're expected to stay with their respective companies, not a lifetime or even ten or twenty years, but four to five years. 'We know they'll leave,'' says Koichi Endo. "We're not far from Tokyo, so about half our girls are from the country, half from the city. They usually stay here until they get married, then they go home to take care of the family.''

Japanese Work Harder.

This is probably the most difficult intangible factor to measure. There does seem to be a sense of cooperative urgency and commitment on a Japanese assembly line that you don't see in most American plants. It's not because of money, line workers make $10,000 to $12,000 a year and the president of Ricoh makes just $200,000—a fraction of what American companies Ricoh's size pay their chief executives.

Some say working hard is culturally ingrained. Confucius taught the samurai that each individual must continually demonstrate his loyalty to the group, or society, in which he belongs. In Japan, your life revolves around your company. Others trace their dedication to the cause of the company back to the perfect role model: the U.S. military, which supervised Japan's reconstruction after World War II.

But you have to wonder how much of the effort is sheer dedication and how much is inspired by management or by electronic scoreboards hanging at the ends of the assembly lines. On the top row of each score-board is that day's production target. One January morning at 11:45 at Konishiroku the target was 170. Below that the scoreboard indicated that seventy machines had been produced.

"If they're not going fast enough, we switch workers around . . . try something new," said one Konishiroku manager. At Minolta, a group leader watches workers closely and can tell by sight who is behind or ahead. Says Yoshitsugu Odagiri, plant manager, "The worker controls the flow of the assembly line with a foot pedal. Some days he works hard, some days he likes to be lazy." When rush orders come in, Min-olta workers can produce 30 percent more machines a day. Edward Lin-coln of the Brookings Institution says, "The workers might not be happy in Japan. That's an exaggeration. But [the Japanese] do know how to manage people."

There is also growing evidence that Americans and other nationali-ties work just as hard as the Japanese. The Nissan plant in Tennessee has been making higher-quality pickup trucks than those made in Japan. Canon based its initial production plans in France on the expectation that the French wouldn't work as hard, then found itself burdened with over-production of copying machines. Quality control guru W. Edwards Deming has found that if a company has production or quality prob-lems, it's not the workers' fault but the "imperfect system" in which they have to operate. Canon's Hiroshi Tanaka, who supervises Canon plants throughout the world, agrees with Deming: "Human beings are all the same. How to motivate them is the question mark."

Quality Control Circles Are a Major Reason for Japan's Success.

Every company seems to have them. Ricoh has quality circle [QC] meetings at lunchtime; Canon, boasting four suggestions per employee per month, splits up into circles after work. Konishiroku's circles com-pete against each other. On the bulletin board at one end of Konishi-roku's copier assembly plant is a poster-size chart listing the nicknames in Japanese for the plant's five- to ten-member quality control circles: the "Mickey Mouse" QC, the "New Frontier" QC, and the "7-11" QC. The top-performing circles are awarded plastic figures of a rose and a Christmas tree, like the stars kids get in elementary school. Sometimes a lucky group gets a couple thousand yen for a suggestion. Konishiroku says it's working: In 1984, workers made 21,606 suggestions, that's 116 per employee. A Ricoh QC reduced the adhesive tape needed to pack-age copier paper. A Canon circle made up of women who drive in 7,000 to 8,000 screws a day suggested rearranging the assembly line so screws go in vertically, not horizontally, to boost efficiency.

Though such suggestions help, they're not a major factor in Japan's success. Takeomi Nagafuchi, general manager of quality control at Ricoh, concedes that "70 percent of quality control is determined at the product design stage. So naturally the biggest effort is made at that stage. If you improve manufacturing only [where most of the quality circles are used], you won't get much improvement."

Japanese Companies, Linked Together By Industry Associations, Are All In Bed With One Another.

That's true, generally, when any industry is just getting off the ground. Edward Poshkus, president of Creative Strategies International, was in Japan representing Dataquest when Ricoh, Canon, and others launched their attack on Xerox: "I was in meetings with the Business Machines Association and invariably I'd get the same questions from eight or nine manufacturers, almost verbatim. So they had to be talking. They'd get together and talk common problems—how to attack Xerox, size of the market, etcetera."

There is considerable evidence, as Zenith and National Union Electric charged in a 1971 lawsuit, that Japanese television manufacturers agreed to set prices so that a $400 television in the United States would cost up to $700 in Japan. The theory is that Japan overcharges in its home market so that it can sell cheaper overseas, in effect subsidizing its export business. It may also have happened in computer chips. A 1978 study by the U.S. Semiconductor Industry Association charged that 16K RAM chips cost twice as much in Japan as they did in the United States. In 1980, when the price of Japanese-made 64K RAM chips dropped from $28 to $5 each, William Sanders of Advanced Micro Devices took out a full-page ad in *The Wall Street Journal* that asked: "Are they dumping? I think so. It sure looks like dumping." Similar charges abound in the industry today.

"That, I believe, was predatory pricing," said Chalmers Johnson, who spent ten years writing the history of MITI (Ministry of International Trade and Industry), "I think the Japanese thought their big American competitors were on the ropes and they came damn close to knocking them out." But what often appears to be predatory pricing, Johnson admits, is just part of the way the Japanese do business. "You just keep moving, it doesn't matter whether you're selling at a profit or not, just as long as you stay in business until conditions improve."

The price-fixing theory also ignores the fact that Japanese firms, once an industry is established, compete as fiercely among themselves as they do with their American rivals. Daniel Okimoto, a Japan expert at Stanford University, said, "You can collude in steel and it's done all the time and that's why there's a trigger price mechanism. You can collude in shipbuilding where there's a small number of producers. But it's awfully tough in multicompetitor fields like radios, TVs, and copiers." In fact, price-cutting is so intense that in 1984 only one of Japan's eight auto companies, Toyota, made a profit in Japan. In 1985, Toyota subcompacts were selling in Japan for less than $4,000, about half what they'd cost in the United States.

"People are not nice to each other here. Toyota's turning the screws on the domestic market," says Abegglen. "The Japanese auto companies make about 120 percent of their profits in the United States, they break even in other markets, and they lose money in Japan."

When Konishiroku was building its Odawara photographic paper factory near Mount Fuji, employees kept seeing a helicopter overhead. Certain that their archrival, Fuji Photo Film, was attempting to spy on them, Konishiroku's people began burning trees all around the construction site so smoke would blind the helicopter's view. Michael Porter, a professor and Japan expert at Harvard Business School, says, "I think the notion that the Japanese home market is cozy is complete and utter bullshit."

Japanese Companies Pay Lower Wages.

In some industries, that's true. Japanese autoworkers make roughly $10 an hour compared with $23 an hour in Detroit. But Japan's advantage in most industries is shrinking. As Jeff Kennard, director of Xerox–Fuji Xerox relations, observes, "It's not cheap labor, that's not been true for years." Several countries, including Mexico, Spain, and Great Britain, pay less. And, in the fast-growing computer and electronics industries, labor costs aren't significant anyway. Payroll accounts for less than 1 percent of the cost of building Apple's Macintosh in Fremont, California. Labor typically accounts for only 5 to 10 percent of the cost of building a copier.

"The labor content in a copier," said Porter, "is trivial, truely trivial." So even if Japanese copier companies pay young girls on their assembly lines less than $12,000 a year, that advantage gets eaten up by the cost of exporting—roughly 8.5 percent of a machine's value for shipping plus a 4.25 percent import duty. And the Japanese even complain about wage differentials amongst themselves. Mitsuo Kubo, general manager of Toshiba's copier plant in Kawasaki, says that because his plant is older, and therefore so are his workers, he has to pay higher wages than Ricoh pays at its newer Atsugi facility just down the road.

Japanese Work Extremely Long Hours.

Generally speaking, this is true for Japanese executives but not those working on the assembly lines. To protect family life, Japanese women are prohibited by law from working after 8:00 P.M. That means Japanese copier companies, even when demand is twice as high as production, can only extend their production a few hours at best. Rarely do they run two shifts. Ricoh's Endo, says "We tell our workers, 'Don't work hard. You'll burn yourselves out. Irrational work won't help.' " Some companies, Minolta for example, are known for sticking to regular hours. It's a point of pride that their people go home on time.

MITI is the Mastermind Behind Japan's Success.

MITI has had some notable successes:

- **Steel.** From 1950 to 1955, MITI-backed government loans provided 40 percent of the Japanese steel industry's investment money, according to the International Trade Commission. That plus tax exemptions, special depreciation schedules, and other breaks helped double Japanese steel production in just four years. According to the U.S. General Accounting Office, in 1957, when overproduction caused severe price cutting, MITI started an open-price system, permitting steelmakers to cooperate in setting prices and production. There's no doubt such strategies helped Japan become the world's biggest steelmaker.

- **Computers.** To help Fujitsu and other Japanese firms compete with IBM, in 1961, MITI established the Japanese Electronic Computer Corporation, a fifty-fifty joint venture between government and industry. Over the next twenty years, JECC purchased more than $7 billion in computers from Japanese firms, then leased them to end users. From 1971 to 1976, MITI provided $260 million to each of three groups—Oki-Mitsubishi, NEC-Toshiba, and Fujitsu-Hitachi—hoping to come up with a competitor for the IBM 370. It worked. Each pairing had produced such a machine by 1975. IBM's share of the Japanese mainframe computer market plummeted from 70 percent to about 40 percent.

- **Semiconductors.** In 1975, MITI organized Japan's leading chipmakers into two groups—NEC-Toshiba and Fujitsu-Hitachi-Mitsubishi—to challenge the United States in the race for the next generation of memory chips: 64K RAMs. Japan won the race easily when Fujitsu introduced the world's first 64K RAM in 1978. By 1980, Japan had six firms involved, the United States had only two and Japan held 70 percent of the marketplace. By 1985, Japan had 90 percent of the U.S. market for 256K RAMs—the next generation of memory chips.

So the degree to which MITI helps varies from industry to industry. Stanford's Okimoto said, "Steel, chemicals, computers, microelectronics, all were targeted by the government of Japan. Color TVs, radios, and cameras were not. Steel was helped the most, watches and precision machines [such as copiers] the least, and computers and semiconductors are somewhere in between."

Generally speaking, said Johnson, "MITI helps get a business started and then there's a stampede to get into it. And the fact that the government has designated it makes it almost riskless . . . the only real risk would be to not go into it."

It is unlikely that MITI is the primary reason for Japan's success. Such countries as France; with its computer manufacturers, have provided even bigger subsidies. Korea has done a considerable amount of targeting and it still lags far behind Taiwan. And, for almost every MITI success, there's been a failure. Some of Japan's best-known companies—Honda, Sony, Matsushita (Panasonic), Casio, Canon, Minolta, and Seiko—have gotten little if any help from the government. (In fact, MITI initially refused to give Sony foreign exchange allocations to license the transistor from Western Electric.) MITI failed to reduce the number of Japanese car firms from eight to two. There is no evidence that MITI helped the copier companies. "We didn't help them at all," said Toshihiko Tanabe of MITI's Machinery and Information Industries Bureau. "They did it on their own."

Lastly, the argument that MITI teams up companies, then controls them like a puppeteer with invisible strings, also is outdated. "Japanese companies are much less affected by MITI than they used to be," said John Sumeola, project leader of a one-year study on the Japanese government's targeting undertaken by the U.S. International Trade Commission. "MITI isn't the reason anymore."

Japan's Home Market is Closed to American Companies.

Thomas Howell, a Washington, D.C., attorney and author of a study on Japan's invasion of the semiconductor industry, argues: "The single biggest factor [in Japan's success] is protecting its home market so its companies have guaranteed sales." Even in consumer goods, which received little support from MITI, the government helped by keeping

American goods out while lifting taxes on Japanese-made color TVs and transistor radios. Says Chalmers Johnson, "This fueled a 'Made in Kasumigaseki' revolution in which, during a particular period, millions of Japanese households bought the same goods: TVs, washing machines, and refrigerators in the early sixties and 'the three C's'—car, cooler, and color TV—in the late sixties. Foreigners think the Japanese are all lemmings, that everybody does the same thing all the time. That's because foreigners can't read the goddamn newspapers. MITI is saying; 'This is the year to buy a personal computer because if you wait two years, there will be an 18 percent tax on it.' "

And it's true that Japan's huge home market, which enabled companies to build up a huge production base, was perhaps its biggest advantage over the cost-cutting Koreans and Taiwanese. However, there are notable exceptions: Through subsidiaries or joint ventures, Eastman Kodak has 10 percent of Japan's film market; IBM has 40 percent of Japan's mainframe computer business; and Xerox has 50 percent of Japan's copier business based on revenues. Texas Instruments is the biggest semiconductor maker in Japan; and Rolm Corporation has sold more than a hundred telecommunications systems to Japanese companies. Though strong arguments can be made that Japan has sealed itself off from the rest of the world, Jim Abegglen said, "You'd have to say that those U.S. companies that really tried, really spent what it took to be here, are here in pretty good shape."

The Japanese Don't Invent or Innovate, They Just Cut Costs.
American inventions, such as the transistor and computer chip, have helped the Japanese immensely: Since 1950, Japanese firms have acquired more than 4,000 technology licenses from the United States. Nearly half were in areas that Japan now dominates. Texas Instruments, IBM, and others were forced by the Japanese government to license their technologies in order to sell in Japan. In computers, Japanese firms learned from American partners. Hitachi teamed up with RCA, Oki with Remington-Univac, and NEC with Honeywell. According to its chairman, Taiyu Kobayashi, Fujitsu learns everything it needs to know about IBM's products from its partner, Gene Amdahl, who developed the IBM 360.

Yet in each industry the Japanese have taken over, they have independently developed a major innovation:

· In shipbuilding, Japanese engineers improved welding techniques, making it possible to build enormous tankers.
· In steel, Japanese companies were the first to turn to basic oxygen

furnaces with continuous casting. Half their American competitors stuck with outdated, inefficient open-hearth mills.

· In consumer electronics, Sony licensed the transistor for just $25,000 in 1953 and, two years later, came up with the first transistor radios. The Japanese also were first to build solid state TVs.

· In memory chips, the Japanese based their 64K RAMs upon a marvelously simple predecessor, the 16K RAM from Mostek Technologies. American firms pursued more complex, and more expensive, designs. As a result, Japanese chips were of considerably higher quality.

Furthermore, not all Japanese companies are price-cutters. Sony, like Konishiroku in the copier business and Fuji Photo in the film industry, commands higher prices based on quality.

The Wholesale Use of Robots Gives Japan its Cost Advantage.

It's true the Japanese use more than half the robots in the world. Most Japanese copier companies have dozens of robots on their assembly lines, but they're not the state-of-the-art, multifunction robots you might imagine. Most punch in rivets, drive screws, make tiny frame welds, or box the product at the end of the assembly line.

Konishiroku, in fact, uses very few robots, primarily because they cost too much. "I heard Ricoh automated and production didn't meet their expectations," said Tsugio Kitahara, a general manager at Konishiroku's copier plant. "As a company, we'd like to hedge that risk."

Canon is staffing its Toride factory with women, not robots, because the life span of products is too short and an automated production line is expensive to retool. Said Nobufusa Tomomatsu, assistant factory manager, "We're starting automation in making the [personal copier] cartridge. I'd like to have the whole line robotized, but it's so difficult to do that and keep things flexible."

Japanese Firms Get Money Cheaper and Easier from Their Lifelong Friends: Japanese Banks.

It's tough to poke a hole in this argument. Japanese people don't spend money the way Americans do. They save. About a fifth of the average income, including their semiannual, lump-sum bonuses, goes into private banks or government-run postal savings plans to save for retirement, pay for university educations, and big-ticket items. In turn, that money is invested in or loaned to Japanese companies, often at low rates, in industries MITI has targeted. So banks and insurance companies own most of the stock in Japanese firms. Minolta's major shareholders in 1984 were Taiyo Kobe Bank (5.8 percent), Daido Mutual Life Insurance (5.3

percent), Sanwa Bank (5 percent), and Saitama Bank (5 percent). It's a very convenient, and important, relationship. Atseo Kusada of Minolta explains, "There is a constant need for cash, because you must keep growing. But for most Japanese companies, profits aren't as high as in the U.S. So to reinvest money, we borrow constantly from the bank. Cash flow is the life of our company, not only to expand sales and marketing but manufacturing, too. That's why each company has at least five or six banks that we keep very good relations with." Keeping good relations also means giving the banks a hand in running the company. "Very often," Kusada adds, "a top bank can have one, maybe two, people sent into the company, not to control it entirely, but [to] have something to say. That happens very often."

And unlike American stockholders, banks and insurance companies aren't worried about short-term profits. Johnson of the University of California at Berkeley said, "We all know that for an American businessman the most terrifying day in his life is when that securities analyst comes to him and says, 'I invest the University of California retirement fund and two more quarters of the performance you've been showing and we're pulling completely out of your company.' A Japanese manager's success isn't judged by that."

The bank-industry relationship does give the Japanese a major advantage. Access to cheap capital (at 5 to 6 percent interest versus 10 percent or more in the United States) is the major reason why Japanese semiconductor firms invested so much in the middle 1970s and subsequently took the lead from the United States in computer memory chips. Sumeola of the International Trade Commission argues that Japan's ability to save and invest is the "single biggest reason why Japan's succeeded." He points out that Koreans save 30 percent, and Taiwanese 34 percent, of their incomes and those countries are also doing remarkably well.

However, some major Japanese firms, such as Matsushita, Nissan, and Toyota, have very little debt to Japanese banks. And Japan, like the United states, is starting to emphasize short-term returns. "It used to be five years," said Kusada, "in three years, you lose money, that's all right. But in five years, can you break even? If you can, let's do that. Now they're talking about, 'You lose this fiscal year, forget about it, let's do something else.' "

So if Japan's biggest reasons for success aren't what we always hear— cheap labor, a long-term view, the mighty MITI, quality circles, or lifetime employment—what are they? Xerox, which claims to have a better window onto Japan through Fuji Xerox than any other American company, has been trying to figure that out for years. "It's a long story, and we've spent countless hours immersed in it. But do you know what they [the Japanese] basically did?" mused C. Peter McColough. "They learned from Dr. [W. Edwards] Deming and Dr. [J. M.] Juran, two Americans, starting over twenty years ago, to apply some new techniques to manufacturing design; particularly manufacturing for reliability, for quality, [and] for cost, at a time when the whole world was laughing at them for going around with their cameras because they didn't have any design capability. They were way behind on that, but they've made some real progress and, very frankly, are ahead of the rest of the world. They didn't make much of a fuss about it, their products in the very early days were still not very competitive, but they really got control of that manufacturing process in a way the world didn't notice.

Harvard's Michael Porter, who has studied three dozen Japanese industries in detail, summed up the reasons for Japan's success this way: "If I had a hundred points, I'd give ten to fifteen to the government-business relationship and the other eighty-five to [their] entering the right segment, worrying about manufacturing automation, introducing electronics [into products] quickly, and taking advantage of economies of scale."

Japan has a knack for entering the so-called right segment—usually at the low end of the marketplace where American industry has left a gaping hole. Japanese-made Hondas and Toyotas, 50-cc motorcycles, tabletop TVs, transistor radios, and small copiers revolutionized America's buying habits. Kim Skidmore of the International Trade Commission (ITC) thinks it's cultural. "It's their ability to see small detail. They find beauty in very small things, very small elements."

Earle Jones, a vice president of Communication Intelligence Corporation who spends half his time in Japan, says it's a matter of focusing. "They don't attack everything. They pick out a market and go after it, not with Nobel Prize kind of stuff. Like the Honda motorbike. Pick one out on the street and it has two wheels and an engine between two handlebars. Inventions? How many patents are there on a motorbike?"

But if you've been to Japan, you know their attention to small things was born of necessity. A country the size of Montana with half the population of the United States can't fill its narrow streets with Buick Regals, or its tiny homes with twenty-five-inch console TVs. A country that imports almost all of its raw materials can't afford to waste resources or energy. The primary motivation for building small copiers and solid-state color TVs, for example, was to save electricity; such cars as Honda's Civic weren't just convenient, they saved fuel. They also fulfilled a need: Japanese companies don't make "ivory tower" decisions about what the buying public wants. Their products are triggered by observation of or discussions with customers. The Walkman, for example, was the brainstorm of a Sony engineer watching skateboarders in California; Canon's personal copier came out of meetings with American customers.

And since the Japanese, unlike a Xerox or an IBM, couldn't offer service from 7,000 miles away, extra emphasis was placed on reliability. Why worry about fixing something that doesn't break? Finally, with shipping costs and tariffs to worry about, the Japanese were forced into products that had high value added—that is, products such as the Sony Walkman, with little weight and material cost, command a high price for the ingenuity (i.e., software) that went into making them. The result is that for most Japanese-made consumer durables, manufacturing cost is only 30 percent of the suggested retail price.

So Japan's strategy has been marvelously fundamental: Start at the low end of a market with a value-added product that's simpler and cheaper to build and use, and through volume production and strict attention to quality, build up the brand name and expertise to take over the industry.

"Toyota did it first, and it took them about twenty years," said Jim Abegglen. "The company had a classic problem of being a small, unknown company going against the biggest companies in the world. But once they did it, others flocked in to see what happened, starting in 1974–75 just after the energy crisis. So it [Toyota's system] just swept through industry here."

Before setting up their existing factories, Japan's copier/camera companies sent teams to Toyota to learn how it had been done. Minolta, for example, sent engineers to Toyota in 1979 before setting up its Mizuho plant, Konishiroku studied Honda. "Those are the companies we learned from," Atseo Kusada said. "We go to Toyota, we go to Nissan, and we see many, many people. Toyota, we believe, has the best system for manufacturing." Toyota's system, known as *kanban* or just-in-time, changed the way conventional manufacturing had always been done, enabling the Japanese to begin building products for up to $1,500 per car less than their American competitors. That price and quality advantage you see—in everything from Japanese-made cars to the Sony Walkman—stems from a manufacturing process so simple, so filled with common sense, that it's a marvel to behold.

"I remember going and visiting the factories at Canon and Minolta in the latter seventies," said David Jorgansen, chairman of Dataquest.

"Compared to the way Xerox made machines, it was night and day. The Japanese were putting machines out once every fifty seconds. At Xerox, there was this huge area at the end of the assembly lines where they did quality assurance and quality control. In Japan, they were put in the box and shipped. It was obvious . . . Xerox was far behind."

Based on Henry Ford's production line principles, Toyota made its assembly lines totally flexible to give them the ability to make any car on any line. Minolta's Kusada explained, "The goal of the manufacturer is a line that can make more than a few models that have more than a few destinations—Japan, the USA, Europe—and indiscriminately assemble [any model] on one line just like Nissan or Toyota are doing."

If American companies are to survive, their factories must be just as cost-efficient, just as flexible. According to Minolta plant manager Odagiri, "In order to make a profitable business in mature markets, you must have a flexible manufacturing system. You must."

7

The Real Reason for Japan's Success

Frankly I hear too many Americans say it's
because of Japanese government help, or lower
wages. The government helps, lower wages
help, but it's much more fundamental than that.
—C. PETER MCCOLOUGH

THE FIRST THING that strikes you when you walk into a Japanese
factory is how clean and quiet it is. No boxes to dance around,
no parts spilling out of containers onto oily floors. It's efficiency
in motion, with mechanical and human arms flashing about, like the quiet
precision of a symphony. Conducting it all is the invisible hand of the
computer and the watchful eye of the quality control manager.

Just as important to the success of a Japanese-style factory are the
unsung players—the product design teams and the vendors who supply
up to 90 percent of the parts that go into a copier. Getting control of
your manufacturing process doesn't start with singing the company song
or plunking robots down onto the assembly lines. It begins much more
simply, with product designers tearing apart existing (usually American-
made) machines to examine each and every part. "We take all 3,000
parts in the copier," said Takeomi Nagafuchi, Ricoh's quality control
manager. "And we extensively test each and every one . . . every nut,
bolt, and screw."

The Japanese have found that this is the best way to determine what
parts are really necessary, and what parts can be replaced. For example,
Canon replaced the dry toner in its early copiers with an energy-efficient
liquid, reducing power consumption from 250 to 110 volts. And
Minolta decided to replace twenty-seven microswitches with a simpler
electronic part. Why? The reason is fundamental: Products with fewer
parts are more reliable, and cost less to build and operate.

More crucial, as Xerox is learning now, is replacing custom-made with off-the-shelf parts. Alan Kay, a former Xerox scientist said, "One of the reasons why Xerox machines and all American products were always so expensive is they liked to machine their own parts for about half the parts in a copier. Japan learned how to work with standard parts that were mass produced. I still remember the shock when Xerox saw the first Japanese machines. One of the reactions was we couldn't build one of those for twice as much."

It's common sense. Some critical components, such as the copier's selenium drum, what some call the "human heart" of a copier, must be made in-house. But buying the halogen lamp or the electric motor that goes inside the machines from a vendor like Toshiba or Matsushita, which makes millions of them a year, has to be cheaper than making them yourself. Kodak, Xerox, and IBM rarely if ever team up to standardize parts and buy them from the same vendor. The Japanese copier companies have been doing that since 1968. "When I was plant manager," said Zene Kumagai, a Konishiroku director, "I visited vendors and saw the main parts for every copier being made there; this line for Konishiroku, this line for Ricoh, this line for Canon. So it's one big family all getting the same part—that drives down the cost."

The result, said Xerox's David Myerscough, is that half the parts in a Japanese-made copier are standardized. "I can take a Canon and a Ricoh box in the same target range and find that 50 to 55 percent of that machine is common. In fact, the goal would be to use the same vendors. If Canon sees something good in a Ricoh product, they'll take it out and say, 'What am I going to add to it.' They'll go to a vendor and say, 'I know you're doing it for them, so if I add another 100,000, can I get a price $10 a part cheaper?' "

The Japanese don't just buy their parts anywhere. They search throughout the Far East to see who is best at making each and every part, then they either buy from them or copy their production methods. Ingrained in the Japanese culture is this desire to be *dantotsu*—best of the best—in every business venture. Japan has approached things that way for over a century. In the 1800s, the government sent secret missions to more industrialized, modernized nations to find out who was the most advanced in every field. The result, wrote Michio Morishima in *Why has Japan "Succeeded"?*, was that the Imperial Japanese Navy was a copy of Britain's Royal Navy, Japan's education system was patterned after the French. The telegraph and railways followed the British example, universities the American. Their constitution was based on Germany's, the criminal code came from France.

The 1,000 vendors who support the Japanese copier industry are the best in the world at making copier parts. They didn't get that way on their own. American companies have kept their suppliers at arm's length for decades, often abandoning partners in favor of competitive bids. Japanese companies find top vendors, whether they are small family-run concerns or such giant operations as Toshiba, and set up a deep and cozy relationship.

"This area is really an industrial park," said Minolta plant manager Yoshitsugu Odagiri as he pointed out his office window at the area surrounding his Mizuho plant. "We're surrounded by parts vendors." Laughing as he sat down, he added, "We can scream for it, 'Bring parts!' "

American companies coldly demand perfect parts with zero defects. If their vendors don't come through, they lose a major customer. Japanese vendors are cuddled, coerced, controlled, and cajoled. "The vendor relationship is so important," said Kusada. "Sometimes we need certain parts very quickly and in huge quantity the next day, [then] we might not need those parts for, say, six months. Vendors have to live with it. But if they depend upon Minolta and Minolta doesn't give them orders for six months, they will all die. We can't afford that. That's why, even when we don't need anything, we try to keep them as happy as we possibly can, even giving them certain orders which we may just have to throw away later. By doing this, you can keep loyalty very high so when we need them, they're there. If Minolta didn't support its vendors, they'd say, 'Minolta has never taken care of me so fuck Minolta. We don't care.' That is what people say, and Japanese people are no different. It's a business so we control them strictly. It's control, total control. Some vendors we own completely. Many we put money in. Very few do we have no capital relationship with. Generally, the smaller they are, the more dependent they are. Probably half our vendors make 80 percent of their business from us."

It's a convenient two-way street. Japanese companies work hand-in-hand with their vendors, teaching them everything from quality control to their secret production methods. Canon buys its key parts from at least two sources, and sometimes sets up pilot production in-house to learn about manufacturing costs, then that production expertise is transferred to an outside vendor. "If you're my supplier," said Jim Abegglen, "I expect to see your books. We're going to be open with each other. Now I'm going to tell you in advance what technology changes I'm going to make. And I expect you to make some investment, too. I expect you to make a profit but I want to know what the profit is. And I expect your costs to go down steadily. Right? Okay? You've got my business. For the next twenty years, unless you fuck up on price or delivery or quality, you're my guy."

This control over vendors varies. Ricoh has no financial relationship with its 350 vendors but gives fifty vendors (who get 75 percent of Ricoh's orders) certificates to assure them that they have a deal. "Then we give them a monthly report on quality," said Endo. "If there's a problem, the vendor comes here to meet with Mr. [Haruo] Kamimoto, the plant manager, to improve the situation. Then we wait a few months to see what they do."

In some cases, the larger company makes sweeping changes. Abegglen was working with a small vendor that was providing machine tool equipment for Toyota, "and they were screwing up on delivery. Toyota sent in a bunch of engineers and they relaid out their factory, redesigned the whole goddamn work platform. Now I don't think they'd do that twice."

This relationship with vendors is crucial to making the Toyota-based *kanban* system work. Toyota bases production upon actual orders, not projected needs. When a car is finished, a small card (called a *kanban*) is sent back to the assembly department. The various departments go to work then, assembling another car, and passing their *kanbans* back to vendors who supply the components. An analogy might be a short-order cook who gets a breakfast order, pulls together the eggs and other ingredients, then checks off what he's used. The system tells the manager what to order from suppliers. Once the vendor arrives with the supplies, he removes his order card from a prominently displayed board at the loading dock.

Japanese factory managers don't talk about a delivery date, they talk about delivery time, like tomorrow at 10:00 A.M. If the vendor doesn't show up by ten o'clock, everybody will know because the board shows he's late. His card is still sitting there. And until he shows up, no one moves his card. Because of the manufacturer/vendor relationship:

- Parts arrive on time. Only rarely does a Japanese vendor show up late. And the parts arrive in tubs, provided by the manufacturer, that can be sent down immediately by unmanned vehicles or conveyors, to the assembly lines.
- Inventory is reduced to the absolute minimum. Three years ago, Ricoh had eighteen days average inventory. Now the average is 2.8 days. Konishiroku's average is just half a day. Canon's is one day. Reducing inventory may not sound like such a big deal, but it is.

Parts sitting idle waste time and energy: American companies now spend about 30 percent of their production costs on warehousing, inventory holding charges, and transportation of parts.

· The assembly-line area is clean and efficient. "Notice how you can look up and down our lines," said Ricoh's Koichi Endo. "We used to have stacks of parts sitting all over this place. Now there's none." As a result, it takes hours, not days, to run inventory checks. Stacks of inventory also have a way of hiding problems.

Yoshitsugu Odagiri said, "Suppose you have a one-month inventory and you have a bucket of defective parts. That's tough to find. With our system, we can pick out any bucket anywhere in the plant at any time."

· Japanese companies get virtually defect-free parts. More than 70 percent of the parts coming into Ricoh's plant aren't even checked for quality.

Of course, you couldn't run the delivery system this way without computers. For example, Ricoh has 1,300 pallets, containing up to 16,000 different parts, delivered by 210 trucks every day. Keeping track of them all without Ricoh's Hitachi mainframe and two minicomputers would be impossible. So once the parts reach the loading docks, and the containers are placed on conveyors, the computer takes over. The vendor inserts his card: If he's delivered fifty buckets of parts instead of a hundred buckets, that's detected. If the delivery's late, the computer notes that, too. Then the computer moves the container, usually by conveyors, to temporary storage in a catacomb of open-ended shelves in a dark corner of the factory. And Ricoh stands ready to make any of six models, in twenty variations, each containing 550 to 3,020 parts. Up until that point in the process, it's pretty standardized. All the Japanese copier companies use *kanban,* or their version of it, to keep inventories low and deliveries just in time. Where you notice the big differences are on the assembly lines.

When something is invented, it's usually very difficult for the average person to use. Telephone calls a hundred years ago had to be made through the operator; problems for computers once went to technicians running room-size mainframes. But as technology advances, it eliminates the people between you and what you're trying to do. Now you can pick up the phone and dial anywhere. Or sit down at a personal computer with ten times the power of those huge, old machines.

The same thing is true in manufacturing. Workers on the assembly line were once far removed from the parts ordering process. Now, thanks to computers, Japanese workers at some plants are in complete control. Above every worker at Minolta is a yellow box, the size of a basketball, with pictures of eight to ten parts from which to choose plus a "Go" button. He no longer has to tell the foreman to tell the parts procurement department to order parts. All the worker does is press the button and, two to three minutes later, they're delivered by a three-foot-tall mobile carrier (about the size of an MG convertible). These $30,000 unmanned vehicles travel about 5 mph, following tracks on the factory floor that resemble cracks in a sidewalk. Totally under computer control, the unmanned vehicle steers itself to a worker's station, pushes a pallet full of parts into place next to him, then picks up the empty pallets and returns to the warehouse.

An ingenius software program, created by a seven-man team from Minolta and the Senkei Company, made this delivery system possible. Keeping track of it all, tucked away in a bright white room far from the factory floor, is a twenty-foot-long electronic map of the factory. Tiny, blinking lights show where parts and products are moving, much the way the New York Transit Authority monitors its subway cars. The result? In January 1985, the assembly lines on the third and fourth floors of Minolta's Mizuho plant were building 800 machines a day, producing three different models: the 350, 350Z, and 450Z.

Ricoh, Canon, and Sharp have advanced the technology a step further, eliminating people from parts delivery entirely. Laser scanners, like the ones used at supermarket checkout lines, read the bar codes on the sides of copier modules as they move through the factory. There's no need for workers to order parts. The computer knows what has been used, and, every two hours or so, sends out what's needed on mobile carriers like the ones Minolta uses. These companies can instantly alternate models. Ricoh's down time (to switch from making one machine to another) has dropped from five to seven hours a month to one hour and forty minutes a month.

The software behind Ricoh's system took forty people a year and a half to develop. And it's understandably in great demand: In 1984, 850 people from thirty countries toured the plant, including DEC, AT&T, Hewlett-Packard, IBM, and Kodak from the United States. "Hitachi wants to buy the software, Apple and Philips wanted to buy it, but we won't sell it to them," Endo said. His concern is that some companies, such as Hitachi, are now or could be competitors in businesses besides copiers. Plus, Endo doesn't think the system would work at factories that don't have all three ingredients: hardware, software, and humanware.

"Humanware," as Endo calls it, and quality control—two of the toughest things for any company to manage—are what makes the whole system tick. It's said that Japanese managers treat their people better, especially those on their assembly lines. And it's true. American companies manage by fear. The Japanese get everyone to work together, and through quality circles involve them in the company. In the factories, everyone from plant manager on down wears the same uniform, usually a full-length cotton jumpsuit plus a cap bearing the company name. As you walk through the plant, workers go about their business, paying little attention to the top brass and their visitors.

Yoshitsugu Odagiri, the personable general manager of Minolta's copier plant, doesn't believe in rallying his troops with fancy slogans or catch phrases. "I respect my middle manager, as a human and as a manager. They read the newspapers, they listen to the speeches so I don't like to interrupt too much. In order to really concentrate our power, our employees must be treated like human beings. On the materials floor, we mechanize, entirely eliminating humans so there are no human errors. But on the assembly line, we humanize. What you have to realize is that equipment has a good point and a poor point and humans have a good point and a poor point. Combine the good points of both and you get effective systems."

Simple enough, but how? Japan has been wrestling with that question for forty years. What they've arrived at is a delicate balance: Konishiroku and Minolta may put the day's production targets on scoreboards at the end of their assembly lines, but ultimately employees work at their own pace. Konishiroku doesn't even use conveyors. Workers pass copiers down the assembly lines on carts when they're finished. Said Tsugio Kitahara, "At most companies, people are rushed."

Minolta's workers control the speed of the assembly line with a foot pedal. "Even an eighteen-year-old girl," Odagiri said, "controls the entire operation herself. A group leader tells by sight who is behind or ahead. Maybe in a hundred years we'll have a robot there, but not now."

The Japanese also seek out the opinions of low- to mid-level managers. In meetings and decision-making, explained Earle Jones, "everything's done by consensus. You walk into a meeting and there's eight or ten Japanese people. You might have the senior technical guy, the product planner, a marketing guy, and then in the back row there's the young technical guys in lab coats. They're not even introduced to you, they're transparent. But they sit back there and take notes. They don't ask questions. They don't interrupt. They just absorb information. And after the meeting, all the Japanese get together and the first thing they do is ask the young guys for their opinions. 'What do you think? What should we do?' And that's all good. It helps them grow, and let's them see how their big bosses behave and their opinions are factored into the decision. You don't have to explain it . . . they've heard the reasons. And when you have a young man who understands, is on the team, his loyalty is so high. It can take time. An American company president who slams his fist on the table and says, 'This is how it's going to be!' can act faster, but he's going to have problems getting people to implement that decision.''

The Japanese also use slogans to promote enthusiasm. At Canon's Toride factory, managers were wearing pins that said, "FRESH"—for Flexibility Reliability Efficiency Speedy Humanity. At another Canon plant, the pins said, "FIGHTING." Konishiroku, in publicity material for a Japan trade show, headlined its envelopes, "ATTACK!"

On the factory floor, where assembly-line workers really get involved, the Japanese buzzword is "TQC"—Total Quality Control. There's a lot more to quality control than meeting in quality circles. Workers are continually trained to check for defects. When a Japanese company starts building a new copier, the lines are shut down, or workers meet at lunch, for quality-control training. Building in quality is everybody's job.

Above the assembly lines at Canon is a chime that workers ring when they spot a defect. Canon calls this "TSS," an acronym for Tomete Sugu Shochi, which means stop for immediate action. Ricoh workers send defective parts to quality checkpoints where special computers trace the defect back to a vendor or preproduction handling. Minolta uses a panel with a warning light tied to production control. If the worker spies a problem, he pushes a button to stop the line and a supervisor comes immediately. Minolta also uses Q-up cards—green cards for assembly-line managers and red cards for inspectors from Quality Control. If there's a problem at a workstation, the Q-up card is filled out by management and the worker fills out his side with an explanation. The card is then posted on a bulletin board. Each morning all the workers gather before the board to see who's having problems. Based on human relations studies in the United States, the Q-up card elevates workers to the status of quality control inspectors.

Konishiroku, which prides itself on quality control, almost goes overboard: Every worker checks not only his own work but the work of the person just before him. The plant has stations just to clean up any toner left from making test copies. And at the end of the assembly line is a station just to check the cosmetics—scars or scratches left during the production process.

Checking quality with test copies varies. Ricoh's manufacturing is so precise that, except when starting production of a new product, Ricoh makes no test copies on small copiers. It does make up to 200 test copies on a large machine like the 6080. Sharp and Minolta, in comparison, make ten test copies, and Konishiroku makes five, during assembly. Sharp uses robots with tiny metal fingers to punch the buttons, and run about ten test copies. Canon runs up to a hundred on advanced machines.

This obsession with quality is the product of the work of two Americans, William Edwards Deming and J. M. Juran. Before World War II, Deming was a determined but discouraged U.S. government statistician who knew the only way to make a high-quality product was to build quality in as you went along, not inspect the product afterward. His idea was to study each and every part, each and every procedure, and then set statistical controls that would prevent wide variations in quality. During the war he taught the system to 30,000 American engineers, but afterward, no one important would listen to him. "Only a few small American companies were interested," said Deming.

When Deming went to Japan in 1946, a group of influential Japanese statisticians dined with him in his hotel room to hear what he had to say. They invited him back, and at Deming's insistence, arranged a meeting with forty-five top Japanese executives. At an American-style beef dinner in his honor, "I told them what to do. And their top people, their top engineers, listened to me." His message was simple: drive out fear; ignore short-term profits; eliminate inspection and build quality into the product instead; institute on-the-job training; and don't think price, think quality. In his lectures, Juran laid the responsibility for doing all this on management. He said 80 percent of quality-control problems could be solved by management decisions alone.

Deming's favorite example of systems management is his bead trick. He fills a container with 3,000 white beads and 750 red ones. Then he asks volunteers ("willing workers") to reach in with a paddle and scoop out fifty beads. Every red bead they pull out represents a defective product. One volunteer gets twenty red beads, another ten, another just two. Meanwhile, Deming paces around like a manager, lecturing employees to avoid red beads or the plant will close. Of course, it's not their fault. No matter how hard they try, they can't have zero defects. The system itself is defective and can only be changed by management. Deming's immediate solution is to set limits, statistical controls, and an average for the number of defects the system should produce. Maybe the upper limit is twenty red beads, the lower limit two, with an average of ten. Then it's up to workers to stay within those limits and, when they don't, to determine the cause. Management's role is to study the entire process and develop solutions. Deming's conclusion: Workers can help but in the final analysis, quality control is up to design engineers and management.

To the Japanese, this made a lot of sense. "We grabbed it because we thought it was good," Atseo Kusada said. "We needed some tool to be more competitive and Dr. Deming offered us that tool. If he wasn't there, Japan would have found something else. But Deming's tool brought us up quickly to this level [holds up his hand waist high]. Without him, Japan would have gone this way, that way, struggling."

Starting in 1951, some major Japanese companies took Deming's Way, they even created the now-coveted Deming Prize for quality control, and began applying it in their factories. Winning the Deming Prize in 1953, an ad for Sumitomo Metals noted, was "the single most important event in the history of [Sumitomo's] quality control. . . . Thanks, Dr. Deming, for helping to start it all."

Deming's statistical controls didn't really catch on at the copier/camera companies until about fifteen years ago. "Our emphasis on quality had always been lower than the other industries," said Ricoh's manager of quality control, Takeomi Nagafuchi. But once Deming's methods caught on, they helped Ricoh start a revolution that almost knocked Xerox out of the small-copier business.

Perhaps the single most important thing the Japanese learned, and many American companies have yet to realize, is that low-quality products cost you money—in lost sales, costly service, wasted materials, and unneeded inspections. (Xerox thinks poor quality could cost a company up to 20 percent of its revenues.) Second, they learned that quality control doesn't begin or end at the assembly line. Nagafuchi says 70 percent of the quality of a product is determined at the design stage. He makes his biggest effort there, giving engineers and designers every statistical tool they need to decide what parts to use. "We take all 3,000 parts and divide them up into A, B, and C parts, in order of importance," he said. "Then we test each and every part. The A parts might be tested 1,000 different ways."

On the assembly lines, statistical controls are applied to manufacturing procedures. Say, for instance, that copier nameplates are sometimes glued on crooked. The quality control group runs a test of all individuals and/or robots performing that task. The test shows that two workers in particular are most frequently responsible for this variation in quality. Instead of admonishing them, the quality control team probes further to find that both workers are having trouble because they're farsighted. The quality control team solves the problem by buying two pair of eyeglasses.

Quality control applies to service, too. Surveys by a Japanese bank, averaging 500 incoming customer phone calls a day, found that callers became irritated because it took too long for bank operators to answer the phone. A quality control team decided to survey only those who waited five rings or more. They found that the major variation (or cause of defects), occurring 172 times a day, was when one operator left the office. So managers started a three-shift lunch system, told all employees to leave messages at their desks and compiled a detailed personnel directory. They eliminated the biggest problem: Such incidents dropped from 172 to 15 a day.

So three key things—vendors, the Deming Way, and just-in-time manufacturing—gave Japan its 30 to 40 percent cost advantage, in general, over American manufacturers. It's that simple. The parts come in, defect-free, from vendors; are checked in by computers; sent for two days or less to a computer-controlled warehouse; and sent just in time to the assembly lines. There, precision robots and workers schooled in quality control handle the assembly. No parts sitting around. No waste. No inventory.

If there remains any doubt to the advantages, look who's following suit: Ford and General Motors have hired Deming. Burlington Industries and Polaroid are also using his methods. Just-in-time manufacturing— widely credited with rescuing Harley-Davidson from the brink of bankruptcy—is now being practiced at 3M, Whirlpool, Hewlett-Packard, and Motorola. Apple Computer takes 400 parts from sixty vendors to make Macintosh computers. At General Electric's locomotive plant in Erie, Pennsylvania, seven men with computers and robots build a diesel engine block in sixteen hours—a task that once took ninety men sixteen days.

And there's also one more American giant, too proud at one time to admit others might have a better way, that's learned a few lessons from the Japanese.

"Yes, Xerox got surprised," says Peter McColough. "But it's the whole damn world. As far as Xerox is concerned, and as far as I'm concerned, we recognize that Japan's gotten ahead of us in certain areas, and we've been scrambling in the last few years to copy everything we think is going to be adaptable to the United States and the Western World.''

8
The Thundering Hordes

How successful you are depends upon how
desperate you are. All Japan has been desperate and will be forever because in Japan, we
have nothing. That's why we're strong.
—ATSEO KUSADA, Minolta

KONISHIROKU'S Zene Kumagai recalls, back in the 1950s, looking
at a prediction that most of the world's silver, the lifeblood of
the company's filmmaking business, would be used up over the
next thirty years.

"We had to get outside the silver halide technology," said
Kumagai, an executive vice president.

That's when his company grudgingly began to diversify and the
copying machine, which has an optical system to record images just like
cameras, was a natural. Kenichi Ohmae, the oft-quoted director of
McKinsey & Co.'s Tokyo office, says their only other option was 8-mm
video. "But 8mm wasn't going well. And Xerox was going like crazy
at the time."

Then near-disaster struck. A technical nightmare, caused by static
electricity, caused dots to appear on the company's photographs and films.
Konishiroku didn't react quickly and its market share plummeted, from
90 percent to less than 20 percent. Its archrival, Fuji Photo Film, took
control of the industry. Then, in 1962, Fuji tied up with Xerox. "This
was a big shock to Konishiroku," Ohmae said. Konishiroku needed help
. . . and fast. Japan's other camera companies—Canon, Minolta,
Ricoh—were in trouble, too. Their cameras were world-beaters, but the
marketplace was saturated.

There was another threat as well. Some thought xerography could
be an alternative to photographic film.

"So we thought, 'we've got to do something,' " said Atseo Kusada, a vice president who started Minolta's copier business. "So what do we do? We have a lens. Isn't there any product that uses a lens? A photocopy is equal to a photograph, right?"

Konishiroku tackled the challenge first. In 1968, it brought forty-eight young engineers together in the top-secret E Project. Their goal was to make a plain paper copier that cut copy cost in half yet doubled copy quality.

"Each morning, everyone gathered for a brainstorming session; there were forty-eight ideas about what kind of copier to make," recalled Tsugio Kitahara, now an associate director. Thirty members of E Project went in pairs to Tokyo offices to find out what people hated about their Fuji Xerox machines. One problem, believe it or not, was copier operators falling down. At the end of 1969, mini-skirts and high heels were the fads in Japan. Young ladies complained that, when they bent down to add toner and someone passed behind, they lost their balance and tumbled. The point was that Xerox machines were too large and too impractical for small Japanese and their packed-in work space. So Konishiroku moved the toner box within 500 millimeters of the top of its machine.

And a year later, at the 1970 Tokyo Business Show, Konishiroku showed eight prototypes, the first Japanese plain paper copiers completely free of Xerox patents. Xerox paid little attention, largely because this came on the heels of IBM's entry. But visitors were amazed by Konishiroku's copy quality. The copies didn't have the Xerox "edge" effect: Copies of a black cat came out black, not white with black around the edges. Because of the toner and development methods Xerox used at that time, its machines made good outlines of characters but were weak on solid areas. The E Project members were treated as heroes and a book, *Takumi No Jidai (Age of Craftsmanship)*, heralded their breakthrough.

Konishiroku's competitors saw this, Ohmae said, and knew they "couldn't afford to fall behind." They thought; "We really have to win this game. We've fought these guys in cameras and everyone survived. We've got to survive in plain paper copiers. So they all got serious about it. This bundle of companies just dashed ahead."

Within two years, five other companies—Minolta, Toshiba, Mita, Copyer, and Ricoh—were readying their attack building prototypes.

Edward Poshkus, who was running copier research for Dataquest at the time, saw them coming: "They came in with the samurai mentality . . . absolute confidence. I've never run into that kind of confidence. They were samurai warriors coming to do battle."

At the beginning, Minolta's Kusada said, "nobody was making money, nobody. Everybody was losing money except maybe Ricoh. But we Japanese are not in the American market for 'quick killing.' Patience was the key . . . we waited, and waited . . . everybody was looking five, six, seven years ahead." Minolta came to the U.S. in 1969, but didn't make any money until 1974.

All the companies focused on the low-end copier business Xerox had ignored. Their strategy was the same as Japanese automakers: come up with a low-price, energy-efficient, small copier that was easier to use, and service, than desk-sized Xerox machines. Because they couldn't distribute or service the machines from 7,000 miles away, the real dilemma was how to sell them.

That's why Ricoh, with Savin Chairman Paul Charlap acting as middleman, teamed up with America's Savin and Nashua, and Germany's Kalle Infotec, and then spent seven years developing the revolutionary Savin 750, introduced in 1975. That was an excellent short-term strategy that, for a time, enabled Ricoh to rule the low-end copier business.

9

Charlap's
Crusade

I'm the one who put the Japanese into this
business . . . man, I didn't do this country
any favors.

—PAUL CHARLAP

MEET Paul Charlap. The man who almost single-handedly brought together eight companies on four continents to build the Savin 750, a machine that revolutionized the copier industry. Shake his hand and you're pulled toward him, he's like a speedboat yanking you off the dock. Then he's down the hall, arms waving, instructions flying, people tailing, everybody vying for a piece of his precious time. Too busy to knock, he pushes open doors and snaps: "Get me the plane to Binghamton at eight. Tell Felix I need to see him. Get Benny on the phone." It's just another day of too few hours for the sixty-year-old, bald-headed former chairman of Savin Corporation. [Charlap resigned as Savin chairman in 1985. He now heads a Savin subsidiary set up to exploit the electroink (liquid toner) technology invented by Benny Landa.]

"Hey, let me tell you something," he says, breezing into a private meeting room. "I'm the one who brought the Japanese into this industry. I take that total responsibility upon my shoulders and when I think back about it, man, I didn't do this country any favors."

It's tough to believe that one man, especially the head of a company less than 1/20 the size of Xerox, could have had so much influence! Though his influence has dwindled as Savin has struggled with its own problems recently, in the early 1970s he was the right man at the right time. He looks and talks like Kojak. And he's shrewd; he's stubborn and he's smart. "If you use the word *genius,* you have to use his name," said Gabriel Carlin, a former Savin vice president. He speaks several languages, including Japanese. He's as hard-driving as a drill sargeant. "Persuasive as a snake-oil salesman," says a Xerox engineer.

Charlap doesn't sit still. He's like a hyperactive kid. At Tokyo's Okura Hotel, the staff keeps a stationary exercise bike for him in storage. Since World War II, he has chalked up 9,000 hours piloting everything from company jets across the United States to a private helicopter between Savin's Stamford, Connecticut, headquarters and its upstate New York factory. At 220 mph average speed, that's nearly 2 million miles—or to the moon and back four times. His secretary gave up trying to keep a schedule for him long ago, so it took four months just to arrange an interview—and that was squeezed in right after he flew in from Europe. That night he was flying to Binghamton, the next day he was off to Tokyo.

He holds a degree in chemistry and one in physics, and his hobby, believe it or not, is bird-watching. He frets constantly about endangered species, and once served as president of the Junior Audubon Society. He hates smoking—calls it "the most disgusting habit in the world"— and loves to nibble, piling tuna fish onto tomato slices and crunching potato chips throughout our three-hour interview. A high roller, in 1982, he personally received $2.5 million when Canadian Development Corporation upped its stake in Savin. On another occasion, just for fun, Charlap bet a co-worker $1,000 that a contract would be settled in a month. He rushed down the hall to collect. His friend blushed, then pulled out a crisp $100 bill. "Where's the other $900?" Charlap quipped.

Charlap's real fascination is with people, friends and foes in every corner of the world. And his biggest strength by far is motivating them, getting them "off their ass" to do something. Fifteen years ago, when everybody envied Xerox and it appeared that the copier giant, shrouded by a web of complex patents, was invulnerable—especially to the invention-poor Japanese—even people at Savin were throwing up their hands. But not Paul Charlap.

"What's the big deal?" a Savin colleague named Gene exclaimed to Charlap, "It [the Xerox machine] only breaks down three times a month."

Charlap didn't respond, but one day when Gene wasn't looking, Charlap had two of the tires taken off Gene's car. Back then, Savin was in Valhalla, New York, and Gene lived way out on Long Island. When he found his car vandalized he screamed and yelled and said, "This is terrible, I don't know how I'll get home."

The next day, Charlap had the wheels put back on the car. Gene came in, couldn't understand it, but went about his business until two days later when Charlap had the tires taken off the car again. After having the tires removed a third time, Charlap called Gene and said, "Hey, Gene, that was only three times this month. What's the big deal?" Charlap had made his point: If someone could make a more reliable Xerox machine, they would rule the industry.

Xerox machines broke down too much, partially because they were too big and too complex. Charlap wasn't the only one to realize this. In Japan, where 90 percent of all documents were still being written in longhand, there was a desperate need for small copying machines. Analyst James Abegglen called it the "soft underbelly of Xerox." In fact, one day in 1970, a group of top Xerox executives gathered in Xerox's New York office to hear what Abegglen had to say. "Everyone was there except [chairman C. Peter] McColough," Abegglen said. "It was a fairly expensive one-day show. I told them that here in Japan was the world's biggest market for copiers. That if you put out a small machine that pumped out copies slowly but effectively, there was going to be one helluva market. That was Xerox's soft underbelly; to come up underneath that animal, the Xerox 914, on price with a smaller machine."

At the end of the day, then Xerox president Archie McCardell took Abegglen aside and said, "So what?"

Abegglen told him Xerox should "just give away the 914, give it away for free and make its money on supplies, in order to head off the Japanese, leaving them no room to come into the market with a small machine. But, of course, McCardell, like those running Detroit's carmakers at the time, just giggled and ignored the Japanese threat." McCardell came to Xerox from Ford.

In fact, the first plain paper copiers out of Japan to reach the marketplace—the NP-1100 from Canon late in 1970 and the UBIX 480 from Konishiroku in January 1971—proved McCardell right. Like the first small Japanese cars, they didn't work very well. Konishiroku's machine literally caught fire; Canon's never made it to the U.S. market. Worldwide, only 8,000 to 9,000 machines a month were sold. Zene Kumagai, a Konishiroku director, says, "We didn't have the technology, or the financial strength to compete with Xerox. We sold very few machines."

Minolta's scientists studied UBIX technology and came up with a machine that was "such a bomb," said Atseo Kusada of Minolta, "that we didn't even try to market it." Even in failure, those early machines proved something. "Before that, we all thought if we start into it, Xerox will just kill us . . . completely. Everybody was deathly afraid of Xerox because of their patents," Kusada said. When Xerox didn't react, "that's what opened the door."

Enter Paul Charlap. And the beginning of one of the most extensive, most successful international product development efforts in history. It's a tale not of dollars and cents, but of trust and real people: Australians, Americans, Germans, and Japanese. Remember, Xerox didn't become the most dominating multinational of its time on ingenuity alone. No single Japanese or American company could muster the technology or the financial strength to challenge them. It would take a combined effort, one orchestrated by Charlap.

Like his Japanese allies, Charlap was itching for years to bust up Xerox's monopoly. In fact, when Savin was founded by Max Low and his son Robert in 1959, its first goal was to develop the world's first plain paper copier. "I was graduating from New York University at the time and I told my father about a device being developed at Minox in Giessen, West Germany," recalled Robert Low. "He talked to me and his accountant about it and we bought the rights to that unit [a diffusion transfer copier that made "wet" copies] and started the company. Minox continued to develop what we thought would be the first plain paper copier. We were shocked as hell five months later when Xerox came out with the 914."

The accountant's son-in-law, who happened to be looking for a job at the time, was none other than Paul Charlap. He was hired and got his first taste of international business as the go-between on technical matters, running back and forth between the Bronx and West Germany. "He [Charlap] had no copying background and I was fresh out of college," Low said. "That's how we started the company."

Three years later, Chester Carlson, the inventor of xerography, came to see Savin's plant in the East Bronx. Carlson told the group, "If anybody is ever able to attack any part of what we've done, it's going to be you," and he pointed at Charlap.

"Why do you say that, Mr. Carlson?" Charlap asked.

"Because you have the stick-to-it-iveness, and the stubbornness, and the scientific understanding. If anyone's going to do it, it's you."

Carlson was right, but it would take Charlap nearly fifteen years.

To get around Xerox patents, Savin in its early years had to stick with machines that copied on what Charlap called sleazy zinc oxide, rather than plain paper. The first was the Sahara 200, a Minox machine that Savin introduced in 1964. Around that time, Low and Charlap decided to sell only in the United States, giving licensing rights to the rest of the world, and to find someone else to manufacture the machines. "We didn't think we could expand fast enough ourselves," Low said.

A marketing license for Australia, South Africa, England, and West

Germany went to Nashua Corporation of New Hampshire. Also licensed in Europe was Kalle Niederlassung der Hoechst A. G. of West Germany. The A. B. Dick Company had a license to sell Savin products in the United States. Ironically, the first Japanese company Savin planned to talk to was Fuji Photo Film, but Fuji's tie-in with Xerox nixed the deal. That's when Savin linked up with Ricoh, giving Ricoh marketing rights in the Far East and Japan.

Ricoh, which had such a commanding share of Japan's coated-paper copier business that people said "Ricopy it" the same way Americans say "Xerox it," claims it took Savin's first product and improved it considerably. "The Sahara had many bad parts; for instance, it used coated roll paper but the cutter didn't work very well," said Iwao Yamamoto, head of Ricoh's research and development at the time. "We corrected those defects in Japan."

Then the Japanese who started Ricoh's American operation came to see Charlap and said, "There's a great man by the name of Kiyoshi Ichimura, and since you can speak Japanese, why don't you go talk to him?" So Charlap took Savin's next machine and went to Japan and met Ichimura, the founder of Ricoh. By 1965, in part because of Fuji Xerox's success in Japan, Ichimura's company was in deep financial trouble, teetering on the edge of bankruptcy. So Charlap said, "Kiyoshi, if you listen to me, if you take this machine we developed at Minox in West Germany and manufacture it, I will buy from you this year $3 million worth of copying machines." Savin eventually bought $10 million, and it saved Ichimura's company.

Ricoh was so poor at manufacturing, Charlap said, that Savin forfeited $5 million in royalties so A. B. Dick could send a team of engineers to Japan to teach Ricoh how to manufacture. Ricoh improved and Savin's sales exploded, reaching $30 million by the end of the 1960s. Several Japanese firms copied what Ricoh was doing with coated-paper machines so completely that when Charlap went to the Hanover Fair, an industry trade show in West Germany, "I couldn't tell where my booth was. There was booth after booth of machines that were exact copies of mine, to the color. And our company soared."

Still Charlap and Low weren't satisfied.

"The sparkle was still in Paul's eye, said Felix Hertzka, then group vice president at Nashua. "We all were so jealous of Xerox and all we could do was nibble away. Everybody kept thinking, if only we could come up with something. . . ."

That breakthrough was about to occur, and not at a multimillion-dollar research facility in Japan, the United States, or West Germany, but at a tiny government laboratory in Australia.

"I went to Australia and put up a $3-million factory for Nashua in 1970," Hertzka recalled. "And this fellow told my manager down there one day that he would put us out of business because he was an Australian. I went to see him and what he had was an absolute joke, a roll-paper machine with a hole punched in the wall to hold the paper. But I got to know him and one day he called to say he had something new. He showed me a postage stamp of black stuff on a piece of paper and said, 'That's a liquid image on plain paper.' I called Paul [Charlap] and the research guy at Nashua, Austin Davis, and asked them both to fly down to look at it."

This was precisely the breakthrough Charlap, who had no research staff of his own, was looking for. He always believed that liquid toner, like the ink in a pen, was far superior to the powder toner Xerox used to make photocopies. "Look at *National Geographic*," he said. "It's a pretty good looking magazine, right? Anybody do that with powder? You know how a Xerox copy comes out warm? That's because a very powerful heater has to melt the powder, turning it into a liquid that's then fused to the paper." Then, says Charlap, "you have to cool the damn thing off. Well, it takes a helluva lot of energy to heat it up and a helluva lot to cool it off. And there's all this powder blowing around.

"Look at it this way: If you drive across the desert, you better change your oil every 1,000 miles because there's all those little particles of sand in there trying to eat up the machine. What happens with Xerox machines is they get dirty, the lenses get filthy and they start putting Band-Aids like vacuum systems on to clean everything up. Still, the copies deteriorated almost immediately . . . after 6,000 or 7,000 copies, it even gets worse."

Liquid toner machines, in which the image fixes on the copy without being heated up, didn't need the Band-Aids. That made them much simpler to build, and considerably more reliable. But they had their problems, too. One constant nightmare for designers was electrostatic pinning, or "static cling" in laundry terms. If you take a balloon and rub it, and put it on glass, it sticks. That's electrostatic pinning. It's a tremendously powerful force. Because of electrostatic pinning, says Charlap, "I can fly our jet that's filthy dirty through a storm at 500 mph and it still comes out dirty, those electrostatic forces are hugging it." In a copier, when you go to transfer an image to the paper, the same electrostatic force behind the paper caused the paper to "whap" onto the drum, squashing the image and creating a mess. As a result, dry toner machines like Xerox's always made much better copies.

But Charlap was obsessed with finding a better way, especially one that would get around the Xerox patents. So with all this running through his mind, he took off for Australia.

"When I got there," Charlap recalled, "I walked into this compound at the Australian Department of Defense and I went up and knocked on the door and said, 'Do you know where I can find Ken Metcalfe?' And he said, 'I'm Ken Metcalfe, but how the hell did you get in here?'

"It was a funny thing. You remember this guy that walked into the White House with the band at Reagan's inauguration? I did the same thing. I walked into their most secret defense facility and ended up at this guy's door. So Ken Metcalfe and I sat down and I told him I was fascinated with what he was doing with liquid toners, and that I personally didn't believe from the physics that dry toning had any chance over the long run versus liquid. As soon as the problems are solved—how do you make an image that doesn't squash, how do you get rid of the pollution, how do you get enough energy to fix the image—'we'll take over the world.' "

Metcalfe's group had heard a lot of this before. Ten years earlier, one of Yamamoto's salesmen was visiting Australia to set up an export deal for Ricoh when he heard about someone using liquid toners to make clear, low-cost copies of X-ray photographs. Yamamoto was suspicious but decided to check it out for himself. "I went there in 1960 and looked it over and thought it had a very promising future. The inventor never dreamed of getting a copier out of it." So Ricoh paid 50 million yen or $240,000 in 1985 dollars for an exclusive license in Japan from the Australian government. Ricoh went on to use liquid-toner technology in several electrostatic copying machines during the 1960s, but was forced by the government to license its secrets to Canon and seven other major Japanese companies. Ricoh kept its work on liquid toners "very secret," Yamamoto said, even from Savin. Thus, Charlap didn't know much about it. Also, Xerox, then Haloid, learned of Metcalfe's research in the early 1950s and sent several people to Australia. Hal Bogdonoff, a Xerox engineer, went to Metcalfe's house and had dinner with him. The company licensed the technology but never did much research on liquid toners because the pure selenium plates it used in the early days were soluble in virtually any liquid, even water. Liquid toner ruined the plates. Plus, said Bogdonoff, "We never saw consistent-enough quality."

In 1970, Charlap made an offer Metcalfe couldn't refuse: "You give me four people, we'll build you a laboratory; you guys go and do what we want done. When you're finished, we will have paid for all the equipment, all the salaries, and we'll give you the laboratory." Metcalfe agreed and that's how it all started. A group of four Australians leaped at the opportunity to be American-style entrepreneurs, a chance to be the first foreigners to knock a dent in the armor of Xerox.

"My theory is you're much better off building a laboratory around a genius than building a genius of a building and hope you'll get somebody in it," Charlap said. "I'm a capitalist deep down and I believe it really does work."

So the Australians went to work. Charlap got Minox involved to help them get started. At the same time, a team of Americans at Nashua, led by Austin Davis, started to develop an organic photoconductor to replace the selenium drum. In the process, they discovered that Kalle, Savin's West German marketing partner, had so many patents on organic photoconductors that it would take years to work around them. IBM, for one, had licensed that technology. So Kalle and Hoechst, which was Kalle's parent company, were invited to join Charlap's crusade. Ricoh, albeit reluctantly, geared up its engineering section.

"We had fights with the Japanese that were unbelievable because Ricoh didn't want to do it," Charlap said. "I said to their president, 'If you will listen to me [bangs his fist on the table], I will give you $50 million a year worth of business.' " To help convince Ricoh, Charlap courted the president of Kalle, Arnold Fischer. "I had refused to work with Hoechst before because I didn't like the goddamn Germans and the place was riddled with Nazis. Only when a friend of mine on their board said, 'Paul, now we have a guy who is one of the finest human beings you will ever meet,' did I agree to meet Arnold. And I sat down with him and said, 'Do you want to sell it? We'll make a deal.' And we did. And then I went to Nashua and got them involved. It was only the combined weight of Nashua, Savin, and Kalle that forced them [Ricoh] to go into it. And we all started to work like dogs. These entrepreneurial guys in Australia stayed up until two or three in the morning— Saturdays, Sundays, and everything else. And at Hoechst in Germany, the manager asked me, 'What are you doing? We never saw our people work past 10:00 or 11:00 P.M.? The lights are on all night.' "

Developing a new photoconductor turned out to be unnecessary because the patents expired on Xerox's selenium-alloy drum. But the researchers ran into some enormous technical roadblocks. One was with the toner. "Everybody in all corners of the world was looking for a way to get around the Xerox patents and that's what the Australians accomplished in theory by using a liquid," Hertzka said. But the toner the Australians came up with "never worked. It was too tacky, it stuck to the drum. So we couldn't get 100 percent of it off the drum." Another American firm, Hunt Chemical, was invited into the group to work on toner (actually a kerosene solvent with carbon black pigment in it). Ricoh, Kalle, and Nashua began to work on toner, too.

Another headache was getting the roller to clean the drum without scratching it. Charlap turned to two old American engineering partners, A. D. Little and SRI International, for help with that problem. "Paul came out with his guys from the Bronx, and boy, was he the original high-energy particle," said Lawrence Lorah, an A. D. Little consultant at the time. What an impressive team he assembled: In the United States, four copier experts at A. D. Little, a dozen at SRI, ten to twenty at Hunt, and a handful at Savin were all working to unseat Xerox. In Germany, there were a dozen more at Kalle and three at Minox. The four Australians plunged forward, and Ricoh's research and development team swelled to a couple hundred people. Yamamoto said, "It became the biggest project in the history of our company." In all, some 250 people in four countries got involved. And keeping everyone in line was Paul Charlap.

"Every couple of months we'd have a meeting someplace in the world—Japan, Hawaii, Germany, New Hampshire," Hertzka said. "We used to have thirty or forty representatives from all the companies come and sit around a room."

In Japan as many as sixty would show up, Charlap said, "including eight or ten Germans and a dozen or so Americans. The rest were all Japanese. And we would sit there on the floor with open kimonos telling our brothers everything. There were no secrets, none."

To create a sense of competition, especially among those working on toners, a progress chart was posted on the wall of the meeting room. Sometimes it showed the Americans at Nashua ahead, the next time maybe the advantage had passed to the Japanese or to the Kalle team in Germany. "That really kept people working hard," Hertzka said.

Of course, Charlap was the ringleader and sometimes that created a problem. Whenever Charlap, who has trouble sitting still anyway, would leave the meeting. "Everything would stop. Everybody would just stop talking," Hertzka said. "It's difficult enough to get all these people from different countries to talk to each other to begin with and there's Paul, as always running around talking on the phone."

So Hertzka would run down the hallway after him and say, "Damn it, Paul, when you leave, everything stops. This thing's falling apart."

Charlap would return and, in Japanese or English, he'd tell each group what he wanted them to do by the next meeting.

The financial incentives to do all this were obvious. SRI and A. D. Little's work was commissioned. The partners paid SRI $100,000 to $200,000 a year. The others funded their own research, knowing that if they came up with a successful machine, Hunt would get a contract for toner; Kalle and Nashua had marketing rights, and Savin, in addition to potential sales, would collect royalties from everybody. Ricoh would manufacture and sell the machine. (The companies eventually agreed to pay Ricoh $25 per machine—$2.5 million amortized over 100,000 machines—for final engineering work and $28 per machine—$2.8 million total—for tooling costs.)

"It was as beautiful a team effort as I've ever seen," said Earle Jones, then vice president of SRI. "Technology is a thing that brings engineers together and, somehow, you get past the language differences. You learn to slow down and do whatever it takes to communicate."

For one of the few times in history, Japanese and Americans placed total trust in each other, Yamamoto said. "Otherwise, it wouldn't have worked."

Like any good team, they learned from each other and built upon their individual strengths. Typical of the Japanese, Ricoh's engineers were outstanding at cutting costs and taking an existing product and improving it. "They would visit here and want to know everything, down to the tiniest screw," recalled Ken Gardner, an SRI engineer. "I'd say, 'Here is where you use this screw,' and they would say, 'Where? What kind of screw?' "

What the Japanese really didn't understand, Gardner said, was the American market. "They had trouble understanding our needs, they were so far removed from the customer." So Gardner established almost a teacher-student relationship with them. "I realized the biggest difference between us and them when I gave a puzzle to a Japanese child. The parents and the child didn't know what it was because they don't learn to piece things together for themselves. Instead, they like to be taught by the 'Master' or the 'Samurai.' "

So, for a time, the Americans gunning for a piece of the Xerox pie were the teachers and Ricoh's engineers were outstanding pupils. Ricoh would run into a problem (such as image transfer, paper handling, or sensing the darkness of an incoming document) and Charlap would call in SRI. SRI would come up with a solution and just three to four months later, Ricoh would add the system to a prototype. "The system was really working well. It was absolutely beautiful," Earle Jones said.

In Japan, meanwhile, Ricoh's engineers were working so hard that they wouldn't even let Gardner visit them. "They worked eight hours a day on quality control and eight more hours a day on the copier," Gardner said. Why? Because in 1971, Ricoh president Mikio Tatebayashi had "ordered" his employees to win the coveted Deming Prize for Quality Control. No copier company had ever done that before and he demanded it be won four years hence, not a year before and not a year after, but in 1975.

"That's because if Ricoh won it in three years, it may be due to cheating or shortcuts," said Takeomi Nagafuchi, Ricoh's energetic manager of quality control. "And he wanted to win it before he died. So he said, '1975.'" Before Tatebayashi's order, Ricoh was running out of steam. "We needed something to take on Xerox since people were switching from Ricoh to [Fuji] Xerox machines," said Nagafuchi. This quest for the Deming created a spirit, and an attention to statistical controls on quality that rejuvenated the company.

Ricoh developed a new "market-in" philosophy, meaning that products would be conceived by those selling, and talking, to customers, and not by engineers, which coincided perfectly with Low and Charlap's philosophy: Give customers exactly what they were looking for.

"I had nothing to do with the research or manufacturing," Low said. "My end was marketing. I would be up until three or four in the morning deciding how to attack Xerox. I designed the machine from a salability standpoint. Then I would more or less give Charlap the marketing specs and, with him pounding the whip, they would see if they could match them. Maybe I'd say, 'Give me a sixty-copy-a-minute tabletop model' and they'd come back and say, 'The best we can do is twenty-eight, or ten.'"

Back then, customers had to leave their offices to look at a Xerox or IBM machine. Low wanted a machine that was so portable and reliable that dealers could wheel it out of their station wagons into a customer's office. "You might say we had a good offensive line [dealers] and we were looking for a rollout quarterback."

Three years after the research began, Charlap's team had most of the technical problems licked. They made some compromises, such as yielding copy quality to get more reliability. Charlap says, "Finally, we decided, 'Who the hell needs a Rembrandt?' So our copies made thinner images, densities of 0.8 while Xerox had 1.3 or 1.4. But we had reliability."

Around 1973, most of the final engineering work was shifted to Ricoh, which came up with two prototypes: a small, simple tabletop model, and a console model about half the size of the Xerox 914. Then, because of Savin's success selling coated paper machines, they decided to go with the smaller prototype, later to be called the Ricoh DT-1200 or Savin 750. (Ricoh won't talk about it, but some of Canon's technology went into the 750. Canon had patented a specially shaped development unit, a cleaning system, and an image-transfer method for liquid-toner machines. "All of these things we licensed to Ricoh," said Keizo Yamaji, a senior managing director at Canon.)

"Then we hired our own industrial designers to design the outside of the machine," Low said. "But Ricoh being Ricoh, and Ricoh being Japanese, just went ahead and did their own body design for the unit and that's how they presented it to us. That was quite a shock. We didn't like the looks of it at all. They said, 'Look, if you want the copier by November [1975], you take it this way. You want it your way, you'll get it in June.' We weren't going to cut off our nose to spite our face so we took it their way." Ricoh later switched to Savin's design when it built a successor, the Savin 770.

In Japan, Ricoh's people were set to go. Bob Luebs of SRI went there in May 1973 to see facsimile machines and remembers being dragged in to see the copier production line. "And there they were: five models of the same machine, in four or five different colors, the same shape but with different nameplates, depending upon where they were going to be shipped. They were so proud that they had broken the Xerox barrier."

Then the machine was test-marketed among American dealers, some of whom were wildly enthusiastic, but others wondered if it would ever reach the marketplace. "We and many others had shown a lot of things that we never brought to market, so there were many skeptics," Low said. "Even in the back of our minds there was the possibility it wouldn't bear fruit." But Low and Charlap were right on target. Their new machine, which took four years and several million dollars to develop, was about to rip a gaping hole through Xerox's virtual monopoly.

Nashua and Kalle introduced their machines in Europe in mid-1973. Savin introduced the 750 in Minneapolis in July 1975 at the National Office Machine Dealers Association (NOMDA) convention. The product, which made twenty copies a minute, made the first copy in 4.6 seconds versus nearly thirteen seconds with a Xerox machine. It had about a third of the parts, and a third of the weight, of conventional Xerox machines. It cost Ricoh about $500 to $600 to build and was to be sold to Savin, Nashua, and Kalle for about $1,600. Low set the price to the customer at $4,995. And Charlap convinced Ricoh to gear up its new factory in Atsugi, Japan, to make 100,000 machines over the next two to three years.

The introduction was timed perfectly. Ricoh, in 1975, won the Deming Prize as planned, and took advantage of the notoriety to give the 750 worldwide publicity. Office managers everywhere, having just gone through a recession and the energy crisis, were eagerly looking for a cheaper, more energy efficient copying machine. People started asking themselves: Do you really want to trek down to the basement to use the expensive Xerox or put Savin machines on every floor? Or, why lease a copier when you can buy one for what that lease costs you every year?

An even bigger selling point was reliability: Ricoh's machine averaged 17,000 copies between failures and took less than thirty minutes to repair, Gabriel Carlin estimated. Xerox machines averaged 6,000 to 10,000 copies between failures and took up to twice as long to repair.

"That's the real reason Savin succeeded," said Monica Camahort, copier analyst at Dataquest. "A lot of dealers had been burned by machines with high service costs. Ricoh's machine didn't break down and dealers really went for it."

Savin and its partners ambushed Xerox in ways the then $3.4 billion giant had never been attacked before. They sold machines instead of renting them; they used dealers instead of a direct sales force; they pitched reliability, not service, and they took Xerox head-on in their advertising. Savin dealers found out when and where Xerox contracts expired, then rushed in with a new sales pitch.

"We positioned ourselves directly against them, challenging the marketplace to decide," said Carlin. "And we were able to get the world to think there were two giants battling for the marketplace, but there was really one elephant [Xerox] and a tiny little mouse."

Sales of the 750 exploded, not just at Savin, but in all parts of the world. Orders in Australia climbed to 500 a month, an unheard of figure. European sales climbed to 5,000 a month, and Ricoh sold another 5,000 to 6,000 a month in Japan. In the United States, entire universities, corporations, and state governments—Harvard, Shell Oil, Mobil Oil, the states of Texas and California—abandoned Xerox's low-volume machines in favor of Savin. The state of Texas alone ordered 2,000 machines at one time. Savin, which had never sold more than 500 or 600 coated-paper copiers a month, watched its orders climb all the way up to 9,000 machines a month at one point. Low recalled: "I remember when my vice president of finance, Dan Giles, came in when we doubled our orders to 1,500 machines. He said, 'Bob, are you crazy? I mean we never sold 1,000 machines a month. How are we going to afford this?' And Charlap just sat there since he wasn't sure himself and I said, 'Danny, I just came back from this dealer show and I was standing on the floor demonstrating the machine and people were grabbing me saying, "We need more, more, more." Danny, we're going to miss the boat if we don't keep ordering.' "

In fact, Savin's biggest problem for the next two years was getting enough machines. Ocean shipments weren't enough. Ricoh began to charter jumbo jets every month, loading them up with 1,000 machines each, to fly shipments to Savin. To keep the momentum going, Low worked Saturdays and Sundays with advertising agents. "They'd call me up at three in the morning, they were so excited and start throwing lines at me. So we started doubling, tripling our ad budgets to really take shots at Xerox with full-page ads in *The Wall Street Journal*, *The New York Times*, and *Business Week*. We had to get Savin known. People still thought we were a coffee company or a trucking company. And the advertising did it. I remember going to our Phoenix branch to talk to the salesmen there. I held up the ads and they stood up and gave me a standing ovation."

All these attacks on Xerox, especially one full-page ad that said, "We are where Xerox used to be: No. 1," worried some Savin people, Low said, "including my father. A lot of people thought that would aggravate Xerox and they were going to react, like Pearl Harbor. I wasn't concerned about that at all. It was like steering a rowboat versus an aircraft carrier. We were beating the hell out of them."

Savin dealers loved it. Said Dave Shearer of Kokomo, Indiana, "Those days were so exciting. I could sell every box I received." By placing just 200 machines a year, a dealer could make more than $300,000 in gross profits.

Where *was* Xerox? Busy worrying about IBM and Kodak, of course, fighting lawsuits, and enjoying its 80 percent share of the worldwide copier market. The low-end market seemed so small: Xerox annual revenues were climbing by more each year than Savin's total sales. "We looked at the 750 and didn't pay a helluva lot of attention," Bogdonoff said. "By our standards, it was garbage. Terrible. Atrocious."

Yet Xerox had nothing in its arsenal to stop the 750. Among its fourteen machines, only the $12,000 model 3100 (the so-called Cadillac of the low end) and the aging 660 compared. Xerox slashed prices but to no avail; even at $4,400, the 3100 was too poorly designed to be competitive. "If we'd have known the Japanese were coming, we'd have done the 3100 totally differently," said Joe Sanchez, who was 3100 group program manager for Xerox. "We could have cut costs on it 40 to 50 percent if we had done cost control."

There was nothing Fuji Xerox could do either. The company had offered to export the 2200, introduced in Japan in 1973, but Xerox turned them down. So with nothing stopping them, Savin, Ricoh, Nashua, and Kalle pushed their machines into offices throughout the world: Ricoh captured the top market share in units in Japan in 1976, producing 77,000 copiers. The next year, Savin's placements in the U.S. exceeded Xerox's for the first time. In just three years, Xerox's share of the units placed in the U.S. copier market fell from 82 percent to barely over 50 percent. Excluding Fuji Xerox, Japan's production of plain paper copiers swelled from 79,000 to nearly 400,000 machines a year. The Xerox monopoly wasn't just cracked, it was smashed. "They were trapped," said Savin's Carlin. "They came to the end of their rainbow."

By the late 1970s, however, Ricoh's cozy relationship with its partners was falling apart. "One day a horrendous thing happened," said Charlap. "Ricoh called me up and said, 'Ah, beginning six months from now, we decided to distribute in America. You go get yourself a different manufacturer. Bye!' And for two years, our only method of communicating with them was through order pads. There was no other way. Nashua and Kalle thought we were the only ones they'd pick on so they didn't stand with us. But then Ricoh went after Nashua and Kalle and almost destroyed those companies, as well as destroying us.

"So I called up [then Ricoh president Takeshi] Ouye and said, 'Hey, Takeshi, you're hurting us for no reason at all. At least tell everyone you're going to supply us.' They wouldn't do it and our stock went down and down, and our dealers were terrified. All our exclusive dealers went running around looking for other suppliers. They thought we'd be out of business any moment. But we fought through and made a settlement with Ricoh in 1979, and it was done under duress. It was not a happy settlement at all. We got a contract to 1990, but we went out and built our own factory at Binghamton. And Ricoh, during that time, did no research and Canon grew. They had no research, no nothing, 'cause we'd always done it for them."

According to Susumu Ichioka, Ricoh's acting manager of overseas marketing, partnerships with such American companies as Savin are fine as long as they're holding market share, but once the competitive battle heats up, Ichioka said, it's tough to cut prices and move quickly in world markets with a partner involved. That's why Ricoh, in 1980, began to set up its own direct-marketing program and then ventured into Xerox's heartland with mid-volume copiers. "We definitely planned to go up against Xerox," said Ichioka. The former partners are now competitors, selling some of the same machines from the same boat. That's left Charlap very bitter about his former allies. Savin has reported losses of more than $125 million since its split with Ricoh as it tried to develop and manufacture its own machine—the ill-fated Savin 8000.

"The only good Jap is a dead Jap," Charlap says now. "They lie, they cheat, and they steal. It's all smiles, all show and display to hide their evil intent. They are good manufacturers, but a person gives up his soul in order to be a part of that. He's no longer a human being. They're the only people in the world today slaughtering baby seals. They hit them over the head with baseball bats and skin them alive. How come? Because they're selfish. They couldn't give a goddamn about the rest of the world. They care about one thing: the Japanese."

The 750 was just the beginning. When the other Japanese companies saw what Ricoh and Savin did, they couldn't wait to grab a piece of it.

"That was when things took off," said Minolta's Atseo Kusada. "We thought we'd never be able to compete with Xerox. Ricoh proved we could, they just cut the machine price in half. So everyone else came in and we started eating Xerox's lunch."

Each competitor came in for a different reason, then adopted strategies that determined where it stood in relation to Xerox today.

MINOLTA

Until the late 1970s, Minolta avoided plain paper copiers altogether, developing instead low-cost electrographic machines, which printed on paper lightly coated with zinc oxide.

"Because of that, we fell behind our competition," said Kusada. "We believed that [electrographics] was the way to go. But with the 750, the manufacturing cost of PPC went down so drastically, so fast, to the cost of our electrographic machines. It was costing us $1,000 to make a unit and we never thought PPC cost would go so low. And people wanted plain paper. So we decided to shift everything to PPC and I went to A. B. Dick to sell it. That was 1977. We were two years late."

Minolta has always prided itself on technology. Chairman and founder Kazuo Tashima has a goal to "give birth to products with originality." And to their credit, the company boasts many firsts: the first copier with fiber optics (1978), a copier with both enlargement and reduction (1980), and the first automatic zoom lens (1983). Minolta's problem has been taking advantage of such breakthroughs. "The minute those things became successful," Kusada said, "we started taking everything easy, started thinking we'd almost automatically be successful with whatever we came up with. And then we went down."

Marketing-wise, Minolta's strategy was to grow slowly and steadily. That stems from the philosophy of Tashima. Before starting Minolta, Tashima was a very successful rice farmer. So he used the Japanese words, *Minoru-ta,* meaning "rice that's ready to be harvested," to name his new venture. He wanted Minolta to reach maturity, too. "So we had a concept," Kusada said. "We wanted to grow this company without risking much. We wanted to use other resources. It was a good idea and the reason we're here now."

Minolta, through the years, sold through a score of American partners: Pitney Bowes, A. B. Dick, IBM, SCM; and through Lumoprint and AM in Europe. But once the Minolta brand name, and an independent sales network, were strong enough, all partnerships stopped. Now Minolta, like Ricoh and Canon, is becoming a first-rate copier company with highly automated plants, strong technologies, and its own marketing force. There's even rumors of Minolta dropping the "Camera" from the company's proper name.

KONISHIROKU

Konishiroku's biggest problem through the years was, and still is, marketing. Konishiroku initially sold machines in Europe through Mitsubishi Trading Company and in America through Royal, a subsidiary of Litton Industries. But sales never got far off the ground: Not until 1978, when they introduced product "V" (Victory), did the company have a real commercial success.

Perhaps because of its disaster in film, Konishiroku staked its reputation on quality. It named its copiers "UBIX," meaning "elegant," and boasts the highest-quality photocopies in the world. Zene Kumagai says the fact that copiers are "so complex, like a human body," lets his company bring all its photographic expertise to bear. "Otherwise, we couldn't compete." Because of that, Konishiroku builds its copiers with human, not robotic, hands. Its assembly lines are lined with workers and the copiers sit atop pushcarts instead of conveyor belts. Several workstations do nothing but clean the machines, and a big quality-control data at the end of the line checks the cosmetics for nicks and scars.

The drawback is that otherwise Konishiroku's copier factory, compared with Canon's or Ricoh's, is in the dark ages. Parts bins clutter the assembly lines; computer use is minimal. At Ricoh or Canon, the finished product flows by conveyors directly to a computer-controlled packaging robot that builds a box around the copier in a matter of seconds. At Konishiroku, some finished copiers are picked off the end of the assembly line with a forklift and carried one at a time to another building about thirty yards away where the driver positions the mid-volume copier on a slat for packaging.

Strategy-wise, Konishiroku's satisfied being a second-tier player. "To have a full line from the low to the high end looks good but our main concern is serving our [current] customers," said Tsugio Kitahara, an associate director.

TOSHIBA, MATSUSHITA, AND SHARP

Toshiba and Sharp, which make everything from stereos to refrigerators, inched their way into the business in 1974 and saw copiers becoming just another commodity. "We wanted a me-too product only," said Takeshi Okatomi, general manager of international operations at Toshiba. The thinking, said Kenichi Ohmae of McKinsey & Co., was "we've conquered the home. Now it's the office. Office is where the future is. And one of the product lines you have to have is a copier. It's become one of the building blocks."

Because of their size and name recognition alone, they remain three powerful forces to be reckoned with:

- Sharp, with the world's most automated plants, places more copiers in the United States than every company but Canon.
- Toshiba, which supplies 3M with copiers as well as selling its own brand, has 10 percent of the world market, in units, and is shooting for 15 percent within five years.
- Matsushita has been struggling, partially because it lacks expertise in paper-handling technology.

CANON

If there's one company that can hold the Japanese electronics giants at bay, and attack Xerox at the same time, it's Canon.

Canon started out like Ricoh attempting to sell through America's Saxon and Addressograph/Multigraph, but it was a disaster. So Canon, in 1974, ventured out on its own. While the others were slugging it out, Canon executives sat back and mapped out their own unique strategy. Until one day, marketing whiz Haruo Murase was called to set Canon's plan in action.

10
Xerox, Here Comes Canon!

If Xerox people are quite happy about their
new machines and they settle down, then they
will lose.

—HIROSHI TANAKA

I T WAS 1978 and, after a tough seven years in the United States and
Canada, Canon's Haruo Murase was looking forward to going back
to Japan. "I figured it was time to go back. My background was
in the camera division and I really wanted to get back into the camera
business." He also was very worried about his children becoming too
Americanized. His sons were learning to speak English better than
Japanese. "Coming home from work and looking at the children, I
wondered how good is it for them?"

Murase came to the United States in 1971 as a marketing representative. Two years later, after Canon ended a contract to sell through
America's Bell & Howell, he went to Canada to set up a national distribution network there. Because the Canadian market was relatively small,
he also was put in charge of the business equipment division, which in
those days meant electronic calculators. In 1974, when Canon ventured
out on its own in copiers, he reluctantly took control of that
business, too.

"I hated how those machines always were breaking down," he said.
"When I was told we were going into copiers, my question was, 'Who's
going to run this business?' Well, I said it's a photocopy so it's a photographic business. And my counterpart in charge of photographic
equipment said, 'No, it's a business machine. That's not mine,
it's yours.' "

So Murase wound up setting up Canon's Canadian copier business
as well. He was very successful, garnering Canon more than 35 percent

of the Canadian copier business, more than twice the share of the market it managed in the United States. While his competitors were ignoring the Canadian market, Murase signed the top dealer in every major city. But after racing all over Canada all day—Alberta, British Columbia, Quebec—picking up dealers, and worrying about his family at night, he was ready for the 7,000-mile move back to Japan.

Then one day he got an unexpected phone call from New York. It was Fujio Mitarai, the longtime president of Canon USA. Mitarai said, "Murase-san, why don't you come to New York to discuss your new assignment?"

Murase answered, "I want to go back to Japan."

Mitarai, who came to the United States in 1966, was an old friend of Murase's from his camera days. Back in Japan, they'd worked in the camera division together and Mitarai became vice president. So Murase agreed to go to New York, thinking that Mitarai, who also was the nephew of then Canon chairman Takeshi Mitarai, could help him find a good position in Tokyo. When they met, Murase found that Mitarai had something totally different in mind. He wanted Murase to come back to the United States to take over the copier division.

Murase was surprised. He asked Mitarai many questions, knowing that Mitarai knew relatively little about copiers at the time. "What do you want to do in copiers? What's the company's commitment to copiers?"

Mitarai explained that he was prepared to make the same commitment to copiers that he had made to Canon cameras in 1976. At that time, Canon bet millions of dollars on the AE-1, the first 35-mm camera with microprocessor control. Mitarai allotted $1.5 million to introduce it during the Montreal Olympics on network television—a first for 35-mm camera makers. That aggressive campaign, featuring tennis star John Newcombe, was so successful that customers began asking for "that camera I saw on television." The AE-1 quickly became the best-selling camera in the world. So what Canon did with the AE-1, it could do with a copier, Mitarai said. Still, Murase wasn't convinced. "That day, I didn't say yes. I still wanted to go back to Japan."

Mitarai didn't give up. After several more telephone conversations, Murase agreed. "If that is your commitment, then I will do my best. That does not guarantee success. We may fail, we may succeed, but who knows?" Murase moved to New York. A smart business decision perhaps, but at a considerable personal sacrifice—the type of sacrifice Canon people trying to catch Xerox have been making all over the world.

When he looked at Canon USA's copier business from Canada, Murase was confused. "We had exactly the same product in Canada, but Canon USA was going slow, doing nothing but having problems. Dealers were complaining and so on. So I thought, there must be something wrong with how they're running the business. I think the management is wrong."

The thing that disturbed Canon people the most was that their copiers were as good as anybody's. In fact, nearly half the copiers on the market were based in part upon Canon technology. Over the years, Ricoh and others have paid Canon more than $80 million in royalties.

Canon started to develop copiers using technology that was not covered by Xerox patents in 1962, after Keizo Yamaji read an A. D. Little report on the copier industry. "When I read that report, two things caught my attention: that Xerox technology would never be broken, and that there would appear imitators of Xerox but those imitators would never win over Xerox," said Yamaji, now chief executive of Canon's copier division. "I had objections to that. I said, 'Let's try to break it.' "

Hiroshi Tanaka, the man some call the "Chester Carlson" of Canon, was put in charge. In fact, for a time, he was the only one working on it. Then, with help from ten others, he started finding some alternatives to Xerox technology. They found that selenium, a rare metal, wasn't the only material that could be used to coat a copier's photosensitive drum. Canon substituted cadmium sulfide, a metal that was very light-sensitive, and added another layer to the drum. "We covered our drum with an insulating layer because these metals shouldn't be touched by human hands," Yamaji said.

It took six years to develop, but in 1968, Canon announced its New Process—the first alternative to xerography, then protected by some 500 patents. Two years later, the company came out with the NP (for New Process) 1100, the first machine based on the new technology. However, the 1100, a ten-copy-a-minute copier, was a failure. America's Addressograph/Multigraph licensed it for $1 million but, following a management change, never marketed it. The only 1100 in North America, Murase said, sits in a display case at Canon's Lake Success, New York, headquarters.

When Xerox's Jeff Kennard, then a product development manager, heard about NP, he invited Fujio Mitarai to meet with him privately on the fourteenth floor of Midtown Tower in Rochester. Kennard was considering licensing Canon's technology, but the two men had difficulty with the language barrier and Mitarai was more interested in the camera business. Then some Xerox engineers went to Japan to study NP. Said Kennard, "The most knowing people in the [Xerox] organization, the technologists, pooh-poohed the whole damn thing. Even when we saw it [1971], we didn't recognize it for what it was.''

Canon, meanwhile, was working on a second-generation NP machine, called the L-7, that used liquid toner. All the major Japanese companies licensed Canon's technology. But when its American licensees, Addressograph/Multigraph and Saxon, plunged toward Chapter 11, Canon decided to market on its own. In retrospect, that was a good decision. But it wasn't implemented well. The disappointing debut of the L-7 copier in 1974 really irked Murase: "That was a remarkable breakthrough, it needed much less maintenance.'' It was cheaper and more reliable than any Xerox machine.

When Ricoh, through Savin, upstaged Canon in 1975 with the Savin 750, a machine partially based on Canon technology, the difference was marketing. Canon was busy setting up its sales network and ignored "offer after offer'' from American firms to sell the L-7. "If we had worked with someone like Savin, we could have had a big success, too,'' Yamaji said. "So we endured that period.''

Yamaji and Tanaka, meanwhile, patiently improved their technologies. Says Tanaka bluntly, "We don't use other people's technologies.'' Their aim was to make a system that used dry toners (like Xerox) as simple as a liquid-toner system (like Ricoh's).

"It was a very painful, methodical way of building a worldwide strategy,'' said Harvard's Michael Porter. "But that's what they chose to do. They didn't take the easy way out. Sure, licensing their technology was controversial. But they needed money and they needed legitimacy. So they got others going down their technological path.''

The critical decision, though it cost Canon millions of dollars over the short term, was to be the only Japanese company since the early 1970s to sell copiers worldwide under its own brand name, taking advantage of the Canon name in everything from cameras to calculators. In the United States, you certainly wouldn't consider Ricoh, Konishiroku, or Copyer household names. "And look what happened to the rest of them,'' Yamaji said. "Konishiroku sold through Copyer in Japan and that fell apart. Ricoh has the same problem now [with Savin].'' Canon eventually acquired Copyer. But Canon's problem, from 1974 to 1979, was that copier sales didn't go anywhere. While Savin soared past Xerox in copier unit placements, Canon struggled for less than 10 percent of the American marketplace.

"Frankly speaking,'' said Murase, "the people in the industry said Canon has a good product, their problem is marketing. I must agree.

Savin took the challenge to Xerox and was so successful. We were so slow." When Murase arrived in New York, he had his work cut out for him.

The company's commitment really meant one thing: money. And Canon chairman Ryuzaburo Kaku provided it. "He made it very clear to us that the center of Canon was to be the copier business," said Tanaka, now director and group executive of reprographics products. "So in copier R and D, money and people and materials are to be invested even when times aren't so good. So when copier development people request hands [people], they are never spared. They hired the people and they gave them to me."

The bottom line was that Tanaka could spend up to 10 percent of copier sales, twice as much as in the past, on research and development. The research staff swelled to 1,000 people. Reassured by this, Murase and Mitarai set two marketing goals. The first was to make the Canon USA copier division number one within the Canon organization. Canon USA already led the Japan and European divisions in calculators and cameras, but trailed in copiers. "He [Mitarai] could not live with that," Murase said. "So that was immediate target, even before talking about market share."

The second goal was to, within three years, make copiers the biggest business within Canon USA. (Murase would accomplish both goals, but the latter took him six years.)

Next he reviewed the records of Canon's 500 dealers. Some were very active, others were just taking up space on the list. So Murase sent Canon representatives into each market to demand of each dealer, "What have you done for us? Do you want to deal with Canon or not? If yes, please do so." Those who didn't react were replaced or deactivated. Murase covered one wall of his office with a map of the United States. Using ink pens and magic markers (green lines for Canon salesmen, red for regional managers, stick pins for dealers), he meticulously restructured the territories so that salesmen served smaller and smaller areas. "We needed more penetration into each market. How could one person take care of the entire area from Georgia to Virginia?"

Then a crucial one-on-one meeting took place. Yamaji made a rare visit to America and, one Saturday, arranged to meet with Murase. "It was raining and we couldn't do anything, so we sat down at the hotel room and got Japanese tea and cake," Murase said. "We didn't know each other well. He was too 'big shot' and he didn't know who I was. He introduced who he is, I said who I am, and so on. So we sat down and spoke. He asked me about the price point [the price Canon USA could pay Canon, Inc., in Japan for the soon-to-be-introduced NP-80]. I told him and he said, 'Judging from the manufacturing cost of that product, the price you are talking about is impossible today. But if your marketing program is going as such and the quantity becomes much higher, I think I can reach the cost reductions. Maybe it's quite impossible today, but I will take your commitment and give you the price today, regardless of the cost. So let's try. Let's do it.' ''

In essence, Yamaji told Murase, "Okay, you count on me."

"And that statement was really the start of our aggressive marketing program," Murase said. "At first, they [Canon, Inc.] lost money. We [Canon USA] made money because the purchase price was good and that's how we were able to start our advertising campaign. And that product [NP-80] was a big success, here and in Japan. And it became a big profit-maker."

Just as important as the new marketing program was the close personal friendship between Murase and Yamaji that began that day, a bond between the American marketing arm and the engineering brain trust back in Japan. Up until that point, Canon USA was "selling whatever was given to us from the factory," Murase said. "The product was provided by the manufacturer and not designed by our request. But that might not work in this market. This market needs different features."

The NP-80, for example, was designed before Murase arrived and did not have a document feeder. In Japan, that's an unnecessary option which customers consider too expensive. But in the United States, people looked at the NP-80 and demanded, "Where's the document feeder?" After their initial meeting, Murase and Yamaji arranged for their people to meet at least four times a year—twice in Japan and twice in the United States—just to incorporate requests from Canon USA into the design and pricing of new copiers.

What saved the NP-80, Murase said, was advertising. To demonstrate its new aggressiveness, Canon coined a new phrase: "The age of Micronics."

"What is Micronics? We don't know, frankly speaking. It gives the impression of the mixture of electronics and precision imaging." (Technically, it refers to a microcomputer that monitors and controls the copying process.)

That was just the beginning. Back in Japan, Canon was preparing a revolutionary new product to ambush the copier market just as it had taken the camera business by storm with the AE-1.

The year was 1980—the same year Xerox woke up to its competition. And the product, the one that really moved Canon to the front of the Japanese pack, was the NP-200, a twenty-copy-a-minute, tabletop model. The NP-200 was priced at $4,000 and featured Canon's patented Toner Projection Development System, fiber-optics imaging and microprocessor control. You could see that Yamaji had kept his promise. With the new system, the toner that creates the image literally jumps across a gap between the copier drum and the developing unit. This created a more uniform layer of toner and clearer copies. In addition, single component toner eliminated mixing chemicals together, bulky lenses and mirrors had disappeared, and the machine was much easier to use.

Canon money was strongly behind it, too. Canon bought 20 percent of Copyer, a giant in Japan, then pumped $13 million into its own Toride factory, making it one of the highest-quality, lowest-cost plants in the world. Copier assembly capacity doubled, from 15,000 to 30,000 units a month. Murase also got $10 million for advertising, two-thirds of it for television. Canon spent nearly $400 per machine (10 percent of selling cost) promoting the NP-200. "The frequency of our print ads was changed drastically," he said. "The size [of ads] changed, and that was the beginning of full back-page ads in *The Wall Street Journal*."

The result? That first year sales of the NP-200 shot past 100,000 machines worldwide, 30,000 in the United States. More importantly, Canon had the machine it needed to crank up production and mount an assault against Xerox in the marketplace. It had taken Canon from 1970 to 1980 to make its first 500,000 copiers; in just two years, from 1980 to 1982, 500,000 more were produced.

There wasn't anything secret about it: "Xerox, Here We Come" said a March 31, 1980, *Forbes* headline. Canon executives talked of "waging total war" against Xerox in a January 12, 1981, *Fortune* article. Canon didn't let up. The NP-120, introduced in the United States in 1981, featured cold-pressure fusing, a 12-cpm model that consumed one-fourth less electricity than its rivals. Then Canon attacked Xerox with the NP-400, a 40-cpm model introduced in late 1981, and the NP-300, a 30-cpm machine in 1982. In three years, from 1979 to 1982, Canon's copier revenues doubled, jumping from $430 million to over $1 billion. By early 1983, the company named for Kwanon, the goddess of mercy, wasn't showing any. Konishiroku, Minolta, and other competitors moaned about price-gouging, charging Canon with ignoring profits to gain market share.

"The manager of Panasonic said to me, 'Hey, Canon, you should make sure you have a profit and don't market at a lower price than ours,' " Murase said. "So I said to him, 'Well, that's wrong. Number one, we're making money. Number two, Panasonic, you should stay as a parts supplier rather than assembling [copiers] yourself. You already have enough products. Why bother to come into the copier industry?' And we both laughed.

"So people say we are the price cutter. I don't think so. An example is the NP-80. If we ended up losing money on it then, yes, I am a price cutter. But within our company, people look at cost efficiency more seriously. We cut design cost, manufacturing cost, material cost. Look at our operation here [Canon USA's main office]. There's no luxury here. Because of all these savings, we reduce the price."

A good example of how Canon works was the company's latest coup: the Personal Copier. Conceived back in 1980, when Canon executives toured the United States to promote the NP-200, the Personal Copier was designed for dealers and customers who liked the NP-200 but wanted a totally new copier for people who currently weren't using a copier machine. One suggestion was a typewriter-size model for the home or office that would be virtually service-free. The copy speed—six, eight, or ten copies a minute—didn't really matter, Murase said. But it should cost less than $1,000. So Canon USA's Mitarai said to Tanaka, "If you are able to materialize such a concept, we will do it."

And Murase promised, "We can sell 10,000 a month." Actually, he says now, "We didn't believe so, but in order for them to do it, we said, 'Sure, 10,000. No problem.' I was not sure, honestly speaking."

Hiroshi Tanaka is a powerful-looking Japanese who, typical of a company with no superstars, hesitates to talk about his own accomplishments. "He doesn't want to make self-advertisement," his interpreter said. But Tanaka thought he could build the machine. What worried him most was making it service-free. "If it wasn't, the servicing costs would kill us. It would immediately prove a great failure." One solution might be to build the copier drum, charging device, toner assembly, and cleaner into a cartridge that a customer could remove and put back into the machine. That would virtually eliminate service calls. However, building the cartridge, and keeping the per-copy costs down, was an enormous challenge. As other companies have learned, the best way to solve such a complex task is with a small team, so Tanaka recruited 140 top research and production engineers from throughout the Canon company and, under highest secrecy, began to develop the machine.

An interesting sidelight is that Canon licensed cartridge technology from Minolta for this project. Yamaji claims Minolta had only one patent for a simple mechanism in the cartridge, while Canon held 370 patents. "With what Minolta had, nobody could make a cartridge." However, Minolta says there was more to it than that. "We gave them the cartridge and, believe me, we won't renew that license when it runs out in 1987," said John Vacca, Minolta's United States advertising manager. Atseo Kusada, a Minolta vice president, said his company couldn't see the cartridge's huge potential. "That's why we swapped patents and gave Canon the right to use it." When asked why Minolta did that, Takeshi Nogiri, Minolta's executive director, turned bright red and asked through his interpreter, "How did you know that?" Then Ted Kato, a public relations man, pointed at Odagiri and said, "Look at his face" and you'll see he can't discuss it further. In the secretive licensing deals between Japanese companies, it's sometimes difficult to tell who gave what to whom. All this is kept hush-hush, not dragged out in the courts, to shield everyone from embarrassment or "losing face."

While one group of Canon engineers worked on the cartridge, another concentrated on the drum. "At the time, conventional drums cost 10,000 yen or more," Tanaka said. "For the cartridge, it must cost 1,000 yen or a tenth as much. Likewise with the developing unit and other components. So targets were set for each part and we tried to do things no one has ever done before. To make a drum for one-tenth normal costs, usually engineers say, 'No, it's not possible.' In Canon, to say no is prohibited. So our engineers are trained and accustomed to pursue to the limit."

Part of this approach was ingrained by Kaku, who took over Canon in 1975. His style is atypical of other Japanese presidents in that he openly criticizes his managers, even at the top levels. He's also known for luring engineers from other companies, and setting people free to try something new. Says Harvard's Porter, "Canon's more of a no-nonsense, 'Let's go out and do it' kind of company. They're young and they don't have all those Japanese rituals. It's not an old-school company where everybody bows all the time."

So Canon's team went out and did it. It took them two and a half years and cost more than 2 billion yen, or $8 million, but they came up with just what Mitarai and Murase were looking for. The only big problem Canon ran into was paper size. American managers said standard A4-size paper was sufficient. Canon salesmen in Japan wanted it to take size B4, a larger paper that accounts for 60 percent of Japanese copy volume. But that would drive the cost up 20 to 30 percent and make it more complex. Instead, engineers built in another feature the Japanese love: Copying business cards.

Then, Canon employees used them in their homes. Amazingly, few people knew what Canon was field testing. Only selected people at Canon USA were told; not even the New York advertising agencies knew what they were mailing press releases for. Murase said, "Until a day before the presentation, most of our staff didn't know why we were having a press conference. The press and Dataquest called . . . everybody thought it was going to be a high-speed copier."

Instead, it was just the opposite: two machines, the PC-10 for $995 and the PC-20 for $1,295; and a $65 disposable cartridge that shocked everybody, including Fuji Xerox in Japan.

Cost-wise, Tanaka had met the challenge: the PC-10 costs Canon less than $300 to manufacture because it was so well designed for automated assembly. The machine contains just eight subunits. The cartridge unit, containing eighty-nine parts, costs Canon only about $15 to make. It can be assembled totally by 146 robots on a $4-million line with no human hands ever touching it. The capacity of that line is more than 5,000 cartridges a day or 100,000 cartridges a month.

The result is that, in early 1985, the PC-10 was sold to American dealers for $400 to $420. That means, even at $450, New York's 47th Street Photo makes a small profit. "I don't like it since I have no business relations with that store . . . I don't know how they get the product," Murase said. Judging by serial numbers, he learned that 47th Street Photo buys from various dealers. "When the order is secured, the dealer ships directly so 47th Street carries no inventory. That saves a lot of money. So if the dealer sells to 47th [Street] Photo for $420, it's possible they can still make money at it."

Marketing-wise, Murase followed his newfound formula, plunking $15 million into advertising in 1983, two-thirds of it for network television. (Minolta's Atseo Kusada estimates Canon's advertising budget was initially $200 per $1,000 machine.) To pick a spokesman, fourteen Canon sales managers were called in to vote. They settled on Jack Klugman, star of TV's "The Odd Couple" and "Quincy" series. The pitch was to the small retailers, executive offices and 6 million Americans who have offices in their homes.

After the introduction, the only real hitch was how many could be sold: To reduce manufacturing costs, Tanaka wanted to sell 10,000 a month immediately. Murase wanted to stick to a scheduled rollout to keep his dealers and sales people happy. He knew they'd be reluctant to sell such a low-profit line requiring few, if any, service calls. "If we disregarded their interests, then this [PC] might destroy our NP business."

So Canon USA sales climbed steadily: 6,000 in January and February; 7,000 in March; reaching 10,000 a month by the end of 1983. By 1985, distribution was widened to Sears and computer stores, and worldwide production reached more than 30,000 units a month. Like Ricoh's 750 eight years before, Canon began shipping machines in cargo jets. Analysts talked of the day when more American homes might have personal copiers, or a copier-printer hybrid, than personal computers.

Canon didn't revel in its success. "We are always awake, never asleep," Tanaka said.

The PC, for example, was a smart move by Canon to head off Sharp and Matsushita, said Kenichi Ohmae of McKinsey & Co. "Canon knows they have the capability of producing a $400 copier for the home or office. I can't see Canon moving into that segment for any other reason than a preemptive move."

Beyond the PC, Canon's plan, masterminded by Yamaji and Tanaka, was to catch Xerox with technology and what they call "global citizenship." Having reached the "top of Mount Fuji"—Kaku's target to become a premier Japanese company—Canon set its sights on climbing to the "top of Mount Everest." The company film, "This is Canon," opened with the Mayor of Bretagne, France, welcoming Canon's new personal copier production plant, joining a Canon production plant in Germany. Joint manufacturing ventures were set up in Korea and China, and a plant will be built in the United States. Canon's non-Japanese employment swelled to a third of its 27,000 employees; outside the homeland, only 4 percent were Japanese. In 1985, at the Toride plant, Japanese assigned to Korea took Korean lessons every other day; to prepare for an assignment in Bretagne, Nobufusa Tomomatsu, assistant factory manager, was drinking wine and learning to speak French. (He skipped a French lesson to give us a factory tour.)

"They're incredibly international, truly a multinational," said Harvard's Porter. "They've gotten over that hurdle that many Japanese companies are just getting to. They want to be number one worldwide, that's their goal, and they want to win."

It's difficult to get Canon executives to talk directly about being number one, but there's no doubt about what they hope to do. "Naturally," says Murase, "we're looking at going higher and wider" into the heartland of Xerox territory. Behind the scene in Canon laboratories, engineers worked days and nights in 1984–85 on the technologies to make that possible: color copiers; amorphous silicon drums that print clearer and last a million copies; and laser copiers that convert images on plain paper into computerized form. Then, at a New York press conference on March 5, 1985, the big three—Yamaji, Murase, and Mitarai—announced Canon's next move into mid-volume console copying (the NP-7000 Series including the 7550 to be sold by Kodak) and the Laser Age. Slide shows captured the moment, touting Canon as "#1" in the world.

Does that mean Canon hopes to be number one someday?

"So we hope," said Tanaka, showing a wide grin bordering on laughter—a typical reaction of a nervous Japanese. "If Xerox people are quite happy about their new machines [the 10 Series] and they settle down, then they will lose . . . ha, ha, ha, ha. . . ."

11

The Americanization of Japan

Japan may think Xerox is the company
we'll never beat. I may think Xerox is piece
of cake.

—ATSEO "AL" KUSADA,
Minolta USA

I T HAD BEEN another long day for Canon's Reiji Shirahase, a good
deal of it spent with two American journalists he'd never met before. The Kirin beer and "Canon" wine were flowing smoothly
and the typical stuff of Japanese-American small talk—New York City,
Japanese food, baseball, and golf—was running short. For a time,
Shirahase's English-speaking colleagues, Eiji Toyosaki and Masayoshi
Hiramatsu, kept the conversation going, chattering about golf handicaps
and Hiramatsu's club championship. Then Shirahase, the manager of
Canon's Ami factory, revealed what he'd been worrying about.

"When I look down our assembly lines, and see everyone all dressed
the same, doing the same thing day in and day out, I worry about the
workers reaching a certain peak." He slapped his right fist up into the
palm of his outstretched left hand. "They hit a ceiling and stop. That's
how you Americans are different."

It has been two decades since Shirahase worked in the United States,
yet he vividly recalled how awed he was by the determination of the
people there. His overseas experience made him deeply envious of
American individualism and creativity, especially New York City's un-
derground telephone wiring and San Francisco's Golden Gate Bridge.
He talks at length about New York City being the finest city in the world.
American record albums, stacked high at his tiny workweek apartment
outside Tokyo, are still a prized possession.

In his heart he believes Japanese people want to excel as individuals,

153

too, but most Japanese companies do little to encourage them. That's why, over the twenty years he headed Canon's quality assurance department, Shirahase avoided using statistical controls to measure quality. He felt that if you set limits on quality control, workers reach them and won't go any further. "Japanese rules, they're too constraining."

When Minolta first came to the United States, Atseo "Al" Kusada knew it would take far too long, "perhaps a couple of centuries," to understand the American market. So Minolta hired dozens of American experts in advertising, promotion, and sales, "because we feel, when you're in Rome, do what Romans do," said Kusada, now vice president of Minolta's copier division. "We run this organization to suit American way." Not that he abandoned his Japanese philosophies entirely. "It's a combination of American way and Japanese way. I have Japanese philosophy in the back of my mind, yet people tell me I'm pretty Americanized. Back in Japan, they don't care. They don't ask me to make $1 million or $10 million, but a reasonable profit. As long as I don't screw up, I'm fine."

As a result, Minolta's strategy in the United States may be totally different than elsewhere in the world. "If I price half that of Europe, then they [Minolta Japan] ask me why. If I say why and I'm convincing, they say, 'That's your job. Do that.' Minolta Europe may think Xerox is the toughest competitor. Japan may think Xerox is the company we'll never beat. I may think Xerox is piece of cake. Sharp is very well known in Japan and here. In Europe, people don't think they exist. So if I apply my strategy to Europe, I will fail. That's why locality is so important. That's why we send people into these countries to learn."

Hiroshi Tanaka, group executive of reprographics products, remembers when Canon opened its first Untied States factory, in 1971, near Los Angeles and had a terrible time. "There were ten different nationalities, and within one year all the [original] employees had left," said Tanaka. "We were embarrassed by that."

So he assigned a new management team, led by a Japanese manager who believed that "skin colors don't count. According to him, we're all human beings. The only difference is Japanese people are more what we call 'dry' or businesslike. American people are more 'wet,' more humanistic." This new Canon manager worked closely with his employees, even bringing a sleeping bag to work. His wife brought hot Japanese lunches for the men to eat at night. And when an employee got sick,

Tanaka said, "the manager rushed to his house, even at midnight, regardless of the time. And he arranged to pay the bills." Gradually, his sincerity paid off. Employee turnover stopped. To Tanaka's surprise, locally hired managers started coming in Saturdays and Sundays, sacrificing their own time. And the manager was forced to give up his golf game and come in, too. So "after all," Tanaka said, "human beings are all the same. There's no difference among ten nationalities."

In their own way, all three of these Japanese executives—Tanaka, Kusada, and Shirahase—have been Americanized. You've heard that business in Japan is more deeply rooted in culture and ritual than anywhere else in the world. And that's true. But to attack Xerox in the United States and elsewhere, they had to change their ways. That meant adopting American-sounding company names (Canon instead of "Kwanon," Ricoh in place of "Riken Kogaku"), American first names (Toru "Ted" Kato), changing management styles and rethinking the way to build and advertise copiers.

"I remember when we first came here," recalled Haruo Murase, vice president of Canon USA. "We had a problem that we'd never experienced before."

The problem, which has plagued Japanese copier makers for decades, was static electricity, particularly during the winter months. Japanese copiers, designed for the humid environs of Japan, produced poor-quality copies and jammed repeatedly. So the American design was changed and, to this day, Canon still field tests its personal copiers in the mountain areas, the low-humidity environs of the United States.

In the United States, you often see ads where Burger King attacks McDonalds, or Diet Pepsi attacks Diet Coke. In Japan, that's unheard of. Japanese are very concerned about embarrassing others—causing them to "lose face." Now Ricoh, considered one of the most Americanized of all Japanese companies, constantly jabs Xerox and IBM in its "Ricoh's bigger" TV and print ads. In a shrewd attempt to counter Canon's hiring Jack Klugman, Minolta hired Tony Randall, the other half of TV's "Odd Couple." (Privately, Minolta had some American-style fun with Randall, too. Marketing reps had a pornographic film made featuring a woman having sex on top of a Minolta copier. Randall handled the narrative of the film, which is shown at some sales meetings.)

In the early years, the Japanese copier-makers kept strict control over their American marketing arms. Sid Reisch, now vice president of Toshiba America, joined Toshiba as that company entered the American market and had a tough time gaining their confidence. "I was a foreigner to them," he explains. That's understandable: Even today, says Takashi Harino of Nomura Securities, "Japanese are very skeptical. Many Japanese still consider outsiders, regardless of where they're from—Spain, Brazil, whatever—as Americans, or *gaijin* (foreign devils)."

The Japanese have a tough time placing trust in American executives because they change jobs so much. Ricoh spent several years building a relationship with John Stuart, their American vice president, only to be shocked when he left suddenly in 1985 to take over Royal's copier division, Konishiroku's marketing arm. But the Japanese really had no choice. When they initially ran Ricoh's copier division they screwed it up because they didn't understand the American marketplace. That's why Stuart was given free reign at Ricoh and Reisch now has full profit and loss responsibility for Toshiba America's copier business. Canon USA is still Japanese-run, but its division chiefs have all been in the same position at least ten years; Canon USA president Fujio Mitarai came in 1966. Having gained more confidence in Americans, Murase worries less and less about finding English-speaking Japanese to run the company. Nowadays, "When I go to Japan looking for somebody, I never ask, 'Can you speak English?' Never. If he can, that's fine. But as a common matter, it's safe to assume he cannot speak English."

Tanaka says he saw the benefits when he came to the United States for a party honoring Canon USA in late 1984: "The party was held over four days, to celebrate Canon USA's tenth anniversary and sales passing $1 billion a year for the first time. About 200 Canon people went, mostly Americans. During this time, I felt very keenly how these people became Canon people. More than ten American managers gave speeches on how they had run the business the last ten years and would compete the next ten years. These people weren't university graduates, not Ivy Leaguers, but they were very impressive. They all put on the same [Canon] red shirts and white sweaters and blue trousers, and it was something to see, quite conspicuous. I was no exception. Now I use that clothing to play golf."

Kidding aside, the Japanese have built up bonds with American managers and their dealers that are awfully tough to crack. "Eventually what evolved was sort of a family relationship," said Joe Castrianni of Sharp. "It became more than just a business relationship, we sort of shared prosperity together." What they've achieved is a delicate balance between disparate philosophies and work styles. "It can be frustrating," Castrianni says. "One of the frustrations, of course, is to try to understand their way of thinking. What we try to do is teach the Japanese how Americans think rather than learn how they think. That's the way Americans do it anyhow.''

Still, there's one thing about working in the United States that Minolta's Kusada could do without. ''I still get mad when a [American] secretary goes to one of our Minolta copiers and says she's going to 'Xerox something!' ''

Of course, as the authors discovered, trying to adjust to Japanese culture and life-style isn't easy either. The toughest thing about visiting Japanese companies wasn't interviewing—or dodging their questions. It was getting there. You don't just call a Japanese company, ask for the press office, and arrange an appointment. Sony chairman Akio Morita's schedule, for instance, is booked six to eight months in advance.

In Japan, there's really no such thing as a one-on-one interview. First you meet one or two English-speaking public relations people who serve as interpreters. Then you're escorted into a meeting room (never the executive's office) where six to eight chairs form a rectangle around coffee tables. You're shown where to sit, usually with your back to a picture or hanging scroll. This seat, one of high honor, is reserved for guests. Two minutes later, the executive and two or three, sometimes five or six, associates arrive.

A Japanese businessman takes your name card with both hands and studies it closely. Then the highest-ranking person takes the seat directly opposite you. The next highest ranked sit to his right.

Interviews last two to three hours. Japanese executives, unlike Americans, who tend to start answering a question before you get it out, often spend several minutes thinking before responding. The other executives may talk, and often confer about answers, but they always defer to the top guy.

Japanese are open and honest about most things. But there are no superstars in Japanese companies. It's tough getting them to talk about their personal feelings. One Japanese public relations guy summed it up best: ''Dealing with the Japanese is like sex with a lot of foreplay.'' A Japanese has to know something about you, understand your personality [*hitogara*] before he opens up.

Ed Poshkus, a veteran Japan watcher and president of Creative Strategies International, explains, ''The Japanese don't do business with a company. They do business with a person. You spend the day talking, negotiating. You go out to dinner at 5:30, 6:00 P.M. and you drink for a few more hours. Then the real negotiating starts. And usually it breaks up around midnight and you go back to your hotel, if you can remember what hotel it was.''

Not knowing the language can be a bit disturbing. We'd ask a difficult question and the Japanese would launch into a long discussion. Back and forth. Back and forth. We didn't know what they were talking about. And then the answer would come back through the translator: "We don't know.'' Out of curiosity, we played our tapes back to an American who speaks Japanese. Generally, we didn't miss much. In one case, what they were discussing was how much they should or could tell us without getting themselves in trouble. Sometimes a Japanese executive would speak Japanese the entire time and suddenly, in English, correct the translator.

Attempts by the Japanese to converse with us in English provided some light moments. Canon managers tried to tell us about the "Berr and Herr'' company; Fuji Xerox managers about meeting "Car Rewis.'' Finally, we figured it out: Bell & Howell and Carl Lewis. The Japanese have trouble with the "L'' sound. The most one Japanese executive could manage with Hillkirk's surname was "Mr . . . John.''

12

Japanese Boxes and Yankee Dealers

> Japanese Incorporated is not our competitor in the United States. The Japanese box is. Our competitor in the United States—outside of the big companies like IBM and Kodak—is a whole series of a thousand entrepreneurs. They don't have a board of directors. They don't have articles in *The Wall Street Journal*. They're in business to make a buck. It just so happens they're selling Japanese boxes. Their whole flexibility or thought process of how they look at selling machines is totally different from us. The dealer is sitting there making cash flow decisions at the end of the day, so his prices at the end of the month could be totally different than they are at the beginning of the month. He may have taken a bank loan out and he comes to the point where he has to make a payment.
>
> —DAVID MYERSCOUGH,
> Xerox

BOB KECK has a perfect view of Xerox Tower from his desk at Kex Copysource, the office products dealership he runs in Rochester. "Everyday I spit at them," he says, pointing at the black tower looming in the distance.

Keck was joking, of course, but his attitude illustrates the intensely competitive feeling American dealers have toward Xerox. In fact, if it weren't for people such as Keck, the Japanese copier makers would still be selling their goods only in Asia and Europe.

Keck's dealership also illustrates the David and Goliath nature of the battle. His Rochester office does about $2 million a year in sales, mostly

Panasonic and Mita machines. Six blocks away at Xerox, Myerscough's group records more outright copier sales than that each day before the first coffee break.

Despite the size of Xerox, or perhaps because of it, American dealers have been very successful. Most of the dealerships were started by former copier salesmen or servicemen, some of whom worked at Xerox and IBM. Ricoh has more than twenty dealers who are former Xerox salesmen; one dealer brought sixteen other Xerox people with him. Many of the owners, with little business background but great drive and ambition, have become millionaires riding the boom in copier sales.

There are about 7,500 copier dealerships in the United States, most of which do between $1 million and $2 million in annual sales. In the early days, when each Japanese maker had a limited number of models, dealerships used to carry several different brands of copiers. Everybody went with the hot box that year. Today, as each manufacturer has developed a full line of products and those machines have become more reliable, most dealers carry only two brands. The ratio of a machine's list price to its landed cost in the United States is about 2.5 to 1, with the cost to the dealer averaging about 40 percent off list. With most dealers, however, there is no such thing as a list price. "They discount like hell," Xerox's Peter McColough says.

IBM discovered just how tough it was to compete against discount-happy dealers when it began marketing under its own label a small Minolta-made machine in 1981. This was really to test whether IBM could expand into all volume segments. "We decided we didn't want to stay in the low end very long," says IBM's Proctor Houston. "It wasn't the arena where we had our marketing efficiencies. Dealers were more effective. When you're dealing with a product in that $3,000 price range and you're trying to do it with a three-piece-suit marketing group looking for a good chit, it's very difficult."

Nothing illustrates the dynamic partnership these dealers have with the Japanese better than the rapid expansion of the National Office Machine Dealers Association. Twenty years ago, NOMDA was basically a loose affiliation of typewriter dealers. Their annual conventions were modest affairs where manufacturers might set up a tabletop display on the balcony of a hotel. Now, the NOMDA convention is a week-long extravaganza, dominated by copier companies clamoring for the attention of dealers. "Eight thousand dealers shake hands with our competition at NOMDA," says Toneo Noda, a managing director at Fuji Xerox. "NOMDA is the enemy of Xerox."

At the convention, the American marketing arms of the Japanese manufacturers construct huge booths to attract the attention of dealers. In 1984, Ricoh spent $1 million on its 6,500-square-foot booth at the Dallas Convention Center. The joke was that Ricoh was going to sell the booth as a condominium after the show. It had 150 employees, 10 percent of its American total, on site and spent another $75,000 on a party for its dealers at Billy Bob's in Forth Worth. Sharp threw a ball for 2,500 dealers and guests.

One of the first things you notice at a NOMDA convention is that all of the Japanese machines look alike no matter who makes them. So it's not a matter of the product itself as much as it is the financing and training support the manufacturer provides and the image it portrays about itself and its products.

The pattern is much the same at each booth: American salesmen out front, Japanese technicians in the background. A Sharp salesman was demonstrating a prototype of a 60-cpm duplicator when it broke down. The original wouldn't exit the machine. A Japanese technician was there within seconds, took the cover off the machine, retrieved the original, and soon had the machine operating again. He then slipped into the background again. During the whole time the American continued his sales pitch.

Another feature at NOMDA, and the other big copier shows around the world, is the private showing. Manufacturers will take a suite at a hotel and invite key dealers and industry analysts to view their latest prototype models. As one might expect, those who view the products first sign a nondisclosure agreement. At a Savin private showing, for instance, in one room sat a stripped down Xerox 1075. In the next room was a Savin 8000 and its developer, Benny Landa. Savin was out to prove that the prototype 8000 produced better-quality copies than the 1075. The prototype did, but Savin has since dropped plans to manufacture the machine itself.

Private showings, elaborate booths, parties, billboards, TV ads—all are intended to convince the dealer that his supplier company is staying on top of the market. And once they have good dealers, the companies don't want to lose them. Ricoh calculates that it costs $100,000 in lost training and promotional effort every time a dealer switches to another brand.

Until recently, there was no national network of dealers. One dealer might have had several branches, but he would not have joined forces with any other dealers. That began to change in 1983 when Alco Standard, a $3.5 billion paper and food distributor, began buying dealerships, concentrating on larger operations in major locations with good profit margins. More than half of Alco's revenues come from paper distribution. By 1985, it had acquired the three largest dealerships in the United States, was doing about $250 million in annual copier sales, and was ready to acquire even more. "I think we can grow to $1 billion in annual sales in ten years and eventually be spun off as a separate New York Stock Exchange–listed company," says Ted Edwards, who came out of retirement at age sixty-two to head the dealer division for Alco. Edwards joined Alco in 1968 when he sold them his paper distribution company, Unisource. At this writing, copier sales account for more than 85 percent of Alco's dealer sales, but Edwards predicts that that percentage will decline. He foresees dealers handling office furniture as well as a full line of office machines sometime in the future.

Kex was Alco's first copier dealer acquisition. "Alco got to noticing that while it averaged an annual pretax return of 3.5 to 4.5 percent on its mainline businesses, Kex was averaging 10 to 14 percent," Edwards explains. "We did a lot of research into the dealership business and decided it was a good business. From that research we decided that we could put together a national chain."

Edwards, whose division is run by a staff of just five out of its headquarters in Valley Forge, Pennsylvania, screened all the dealerships in the country looking for those with minimum annual sales of $8 million, a pretax return of 8 to 10 percent on sales, and a return on capital of 25 percent or better. He identified 173 candidates. Alco quickly acquired A-Copy of Glastonbury, Connecticut, the largest dealership in the country, and the next two largest dealerships—Modern Business Systems of Jefferson City, Missouri, and San Sierra of Sacramento, California. "They are a hard-hitting, entrepreneurial, tough bunch of guys to manage," Edwards says of the dealers. "They don't know what 'no' means. They would sell their grandmother if they had to."

Both the Japanese and Xerox are keeping a close watch on Alco, a company they consider a major new force in the American copier industry. Alco's strength is its proven ability to market products. It also gives these relatively small, independent dealerships the backing of a huge company. That means stability—the same stability offered by Xerox, Kodak, and IBM. That means instead of doing business with a small dealer with limited resources, a customer is now dealing with Alco, a multibillion-dollar company.

Alco's management style is hands-off. "We don't know the copier business," Edwards says. "We just know how to run these dealerships." The parent company sets sales and profit goals, but the dealers make their own decisions on what machines they will carry. Edwards tells of a New York City–area dealer who asked when Edwards planned to visit the operation. Edwards answered, "When you fuck up."

"We're professional distributors," Edwards says. "We don't really care what the stuff is. If somebody calls us up and wants something quick, we don't panic. We plan to get it there tomorrow anyway."

Edwards sees the trend toward mass distribution accelerating. "It's going to be more and more costly to get stuff to the marketplace," he says. "We used to pay our warehousemen two cents or three cents a minute. Then we could go and hand pick the paper and give it to the driver who was making four cents a minute. We could afford to do that for the small customer. Now, with a warehouseman making fifteen cents a minute and a trucker making twenty-two cents a minute, it costs you a buck when they go to take a piss.

"I have no idea what Xerox thinks about us. They probably see us as just another competitor. I think it's becoming clear that IBM, Xerox, and Kodak can no longer handle the Segment 1 and 2 boxes, the under-$10,000 machines. They can't afford to send a guy in a blue suit and a white shirt, to use IBM as an example, out on a call to sell a small machine. We can. As we see it, they're going to need people like us in the future. I could see even taking a low-end Xerox machine in our dealerships some day."

When it bought A-Copy, Alco also acquired the services of Herb Chambers, probably the most successful copier dealer in the United States. Chambers began as a copier serviceman with APECO (American Photocopy Equipment Company) in 1962. In 1965, he started his own dealership with a $1,000 investment. By 1985, A-Copy had twenty-three outlets and 900 employees, including 300 servicemen, and total annual sales of $70 million. Chambers is president of A-Copy and a senior vice president in Alco's's dealer division. A-Copy handles both Canon and Ricoh machines, with a separate sales force for each.

"You talk about a tough guy to compete against," says John Stuart, head of Royal's copier division in the United States. "I mean he's the cobra. For a big call, Xerox brings in their regional manager. A-Copy brings in the president. And he is one of the best salesmen I have ever seen in my life."

Stuart and Chambers remember their first meeting. Chambers called Stuart when he headed Ricoh's copier division. "I heard you're running Ricoh now. I've been trying to get your line for two years. When can we meet?" Chambers asked.

"How about today?" Stuart answered.

"Fine, I'm in Philadelphia now, I'll be there in forty-five minutes."

"You can't drive here that fast."

"I know, I'm taking my helicopter."

For Chambers, a helicopter is the only way to keep up with the fast-moving copier business. "The time was right. John was in the right mood. We made the deal. I don't think we would have gotten the franchise if it hadn't been for the helicopter," he says.

Chambers likes Canon and Ricoh because those companies have committed substantial resources to copier research and development. "The past four years or so, Canon has always managed to stay six months ahead of everybody," he says. "And they stay six months ahead with reliable products. I have seen others rush to market with machines and then fall flat on their face because the machines weren't reliable."

Chambers echoes the anti-Xerox feelings of many dealers: "There is a certain animosity toward Xerox. They gaffed people for so long. They charged outrageous prices for so long. Now they are trying to change and get back into the picture. But people have longer memories than that."

Sid Reisch has been competing against Xerox for most of his career. He started in 1953 selling diffusion-transfer copiers for Kalmac in New York City. He went to SCM, Savin, and then began Toshiba's copier business in the United States in 1974. He has a photograph from a promotional campaign at SCM in the sixties showing him in boxing gloves taking on the champ, Xerox. "The salesman that was required to compete against Xerox was really a tough individual," Reisch says. "Tough skinned. A cross, in the early days, and I want to make this clear, between a horse trader and a used car salesman." Some of the salesmen he worked with, Reisch says, thought Xerox was impossible to beat.

Reisch has never agreed. "I've been in management in the copier business for over twenty-five years," he says. "In my early days I hired Xerox people. They always looked good, clean cut, well spoken, good educational background, but frankly—and this is not a knock, it has just been my experience—for the most part they couldn't compete in the dog-eat-dog world of downstreet sales in the copier business. They operated for many years in a vacuum. I would put a copier salesman from a dealership head-to-head with any Xerox person any day of the week and they'd beat them every time."

Reisch's competitive spirit helped Toshiba's 250 dealers almost double their copier sales in the United States in 1984 over 1983, the best percentage increase in the industry that year. Sales increased another 25 percent in 1985.

Sharp has about 500 copier dealers in the United States, the most of any Japanese manufacturer. Joe Castrianni, who runs Sharp's copier business, began working with dealers in 1960 while at Olivetti. Later, he switched to Saxon and then founded Sharp's U.S. copier division in 1975. Castrianni echoes a common sentiment among the Japanese companies. They are more wary of each other than they are of Xerox. "Sure, Xerox is everybody's competition," he says. "But our direct competition is Canon." Sharp and Canon have held the top two spots in the United States in terms of copier placements since 1981. Canon took over the number-one spot in 1982 and has increased its lead with the introduction of the personal copier.

Dave Shearer's dealership is in Kokomo, Indiana, the heart of UAW country. He handles only Savin copiers. It can be a problem selling a Japanese-made product in a staunchly American-made environment. Customers even call him and ask who makes the pencils and pens he sells. Shearer also handles Olivetti (Italian) typewriters. He recalls a time when he was trying to sell them to General Motors. "The IBM salesman drove into the GM parking lot in a foreign-made car," he said. "He was out of it." GM bought Shearer's Olivettis.

PART FOUR
RECOGNITION

13

1980—
The Awakening

We had this gigantic cash cow and we almost milked it dry.

—FRED HENDERSON, Xerox
vice president

IT LOOKS innocent enough on paper. Just a graph with one line going up and another going down.

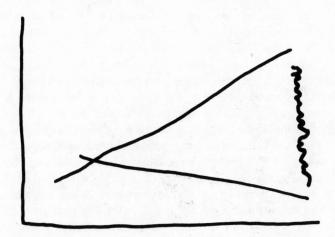

At Xerox it was called the Jaws Chart, after the movie. At one time Xerox executives drew it to illustrate what *would* happen to their copier business. They draw it today to show what *did* happen. The line going up represents profits. The line going down is the lease base, what the company always referred to as its annuity for the future. Toward the end of the seventies and into the eighties, the company cannibalized its lease base, converting the machines to sale. This made the yearly profits actually look better than they should have at the expense of future profits from the rental machines. A company can only do this for so long. If nothing comes along to fill the gap, like new machines, Jaws will eventually take a big bite out of earnings. "Customers are sophisticated," Xerox scientist Bob Gundlach says. "Even with the best marketing force in the world, you can't keep pushing old technology."

Everybody at Xerox kept staring at that Jaws Chart. They knew what was coming. In 1977, Rank Xerox under Bill Glavin began selling the leased machines it had in place, because Rank Xerox was anticipating a new line of products in 1979–80 (that's when the 1075 and 1045 were originally scheduled to be launched).

The new products didn't come until 1982. Jaws chopped Rank Xerox from £255 million of operating profit in 1979 to £200 million in 1981 and £105 million in 1982. "During that period of time, Rank Xerox went right down the tubes from the standpoint of their ability to sell large- and medium-volume machines," Glavin said. "They really didn't have them. We had a superb strategy. The only problem was we didn't get the products when we were supposed to and we ended up sitting out there left to dry. The ability to recuperate from that has taken a long time. A lot of that is due to the currencies and the economic situation. Currency alone cost Rank Xerox a billion and a half dollars in revenue from 1980 to 1984. But there was a very clear strategy, very well thought out. We knew what we were trying to do. It just didn't come together for us because we couldn't get the products when we needed them."

Xerox in the United States went to the same strategy later. It first tried to plug the holes in an aging product lineup with stopgap (called the second-and-a-half generation) machines like the 8200 and 2600. The 8200, basically, was a 9400 cut in half. The machine worked, but the strategy didn't. Xerox Corporation in the United States reported an all-time record net profit of $598 million in 1981. The next year, the Jaws phenomenon, along with the costs of a massive employment cutback campaign, chopped that profit to $424 million. The third generation machines—the 10 Series—didn't begin to reinvigorate company profits until late 1983.

For Xerox, 1980 was the year the message finally hit home: It was living on borrowed time. After years of denying that the Japanese were a threat, and then thinking they had the threat licked, company executives finally realized that if they didn't act fast they could lose the entire copying franchise. It was time to start paying for the mistakes and excesses of the 1970s so Xerox could survive as a world-class company through the eighties and nineties.

The precise turning point for Xerox came during the summer of 1980. The change in mood of the company's top brass was remarkable. In May, at an idyllic annual meeting under a circus tent in Webster, Peter McColough and David Kearns told 2,000 shareholders that Xerox was beating the Japanese. Xerox has "plugged the holes" in the low-volume market and "broken new trails" in the high-volume market, McColough said. "We can produce a new copier for the same amount that it cost five years ago," Kearns boasted. "That's like being able to buy a 1980 automobile at 1976 prices." Kearns talked confidently about outrunning the Japanese in all parts of the copier business, the same message he carried to shareholders at the two previous annual meetings.

By August, however, a memo from Kearns was posted on all company bulletin boards: "We are determined to change significantly the way we have been doing business."

"What do you mean?" workers joked to one another. "Is there trouble in Camelot?" Trouble indeed. Xerox thought it was narrowing the production-cost gap with the Japanese when all the time the gap was actually getting larger. No one fully comprehended just how good the Japanese were or how quickly they were improving. Market share was evaporating faster than ever. "I can remember a company conference in 1977 when I talked a lot about costs," Kearns says. "I'll tell you that my idea of what we needed to do about costs then and in 1980 were a lot different. What we started to do in 1980 we should have done in 1975."

That recognition came none too soon. While Ricoh and Savin were experiencing some difficulty in their partnership, a new and stronger Japanese challenger was emerging. Canon was expanding its factories and strengthening its marketing to make a run at the leader. The Japanese were no longer content to control the low end. They began moving up market. For the first time, Xerox began seeing national television ads for copiers from the Japanese companies themselves. The pace of competition accelerated. Between 1971 and 1978, seventy-seven different plain paper copiers were introduced in the United States. From 1978 to 1980, another seventy were introduced.

Four factors came together in 1980 that let Xerox see the true severity of its problems and provide some guidance for solving them.

The Cost Gap

The manufacturing group in Rochester discovered that the Japanese were able to produce copiers for about half as much as Xerox. "We were horrified to learn that the selling price of the small Japanese machines was our manufacturing cost," Kearns says. "We discovered that some of our assessment methods of looking at the Japanese were not good enough. We were not tracking the rate of speed of their improvement. We tended to put a peg in. By the time we thought we were catching up, or thought we were close, we found ourselves still far off the mark." That was the beginning of competitive benchmarking, a strategy that is now used throughout the corporation. (Benchmarking, comparing yourself to your best competition, is discussed in greater detail in Chapter 18.)

The next year, a group of Xerox engineers went to Japan and made a similar discovery. It was taking Xerox about twice as long and costing about twice as much as it cost the Japanese to develop a product. The actual burn rates—R & D dollars spent per day—were similar, but Xerox simply couldn't push a copier out the door as fast as the Japanese.

Fuji Xerox Success

Kearns and the rest of Xerox began paying even more attention to Fuji Xerox, their Japanese partner. Fuji Xerox had perceived the threat from other Japanese copier manufacturers earlier and had already started to change. Total quality control was the focus of its New Xerox movement. Since that movement began, Fuji Xerox's year-to-year gains in revenues and profits have paced all of Xerox. The New Xerox movement became the model for Xerox Corporation's own focus on quality.

New People, New Attitude

Several top executives including Bill Glavin, Dwight Ryan, and Wayland Hicks returned to the United States from jobs at Rank Xerox in Europe. These people had more firsthand experience in competing against the Japanese for market share. The European market is geared toward small machines, the Japanese specialty. The Xerox strategy had been to maintain profit margins, which kept prices up and provided an umbrella under which the Japanese and even IBM could sell. That avoided the basic problem: Xerox's costs were too high. "By the time I got to Europe in 1977, I had leapfrogged from what was an incursion into the territory to a full-fledged war,'' recalls Ryan, who was regional manager for the West Coast of the United States before transferring to Rank Xerox.

For the first time since the atomic decade of the sixties, Xerox had a strong group of homegrown managers who understood each other, the copier business, and the international scene. They began to work together against an external enemy instead of competing against each other to become the next president of the company.

A McKinsey Study

Ryan, with the aid of the consulting firm, McKinsey & Co., launched a study that eventually led to the reorganization of Xerox into entrepreneurial business units and massive personnel cuts. The main target was the giant bureaucracy that had stifled copier product development for more than a decade. By this time, the Office Products Division in Dallas began to have some success developing new products, such as the Memorywriter, with small teams of personnel. The Ryan/McKinsey effort brought together in early 1981 two dozen Xerox managers who had impact and clout. That gave Kearns a team that could implement the changes he thought necessary.

"I went into that study with very strong feelings of how the company should be organized and we ended up doing that,'' Kearns said. "But I thought the changes were substantial enough that I really wanted a lot of input from a broad range of people—manufacturing, engineering, product planning, as well as marketing. Sometimes you use an organization change as a catalyst just to get things going. There was some of that involved, but the main thing was to get more of the pieces put together at a lower level where people could make decisions. I feel that the guys came out of that very comfortable. The biggest issues were where the power was, marketing or the SBUs [strategic business units]. I think we're working our way through those fairly well.''

After a decade of denial and ineffective action, Xerox was finally doing something about the Japanese.

Ryan returned to the United States in early 1980 as a marketing vice president at the Stamford headquarters. In August of that year he was put in charge of a new program, called Business Effectiveness, that was supposed to use benchmarking and employee involvement as the two major tools to improve productivity and increase customer satisfaction. When the McKinsey organizational study began, he also headed that. Glavin, who had been managing director of Rank Xerox, returned to the United States as executive vice president in July 1980.

"Much to my amazement, the staff at the headquarters group and the management there was really lacking any coherence, I guess that's a nice way to say it," Ryan recalls of his first impression on going to Stamford. "Therefore, they were all at cross-purposes. And things that seemed from afar to be funny became absolutely apparent to me as to why we were in that situation." While one faction argued for cutting prices and holding market share, another argued to maintain high profit margins. No one got to the real problem of producing good, low-cost machines that could compete against the Japanese and Kodak. The predominant mood was indecisiveness and frustration at the lack of any action.

"So Glavin comes over from Europe and he was like the Germans marching through the Ukraine," Ryan says. "I found it exciting working for him. He started to make changes and make things happen."

Glavin, vice chairman of Xerox, is a big man, about six-foot-six. His size complements his forceful personality. He joined Xerox in 1970 from the Service Bureau Corporation, a subsidiary of IBM, to be executive vice president of Xerox Data Systems, the computer business Xerox acquired through Scientific Data Systems and eventually abandoned in 1975. In 1972, he came to Rochester as a group vice president and, in 1974, went to Rank Xerox as managing director and chief operating director. He helped bring a new philosophy to Xerox, first in Europe, then in the United States: market share. As Ryan says, "Xerox never forgot market share in the late seventies, but it sure didn't emphasize it."

Soon after Glavin arrived in Europe in 1974, the Japanese began their big push there. The economies were all in recession. Companies in the United Kingdom were on a three-day workweek. "We were blaming everything on those things," Glavin remembers. "What was really happening to us was that the competition was killing us and we didn't know it. In those days we didn't have competitive benchmarking and market research. We had so much of the market we didn't care: It wasn't until 1975 that we clearly understood what was going on. And by that time it was tough to react. You go to the engineering organization and ask for help and all the engineering organization is worried about is the Kodak threat. We don't have a product answer for that.

"In Europe, we didn't see Kodak. They weren't there yet. But in the United States they [Xerox] had Big Yellow hanging all over them. Everytime you talked to anybody, that's all they could talk about. I kept saying, the Japanese are coming, the Japanese are coming. But in the U.S. the real threat was Kodak. As it turned out, we had our eye on the wrong ball in those days in the United States. And that, consequently, was driving the research and development efforts, and it made a big impact on the rest of the world. Tony Kobayashi [president of Fuji Xerox] is chugging along, doing his product, winning the Deming Prize, and getting his company going and he's out there doing it all by himself because first the engineering people in the United States didn't believe he could do it, and second, they really didn't want the products that he was making."

In Europe, the Japanese were especially attracted to those countries with hard currencies. They took advantage of the favorable exchange rates against the yen to help lower prices and gain market share. Glavin wrote a report in 1977 describing where he thought the Japanese companies were heading. There wasn't one explosive company in Europe at that time to parallel Savin in the United States. They all seemed to develop their markets slowly but steadily, with different strategies in different countries. Glavin predicted Canon, which was not a major competitor at that time, would be the primary competition over the long term. Canon would be able to move up market because it understood the distribution and service requirements of highspeed, dry-toner copiers, he said. Canon was buying up dealers and distribution channels in some European countries, a practice since abandoned. The reasoning for Glavin's conclusion may have been flawed, but certainly not the conclusion itself.

Fuji Xerox had produced its first small copier, the 2200, in 1972. In 1977, it introduced the 2202. The United States didn't take it, but Rank Xerox committed itself to taking 25,000 beginning in October 1978. "We told Tony, just keep making them and shipping them to us, and we will sell them," Glavin says. "We did. We sold almost 24,000 units in that twelve-month period. We had never sold 24,000 of anything in a given year before. The operating units couldn't believe they could do it because it was 100 percent incremental, I didn't let them cut back on anything else. That's when we started to go back toward a market share strategy.

"It demonstrated to us that first of all our sales force could sell high volumes of machines if the price was right. It also demonstrated we could compete against the low-end competition if we had product. This product was not a smashing product, but it was not a bad product in those days."

When he returned to the States, Glavin committed Xerox to pricing its new 10 Series to the market, wherever that level was headed. This was during the period Xerox was shrinking its overhead and getting its costs down to meet the Japanese. The process had begun, but was nowhere near complete.

"I was convinced that what we needed to do was get aggressive in the marketplace, get back our share," Glavin says. "I was convinced the problem was price. Now we have our costs in line to allow us to be aggressive on price. We couldn't before."

14
Turning Point:
The McKinsey Study

Mention the name Eddie Miller to Dwight Ryan, and Ryan immediately starts laughing. "Eddie Miller, oh, my God, the bane of my existence for a while," he says.

Miller admits he wasn't too popular with Xerox executives when, as a McKinsey & Co. consultant, he worked with Ryan on a study of the company. "I had really broken my pick," Miller says. "I even pissed off Kearns in the process at various times. I had decided if this fails it is not going to be because I could be accused of not telling a client what he should hear versus what he wanted to hear. I was not going to mince words about personalities or anything else."

Today, most people in top positions at Xerox, Ryan included, agree that this study was the pivotal event in changing the way the company does business. It helped implement a wholesale reorganization in the company and brought together the people who would play key roles in the new Xerox. David Kearns says he knew the types of changes he wanted to make, but he had to get his people behind them. This is the vehicle he used.

Miller was in McKinsey's London office when he first started consulting to Rank Xerox. At one point, he commuted back and forth across the Atlantic thirty times a year. He met both Bill Glavin and Wayland Hicks at Rank Xerox—Hicks while on a fox hunt. He left McKinsey in 1982 to join a venture capital firm.

Miller's view of Xerox is unique because he was an outsider allowed to observe the inner workings of a huge corporation during a period of great upheaval. The power was shifting at Stamford. Jobs were at stake. As a consultant, he had a vested interest in the situation to the extent that he wanted his recommendations adopted. Yet at the same time, Miller could take a more objective view because he was not a direct employee of Xerox and was not caught up in company politics. Here is his insider's account, taken from a three-hour interview in his Madison Avenue office, of the events that led up to the 1981 Xerox-McKinsey study and the subsequent changes at Xerox:

Xerox was an incredibly difficult client, the hardest client I worked with in thirteen years. It was about the hardest company to do change in. It was also a lot easier to get change done in Rank Xerox or Fuji Xerox than in the U.S. The reason was that you had profit and loss responsibility over there. In the U.S., you had a larger and larger number of staff people. Everyone had a function. Inevitably, when you made some recommendations or tried to change some things, you were trampling on someone's turf. In the U.S., everybody had a functional perspective. There was no one, save for Peter McColough himself, who had a profit and loss responsibility.

Joe Wilson was first and foremost a businessman. He was good with people. He saw the big picture. He focused on the customer. McColough was a salesman, pure and simple, with all the pluses and minuses that entailed. He was very responsive to the stimulus of the moment. Every day he was managing the biggest company he had ever managed. He was a risk taker, [but] I'm not sure he was an effective risk taker. His golf course acquisition deals were legend. He was a venture capitalist's best friend. The real strength of Xerox, even today, is its sales force, which McColough started. You start off with a guy who had that orientation. He had never worked at Hewlett-Packard or a General Electric. When the company started getting some size, for whatever reason, it chose to bring in Ford people, like Archie McCardell. Ford was a monolithic, functionalized, bureaucratic, centralized organization. Belief in analysis overcomes all. I expect that Peter thought he was doing the right thing. It didn't really matter until about 1975, because Xerox was the only game in town.

One of the interesting things that I observed was that the problems of Xerox and British Telecom were identical. Different countries, different businesses, but their responses were the same. The reason was they were both monopolies. Companies that are monopolies in their industries seem to develop in similar ways. Typical monopolies are very profitable. There is a lot of cash around. They tend to attract a lot of bright people. Xerox was an exaggerated case. Most companies do not start off as monopolies. Most companies don't have as many bright people as Xerox did. In sheer brightness they were right at the top. Also in sheer irrelevance they were right at the top. Bright people have to do something. If there is no inherent challenge in the marketplace—competition— all that brightness gets focused inwardly. The only thing that people have to maximize is their responsibility.

No place was that more evident than the technical and development side in Rochester. The reason the U. S. never brought in a Fuji Xerox machine until very late was that the engineering organization there had convinced themselves, again because of lack of any competition, that they possessed this incredibly complex technology. Mere mortals could not develop these machines. The machines showed it. Everything inside a Xerox machine was special. You could not go out and use a normal nut. It had to be a specially designed nut. The concept of using as many standard parts as possible was not even thought of. Everything was different. In that environment, the people in Rochester literally could not believe that anyone else could know as much about xerography as they did. It just did not enter their minds. Their view of the world was that you couldn't possibly design anything any good without having 1,000 people working on it. It was easy for them to find any kind of fault with Japanese machines. They wanted to look for things that justified their point of view. In Rank Xerox, they were more like businessmen looking for markets, and because they were 3,000 miles away from headquarters and not caught up in the turf battles, they could be more objective.

I can remember as late as 1975 looking at internal Xerox reports showing that market share was a word they had never heard of. They did not have any formal market share information. It had always been 100 percent. Right then, some people started to accumulate some information and the Japanese weren't even listed in 1975, even into 1976. Kearns will be the first to take the blame for this. The whole company, in terms of competition, was focused on IBM at that time. Everybody was convinced that if they were going to have any competition, it was going to come from IBM. When IBM came out with its first product, a shudder went through Xerox. Later, it was Kodak. Xerox totally missed the fundamental strategy of the Japanese, which was going in at the low end of the market and working up, going for the soft underbelly.

At one time I think McKinsey might have had as many as twenty-five or thirty people working on Xerox around the world. We had the Tokyo office working with Fuji, the London office working with Rank, the New York office working with headquarters, and a variety of efforts going on in each location. Sometimes, as a client, it was very hard to get people at McKinsey to work with Xerox. It was very frustrating. There had been a series of what I call nothing studies in the 1960s and early 1970s.

Then, a kind of new guard came into the McKinsey-Xerox world, including myself. We were doing good work, we were doing what the client wanted us to do, but we just weren't helping anyone. The client was happy but we were not. I agitated for and eventually got a worldwide meeting of every significant partner who was working on Xerox. It was a two-day meeting, transferring McKinsey technology as it were. We were all seeing the same thing. It didn't matter whether it was Fuji or here in the United States. The problems were the same worldwide. It all added up to how do you change this beast.

Somewhere around 1977 we had a couple of meetings. At one of these meetings we wrote a position paper to Xerox which in effect said, time after time these are the problems we see, referring to the turf battles and bureaucracy. The result of that was Archie McCardell left, Kearns came in as president.

The Kearns for McCardell move was received very well at Xerox. Archie was very uncomfortable sitting in a meeting with its give and take. Kearns and

Archie couldn't have been more different. Archie would go into a meeting with his analysts and come out with the answer. It was all planned out ahead of time. Kearns liked sitting in meetings, liked getting input from people, liked the give and take. To a fault. The joke at Xerox was that the last guy who got to Kearns wins the bet. Whoever put an idea in his head at the last minute would get his way. Kearns believed in people.

The bureaucracy of Xerox began to change after Kearns came in. No question about it, Kearns was a change agent. His problem was that he didn't always know in which direction he wanted to change. To be fair to him, he was operating in a difficult environment in what he had inherited from Archie. Kearns is a pretty damn good politician but he had to tiptoe through those tulips carefully. That Stamford bureaucracy was a hotbed of politics.

Of course, the thing you have to understand about Xerox is that there were very few decisions made on a rational basis. They were almost all made on a political basis. That was no different than in a lot of big companies. You don't have to study the *Fortune* 500 very long to come away with a pretty jaundiced view of American management. The *Fortune* 500 long ago ceased being a business environment. The premium is on political maneuvering. There are far too many staff groups, to the detriment of judgment. Most of the decisions are made around the issues of turf, career advancement, and those kinds of things. The big companies have ceased to be technical innovators. They are now just large distribution organizations. It was a bit more extreme in Xerox because you had so many bright guys fighting with each other and you were dealing with relatively weak leadership before Kearns.

David was and still is a very charismatic guy, particularly in a sales and marketing sense. After the first six or twelve months that Kearns settled in, there was a great wave of disappointment. Kearns was trooping all around the world giving these upbeat messages, but nothing was really changing. We as consultants were still beating on him and everyone else to try to break down this syndrome of staffitis, one analyst checking on another analyst. We made some progress in Rank Xerox and the Tokyo people made some progress in Fuji Xerox, but in the States there was no progress.

The pressure was really building on Kearns. His people were getting very depressed. Nothing seemed to be happening. They were getting their lunch eaten by the Japanese and others in the copier business. There was this big fight between the Office Products Division and the rest of the company. Their meetings were a joke. Fighting is an emotive word. One of the problems at Xerox was that people didn't really know they were stabbed until they saw the knife coming out. The meetings were always super-gentlemanly. You wouldn't be aware there was a fight going on; it was all below the surface.

Sometime in early 1980, Kearns came to us and said, "Listen, I gotta change this company." There had been a significant amount of time that Kearns had been on the job and there was just a lot of disappointment around the company because nothing seemed to be happening. He was aware of that. Basically, the general feeling in the company was that nothing was going to happen until they got rid of the Old Guard.

Kearns knew he wanted to change the company. He didn't really know what it was he wanted to do. I think he was very conscious of the fact that he had Peter looking over his shoulder. He asked us in early eighty, he said, "Look, why don't you guys just go around and talk to key people in the company, all over the company, and try to see what is really on people's minds and feed it back to me." [Tom Peters, co-author of *In Search of Excellence,* did some of this work.] Which we did. But frankly, it was a ho-hum kind of thing. There was nothing that we could have said that would have been news to anybody. I guess we were kind of frustrated by it. If I would have been Kearns I would have said, "Jesus Christ, these guys just spent two months going around talking to everybody, so what else is new."

We were equally frustrated. We had a growing feeling that everybody analyzes the problems, they talk about the problems, everybody knows what the problems are, but the real problem is that nobody does anything. One of the reasons that nobody does anything is that the environment is so political you can never build a consensus of action and, by the way, virtually everybody believes that Xerox is going to go down the tubes before Rochester gets any new products going. The bureaucracy is stultifying to everybody.

By this time, I guess, Kearns had already toyed with the idea of changing the organization. What is now the basis of the 10 Series line of copiers was mired down. Schedules were slipping, product costs were increasing, and everybody kept staring at the Jaws Chart. They all knew what was going to happen. Pretty soon the jaws would clamp shut. The big earnings decline was no surprise to anybody in Xerox.

So Kearns was really thinking about changing the organization, partly inspired by the fact he knew there must be a better way, partly inspired by the fact that by this time the Massaro organization had begun to take hold in Dallas and it was just amazing everybody how quickly they were able to produce products and get things moving, high morale, and so on. Over a three-year period, they had firmly established Xerox in office automation. They had created the de facto standard in local area networks, and they did that very wisely by making it an open system. They firmly established Xerox in the typewriter business, which at the time everybody thought was a joke. In 1979, those Dallas guys were going around talking about a 20 percent share in the typewriter business. Everyone laughed. No way. IBM owns that market. They set up an efficient, automated factory. Nobody in Stamford or Rochester believed the factory existed. Of course, Xerox just cleaned IBM's pocket in typewriters.

So Kearns came on and said, "Hey, if it works in Dallas, why wouldn't it work in Rochester."

The other influence was the Japanese, who had shown what they could do with a relatively small number of people. The forces were building to say, this engineering bureaucracy that we have up in Rochester just can't be right. And there was also, I'm sure, in Kearns's mind, the idea that this would be a convenient way to change some of the players. Bill Glavin had come back from Rank Xerox at that time and was a chief staff guy. While Bill is fairly political, basically he's reasonably astute in management in many ways. Glavin was beginning to whisper in Kearns's ear, "There is something wrong here."

Kearns asked us if we could undertake a study to fundamentally look at the whole product development, product marketing, product introduction process. We said we think the problem is bigger than that. We're really talking about a question of corporate culture. We want to really do something that will change the company. If you're prepared to do this, make changes in players, then we will.

There have been countless McKinsey studies done. We write them up, Xerox has looked at them and says good, but nothing much happens. The reason not much happens is the organization doesn't buy it. The only way to make the organization buy it is to let them be part of the process and figure out what the answer is. We told Kearns that what we wanted to do was create a very, very top level McKinsey team with our best people on it. We wanted that team matched by a Xerox team. I led the McKinsey team. Dwight Ryan led the Xerox team. We very quickly hit upon the idea of engaging the ideas of the opinion leaders of Xerox and the people who would be part of implementing whatever change came out of this effort. So we came up with the idea of having a couple of week-long retreats. Xerox would bring in a couple dozen people clearly identified in everyone's mind as being the movers and shakers, the young Turks, the guys who were on their way up. We would match them with McKinsey people.

During the first retreat we looked at Xerox's fundamental economics, and we played back to them what we saw as the issues, the same issues we had been raising for years. We also wanted agreement on what Xerox's fundamental mission and strategy ought to be. Unless you can agree on that, nothing else is going to work. One of the problems of Xerox was that they've never had strong management leadership like a Hennessey at Allied, or a Gray at United Technologies. Someone who would say, "Goddammit, this is what we are going to do. Either follow it or get out of the way." Everybody had their own opinions. A decision would be made, then all the staff people would go back and start rehashing the decision if they didn't like the way it came out. The only way you can get any kind of change is to get enough of the people pulling in the same direction so you can stop that. The whole point was to get these guys to believe that something was really going to happen this time.

Essentially, what came out of these sessions was we gotta break up Rochester. The proposal eventually emerged as let's break this thing up into high-, medium-, and low-range copiers, with each one of those units having worldwide profit and loss responsibility for that part of the product line. Let them be responsible for identifying what products are needed, see to developing them or getting them sourced from Fuji Xerox or Rank Xerox. The source could even be totally from outside of Xerox. The important thing was to have the product out. And they will have under their control engineering, analytical, marketing, pricing—all those functions that are necessary to run a business. The theme that we were trying to pound into Xerox is get away from having a bunch of staff guys do something in their specialty, get into arguments, and then have to resort to huge meetings to resolve these differences. Put a businessman in charge. Clearly, the business was too big to run with just one businessman.

That was heretical thinking. For the first time, the headquarters staff wouldn't be kingpin of the organization. Somebody else was going to give sales objectives to the sales force, and somebody else was going to determine prices.

From an engineering side, it was equally heretical. The reaction was, "You can't do this. You don't understand it. If you try to break up the technology base and put it into these three groups it will wither away. You have guys that are too superficial; they don't understand all the engineering issues. Three years from now Xerox will not be competitive. Blah, blah, blah, blah."

It was painfully evident to everybody except the two or three diehards that this thing worked. But nobody wanted to stand up in a meeting and tell David that's what they thought. So they volunteered Don Massaro for it. In typical Massaro fashion, he started his preamble off with: "David the guys have asked me to report back to you and tell you what we have been doing these last few days. I'm very happy to do this because, now that you're finally getting some general management experience, we thought this would be very useful to you."

David had just reorganized the company to where he had everything reporting to him. Literally, it was true, it was the first time in David's life that he had ever been a true general manager.

The house collapsed in laughter. David shot back, half irritated, half bemused. "Well, goddammit Massaro, if you don't improve your numbers you're not going to be a general manager anywhere." [Massaro left Xerox in 1982 to start his own company.]

Our concern at McKinsey was, Okay, great, now we have this semblance of an organization structure. This was always the point in the past when Xerox said, "Terrific, problem solved, let's get on with business as usual." And they'll change the chairs around and so forth, but nothing really happens. We were making ourselves very unpopular by saying, Hey, you guys haven't even started. You are only 1 percent of the way, not 90 percent of the way, because you have all these other things to deal with like cultural issues, all the systems issues, all the people issues, and so on. It is true in any organization that once the organization kind of gets clear, then the turf battles start. Everybody gets totally focused on that. They literally can't think about anything else until those people battles get fought.

The big thing we were always fighting for was to trim that corporate staff. When we started, it was something like 1,000 people at Stamford. We could see no good reason for more than 150. Of course, everybody is all for that until you start screwing around with their particular part of the staff. What I'm trying to give you is a feeling of tremendous turmoil, tremendous emotion, tremendous vested positions; most decisions being made on the basis of how is this going to affect me rather than the company.

Nevertheless, it's happened and it's happened pretty much the way it was set forth. McKinsey achieved a majority of the objectives it wanted to achieve. Does that mean I think the place runs today the way it should? Absolutely not. There's more to be done. Possibly the biggest thing that came out of that study was a genuine belief by virtually everyone that the company had to be run in a different way. And there was a general consensus about what that meant. Second, I think it became clear to everyone, even some of the victims themselves, that a wholesale change in management at the top was needed. Third, it positioned a lot of the young Turks into positions of responsibility. I think it convinced Kearns that some of the guys he was really nervous about could hack it. It gave David the confidence that he probably ought to bet on these young guys.

15
The Chicago 7

I absolutely guarantee you that Xerox
would not be in the typewriter business without us.

—JIM KEARNEY, Engineer

THIS IS a story of how one determined product designer, with the help of five other engineers and a secretary, ambushed IBM and helped Xerox change its entire approach to product development. It is also a story about the beginning of what has grown to more than a $500-million-a-year business, a *Fortune* 500 company all by itself, if Xerox chose to spin it off.

Jim Kearney and his group—which came to be known as the Chicago 7—developed the first Memorywriter electronic typewriter. In effect, they were Xerox's first strategic business unit.

It was mid-1978. Xerox wanted to go big into typewriters. It wanted to sting IBM. But two groups involving hundreds of Xerox employees had failed to develop a viable product. Xerox wanted an entry-level machine it could sell for $1,200. When it initially scoped the project, the best unburdened unit manufacturing cost (UMC) it could meet was $900. No good. With the most automated factory, Xerox thought it might be able to reduce that cost to $600, still not a viable project by Xerox's return on investment standards.

Enter Jim Kearney, who at the time was an independent designer. Xerox offered Kearney, then forty-six, a five-year contract with bonuses and incentives based on the final UMC of the machine and its eventual sales. Kearney is an independent sort. He shyly admits that he is a regular Xerox employee now with, perish the thought, retirement and profit-sharing benefits. However, he still relishes the fact that he is the lowest-ranking manager in Xerox. He loves to tell how he has been able to circumvent the corporate mentality. Once, during a company-wide spending constraint, he wanted to rent an additional 1,000 square feet of laboratory space. The official word was no. He went out and rented a totally new facility with an additional 2,000 square feet. "Once you do it, what can they say?" he says.

The Chicago 7, working in a small office outside Chicago with a sign on the door that read EMD for "Every Man's Dream," were pitted against "Centaur," thirty-five Xerox engineers in Dallas and Hayward, California. Both groups received the same product specifications. Centaur drowned in paperwork and cross-checking bureaucracy. By contrast, Kearney's motto was KISS or "Keep It Simple Stupid." A retired, seventy-one-year-old German toolmaker brought in his own lathe to build a working model. The number of parts was reduced to a minimum and built into modules. The closer Kearney got to a UMC of $300 the more incentives he would receive. "If the product cost ended up being $600, I didn't get a penny," he says.

Just six months after they began, the Chicago 7 had a working model. Within a year, they had a prototype with a UMC of $364. The Centaur effort wasn't even close. Since the machine met and exceeded its sales goals, Kearney collected more than $1 million in incentives over three years; his five designers another $1 million. The company got a winner. The Memorywriter, introduced in November 1981, soon surpassed IBM as the leader in electronic typewriters with more than 20 percent of the market. The module concept enabled about 200 employees working in two shifts a day to produce more than 1,000 Memorywriters in fifty or sixty configurations.

Kearney blames three factors for slowing product development at Xerox in the 1970s. The symptoms were shared by many other American companies:

1. **Rapid Growth.** People were getting, and expecting, one or two promotions a year. "No one stayed in the same job for a year or more without being promoted," he said. "If it takes two years to design and develop a product and no one is ever there two years, doesn't that say you aren't going to do it?"
2. **Matrix Management.** "The Brave New World of management," Kearney says. "No one takes the blame for anything. Everyone opens their kimono for everyone else to see. Everyone shares. No one really cares about actually completing projects. In fact, people think it's their job to not complete projects. You're promoted for not taking risks because the company never is exposed."

3. **Staged Program Management.** This is the NASA system of endless project reviews and evaluations, adopted in the sixties and seventies by many companies, including Xerox. "That's not the way
products are developed," Kearney says, because not enough attention is paid to the key phase of design. When the Memorywriter had
its first program review, Kearney was anxious to get good suggestions from outside engineers. Instead, they told him why the design
wouldn't work. When the next review was scheduled, Kearney did
it himself, "I bought a new pinstripe suit and wrote a seventy-five-
page review manual. That's what the system wanted."

Kearney's group is still together. They designed the second generation of Memorywriters, which was introduced in late 1985. The new model
costs about half as much as the first generation to produce.

"Now, I'm working on the next job," he says. "If you wait for
someone to give you an assignment, they will. You can't wait."

16
The McColough Years

"You've heard the famous story about the monkey, haven't you?" Peter McColough asks.

"No."

McColough laughs.

"That was not one of our notable successes," he says. "We had a series of early commercials that turned out to be quite famous. The little girl, whose father worked in the office, made copies on a 914 and that demonstrated how easy it was. It was a cute commercial and it was very successful. Somebody then had the brilliant idea that if the little girl could demonstrate how simple this really was, wouldn't it be great if a monkey did it."

The interviewer laughs.

"You haven't heard this story?" McColough asks again.

"No."

"Well, the agency in New York found some monkey trainer and produced a marvelous commercial where a monkey was given an original document and it shows him walking up through an office and he climbs up on the machine and he makes a copy. It wasn't faked. The monkey did it.

"We thought this was an absolutely superb way of demonstrating how simple this machine was to make letter perfect plain paper copies. We were delighted with it. Ecstatic with it. So we put it on a "CBS Reports" one night. We thought it was great. But the next afternoon we started getting phone calls from the field saying, 'Christ, are you guys stupid. We're starting to hear from the customers.' Girls who operated the machines were finding bananas on them. Signs said, 'If we can hire a monkey, why do we pay you $40 a week?' "

McColough is laughing as he finishes the story.

"We never ran the commercial again. Never again."

C. PETER MCCOLOUGH, the C. is for Charles. Few American businessmen have known such success. Few have known such frustration and failure. Few have been praised so highly, and criticized so strongly. And certainly no one in industry has had quite the same wild ride to and at the top.

It was 1954 when the Halifax-born McColough joined Haloid as a $17,000-a-year sales manager. He was thirty-two. Haloid was forty-eight. The 914 was still six years from the market. McColough wasn't impressed with the crude xerographic process Haloid demonstrated for him. He didn't see much future in making paper masters for offset printing. But Joe Wilson was impressed with McColough and Wilson's optimism about Chester Carlson's process was contagious. Even then, Wilson was talking about a xerographic machine that would do the work of offset, not just make the masters. Besides, McColough, a 1949 Harvard MBA, was looking for a company with growth potential. Even xerography had to be better than selling coal, which he did as a vice president of Lehigh Navigation Coal Sales Company in Philadelphia.

Haloid had revenues of $17 million and earnings of $884,000 in 1954 when McColough went to Chicago to start the little-known company's first reproduction service center. "I had a hell of a time getting a half decent office to work in back then," he says. If the company wanted to play in the major leagues it should have a major league field, he argued. When he became president of Xerox in 1966, revenues had grown to $534 million and earnings to almost $80 million. Xerox had already become a business legend. Wilson was still running the company, but from early on it was clear that McColough was the chosen successor. He was manager of marketing in 1957, general sales manager in 1959, and vice president in charge of sales in 1960, the year the 914 was shipped to its first customers. McColough became chief executive officer in 1968— "Peter is now the boss," Wilson said. He held that position fourteen years before giving the title to David Kearns in May 1982—"David is the boss," McColough said. During the time he was CEO, revenues went from $739 million to $8.5 billion and earnings from $100 million to almost $600 million. Today, Xerox is a $14-billion enterprise worldwide. The company grew by a factor of 1,000 during the McColough years.

The New York Times, in its story on the transfer of power from McColough to Kearns, called McColough "one of the last links to the company's glorious past and one of the major architects of its troubled present." Others have been more harsh, saying McColough's success was luck. He was in the right place at the right time. He was a weak manager. He was a venture capitalist's best friend because when he made up his mind he had to have a company, he was blind to its weaknesses.

He personally made the decision to buy Scientific Data Systems in 1969 for almost $1 billion in stock. With SDS and an earlier offer for CIT, McColough and Xerox initiated the era of megamergers in American business. He also, at one time or another, considered buying DEC and Control Data. At the same time, it was McColough who built the Xerox direct sales and service force, which is still considered one of the main competitive advantages of the company.

He made the critical decision in 1972 not to import a low-volume machine, the 2200, from Fuji Xerox. He wanted to develop a similar machine in the United States. It wasn't until seven years later, after many failures at developing its own low-volume machine, that Xerox finally imported a Fuji Xerox machine. That single decision, perhaps more than any other, helped open the door for the Japanese.

McColough focused Xerox on the mid- and high-volume segments of the copying market, concentrating on the threats from IBM and Kodak. He pushed forward the development of the 9200, at a cost of more than $300 million, to compete with offset printing in 1974. The 120-cpm machine was slow to gain acceptance in the market, but today the 9000 family is responsible for more than $1 billion in annual revenues and more than $250 million in operating profits.

He championed Archie McCardell for the position of Xerox president. And today at Xerox, almost no one has anything good to say about the McCardell years. He also selected Kearns. Today, almost everyone speaks favorably of Kearns.

Above all, McColough is a gentleman. When you talk to him you get the impression he is not distracted by anything else, you have his full attention. That trait causes secretaries, who don't work for him, to say, "I just love the man." Others in the company refer to him as, "The elder statesman of Xerox. People are kind of in awe of him." McColough is accessible to anyone in the company. In 1975, a Xerox employee who had been fired caught the next plane out of Rochester and went to Stamford, armed with his résumé, insisting on seeing McColough. The employee explained why he deserved to stay with the company. McColough agreed. The employee was reinstated. When he was chief executive, McColough had a rule that anyone who had been with the company eight years or longer couldn't be dismissed without his personal, written approval. The company had an obligation to long-time employees, he said. If the people weren't any good, they should have been dismissed in their first year or two with the company. Despite that compassion, many Xe-

rox employees blamed McColough personally for the company's problems in the late seventies and early eighties.

McColough recognizes that disparity of opinion and addresses it head-
on: "I think part of our problem, even today, is there's a disappointment in Xerox doing things because the expectations, right or wrong,
are very high. People should look at your record rather than looking at
your failures. Certainly we've had failures, but if you haven't tried anything you won't have any failures. Maybe this is a defensive way of
looking at it, but I sometimes look at Texas Instruments. It is about the
same age as Xerox. I think many people think TI has been a more successful company than Xerox. The fact is, TI is less than half our size.
They have had periods when they go into horrible losses for a year. We
haven't been close to a loss. But maybe people didn't expect as much
from TI.

"When somebody asks me the one trait an executive needs more than
anything else I tell them a thick skin. One of the things that I point out
to my friend Kearns is to get used to the bad publicity and criticism and
not take it too seriously. When you're the boss, you're going to be blamed
for everything and given damn little credit for anything. You have to
get used to it."

McColough thinks it's important for a business executive, everyone
in fact, to have a balance in their life. He didn't discover that need until
he was in his forties. Now he sails—a fifty-seven-foot Finnish Swan,
ketch rigged—swims, rides a bike, and is involved in fund-raising activities. He has a home in the Catskills where he skis most every winter
weekend. In 1968, he was active in Hubert Humphrey's campaign. Jimmy
Carter wanted to name him secretary of commerce. McColough declined. If the Democrats ever win the White House again, he would be
a leading candidate for a cabinet post.

He is a member of the board of directors of Citicorp, Citibank, N.A.,
Union Carbide, and Knight-Ridder Newspapers. McColough owns more
than 17,000 shares of Xerox stock and has option rights on another
50,000. His highest salary at Xerox was $913,000, in 1978. When he
retires, his Xerox pension will be about $400,000 a year.

During the course of writing this book, McColough, a balding man
with a medium-size build, who smokes Kent cigarettes fairly constantly,
granted us a series of three lengthy interviews. He got choked up once,
when he was talking about the last day of Joe Wilson's life. Wilson was
his mentor, and McColough calls him his "very finest teacher." There
is still a great affection.

McColough's sense of humor was also apparent. "When you finish the book, send us one," he said. "We'll make 10,000 copies."

E. Kent Damon, the retired treasurer who joined Haloid in 1949, worked closely with both Wilson and McColough. "Peter was always much more relaxed than Joe," Damon says. "I had the feeling that they were equally bright. But with Joe you realized it right away. Peter was a little more old-shoey. He didn't come off quite as fast. Joe was a real scholar."

When asked what gave him the most satisfaction in his years at Xerox, McColough began talking about the company's overall revenue growth and then said: "We've brought a lot of products to the world that made life more pleasant for people in offices. They enabled people to communicate with each other much better. You sort of feel proud of the fact you were in that business. Naturally, I think I would rather be doing that than making rubber bands all my life."

That sounds much like a statement he gave *Newsweek* magazine in 1965, when it became apparent that he was Wilson's successor. "We still want to offer products and services that really do some good in the world," he said. "And if you want to do good, you have to make some money to do it with."

Here, compiled from the interviews, are McColough's comments on some of the major issues during his tenure at Xerox. He talks about Joe Wilson and Chester Carlson. He talks about the FTC's vendetta against his company. He talks about trying to maintain the advantages of a monopoly as long as possible. He talks about the companies that got away— DEC and CIT—and the one he reeled in but shouldn't have—SDS. He talks about the old days, the new days, IBM, Kodak, the Japanese, and American industry in general:

Q.: Thirty years with the same company is a long time. Did you ever think about leaving Xerox?

A.: No. I never had any rows about anything. I always had a philosophy, though, when I was younger and didn't have any money, that I should always be prepared to walk out of a job any day and never have security or the paycheck ever influence me if I felt there was a conflict of some sort. Either a basic philosophical difference where I couldn't balance my view with somebody else's or certainly if there was going to be an ethical question. But I never really was tempted to leave the company.

I can tell you a personal comment which people find hard to believe. Like a lot of younger people, I was ambitious to move ahead. I can remember when I was made president of the company in 1966, I went through about six months of getting congratulations. Instead of feeling elated about it, I was really rather depressed. Up until then I always felt I had the option if I wanted to do something else. I was interested in politics. I had the freedom, if I wanted to, to move into a government job. But then, after planning with Mr. Wilson the succession of the company, I realized I had taken on an obligation that no matter what I wanted to do, I couldn't leave. I remember, for example, being very active in the 1968 campaign with Senator Humphrey. Certainly, if he had won I could have done something fairly significant in Washington. But I didn't really have that option any more. I lost my freedom of action.

Q.: What do you think of the guys running the company now?

A.: They're working hard on problems. I think they are doing the right things. David has a young team now—Dwight Ryan, Wayland—almost all the key people. And they all have worked outside the U.S. If you don't work outside the country, I don't think you get a true understanding of the fundamental problems of a multinational company.

Q.: Today, does Xerox have the strongest management team it has ever had?

A.: When you talk about management teams you can't just talk about individuals. I suppose by today's standards of education you might say that some of the guys around Mr. Wilson may not have been the strongest managers in the world, but he had a team that worked together. If one guy had a strength and another guy had a weakness, one guy would buttress the other. Together, as a team, they were very, very strong. I think we've had strong teams over the years, and I think we've got an extremely strong team now. We've got a new team now. That's both good and bad. The good side, obviously, is they're enthusiastic, they're aggressive. The other side of it is that they haven't had as much experience as they are going to have in a couple of years. You know, you learn in life by making mistakes, mostly. They've got to make their fair share of mistakes. I am a great believer in younger people. You can overdo this experience business. One of the problems with experience is that you can be applying the experience of the fifties to the problems of the eighties. It's not always relevant.

Frankly, one of my great satisfactions is the management team today. My greatest responsibility in the company as I got older was to make sure there was a very strong management team to carry on. Maybe some chief executives like to go back and say, "They aren't as good as

I am, they make mistakes." That's a very ass-backward way of looking at things. Properly, you should have pride in what succeeds you in the company. I feel very good about the team we've got today.

There's no greater responsibility for a chief executive officer than to try to leave a company in good hands. One of the problems very often of the so-called very strong chief executive officer—Harold Geneen perhaps being the notable example at ITT—is the guy who thinks he's so strong, therefore makes so many decisions, is so powerful that he invariably leaves a weak organization because the only guys who stay around him are the "yes" men; the good guys leave. That type of chief executive officer leaves a real vacuum after him.

Q.: One of the criticisms made of you is that Xerox never had a strong leader while you were in control.

A.: I never really believed in that. People said the same thing about Mr. Wilson, who was a very modest man. Take a look at General Motors and the Ford Motor Company. Ford has had very strong, prominent leaders. Henry Ford was of that nature. Bob McNamara was very well known. The recent chairmen of General Motors, on the other hand, have not been what people would say are strong leaders. And yet, if you look at the performance of the two companies, GM is perhaps not as colorful, but for thirty years Ford has made no inroads on them. In fact, GM is probably stronger today vis-à-vis Ford than they were thirty years ago.

I think there is a great tendency in management assessment to confuse a lot of noise with strength. Noise does not make strength. I think, over the years, Joe Wilson, who founded this business, myself, David Kearns, most of the top management, have not been noisy people. Most of them are reasonably quiet people.

How many organizations in thirty years have come from $17 million to where we are today. Not very damn many. If you look at the overall record, I don't think it's bad. I think it's damn good.

Q.: You have regularly been involved in outside activities, such as politics. Has the number of your activities increased the longer you have been at Xerox?

A.: I was pretty narrow in my focus on outside activities, recreational activities, even vacations, until about twenty years ago when I was in my early forties. Like a lot of people, I was working, had a young family, didn't really take my vacation. Then I realized that perhaps that's a mistake. You really should try to relax a little bit more, take vacations, have more time to think about things. And also, I think under Mr. Wilson's influence, I realized that I really should try to play a broader role than just a businessman and try to play a role in society. I had an obligation to work for United Way, which I had never done before, to perhaps go on some nonprofit boards, which I hadn't done before. I got interested in politics. A lot of that had to do with Mr. Wilson's influence. He deeply believed that you really had an obligation in life if you were privileged, had a good education, making some money, to put something back for other people. Not just to take. He also felt very strongly—I came to realize he was absolutely right—that the best forum for the development of leadership is to go outside the company. In the company, if you have a certain position, you don't have to give an order. You suggest something and people tend to follow. If, on the other hand, I had to work on the Community Chest, people who worked with me didn't give a damn about who I was, they worked for another company. I could only lead by persuasion and selling. That's a pretty good way to learn and then come back in the company.

You mentioned earlier, people have said Peter McColough was not a very strong leader. That's not the usual criticism I have gotten. The usual criticism over the years is that I was too involved outside the business trying to build my own reputation. That I should have done fewer of those things, served on fewer boards, not been involved in the Democratic party. That if I had minded my knitting in the company more, the company might not have had some of the problems it had. I don't agree with that but that's what I have heard.

Q.: Some of that criticism has been in the press. Was it unfair?

A.: The press has a duty to write. By and large, they try to be fair. Sometimes they inadvertantly make misstatements. I suppose this sounds rather arrogant, but I basically feel I am the guy that's playing in the game. I'm bloodied and I'm beaten up. The press is the scorekeeper. And I got to remember that I shouldn't get too mad at the scorekeeper, but to also remember that it's very different when you're playing in the game. With that philosophy I have never been bothered by public and press criticism.

Some guys I know, top business leaders, are extraordinarily sensitive to the press. Of course, when you're reading an article about your own company or yourself you're reading every line. When the public reads it they don't remember everything. I know guys who have been very, very upset, they're not sleeping at night because they got a bad *Forbes* magazine article or something. It just ain't worth it. I think it also comes down to basic philosophy. To get by in life you have to have certain basic philosophies or you're going to get in trouble. I have always believed that on a day-to-day basis, as head of big business concern, I make mistakes. First of all, you have to realize that day after day you've got half an hour to make a big decision. And you never quite have all the facts you want. If you don't make it in half an hour, let's say you're more comfortable with three hours, the first thing you know you have a backlog. So you've got half an hour to bang out that decision. You're uncomfortable, but you have to make a decision. Sometimes you're right. Sometimes you're wrong. You hope that your batting average is over .500. All you can do is the best you can with the brains God gave you in the time that is available. You can't really crucify yourself as to whether you were right or wrong all the time. If you have the satisfaction at the end of the day of saying, I just did my best, I didn't have enough time but I did my best, that's all you can do. There's no point in coming home and saying, "Oh, God, I made another mistake."

If you have a pressure position you really have to try to hit a balance in your life. Sports, recreation. If you don't hit a balance, you're going to have trouble, whether it be a heart attack, ulcers, or family problems. The usual comment about the guys who jumped out of the windows on Wall Street when the stock market crashed in 1929 was, "How could those guys commit suicide?" I think that's absolutely the wrong question. Because if you were on Wall Street forty years before 1929, and your only objective was to make money, and you took no vacations, and you had no friends—many of them didn't—and you probably had two or three wives, and your kids wouldn't speak to you, and your whole life was making money, and then the money disappeared—well, you jumped out the window. The mistake is not jumping out the window. The mistake is to make that your life.

Q.: With the FTC, the private antitrust lawsuits, IBM, and Kodak all clamoring for management attention, where did the Japanese threat rank in the 1970s?

A.: I would say they had pretty high priority. The antitrust suits were very, very serious. The cost of those lawsuits was not the legal fees, which were very significant in total dollars, but the time constraints that were put on me and a few other people. The other thing that was very serious about them was that we couldn't respond, while those lawsuits were underway, in the marketplace in the way we would have liked without jeopardizing our chances of winning or of settling the case with the FTC. I used to travel in the field and the salespeople would say to me, "Look we ought to be doing this. We ought to be offering four-year contracts. IBM offers a four-year contract. Other people do it. Are you guys dumb down there in Stamford? You guys must know that we are losing market share. Why can't we do that?'' I said, Well, maybe we are dumb. At least I know how you feel and I agree with you, but we have a very serious attack on the company from the FTC, also from SCM, Van Dyk, and some others, and we've got to win those lawsuits. And we cannot do things that are going to make us be in a position of jeopardy in those lawsuits. They've got to be won. And we did win. We didn't do some things and we were criticized in the press. "You're asleep at the switch," they said. I had to stop on a lot of the things I would have naturally wanted the company to do because of the damn lawsuits. In essence, we were holding back.

Q.: In particular, against the Japanese?

A.: The whole marketplace. We were not as aggressive as we would have liked to have been. In terms of pricing, in terms of contract terms, many other things. It was a very frustrating time for the people in the field who were trying to sell. It was a very frustrating time for all of us. And obviously, when you go through those things you can't talk about them. We had a suit against us from SCM for $500 million. If we had lost, that amount would have been trebled. The problem with these antitrust suits is that when SCM or somebody comes in and demands a million documents or so from Xerox, and gets a million documents, they can find enough paragraphs or sentences in those documents, written by guys who have no knowledge of antitrust, a branch manager in Charlotte or some guy in Rochester, that they can literally stand in front of a jury and read terrible stuff for weeks. And it doesn't mean you really violated the law. For example, a branch manager would write, "This week is killer week, we're going after IBM. Do everything you can." I wouldn't talk that way. But when you can quote that sort of stuff in front of a jury or judge, God, do you sound terrible.

You can't make everybody sensitive to what you should say or shouldn't say. Particularly the sales force. The whole purpose of sales meetings is to excite people. Even some Xerox lawyers had written documents they had considered privileged. They were ruled not privileged at the SCM trial. What a lawyer might say to you, if he really is trying to get your attention, is that "we've got serious antitrust problems" and then develop the argument for it. Now, he may not really believe that, but he wants you to pay attention to it and change your policies. When the privilege gets broken and that gets into court, you can imagine: "Here's even your own lawyer telling you that you have problems." You can't say he was just trying to scare us to change our policy.

Q.: Your antitrust problems, of course, came about in part because of the strong patent protection you built up. Did Chester Carlson's background as a patent attorney have an influence on setting up your patent protection?

A.: I would say Joe Wilson was really the driver. Sol Linowitz implemented the thing, but Joe Wilson was the guy who really believed that if we were going to spend money on inventions and research that was risky, we should get the best patent protection we could. Linowitz, for many years, was not even full time with Xerox, which is another thing that people don't understand. As a part-time employee of Xerox and as a full-time lawyer in Rochester he played the sort of unusual role of overseeing our patent department.

We felt it was very important to get strong patent protection, particularly on basics. We were concerned that without that we were a very small, very weak company. If somebody else came into the market—IBM, RCA, somebody like that—we would not have had the marketing strength, the size to fend them off.

Carlson did do an unusual thing because he was able to get basic patents that were very difficult to get around. In fact, nobody ever did get around them. We also used to do patents on widgets, various features on machines. But those are patents people can redesign around in many cases.

I think Chester did probably influence Joe Wilson. But then the orders came from Wilson and the money came from Wilson. Wilson was very wise. His philosophy was not only to get patent protection, but he was also unwilling to license people for copying and duplicating. He felt we had worked to get them, that we had to keep those to ourselves until we could develop sufficient size. We were approached by many people and he kept putting everybody off. He never would quite say no. IBM used to come up to us regularly, every two or three years, for a license. He never would say no forever, but he would say, "the time's not right. If I license you I've got to license everybody else and I'm not ready for that."

On the other hand, he pursued another interesting policy of saying that where we weren't going to be interested in using patents, we ought to license other people aggressively. So he licensed GE in xeroradiography. He gave IBM a license for their old computer equipment. He licensed Bell and Howell in microxerography, the reduction of images so they could be put on microfilm. These companies were in areas that weren't going to compete with us. He felt we might get some real revenue from them if their products worked out. None of them worked out. He also felt that by licensing a lot of companies he was protecting his company because if anyone ever tried to take us over—for years, we were afraid of being swallowed up by some big company—there would be a lot of alliances that would make it more difficult, particularly from an antitrust point of view. That wasn't perfect protection, but it made the waters muddy if someone tried to acquire the Haloid Company. He was nervous of that because Rem Rand at one point, in the late forties, made a run at the company.

A.: How important, really, were the patents to Xerox?

Q.: We never really talked about this very much because when the lawsuits were going on, frankly, I didn't want to talk publicly about it. What I tried to do and what Mr. Wilson tried to do—it really extended into my regime here—I tried to hold onto the patent situation in terms of not licensing as long as I could. I felt we had the patents. The purpose of the patent is to give you an exclusive. And there was no reason in the world why we had to license somebody just because they asked for a license. From my point of view there is nothing wrong with having a monopoly if your patents are legitimate, which they were. I think we were vindicated in that in some of the court cases.

However, at about the time we settled with the FTC in 1975, I had come to the conclusion that even though in a strict legal sense patents were given to you for exclusive use, the policy of not licensing had become counterproductive. And one of the reasons I settled with the FTC was not because we were cowardly or afraid. I felt that, generally speaking, we had to change our policy. What we found was that by not licensing, people were then claiming we had a monopoly. We had to sue a lot of people for patent violations and we, in turn, were being sued for antitrust violations. So I had come to the conclusion that it was a counterproductive strategy, involving some enormous lawsuits. It wasn't the legal fees that were most costly, but the time it took. I think I gave, just to give an example, about forty days of depositions in just the SCM case alone. I was on the stand for about ten days. And before I went on the stand our lawyers—over about four or five months—required thirty days of preparation to go on the stand. You can just judge from that. I had Van Dyk and some others going on at the same time. It was an enormous burden on my time. I hated day after day going to depositions. I had to rush from this office, come in early in the morning, spend the whole damn day in depositions.

Q.: In a way, though, weren't the lawsuits a sign of success? When you're successful you become the target.

A.: Well, I've said sort of facetiously to David Kearns and others around here, I almost half hope that at some point in the future we get some antitrust cases against us again, because if we don't it will mean that we aren't doing as well as we should. I also hope that I won't be a witness. I'm sick of it.

Q.: You're not patenting as much now as before. Why is that?

A.: One of the reasons you take out patents is to make sure no one can stop you from doing what you want to do. But there's a cheaper and easier way to accomplish that—make a disclosure. You just have to say you have invented a mechanism and you intend to use it. That means if somebody else tries to get a patent on it to stop you from using it, it won't be allowed because there is a prior invention. They can't stop you from using what you have invented.

Q.: Does a monopoly inherently lose sight of the customer?

A.: I don't think there is any question that as we got bigger and successful and a monopoly in plain paper copying, we got away from the customer. There's a tendency to say, here's a new machine we're going to do and we know better and the customer will like it. I think we really fell into that trap.

Q.: You said you were worried about IBM in the early days. Now it seems to just be hanging on in its copier business. Did you expect them to be a more formidable competitor?

A.: I would say IBM has not been particularly successful in the copier business. Nevertheless, they are somebody you have to fight all the time. A thorn in your side. They're Copier I was not a great machine. It had the IBM name on it so it did probably better than it should have done. They have never had a big market share. We feel we have been fighting the two strongest American companies, IBM and Kodak, plus Japan Incorporated.

Let me tell you this, too, there's no question that IBM changed its strategy in copiers. In 1970, we know from patent searches and other information that IBM's plan clearly was to have a complete line of copying machines. They changed their strategy. I think our response was partly responsible. I also think that as we went through the seventies and as the industry became extremely competitive and they didn't do very well, they changed their thinking. I don't know what they are doing now, but I know in the early days they didn't make any money in copiers. I know they lost money. Their machines weren't very good. I suspect also, knowing IBM people and their thinking, when things got tough in the copier business, IBM said the way to succeed in business is to leapfrog. And the thing that would be important in the future would be electronic copiers. I think they genuinely said, Well, let's get to the next round because electronics are going to take over. They haven't done a hell of a lot there either.

Q.: But you were concerned about IBM?

A.: Sure, IBM was gigantic compared to us even then, still are now. There was even more concern in the sixties, when IBM talked to us about going into the copier business, because we were still pretty small then. We felt that if we licensed IBM and they had our technology that we probably couldn't equal them in the marketplace because they would be so much stronger.

Q.: In the early days, did you think xerography would ever be this big or last this long?

A.: Let me go back to what our fears were in the fifties. Joe Wilson's fear in the beginning, and I certainly agreed with him, was not so much that we were going to have intense competition from other people in xerography. Our real fear was that we felt we had no right to think Carlson, Battelle, and Xerox had a monopoly on invention, and that Carlson's invention would be the only good way to make copies. That doesn't usually happen. Usually, somebody finds another way. We felt that the real competition would come from somebody being inventive enough to find a better way, maybe a chemical way or some other technique completely different, to make copies. We thought it was arrogant to think our system would be the one that survived. Now, I relate xerography to the internal combustion engine. It was developed around 1900. Who would think that would be the only way to power automobiles for the next eighty-five years? The xerographic process has turned out to be the same thing. Nobody has found a better way to make copies. Frankly, thirty years later, I am surprised the xerographic process is like the internal combustion engine.

Q.: Early on, you and Joe Wilson started talking about diversification. In the early 1960s, you said, ten years from now Xerox will be a totally different company.

A.: That never happened.

Q.: You didn't see the true potential in xerography. No one did. Are people still underestimating the market?

A.: A lot of people say the copying market is not a growth market. I don't think that's true because it deals with information, which is a real growth area. One of the reasons, I suppose, we never did the diversification percentagewise in our revenue that we thought we could do, was that the copying business became far bigger, far quicker than Joe Wilson or I ever imagined. We had hopes of building a very substantial business. But I think we would both be liars if Joe were here today and we said we thought it would be the size it is now. Today, Xerox probably has a couple billion dollars—leaving out financial services—in revenues outside the copying business. Compared to the total business, it's not very big. But a $2 billion company is still a pretty big company.

Q.: Even the 9200 was a diversification, in one sense, because it put you up against offset.

A.: I'll always remember when I first went up to Rochester to be interviewed by Joe Wilson for a job. That was 1954. I wasn't very interested in the job. I had seen the flat plate equipment—we called it the Standard Xerox—at the old Haloid Street plant. I wasn't very impressed with it. It was manual, very crude looking. It was designed as a copier but it missed the mark. We found out that it was so manually demanding in terms of rocking the trays back and forth that people wouldn't use it for copying. Somebody by accident found out it made very good paper offset plates. I didn't see much of a future in it, just for making plates for offset. But Joe had the vision then, based on that crude equipment, that someday we would have that equipment automated and it would do the same job as offset. It took us twenty years to do it.

Q.: Do you remember much about Joe Wilson's last day?

A.: We had a management meeting of some sort. We used to have offices in the Bankers Trust Company building in New York. At the top of the Bankers Trust we had a boardroom. Joe was there that morning—he came down the night before from Rochester—then we had a luncheon meeting with the board. The board meeting was scheduled in the afternoon. Joe had a date for lunch with Nelson Rockefeller. I remember him tapping me on the shoulders when he left the office and saying, "I'm going to have lunch with Rockefeller. I'll be back for the board meeting at two-thirty." I was at lunch with the board members when the telephone call from Rockefeller came through saying Joe had died.

[McColough slowed his speech at his point. He paused, fighting a tear.]

Very unexpectedly. He was with me all morning. His death was unexpected. I know that. I had had a conversation with him just a week or so before the meeting. I had told Joe that I wanted to be chairman. The only reason I would want to be chairman was not the title. It didn't mean anything to us. It doesn't matter whether you're CEO, or president, or chairman. I always had the understanding with Joe that he would stay chairman unless I felt that I should be chairman, only because that enabled me to make somebody else the president and chief operating officer. A few weeks, no more than two weeks before Joe died, we had a meeting in my office, and I told him that finally I felt I had to make a chief operating officer. To do that I would have to give that person [Archie McCardell] the president's title—I was then the president—and then I should take the chairman's title. This was always agreed between us. I should do that when I was ready. I felt the burdens were pretty heavy at that point. Then I had a long conversation with Joe as to what he wanted to keep doing in the company. What role he would play, what title he would have, and I noted from that conversation that he wanted a title that he would just keep until retirement. He was really thinking for many, many years beyond that, so I know that he had no inkling that he was going to die or had a serious health problem that meant certain death. I have always heard around Rochester that Joe knew he was going to die. That was nonsense. It was totally unexpected. He didn't know about it. He just sort of slumped over and that was it.

Q.: Did he have any qualms about taking another step out of the company?

A.: No, because it really didn't change his role. It was more of a title change. And he repeatedly said to me over the years that when I became chief executive officer, just as I have said to David Kearns, when you need that title let me know. It doesn't make any difference to me. I'd like to play a role but the title doesn't mean anything.

Q.: Sol Linowitz tells the story about when he and Joe Wilson were out for one of their Sunday walks and hit on the name Xerox. Was there much discussion in the company about adopting such an odd name?

A.: We had a big debate. It was such a funny name. We said, Yeah, it's going to be unique. Maybe we shouldn't do it if we aren't going to be successful, because we'll never have the advertising power to get it across. And then we were arrogant enough to say, We're going to be successful.

Q.: Joe Wilson seemed to have the ability to step back from the emotion of a situation. It was your decision to move to Stamford, for which you have received a lot of criticism. The move must have been difficult for him to accept. Yet he didn't say anything about it.

A.: Yes, sir, I understand that criticism. I've never been able to explain that in Rochester. I've heard people say, "Peter did that when he took over. Joe Wilson disagreed with him and wouldn't have done it." No, Joe Wilson never liked it. Joe Wilson never would have done it because he lived in Rochester, but he didn't disagree. You can't explain that in the town. You want me to tell you why we did it?

Q.: Sure.

A.: I've said this in Rochester, but they never paid any attention to it. What happened was that by 1969 we had taken control of Rank Xerox. We had major operations on the West Coast with Scientific Data Systems and other things. I and other key people on the corporate staff found as we traveled around, people would say in London, for example, and California, "How is your business back in Rochester." I'd always say it's not our business in Rochester. We're corporate staff. The whole thing is our business. I also got a lot of complaints from people saying, "Look, unless we work for this company in Rochester we're second-class citizens. We don't get the same capital considerations for expansion. We don't get the same promotion opportunities." After about a year or so of traveling around and getting this reaction, I said I really think this company could operate better if we take the corporate staff—which was then doing an awful lot of stuff that really shouldn't have been done by the corporate staff—and we move it to neutral ground. Also, as long as we're in Rochester, the local management will never develop. The top guys are there and you sort of smother the local management. I didn't really care where we went. I made the decision fairly quickly. The choices were Chicago, which is the central place in the country, maybe the Washington area, or the New York area, which is the most convenient. That's why we moved. It had nothing to do with any personal reason or disagreement with Mr. Wilson. That's not what you hear in Rochester, though. When you ask them they say it was a personal thing, that I didn't like Rochester, or the taxation was better in Connecticut.

Q.: But that really is a rare talent in an executive, to be able to step away from a company that you built up.

A.: Sure, it was a very tough decision because Joe was emotionally involved in Rochester. I recognize it was not particularly good for Rochester. I also want to tell you I had a very difficult time. I had to tell my wife and my children that we were going to move. They wouldn't speak to me.

Q.: So it was a good decision?

A.: Yes. If you ask almost anybody in the company they will tell you it was the right decision. I think you get a more impartial perspective of our total operation around the world than if you are right by one particular operation. You get drawn into that operation too much.

Q.: At one point in the mid-seventies was Xerox actually considering abandoning the low end of the copier market?

A.: It's true that certain people in the company, some of them reasonably high up, said we can't make any money there and therefore we ought to be out of it. But it was never accepted by top management. I don't know anyone in top management who ever felt that way.

Q.: Then why didn't Xerox take a small copier from Fuji Xerox before 1979? What was the thinking in Stamford?

A.: Xerox, despite what a lot of people think, was never very big in the small copier business. I hear statements that we had 100 percent of the plain paper business when we had the 813s and 660s. Perhaps that was 100 percent of the PPC business at the small end, but when you include everything, we were always a very small segment of it, going way back. The Japanese, with coated paper machines, were pretty strong in the small copier business back in the sixties. So we didn't have a great interest in the low end because while the volume of machines was substantial, the total revenue was not substantial compared to the middle and high end. More importantly, the margins were much worse than the other areas. It was not that attractive. Also, Fuji Xerox didn't really have very competitive plain paper small copiers until about 1978. I think if they did have machines with the right features and the right cost, we probably would have been more receptive to taking them. But they themselves were really just getting into it.

There still isn't any great money in the low end. No one's making any money of consequence. We can see how Canon is doing in various countries. They're not making any money. I would question whether there is much money made around the world in the eighteen-to-twenty-copy-a-minute machines and slower. There is a lot of investment. If there is money made, it's very small. There are a lot of machines. That's why Savin could say, at least with half a grain of truth, "We place more machines than IBM and Xerox combined." But if you look at Savin's total sales at that time, they were somewhere around $400 million. We were adding more than $400 million a year to our business. Ricoh has done the same thing recently, claiming to be the biggest copier company in the world. That may or may not be true in terms of total units. But in terms of volume, they certainly aren't the biggest, or anything like it. And in terms of profit, they aren't in the ballgame.

Q.: Why did it take so long for Xerox, even Fuji Xerox, to realize the threat from Japanese copier makers?

A.: A major part of the problem is that if you're in a business that is growing so rapidly, and is this great success, and your competition has shown some signs of getting tougher and making some inroads, but they are still pretty small and still pretty puny, it's difficult to get very concerned. I think that's the major factor.

Q.: Was there a time when market share was eroding so quickly that management here was afraid it had gone too far? Maybe Xerox couldn't bounce back?

A.: No, I don't think so. I think we felt that we had a real strength in marketing operations around the world. We had an organization which still nobody has. And the right product. Let me say something we've never really talked about: In the late seventies, we were criticized a lot for not seeing the Japanese challenge, or not meeting the competition from IBM and Kodak. That wasn't our biggest problem. What we didn't say, with all the criticisms, was that our strategy was not right. The biggest problem we had out of Rochester, frankly, was not that the strategy was wrong, but we had one hell of a problem for a while trying to implement the strategy. We just didn't do it very well. We had a strategy for the right products at the right price. Some of those products were killed in development, as you know. Others slipped and became too costly. We had, you might say, an organization failure. I don't walk away from that. We are responsible for pulling things off. I'm just saying our strategy was right.

Q.: Archie McCardell and the other Ford guys you hired catch a lot of criticism for ignoring the Japanese. Why did you bring them in?

A.: I brought McCardell in because the company was exploding so rapidly that we didn't have systems and controls, in fact, just about the time that McCardell came in [1966] I was concerned that we couldn't pay our bills even or pay our salesmen. Not because we didn't have money, but our records were so lousy. The whole system was falling apart. We couldn't bill our customers. McCardell and some of the other people put very good controls in the company, but toward the end of the seventies I felt we were stifled by controls. It was really holding us back. It was too well organized; it was too efficient in terms of controls and it was killing us.

The other very difficult problem, and it's easy to say and hard to correct, is trying to galvanize an organization that had grown rapidly with tremendous success. We had a success in the sixties and early seventies that was almost unparalleled. IBM, I think, would be the only other comparable company. If you try to tell an organization that had grown to over 100,000 people that you got to change, that things are changing in the marketplace, and they don't see it because your profit is still jumping $100 million a year, it's almost impossible to galvanize that organization. It's only through the adversity that we've been able to persuade masses of people that we have to do things differently. Just like a racehorse runs his best race when the other horses are right on his neck. It's very difficult to change; that's just a human factor. The adversity and the difficulty have been very good for Xerox. Many Xerox people have said to me over the years, "Why didn't we do it earlier? Or, if you disagreed, why didn't you issue an order?" Hell, it's simple to issue an order, but I can tell you in a big company things don't work that way. You've got to sell thousands and thousands of people that you have to do something differently. It's not easy. Yeah, we should have done it earlier, but I think if you want to be really practical and pragmatic, you can't do it until you have some of these problems. Today, people are receptive to the idea of cutting costs in Xerox. But only when they saw it was necessary, that their job was on the line, other peoples' jobs were on the line, did they respond. I think that's human nature myself.

Q.: Was Kodak's Ektaprint announcement a surprise to you?

A.: No, the announcement was not a surprise. We knew they were coming about that time. You always know these things because of patents and so forth. I would say the machine was better than we thought it would be. Two things on that that were a surprise: The quality of reproduction was better than our people anticipated—we knew Kodak would have very high quality. But the bigger surprise was their recirculating document handler. When you recirculate documents you obviously don't have to have these elaborate sorters at the end. Our people were convinced, until the Kodak machine came out, that you could not recirculate documents without damaging them, and if you damaged them you were in deep trouble with the customer—that goes back to the early days. We had some machines where we would feed documents and have some damage and lose customers. We said you can't take that chance. They did and it worked.

Q.: Were there any Xerox people who worked on the Ektaprint?

A.: I think there were a few who transferred over.

Q.: Was it a concern at Xerox?

A.: No, we have never been concerned about Kodak. We hired people from Kodak and Kodak from us. They are very ethical saying you can't bring your knowledge with you. Where you get worried is not so much that people take ideas and apply them at another company. Someone could simply say, "I cannot tell you anything but I would not try that approach."

Q.: Xerox has always been a leadership company, an example for other companies to follow. One of the raps against you, however, is that you haven't profited from all your leadership; PARC, for instance. Do you agree with that?

A.: I think there is some truth in that. We have talked about this a lot around here. One of the things that's difficult to overcome, because it is sort of the final net, net, net figure, is if your stock is low, no matter what else you do, it's very hard to establish leadership today. I see the lists of the ten best-managed companies, and those are usually arithmetically derived. I remember some years ago, when Xerox was soaring, two or three years in a row I got an award for Xerox being one of the four best-managed companies in America. I've got them at home in my library, from magazines, from *Dun*'s and what not. I didn't believe it, but the arithmetic was good. Our basic problem right now is that we are in a very competitive marketplace and we have some drags on. We should be earning $150 million dollars a year normally in Latin America. But we aren't earning much there, if anything, and we can't do a hell of a lot about Latin America. We have a good organization there, and we are set if Latin America goes again. The dollar has hurt us. We have brought out a lot of new product at great cost and we have deteriorating prices. I think when these things start to come together, earnings will be better, then I think you'll see our stock price better and the way people talk about us will be much better. Mind you, the fundamentals aren't any different, it's just that the arithmetic will be different. I'll be very happy to see it.

I think things always go too far. Joe Wilson and I used to get nervous years ago when we were growing in the mid-sixties and seventies, all the stuff written and said about Xerox made you think we could walk on water. We didn't believe it. We felt we had a pretty good team, a pretty good company. But we knew we were as human as anybody else. So I think it was overdone. Then, when it turns a little bit, I think it goes down too damn much the other way. I think there are excesses.

Q.: Philosophically, how importantly did you and Joe Wilson view the direct sales force in selling this new technology called xerography?

A.: We thought it was very important. We thought that, with the 914, not only was the technology a breakthrough, but also the pricing. If you quantify it, Joe Wilson and I felt the success of 914 might be 50 percent technical breakthroughs and 50 percent pricing breakthroughs. You just couldn't have done it any other way. We both also felt that it was fortuitous that we had a direct sales and service force from the old photographic days. We felt that was crucial. The 914 was incredibly more expensive and complex than anything else on the market at the time. The usual way of selling those copiers was through dealers. Dealers would not really be prepared to make the investment in parts that we required and certainly not be willing to make the investment in servicing that we required. We were convinced that the only way to proceed with that was a direct sales force.

We were also convinced that people would not necessarily be able to understand or even believe our claims in print advertising about the machine. It was hard to get it across. We would do the best we could, but you really had to demonstrate the machine. With our limited sales force—I think at the time we introduced the 914 we only had seventeen branch offices and about 125 salespeople—we had only limited coverage of the country. We didn't have offices for customers to come to. That's why in a marketing sense, very early and that's unusual for a small company, we went to television. We found television was an ideal way to demonstrate what the machine was and what it did.

Today, the greatest strength of the company is that we are around the world in a hundred countries and have contact practically daily with law firms, industries, and governments. We have a knowledge of the customer, relationships with the customer.

Q.: Has the dealer network gotten any stronger, more aggressive in the last few years?

A.: The dealer network was strong when we came in. Probably got somewhat weaker over time, because a lot of companies came in with their own direct sales force—IBM, SCM. In recent years, with the advent of more reliable small copiers from Japan, the dealer network became stronger again.

I'm jumping way ahead, but it's part of the story. One of our problems these days is that in 1960, because you didn't have so much inflation, we could afford to sell by a direct sales force a relatively small machine. We sold the 813 directly. Costs for sales were much less than they are now. You could afford to do that. What's happened recently, and it's not just true of the office copying business, it's true of everything in the office equipment field, the dealers now are stronger and give wide coverage because you can't afford with a direct sales organization to sell what we call onesies and twosies of low-cost products. You can't afford to sell even a $1,000 machine directly. You can go to GM, of course, and sell a $1,000 machine, because you'll maybe take an order for 400 or 500. IBM is facing this also. Twenty-five years ago, I think they would have sold their PC directly. Now the great bulk go through dealers.

No matter how big your sales force is today, there are so many dealers out there that they outgun you in the numbers of people on the street.

And they are selling a lot of stuff. Typewriters, personal computers, etcetera. There's an enormous number of people out there selling stuff against you.

Q.: Do you think Japanese copier manufacturers have ever been guilty of dumping machines in the United States?

A.: We don't think so. We can't prove a dumping problem. The Japanese are also very tough competitors at home, so there is no evidence that they are underpricing their products overseas. What may happen is that a dealer gets stuck with excess stock and then he gives some very attractive prices to get rid of it.

Q.: You've done a lot of negotiating with the Japanese, including setting up the transfer of the plants from Fuji Photo Film to Fuji Xerox. How are the Japanese to deal with?

A.: In general, I think American companies are used to a system that says when the agreement is struck that's the end of it. Japanese negotiate somewhat differently. I think that is one reason some American businessmen accuse the Japanese, unfairly, of being tricky in negotiations. In the Japanese mind, that is not the end of the negotiations. After the Fuji Xerox transfer was agreed to, the Japanese brought up other issues that we would not normally consider part of the negotiations.

For example, they wanted to know who was going to pay severance pay to the employees at the plant, even though they would still be part of the Fuji family. Also, who was going to pay the tax on Fuji Photo's profit on the plants. There was a whole series of items that unless you understand the Japanese, you thought you were being nickeled and dimed to death. That's what took so long.

Today, the two companies understand each other so well that they can cut right through the difficulties. In the old days, we had small committees that worked things out behind the scenes. If we reached an impasse, we called a halt. The Japanese would meet privately, someone would tell them exactly what the problems were. They would work something out and we would get back together a day or two later. We can cut right through that now because of the long relationship. I don't know if that's true of other American-Japanese business relationships.

People tend to say the Japanese are shifty, but I think that's unfair. You have to recognize, that's their style.

People have to understand about a partnership. People even in this country don't understand it. I've had many people say, Why didn't we get 51 percent control of Fuji Xerox? It's fifty-fifty now. I explained that if we ever have to vote, the partnership is over. The only purpose of having that vote is to control the dissolution of the company, because with a partner you've got to agree. We have partners in Latin America where we have 75 percent of the vote. We don't vote. Sometimes we have disagreements, we have to sit down no matter how long it takes and make sure that through compromise, better communications perhaps in some cases, that we come to an agreement. You can't vote.

When we went to Japan, we had a list of twelve companies that would be possible partners. Toshiba was high on the list, Fuji Photo was well down on the list. We didn't know anybody over there, but we thought other companies that were more into electromechanical devices would be a better partner. Fuji Photo was a chemical company, like Kodak. The reason we made the deal with Fuji Photo was we had a deep trust in Mr. Kobayashi's ability, his honesty, and his integrity. And we really picked our partner on the basis of personal qualities rather than company qualities. Not that Fuji Photo is a bad company, it's a good company, but it was not the ideal company for us in some ways.

Q.: Some people in your copier community in Webster really wonder whether Fuji Xerox is more a competitor than a partner. They see Fuji Xerox taking jobs away from Americans. They think the flow of information is more one way than it should be.

A.: I don't think that's accurate. People are talking just from their own limited perspectives. It really isn't a one-way street. We get a great deal of corporate intelligence on the ground from them in Japan. We wouldn't have access to a lot of that if it weren't for them.

The guys in Rochester who complain about that don't really see the bottom line. They don't see that we're getting 50 percent of the profit from Fuji Xerox. That we're getting royalties from Fuji Xerox. It's a major benefit to the company.

Fuji Xerox is getting more independent. And I think as you look down the pike ten years that Fuji Xerox more and more will stand on its own two feet. I think it's really a process like your children growing up. I don't think it's a bad process. It does cause some problems some times, but it is a good process because at the end of the path there will be a bigger, stronger Fuji Xerox that we own 50 percent of.

The fact is, I don't think you can point to anything like the successful partnership that we have with Fuji Photo in Fuji Xerox at any other American-Japanese company. It's by far the largest, to my knowledge. I don't know anything comparable to it. It's over twenty years old, so it's not new. I think it's really a great strength of Xerox to have a major, strong company in Japan, strong and competing in the Japanese home markets. I think it's a better relationship than for Kodak to have to go outside the family, so to speak, to Canon. Or for IBM to go to Minolta.

Q.: Do you think you're ahead of other American companies in figuring out how this game is played today against the Japanese?

A.: I think generally we've had an earlier, better understanding of it because we faced tough Japanese competition earlier than many other companies. Fuji Xerox got the message before we did. I remember some of the early warnings from Tony Kobayashi that perhaps we didn't take as seriously as we should have. My impression is, with some exceptions, that we probably have a better understanding of that competitive nature, the need therefore to be more efficient, the drive for productivity, than a lot of other people. I still hear too darn many Americans say the Japanese are successful because the government is helping them; they are closing their markets. All of which is true, but the basic fact is that the Japanese are very tough competitors because they are damn good. No real excuses. They have done a helluva good job. I think we have been ahead of most people.

Q.: Have you ever had any private discussions with the government about protection in the copier industry?

A.: No; We're for free trade. We have never pushed for protection for the industry. We don't believe in it. We're a multinational company. We deal around the world. We're tempted some times, but we don't think that's the right way to go. The only thing we've ever done is try to make sure the Japanese competition is fair, that they aren't dumping in this country. We have looked at that. We do not see it. We think their prices are low, but as you well know, it's a dog-eat-dog business in Japan just as much as here. If we thought they were doing unfair pricing practices in this country, we would probably lodge a protest.

Q.: Some people criticize the *Fortune* 500 companies for not being innovative. They are just large marketing organizations. Do you agree?

A.: I don't think there is anything new in that. It has been true for a long time. The strength of big companies is certainly not innovation. It's financial, marketing. On the other hand, and I know because I have bought some of them, when the smaller, innovative companies have to go beyond developing that first product into the business of building a business, labor relations, etcetera, very few of them ever make it. They reach a certain point when other skills are required and they don't make it. So I agree, but I don't think that bodes ill for the U.S. There are still lots of start-ups here. Most of them fail. Besides, if there were no big companies, who would the smaller companies and the venture capitalists sell out to?

Q.: That does seem to be the case. A lot of those people just seem eager to cash in, not to build a lasting corporation.

A.: What George Eastman was and what Joe Wilson was is something different. They both started small companies with a good product.
What was unusual was that both of them had the skill to go beyond just
product development. They had the other skills required to build a big
company. That's what most people can't do. Joe Wilson was able to
finance the company. He had skills in negotiating with the unions. He
used to do that personally.

Joe Wilson was always looking ahead twenty years. Where will we
be in twenty years? But you know a lot of venture capital people, the
people raising money, they're really get-rich-quick artists. Try to get a
nice fancy name for the company. Get some product out there that looks
like it's in the forefront of something that's hot. Whatever hot means at
the moment. Try to float the stock to the public. Whether the public is
going to be zapped two years later or not. I think they're playing that
game. They're financial entrepreneurs more than great innovators. Venture capital always goes through cycles. I can remember the bust in 1970.
It has come back. I think there is so much money being thrown at product concepts, questionable market opportunities, questionable technology that an awful lot of people are going to be burned. I think you'll
see it go through another cycle where venture capital will dry up again.
It seems like every second guy I meet is either in venture capital or
leveraged buyouts. And there are a lot of suckers out there who put money
into it.

Q.: What about the experiences you have had with venture capitalists? Art Rock was in on the SDS deal, wasn't he?

A.: Art Rock has been very successful. He's a different kind of venture capitalist. Very different.

Q.: How about Max Palevsky?

A.: Max Palevsky was an operator, he had a good product idea. But
Arthur Rock was not the type of guy I was talking about. Arthur Rock
very carefully evaluates the opportunity. He has put his money into relatively few things through the years, but then he goes in and gives skills,
particularly financial skills. He usually joins the board. He's not just
throwing his money at Max Palevsky and walking away and saying, "I
hope he makes it." He goes in and he works with that company, with
all of his experience on financial controls and how you operate the
company. He's the right type of venture capitalist. He's also very
smart.

Do you want to ask me about SDS?

Q.: Well, yes. Maybe the questioning method was a little too delicate?

A.: No, no, no. You don't have to be delicate. I made my mistakes and I'm not the least bit sensitive.

Q.: Do you harbor any ill will toward these venture capitalists?

A.: No, they didn't oversell. Let me give you the background. In 1963, I guess, we had under development the next of the xerographic devices. We had seen a lot of growth by then. Joe Wilson had very broad objectives for the company. When I first interviewed with Joe Wilson for my job, he persuaded me that there was an opportunity within Haloid for two reasons: First, he was convinced there was going to be a great need in the world for communicating information. It was going to go up dramatically because the need was there. It was pretty obvious that the amount of information, the amount of knowledge, in the world was growing exponentially and with it the need to get it from one place to another. Second, he convinced me that perhaps xerography, very unproven then, might be one way of getting that written information from one place to another, one person to another. About 1963, we felt we could develop a whole series of xerographic machines. Joe Wilson said, "Look, we're only communicating graphic information. Things that have been written down that you can copy and send from one person to another so they can share that information. But in looking at the future, all information is not going to be graphic. The computer is coming along. The computer handles information in a totally different way, in digital form. And if we're going to be big ten years or twenty years out we also got to be able to handle information in digital form as well as graphic form." And there was a lot of discussion in the company around sixty-three, sixty-four about that. There was universal agreement that if we were going to be very large in the future we also had to have that digital capability.

Then the debate occurred, how does Xerox get the capability to have the information in digital form, already having had it in graphic form in copiers and duplicators. This took quite a long time—actually several years. We thought one way to get it was to start building up our skills in research and engineering, adding people with different skills than we had at that time, who would take us into digital information handling. Obviously, the other way to do it was to acquire somebody, all at once, a computer company. But there was no disagreement in the company that digital information handling was important and that Xerox had to get into it.

I'm leading up to SDS, slowly but surely.

I think almost everybody in the company in the end accepted the fact that we were scrambling so rapidly to add engineers to plan and bring out the new copiers that we had a full plate. We did not see how we could handle the expansion of our engineering force. At that time we were probably growing at 40 or 50 percent a year in terms of people. That's quite a job. Remember that for every guy you hire you've got to interview ten. Managers were spending almost more time in hiring people than they were in running their job. But almost everybody, I can't remember anybody who disagreed, came to the conclusion that it would be too difficult and too slow and really not very practical to try to build in-house a digital capability. Therefore, that led to the conclusion that we should go out and buy a computer company. I think we finally made that decision in 1965.

I don't think it has ever been publicized. Joe Wilson and I, really as our first choice in 1965, went to Boston one day and spent the better part of the day with a guy named General Doriot. He happened to be a professor of mine at Harvard Business School who ran a company called American Research. We went to see him because American Research was sort of a venture capital firm that backed DEC, Digital Equipment Company, and at that point, the time that Joe and I were talking to Doriot, he owned 70 percent of Digital Equipment. We assumed he could have sold us Digital Equipment—that was the purpose of our visit: Try to buy Digital Equipment. We had a good day with Doriot. He really pretty much agreed that the need could be developed, that Digital Equipment was a small company that would be stronger if they joined Xerox. And he in principal agreed that that would make sense. He said, "I own 70 percent of that company, but I'm not going to force Ken Olsen, who still runs Digital Equipment, to do this if he doesn't think it's the right thing to do." So he talked to Olsen, and Olsen said he didn't want to do it. Doriot got back to us and said, "Well Olsen doesn't want to do it. That's the end of it."

So from sixty-five on we kept alive the subject of acquiring a digital capability, buying a computer company. We had some preliminary discussions with Max Palevsky in 1965 about Scientific Data Systems. And I think at that time we weren't quite ready to make a quick decision. He had some reluctance, so nothing came of those discussions. By 1968, we really felt that we had to get a digital company. We had not developed any in-house capability. It was clearer than ever that information was going to be handled more and more in digital form. We had to make a computer acquisition if we possibly could.

I sounded out some of the other companies to see if they would be interested in being acquired. Control Data. I did it indirectly; it wasn't done directly. It was done through people on Wall Street. Burroughs, not National Cash. There weren't many of them in those days. They weren't interested. Once we decided we had to acquire a digital company, we knew it would be a big investment for us, whether it was Control Data or anybody else, it would cost a lot of money.

It was then that a guy, a finder from Wall Street, brought us CIT. We really felt we should acquire digital capability, but maybe first we had to acquire some other larger base of capital, because we felt that going into the computer business would require a lot of money. We didn't have enough capital. We got out of sequence because CIT became available. I happened to negotiate that deal. I was criticized a lot for it, and we really couldn't say why we were going to do it. We were really doing it to build a bigger financial base to later acquire a computer company. We got criticized because we were offering a 50 percent premium for CIT. At that time, it was the biggest acquisition that had ever been discussed. It was roughly a billion dollars. We had a lot of opposition from Wall Street on it. We could have put it through. It always has been claimed that we backed off because of Wall Street pressure. That's not right. The deal with CIT, which really was part of our computer strategy, fell through for other reasons, not because of Wall Street pressure. We would have gotten the vote to put it through, but because we were paying such a high premium a lot of people thought it was terrible. What they forgot about was that Xerox was trading for a tremendously high PE ratio, and we weren't really giving that much up, frankly. But you know, when you go through these things, you can't always say, "We're overpriced, we're trading cheap paper for something." That's one of the problems of running a company.

All right, CIT fell through and the pressure was on from all through the organization. I don't care what people say today, but I don't know anybody who disagreed then. "Dammit McColough," they all said. "You got to buy your computer company." The only ballgame left in town was Scientific Data Systems.

I picked up the phone, I took the initiative, and called Max Palevsky. I flew out there and met with Max and Arthur Rock. I told them what I wanted. They were agreeable. We dickered about price. To digress for a second, it has been said that Max Palevsky took advantage of Xerox; that as soon as the acquisition was made he walked away from it. Max Palevsky was not dishonest about that. He said to me very clearly in the negotiations, "Peter, for years I have been working eighty hours a week trying to make this thing successful. I've gone down to fifty. And, whether you buy this company or not, I'm going to be down to ten in a year or so." There was no misrepresentation at all. It was a company that had been started in 1962. It had been successful. It had been making profits every year after the first or second year. The growth record was great. The profitability record was great. So we made a deal.

It was clearly a mistake; I don't make bones about that. They were in a lot of areas in 1970 that were related to government funding. They were supplying a lot of things to military contractors that were indirectly paid for by the federal government. They were also very large in the service business, supplying equipment to people in the service fields. Subsequent to the acquisition, around 1970, the computer business generally went into a slump. SDS was hit particularly hard. The service companies weren't buying computers. The defense industry stopped buying. SDS went into a slump.

It has been said that Xerox wrecked them. The fact was that we didn't change them at all. They got into trouble and only then did Xerox come in.

By 1975, we were losing money on it—it was only about a $100 million business. We felt that if we were to stay in that business we had to invest money. We, at that point, had changed our idea on our strategy, changed our notion of what we really had to do. We said we don't really have to be in the mainframe, CPU area of computers. We have to be able to handle information in digital form, but we don't have to sell stand-alone computers. And we aren't willing, because we have other things we want to do with our money, to lose 20 million bucks a year and make a several-hundred-million-dollar investment for the next line of SDS equipment. The result was that, in 1975, we said we're getting out of the mainline computer business. We didn't get out of everything at SDS. People don't remember that we got out of about half and kept the other half.

I don't even want to say this because it sounds defensive. SDS was a mistake, no question about it, I shouldn't have done it, but we really didn't lose anything like a billion dollars. First of all, we gave very high priced stock. Second, SDS had a good balance sheet, so we picked up a lot of assets and no debt. We got a big tax break when we sold it. More importantly, we also got a nucleus of people, many of whom we are still using, whom we never would have had. So in essence, we did acquire digital capability. I don't say it wasn't an expensive way to do it. I try not to defend it because you only sound like you are being defensive, but it isn't as bad as it has been portrayed.

Q.: Where does this reputation you have for so-called golf course deals come from?

A.: I guess because people disagreed with something. The guy who said that was not involved in the decision-making process. The decision certainly involved the top twenty or thirty people back in the sixties and they knew it wasn't a golf course deal. I can understand how people feel that way. Things are going on now that we're having a lot of serious discussions about, but the rank and file don't know it until they read about it in the paper in the morning. They don't know how much thought went into it. People did not understand CIT because we never told them why we were going to buy CIT. I could never tell them why we were going to buy CIT.

Q.: Why did you drop the CIT deal?

A.: I can't tell you. I told them when the deal fell apart that I would never say why we didn't do it.

Q.: That's forever?

A.: Yeah, I really can't break my promise.

Q.: Is it a major thing that would cause people to ooh and ahh if they knew.

A.: Yep. Yep.

Q.: It is?

A.: It had nothing to do with Wall Street pressure. It was our decision and I really can't tell. I promised them that I would not do it.

Q.: But it was something that came up on their end of the deal rather than on your end of the deal.

A.: (Very long pause. Then he said with a little laugh): I don't want to get sucked into this. I gave my word and I've never broken it. Also, very seldom can you do these things without having the thing leak out. It has never leaked out. I told them at the time that I would not tell. There were a number of reasons that usually are given. It had nothing to do with any of those things. I'd like to tell you, but I won't.

I've told very few people. I think it was only when David Kearns became chief executive officer. I said do you want to know something, do you want to know why that deal fell apart?

And, incidentally, contrary to what the Wall Street people thought, CIT would have been a good deal for Xerox. It would not have been a bad deal at all.

Q.: Wall Street seems to have a different opinion or attitude that in a lot of ways seems harmful to businesses long term. Wall Street was looking at Xerox-CIT as a super-growth company slowing down, but really what you would have had is a tremendous company coming out of it.

A.: What we were looking at is where we would be in ten years. We weren't concerned about that year's earnings or the next year's. Wall

Street has a very short range, and they are a bunch of sheep. I think that's a real problem for American industry, unlike the Japanese. The Japanese companies, because their stocks are held by banks and institutions, aren't going to show much growth in five years. They are going after new business; they are going to invest heavily, and their shareholders go along with that strategy.

In the U.S., even now, if you have a bad quarter your stock will probably take a beating. People in the company will say, "Why worry about it? The hell with Wall Street." But if you have to raise money in bonds, or have to raise money for acquisitions, Wall Street can affect your bond rate or some other thing that could keep you from getting the money, to say nothing of irate stockholders dumping your stock and so forth. I think it's a serious general disadvantage for American industry because Wall Street is very short run. And furthermore, if one guy does it the other guys do it. They say I don't know that Xerox is going to be a bad investment, but the XYZ fund thinks they are and I want to get out before they do. It's a tough problem.

I'm not sure that some of these big financial institutions pay a helluva lot of attention to some of these analysts, which may be good, it may be bad. I'm not sure that Citibank will listen to an analyst's report from Goldman Sachs or Salomon Brothers, but if they are going to put a negative out on Kodak or Xerox, they might say, "I don't believe it, but other people are going to believe it, and I'm stuck with my stock and I have to react." It isn't that they believe it.

Q.: What kind of a person was Chet Carlson?

A.: Carlson was a very quiet, private, very, very humble man. He had no airs about him. I remember when I used to go see him; he had an office in a laboratory at Xerox. I was quite young. He didn't have a title. Obviously, he was a very senior person. He would be sort of apologizing for taking my time. I was thinking just the reverse, I was taking his time. He was a thoroughly delightful guy, but very modest, very shy. I'm not sure that a lot of people understand that he really played no role, it was at his request, in the management of the company. He had a lot of influence in the company in terms of the development of xerography, suggestions in the technical area, but he was not a businessman.

I think he was quite anxious to make an invention because I think he realized that only through an invention would he ever have any money. He recognized that he was never going to be an executive or have a high post in a company, but I think his main ambition was to make an invention just for the satisfaction of doing it.

I think the amount of the money he eventually made became much greater than he thought. I had some discussions with him about this. The money didn't come until later in his life and I think the amount of money he made was a great burden to him. He used to talk about the many millions he made, about the responsibility of using that money wisely. How could he give it away wisely? I had the impression that he might have been a happier man if he had made 2 million bucks instead of the very large amount of money he made [more than $200 million]. I think he is the wealthiest inventor of all time. Other people made money, Henry Ford or Dutch Land at Polaroid, by making an invention and then making a product. But they really made their money in the manufacturing and sales end of it. Chester had nothing to do with that. In terms just of a guy making an invention or several inventions and reaping the awards of inventions alone, Chester Carlson is probably, to my knowledge, the wealthiest inventor of all time.

Did you ever hear the black bird story about him?

Q.: No.

A.: That's a damn good story. Inventors are different people from you and I. If you look at this cup and saucer, say, I think your mind immediately jumps to the conclusion that's round. A true inventor doesn't. He looks at it and says, "Well, it kind of looks round. I wonder what it is?" The black bird story really shows the mind of an inventor. Chester was a young guy, I think about a junior in high school in California. He had a cousin who was then a junior at Cal Tech. One weekend, this cousin, who was quite close to young Carlson, was spending the weekend at the Carlson home, and the two boys were looking out the window. The older boy looked at a tree and said, "Look Chester, look at that blackbird." And Chester says, "How do you know that's a blackbird?" His cousin says, "You idiot, it's the shape of a blackbird, it's the size of a blackbird, and it's black. It's a blackbird." And Carlson, very seriously, said, "Ah, but you haven't seen the other side."

That is one of the best examples I know of the mind of a true, true inventor. I think that really tells you how they think differently. They have to think differently. And really, if you think of his invention, he took physical phenomena that were already known and just put them in an application that nobody had ever thought of. Photoconductors weren't new. People had known about photoconductors for years. They didn't have very good photoconductors. He didn't invent photoconductors. He just used them in a different application.

PART FIVE
THE NEW XEROX

17

$1 Million Change

I don't know whose idea the new name was
over there at Xerox, but whoever did it, it was
a brilliant move.

—MIKE MURRAY, Kodak's
chief copier marketeer

BILL GLAVIN huddled in a hallway in Henrietta, New York, with
Shelby Carter and Wayland Hicks. It was September 8, 1982.
In just fourteen days, Glavin, then executive vice president of
Xerox, was scheduled to go before the press at the World Trade Center
in New York City and announce a new era in copying, a new generation
of machines that would become the most significant Xerox achievement
since the 914.

But he still didn't know what he wanted to call them.

Oh, they already had names—the 8600 and the 3850. And all of the
promotional and technical materials, including announcement films, had
been made. But Glavin wasn't satisfied with the names. He wanted to
change them. Such a decision, he knew, would cost a chunk of money,
would cause a lot of grumbling from the product teams, and set off a
mad scramble on two continents to make the changes in time.

"Can it be done?" Glavin asked as they were about to go into the
launch preview session on the 8600 at the suburban Rochester engineering site. Hicks was in charge of the development teams for both copiers.
The 8600 would be announced in New York and the 3850 at a product
show in Paris on the same day. Hicks had alerted his chief engineer in
London, Bill Drawe. Drawe, in turn, had brochure printers on standby.
As they entered the conference room in Henrietta, demonstration models
of the 3850 were on their way to Paris.

"It won't be easy but it can be done," Hicks said. "It's not inconceivable that we will screw up and inadvertently have a name wrong someplace in a tech rep manual or somewhere. You're going to hear it presented as a problem at this meeting but just remember, if you really want to do it, we can."

"We will never have this opportunity again in our careers," Carter said. With one crucial but expensive decision, Glavin had a chance to create the kind of marketing magic that hadn't existed at Xerox since the glory days of the 914.

The idea of changing the names had actually been kicking around Glavin's office at Stamford headquarters for several months. The new machines, and those to follow, represented the so-called third generation of Xerox copiers. They were new technology. They had sophisticated microprocessor controls that made them easier to use and more reliable. Glavin worried that this message would get lost if the names did not stand out. Xerox already had copiers called the 8200 and 3450. Carter, who had been featured in the 1978 book *Ten Greatest Sales Persons* by Robert Shook, would periodically stick his head in Glavin's office to remind his boss: "You're going to blow a big chance."

Despite the uneasy feeling that they were missing a great opportunity, there were no acceptable brainstorms on new names. The American advertising group had decided to lump the machines under the theme of Marathon copiers, keeping the original machine names. In Europe, meanwhile, Dave Springett was trying to come up with an advertising theme for Rank Xerox. He didn't like the Marathon idea. "In some European countries, people laugh at people who run," he said. Springett was thinking more in terms of the X-Series, still keeping the original machine names.

"We had these new products coming out, which were really a new dimension in copying, but they had no connection," Springett recalls. "It was just a hodgepodge of numbers." Xerox morale was low on both sides of the Atlantic, where massive job cuts were taking place. "I was trying to work two problems," Springett says. "I wanted to make everybody inside the company feel better. We really needed a boost. And, I wanted to tell the world, 'Hey, we're in this business to stay.' "

Springett went on vacation the last week of August. "I was sitting in the south of Spain literally looking at the Rock of Gibralter wondering how do I relate all of these products," he says. "There was no way around it, we had to change the names."

His proposed solution was to call the new machines XD-100, XD-200—XD for Xerox Dimension.

Springett knew that at this late date the product development teams would scream about any name changes. The only guy who could make the decision was Glavin. When he returned to London, Springett called Carter. "Dave's just the kind of incentive a staff guy like me needed," says Carter. "He's all charged up about the prospects and comes right out and says, 'Have you got balls or don't you.' I just sucked them up one more time and went into Bill and said, 'Goddamn it, we should do it.' "

By the September 8 meeting, Glavin had made his decision. "I was convinced we might be losing a marketing opportunity we could never recover," he says.

Among those attending the meeting were Eric Steenburgh, product manager on the 8600; Dwight Ryan, head of the United States marketing group; and Frank Pipp, then head of manufacturing and engineering. Xerox holds these preview meetings as close to the launch date of a product as possible. The status of the product is examined in detail from every viewpoint: engineering, marketing, manufacturing, service. The facilities for the product announcement have been rented, but the press invitations have not yet been sent. If there is a problem, the announcement can still be postponed. Usually, the meeting agenda doesn't include changing the product's name.

The feeling among the group, Steenburgh especially, was that the name shouldn't be changed at this late date. There were enough natural problems that would arise without creating more. In a slide presentation, he listed the work that had to be done to change the name on the 8600, along with his cost estimates: new nameplates and data plates, $40,000. The quickest he could accomplish that was one month. New labels for supplies, $20,000, four to six weeks. Remake introduction movie, media materials, ads, brochures, $200,000, one month. Remake operating training manuals, $25,000. Remake service education materials, $100,000. Remake manufacturing education and packaging materials, $100,000. Remake human factors operator cards, $50,000. The 3850, of course, needed similar attention.

"I appreciate the difficulty of making a change at this late date, but that's what I want to do," Glavin said. "Of the things I've heard, I like the X-Series idea best. So let's think in terms of X-10, X-20, and so forth on the machines."

"The best I can do to make all that happen is one month." Steenburgh told Glavin. "We'll have to slip the announcement two weeks."

"I don't want to slip it," Glavin said.

"Bill, you don't understand, I got to go out and have nametags specially made. If this is such a good idea why didn't you guys think of it months ago?"

"Sometimes good ideas come late, Eric. I don't care if you have a jeweler make the nameplates. I want this to happen."

The names still weren't set. Xerox lawyers had to check if any one else around the world was using an "X" in a product name that would conflict with the X-Series, and the company had to make sure there were no potential problems with foreign translations of X-Series.

"We're going to change the name," Glavin told the group. "Wayland and I will be back to you within twenty-four hours to tell you what it is."

Glavin flew back to Stamford on the company shuttle. He remembers the next morning when the lawyers and corporate marketing staff came into his office and told him that X-Series was out.

"That was stupid on my part," he says. "I should have known that because Agfa had used X for a long time. I said, 'Okay, then I want to go with something like thousands.' I said I'd like to call them one zero forty-five and seventy-five."

Glavin told his group to return after lunch with a numbering plan for the other new machines. Fuji Xerox had announced two low-volume copiers in Japan in mid-1982 (the 2100 and 2970) that he wanted to include, as well as several new machines using the same technologies then in development. The group returned at one o'clock.

"While we were sitting there, I said, 'What about calling it 10 Series?' " Glavin recalls. "Call it the 1075. Call the whole thing the 10 Series so that every number you have has to have a 10 in front of it. That was the first time 10 Series had really come out."

Steenburgh, who was expecting to hear the new name by noon on September 9, got impatient and called Glavin directly.

"It's the 1075," Glavin said.

Steenburgh gave the word to his task force.

Hicks called Drawe in London with the news that the 3850 was now the 1045. Drawe had expected an X-Series name.

"Hicks, I've worked with you for a long time, and that's the dumbest thing I've ever heard," Drawe said. "What's so magical about those four numbers?" Hicks then explained the 10 Series concept, the need to have a name that would link this new generation of products. Drawe started his group working on the changes. New nameplates had to be handmade in London and flown to Paris. They caught up with the machines after they had already been set up on the display stands for the introduction presentation.

Steenburgh estimates it cost about $1 million to make the last-minute name changes for both the 1045 and the 1075, not counting employee salaries. The Fuji Xerox 2100 and 2970 were easier. They were simply renamed the 1020 and 1035 when they were introduced to the United States in 1983.

"It also cost a lot of heartburn and a lot of sleepless nights because people literally worked fourteen days around the clock to make that list of things happen," Steenburgh says. "I took a very hard position that we shouldn't do it. From a technical and manufacturing standpoint I didn't think we could implement it in the time we had left. As it turned out, there is no question that it was a brilliant marketing decision. It was a new technology. It was something people could sink their teeth into. Our people as well as customers."

Hicks says he was ambivalent about the decision at the time. "I give Bill Glavin a lot of credit. I didn't try to fight the decision because I could see some value to it. On the other hand, I have always felt the value of the product should be the value of the product. What you say about it, the words you put around it are all fleeting and temporary. The real thing that counts is, do the doggies eat the dog food? Does the customer like the product? The hoopla that goes around it is a lot less important. In this case, however, it became very important. It telegraphed a very strong message to the outside world and also telegraphed a message inside Xerox. It gave our own organization a rallying point."

When Springett heard about the 10 Series, his first reaction was, "Good, when can we get Bo Derek to open the show." For him it was the beginning of a new attitude within the company. "Frankly, it has put us back in the copying business," he says. "If we hadn't linked those copiers together, it would have been a significantly different business for us today."

Glavin got calls at home, complaining about the money the company was wasting. No one complains now. "The interesting thing about this case is that when you ask the question, how do things happen in companies," Glavin says, "sometimes, they don't happen with a lot of forethought."

On September 22, 1982, Bill Glavin unveiled the 1075 at the World Trade Center. "This is the most significant announcement Xerox has made in some years," he said. "The 10 Series of Marathon copiers ushers in a new era in copying for Xerox."

Steenburgh and Drawe had done their work well. The movies had been remade, the manuals rewritten, the toner bottles relabeled without a hitch. Almost. The copier folks at Kodak still chuckle about the 1075 press kit they received. In it were photographs of the new machine. The nameplates had been retouched to say just "Xerox." But if you looked closely at one of the photographs with a magnifying glass it said "Xerox 8600."

No matter. In retrospect, this eleventh-hour, million-dollar name change, which may have seemed like useless number juggling to even sophisticated businessmen, was probably the single most important decision in creating a new mood at the new Xerox. The "10 Series of Marathon copiers" told the outside world that Xerox was finally unveiling new copier technology that would once again set the industry standard. It told Xerox workers, frustrated by a decade of indecision, that there were finally some new executives running things who weren't afraid to make bold moves and take some risks.

18

Learning from
L. L. Bean

We have to recognize that we don't have
any monopoly on innovation and brains in the
world.

—PETER MCCOLOUGH

A T its Webster engineering site, Xerox has a competitive analysis laboratory where sixty or more of the latest competing copiers are on display. On the wall above each copier is its "window sticker"—a listing of its features, options, and price. Company engineers are encouraged to come in and see what the other guys have to offer.

"The toughest part of competitive benchmarking is communicating to your people just how tough the opposition is," says Paul Regensburger, manager of benchmarking for the copier division. "When you come back from Japan and tell someone they have a 50 percent problem in cost, they tend to be defensive. People have to see for themselves. We like to say there are four phases to the implementation of benchmarking, based on people's reactions. The first is 'bullshit.' They don't believe it. The second is 'ah shit.' Then frustration. And, finally, action. That's the good phase; when the ball starts to roll."

Competitive benchmarking, in short, is keeping up with the Joneses, corporate style. The idea is to find the best competitors, those companies that do something at the highest quality and lowest cost, and then figure out how to do it even better. The goal is to be best of the best in all categories.

Most companies practice some form of benchmarking. Even Haloid purchased Kodak photographic paper and compared it against its own brand. But no one in American industry benchmarks as extensively as Xerox. Every department in the company measures its performance against similar operations at other companies, even lawyers and strategic planners. Walk into any Xerox facility anywhere in the world, mention benchmarking, the employees will know what you are talking about. David Kearns has made it one of the foundations of the New Xerox. Benchmarking, which really is nothing more than admitting that someone else is capable of doing something better than you, is the one factor that sets Xerox apart from those companies that have tried to battle Japan Incorporated and failed. It helps the company set targets and determine exactly how to reach them.

Xerox thinks about its competition in the broadest sense, not just the Japanese, IBM, and Kodak. In fact, some at the company think the term "competitive" is an anomoly. "From our point of view, it should be dropped," says Bob Camp, who has been a distribution manager at Xerox for more than twelve years. "You have to look at the competition, but you also have to go beyond. We're trying to find the functional best practices in business, no matter who does them."

Camp's benchmarking quest took him to L. L. Bean, the huge mail order distributor in Maine, which had instituted some computer controls to more efficiently run what Camp calls a conventional warehouse. Full automation of warehouse operations is often not practical because of the diversity of items handled. At Xerox, as at L. L. Bean, the warehousemen aren't handling full pallets of items. Instead, they often pick one item—sometimes as small as a screw—from a variety of locations. What Camp discovered at L. L. Bean was a computerized system that arranged orders to minimize the work loads of the pickers, the people who actually fill the orders. The computer literally measured the distances the pickers had to travel to fill an order and then matched the orders to the way the warehouse was stocked.

After observing the warehouse operations of several other companies, including General Electric, Xerox had its own software written to adapt the Bean method of computer-directed picking to Xerox warehouses. "I think we learned a great deal from Bean," Camp says. "It really shows the nature of benchmarking. In a lot of ways it's like a dog breeding competition. We're looking for the best of breed for a particular business practice even if the company has nothing to do with copiers."

Some of the measurements Xerox uses in benchmarking are: cost of a function—such as sales, service, distribution—as a percentage of revenue; labor overhead rate; material overhead; cost per page of a publication; return on assets; number of problem-free machines; billing error rate and service response time. Through benchmarking, Xerox will determine where the competition is today and then project where it will be in five years. Those analyses are built into the strategic and operating plans of the various divisions.

Xerox has used benchmarking as a tool in its drive to lower manufacturing costs, reduce employment levels, accelerate product development, and pay more attention to what the customer wants. It also uses benchmarking to spot other business opportunities. In 1983, Xerox began manufacturing photoreceptors for use as replacement equipment on Savin and Royal copiers. As the lowest-cost manufacturer of these items, Xerox turned a low-end disadvantage into an advantage.

Some other examples of benchmarking:

· When the competitive analysis lab has a problem with a Kodak machine they call in a Kodak serviceman. They keep a clock on the repairman to see how long it takes him to respond, how long it takes to discover the problem, how long it takes to fix, how often the repairman has to break away to get a part he doesn't keep in his inventory.

· When Canon first introduced its Personal Copiers, Xerox bought ten and gave them to customers to gauge their reactions. The customers knew the machines were Canon but not that Xerox was conducting the test. At first, Xerox found a great reluctance to take the machines, even though they were free. Customers didn't know what they would do with them in their homes. After the people had them for a while, however, they didn't want to give them up. Copy usage increased dramatically. The copy quality was good. So good, in fact, that some customers began to spurn the small convenience machines from other manufacturers in their offices because the copy quality was worse than on the PC. In a separate test, Xerox engineers determined that a Canon PC would probably run five years before breaking down. The photoreceptor on the Canon PC is a small seamless aluminum cylinder, manufactured the same way as a Coca-Cola can. Xerox never thought such a method could be used because the cylinder wouldn't be strong enough. After seeing it could be done, however, Xerox engineers are now asking themselves: If aluminum, why not cardboard or paper? Do we really even need a photoreceptor? That's the type of thinking Xerox wants to foster through benchmarking.

· As a result of studying Japanese inventory methods, Xerox has adopted what it calls central commodity management. It has reduced the number of vendors it uses for major material buys from more than

5,000 to less than 300. It balances lower costs from single, mass purchases against lower material inventory levels. In a period of two years, it reduced product cost in Webster by $100 million.

- Scientists engaged in basic research have compared themselves to Kodak, IBM, Bell Labs, and Japanese competitors. The median time from the inception of research to when the concept appears in a product has declined from seven years to six and a half. "More and more of those are software products, and software has essentially zero manufacturing time," said George Pake, founder and president of the Palo Alto Research Center. "But we are getting better."
- Xerox bought service training—where a customer is trained to take care of his own copiers—from IBM to learn what methods, learning materials, and visual aids IBM uses. Xerox has been trying to buy the same service from Kodak since 1975. Kodak won't sell.
- The Printing Systems Division in El Segundo actually took a prototype of a new product (the 4045 laser printer, introduced in early 1985), scheduled to be built at Fuji Xerox, to several companies with plants in Taiwan and Singapore to get their estimates of manufacturing costs. It found that the outside companies could build the product for half the cost. PSD president Joe Sanchez told Fuji Xerox to get its price down.
- When Kodak introduced its Ektaprint 250 in 1982, Xerox was so concerned about the possible threat that it purchased one of the new machines, for $116,000, in the first location it became available, Washington, D.C. (Though the machines may be made in Rochester, Kodak and Xerox will only place a new machine where the service force has been trained to support it.) Over the next three months a team of forty Xerox engineers, led by Hal Bogdonoff, checked out the new competition. They observed it in operation and they analyzed how it was put together. "We looked at thousands of parts, down to whether the screws were flat or Phillips head," he says. The first wave of seven engineers spent a week of seventeen-hour days tearing down the machine. "We wanted to see how it was put together, but we didn't want to get it to the point where we couldn't put it back together," says Bogdonoff. His benchmark report to Xerox management: From a technical standpoint, don't worry.

It's a tough call to buy an Ektaprint, even for Xerox. One machine can account for about half of the competitive lab's annual machine purchasing budget. Xerox could buy twenty-five or thirty small Japanese machines for the price of one Ektaprint. The joke in the industry is that

Kodak sells only two of every high-priced copier model it introduces, one to Xerox and the other to IBM.

Xerox doesn't use benchmarking as a guide to copying the competition. "That way you're always shooting behind the target," Bogdonoff says. Kearns, in his speeches, sometimes uses a story about Thomas Edison. Someone praised Edison as being a unique genius. "Actually, I'm a good sponge," Edison replied. "I absorb ideas and put them to use. Most of my ideas first belonged to people who didn't bother to develop them."

Xerox uses competitive benchmarking to foster that same attitude, to purge itself of the not-invented-here syndrome. "In 1979, when we looked at what the competition was doing, we would kind of sit back and laugh at it," says Bob Willard, a strategic planner in manufacturing. "Maybe that was part of the behavior change. We don't laugh at it anymore. There are some incredible products out there against us." Some engineers still get upset when they hear about how somebody else does things. "They often say, 'Xerox wouldn't have let us do this,' " says Lyndon Haddon. "It's almost a mystique about the old days at the company."

Haddon says a company tends to begin benchmarking when it is threatened. "Where companies go wrong is that they don't start before they're threatened," he says. "Also, companies tend to start and they quit when they feel they have gotten where they want to be. Actually, this is an ongoing process that you should never stop."

The company issues a little red booklet on benchmarking to employees. You see it in offices everywhere. It explains how each department and employee can determine what to benchmark, how to benchmark, and how to use that information to improve Xerox. "We must understand that Xerox does not, and cannot, always have the best answer to every problem we encounter. We can and should learn from others and measure ourselves against the best they can do," the booklet says.

Benchmarking began as a formal process at Xerox in 1979 in the manufacturing division. The first detailed study of Japanese methods was begun in 1980 when Charlie Christ sent a team to Japan to benchmark Japanese competitors using Fuji Xerox. At that time, Christ was a vice president for copier manufacturing. He went on to head that division and is now a corporate vice president in Stamford.

"The issue was how in the world could the Japanese manufacture it in Japan, ship it over to the States, land it, sell it to a distributor who sells it to a dealer who marks up the cost to the final customer, and the price the customer pays is [still] about what it would cost us to build the

machine in the first place," Christ says. "We didn't understand that."
One reason Xerox was so surprised about the low Japanese costs was
because it was figuring out how much it would cost Xerox to build them,
not the Japanese.

After getting the results from his Japanese study team, Christ brought
a proposal to the senior management of the manufacturing group in January 1981 that he called a "Blueprint for Survival." He characterized
the Japanese as a new challenge for the 1980s. He said the Xerox goal
was to become the low-cost producer throughout its product line. He
quoted a January 12, 1981, *Fortune* article that said Canon's goal was
to achieve a leading position in office machines and wage total war against
Xerox. "We had to aspire to world-class benchmarks in every aspect of
our business," Christ said. "We had to develop an external focus instead of an internal focus. Up to that time we had been putting in 8
percent productivity gains each year, which we thought was pretty good.
But we had been benchmarking against ourselves. We weren't looking
outside." As a part this early productivity effort, Xerox had eliminated
2,500 jobs in its North American Manufacturing Division, reducing from
12,500 to 10,000, from 1975 to 1980. It wasn't enough.

"I was convinced if we didn't change that, long term, we wouldn't
survive as the kind of company we would like to be," Christ says.
Looking out five years, planning productivity gains for Xerox and as-
suming the Japanese improved to offset inflation, he told senior management that at the end of the period Xerox would still be 21 percent
disadvantaged in productivity. He created a new curve for productivity
that would reach parity with the Japanese in 1985. That meant 18 percent a year improvement. "Personally, I thought a better assumption for
Japan was that they would offset inflation and improve about 6 percent
a year. So our curve became more like a 25 percent curve, over time,"
Christ says.

He set these performance ratio goals in order to reach 18 percent
productivity improvement each year on UMCs:

- .6 overhead worker to every direct labor hourly worker. At that time
  Xerox was at about 1.3.
- 99.5 percent on quality. Subsequently changed to 99.997.
- 1.0 month of parts inventory. Xerox was at 3.2–3.3 months.

"Frankly, the difficulty back then was the concern, 'Was it enough?' "
Christ says. "Japan is not standing still. They were at 1.0 on inventory,
and our guess was they were going to drive to .5, .6. Parts quality they
were at 99.5, and we saw them going to 99.95. Indirect to direct they

were at .8, and we saw them going to .6. In electronic components they were at one failure per million, and we saw them going to one failure per 10 million. In some cases, Japan at that time was where we wanted to be. So we went back and cranked up the requirements a little tougher.''

On October 12, 1983, Christ made another presentation, assessing how Xerox had done against its goals. Now it wasn't a question of survival, he said, but the challenge of leadership.

- By end of 1983, benchmarked to 1980, Xerox had improved product quality by 70 percent and was aiming for 93 percent by the end of 1985.
- Inventory levels were at 1.4 months. The 1984 goal was 1.1, the 1985 goal .9. Through 1983, Xerox was able to squeeze $176 million out of its copier manufacturing inventory levels. Through 1985, the goal was $225 million. This is a one-time collapse, meaning the company has that much more money to use elsewhere.
- Overhead spending had been reduced by $200 million a year, from almost $500 million a year in 1980. By the end of 1985, Xerox reduced overhead spending in the manufacturing group by $275 million, mostly by reducing manpower levels.
- In 1980, Xerox had almost 18,000 people in manufacturing in the United States and Europe. At the end of 1983, that had been reduced to 12,000. By the end of 1985, to 9,000. All of that has come out of overhead, not direct labor. All the while, output has remained about flat in terms of standard hours.

Regensburger took his first group of engineers to Japan in 1981. He took a second group to "recalibrate," as he calls it, in 1983 and now returns once a year. The basic finding in 1981 was that the Japanese were able to produce products in about half the time at roughly half the cost. Their burn rate—dollars spent per day—wasn't much different than Xerox. But the duration of the burn was much shorter. It took Xerox almost twice as long to design products. Regensburger says benchmarking has helped Xerox reduce product development costs to as little as one-third their historical cost. This has led to cost savings of as much as $30 million on a single copier program, and more than $120 million a year on the entire design process:

- Production lead times have been reduced from fifty-two weeks to eighteen weeks and less by using a selected supplier base, eliminating price quotes, concentrating on critical parts, and utilizing vendors for design suggestions.

- Prototype and model costs have been reduced up to 50 percent by using simple parts and tools, standard parts and subsystems, and early supplier involvement in parts design. This alone has saved $8 million on a single copier program.
- Quality on the 10 Series was improved by three to five times over previous machines by training suppliers and getting them to also commit to manufacturing excellence. Defects per machine were reduced by two-thirds, parts defects were reduced by 80 percent.
- Tooling costs were reduced $15 million on a single machine by avoiding expensive redesigns, selective hard tooling, and a better understanding of the critical parts in the copier.

Machine prototypes, historically, have cost Xerox about $200 a part. That was reduced to $70 a part in 1984. The benchmark target is $40 a part. Tooling costs reflect an equally dramatic decline. The best Japanese copier makers spend about $3,800 per part drawing on tooling. Xerox spent $14,000 per drawing for the 1075. A typical clean sheet, low-volume copier can have 600 to 800 drawings, mid-volume 1,400 to 2,200, and high-volume 4,000 to 5,000.

Product development time benchmarks are just under two years for a clean sheet, low-end product to three and a half years for a high-end product. Variant products are less.

"The Japanese get up to what we call form, fit, and function very early in the design process," Regensburger says. "They put a system together as fast as they can, put a prototype together as rapidly as possible, and then use that as a learning vehicle to understand the problems. The Japanese style is to get all the machines as close to production machines as they can. We used to try to figure out all the problems before we made a prototype."

A major difference was in relations with vendors. There is commitment, trust, and rapport between Japanese companies and their supplier companies. Xerox is trying to emulate that by cutting down on the number of its vendors, making early commitments to them, and bringing them in early to actually help design some parts. Another big difference Regensburger found was in the nature of the engineers themselves. In Japan, the engineers aren't as specialized as in the U.S.

"We're close to parity now with the Japanese in terms of manufacturing," Christ says. "Every product that now comes out is closer and closer to achieving that ideal in a product design sense. The thing we didn't anticipate in 1979 and 1980 was the intense pricing pressure in the marketplace. Prices are going down on average about 10 percent a year in the copier business. That tends to be loaded primarily at the low end because that's where most of the competition is. But it tends to come up market as the competition moves up market. It shows up in two ways. An absolute price decline on a given box or for a given price you can buy a better box with more features and better performance. I have assumed the market price levels will continue to decrease about 10 percent a year for the next three to five years. That has increased the challenge to us because it has put increased pressure on the margins in business.

"Dave has said it many times, we are no longer the company we once were and we are not yet the company we must be. We're in a period of transition. We're pleased by the progress we have made but frustrated that the price levels in the industry have continued to go down so that the results of our work are not obvious to a lot of people.

"We worked our way through the process of anger, denial, rejection, and acceptance of being behind the Japanese. Other companies have simply rejected that fact. A lot of companies have said Japan is dumping, or they try to fight it in the courts. I don't know of a company that has succeeded by doing that. Other companies retreat to the high margin business and by doing that just perpetuate the umbrella under which the Japanese operate. This company accepted the fact that we were getting kicked. We knew it was going to be difficult to change, but the alternative could have been worse."

Christ thinks Xerox can be as competitive as the Japanese from any of its manufacturing sites in the world. With its central commodity vendor base, Xerox can buy as cheaply as the Japanese. Labor rates are still a problem in the United States, about twice the levels of Japan, but labor is being designed out of products, down to 10 percent in copiers, so this advantage is declining. In Europe, wage rates are roughly equivalent to Japan. And because of freight, duty, and insurance to import to the United States or Europe, if Xerox can get within 10 percent of Japanese production costs it will actually be at an advantage in those countries where it manufactures.

An interesting outgrowth of the benchmarking and employee involvement processes are the Xerox Horizon Teams. Christ started these in 1983 as a way of getting the manufacturing group to think about what kind of environment the company would be operating in beyond its normal planning horizon, to 1990 and beyond. There are five teams. They focus on manufacturing assembly operations, quality improvement, materials acquisition, human resources, and scenarios. Christ picked the captains, but then each captain had to recruit his own team members. At first, team members were all salaried workers, but now even hourly production workers are joining.

"You might rationally expect over the next several years that governments that are in high-tech, information-type businesses will start to worry less about regulating trade of hard goods across their borders and start to be more concerned about regulating, taxing, and dutying information flows," Bob Willard says of the areas his scenarios team is studying. "How do you cope in a world where there's less emphasis on the shipment of hard goods in terms of duties, and instead countries try to put regulation on the flow of information, which is the business we're in?"

The materials acquisition team is focusing on how Xerox works with its suppliers to make them feel more like part of the Xerox family. "It's not let's negotiate harder, beat the price down, and shave our suppliers profit type of thing," Willard says. "It's how do we build all the right relationships with the companies that supply us so that we both do well. We use their expertise to help us design better in the types of things they are expert in. We link our information system to theirs so that drawing changes, spec changes show up directly on a vendor's computer terminal."

The quality team is focusing not only on production quality but also management quality. "Quality management is also free," Willard says. "We don't have to scrap decisions or make up for management mistakes."

19

"Can We Knock Out Kodak?"

This is a prototype of a new Xerox copier. Do not discuss it with anyone.

—XEROX WARNING SIGN

THE BLACK CADILLAC LIMO rolled onto the expressway from O'Hare. It was 8:30 A.M. The road was slippery and clogged with cars. A light, but threatening, snow was falling.

"Look at that," Chuck Otto said, motioning at the snow. "This was supposed to have passed Chicago already. How many times have we come out here for a day and had to spend the night? Better get ready to get snowed in boys."

Otto had flown to O'Hare that morning from Rochester with Wayland Hicks, Joe Marino, Sarsfield "Sars" McNulty, and George Hebert. It was January 10, 1985. In thirty days, Xerox was scheduled to launch a new high-volume copier. They had come to review the project with servicemen, salesmen, and customers who had been testing it. The review would conclude with a focus group session at a midtown market research company: Xerox people on one side of a one-way mirror, a professional interviewer and actual users of the machine on the other. Otto, Hicks & Company wanted to make sure the product was right before it was released. Preliminary results were good. If the reaction today was positive, the launch would be on February 12 as planned. Xerox had been building the machines in Webster since September. The first official installations were scheduled for March. The copier would be called the 1090. The people in the car knew that. The people they would talk to, even from Xerox, did not. They knew it by its code name, Polaris.

"One question I want to be sure we ask today is, can we knock Kodak machines out with Polaris?" Otto said. He is vice president and general manager of Xerox's high-volume business unit, which competes directly against Kodak. "The 1075 did well on new business, but not so good on rooting Kodak out once they were entrenched."

Polaris makes up to ninety-two copies a minute. Its primary target market is centralized copying departments of large companies, law offices, and government agencies. The same target as the Kodak Ektaprint 250. Polaris also has improved electronic controls and a new document handler that make it easier to use for a casual, walk-up customer with limited training. That makes it a threat to the entire Kodak Ektaprint line.

"Another question we should ask," Marino said, "is about the 225. What is Kodak doing with it? Have any of our salesmen run into it?" Marino, who had been with Xerox nineteen years, was the chief engineer on Polaris and the chief technical engineer on its predecessor, the 1075.

"I think Kodak is having some problems with the 225," he continued. "It's been almost a year since they announced it and from the information we're getting they're just now testing it on customer sites. They haven't even got their pricing completely figured out yet. When they showed it to us in Rochester they really went through a pretty standard demonstration. I wonder if they aren't having some software problems?"

"You're probably right," Otto said. "It sure seems like they have moved slowly, even for them. I don't think the 250 is going very well either. Certainly not as well as they expected."

"I'll bet the 225 will be priced right on the 1075 in Europe," Hicks said.

"I know, I know," Otto said.

He and Hicks had returned from Europe the night before. They had wagered dinner on the pricing question. Otto had bet Hicks that the Ektaprint 225 would be priced above the 1075. Kodak was in somewhat of a quandary with its machines. Even though the 225 was slower than the 250, it was more technologically advanced. It could automatically make two-sided copies of two-sided originals. The 250 couldn't.

"Do you think Kodak knows about Polaris?" Marino asked.

"I think they know something is up. They have to," Hicks said. "But they don't know just how powerful Polaris is."

"They don't know how fast it is," Otto said.

"I hope not," Marino said. "If this gets out, the boss [Hicks] will have my neck."

Everyone in the car laughed. Marino's concern about security was based in part on a bad experience with the 1075 two years earlier. A large customer in Chicago had two 1075s on test. The operators liked them. In fact, their affection was such that they nicknamed them E.T. 1 and E.T. 2, after Steven Spielberg's movie. "The machines looked so modern with their visual displays and were so friendly to use," Marino explained. Unfortunately, however, an employee of the test site company, who was about to leave the firm, let a Kodak service technician see the Xerox prototypes. So the major competitor to the machine got a sneak preview of the 1075s speed and document-handling capabilities.

Xerox had fifteen Polaris models on test in Chicago and another sixty in Rochester. Most of the machines in Chicago were located at established Xerox customers who were paying 1075 rates for the new product. "We charge for the test machines because there is some question about the quality of the feedback you get if you let them out for free," explained Hebert, a program manager for Polaris and the 1075 in the American marketing organization. Most of the machines in Rochester were in Xerox offices. The original plan was to put fifty machines on test in Chicago, but Hicks had argued against it. He felt Xerox was large enough to test its machines in-house. Once they got out, the chance of a security leak increased. "Why telegraph to your competition six to eight months in advance what you are doing?" Hicks argued.

"If we're doing the job right in Rochester on quality, we don't need such extensive outside testing," Otto said.

The few outside customers who tested Polaris argeed to place the unmarked machines in a secure area and not talk about them with anyone. Only the procurement managers were supposed to know they were Xerox machines. Even the machines tested at Xerox's own offices came with signs that warned Xerox employees: "This is a prototype of a new Xerox copier. Do not discuss it with anyone."

About thirty of the test copiers had "black boxes," modems hard-wired into telephone circuits, that transmitted information to Marino in Rochester on daily copy volume, paper jams, failure rates, service calls, and other problems. His small briefcase was filled with computer printouts on the Chicago 15.

"I can't believe the copy volume they're getting," he said. "We have a machine here that made 600,000 copies in three weeks. I thought it was a misprint when I first saw it, but I guess it must be a commercial printer."

"I think we're right to increase our volume estimate," Otto said.

"Ninety K a month seems a little low with the reliability we're getting. That's another question we should ask. How much volume do the people working with the machines think we can get and still maintain reliability?"

Xerox regularly uses Chicago as a test site and as an initial launch site for new products. The 9200 and 1075 were both tested and launched in Chicago. Xerox likes Chicago because it is a large market capable of swallowing all of the company's initial production, and it has a diversified set of customers. If you can satisfy the needs of Chicago you can satisfy the needs of the United States and a large part of the world. It's also just an hour and a half from Rochester by air, so if there are any problems engineers can be there quickly to solve them.

"Was your December as hectic as everyone else's in the Tower?" Otto asked Hebert, referring to Xerox Square in Rochester, headquarters of Dwight Ryan's sales and service group.

"Hectic?" Hebert said. "We haven't caught up yet. We took 3,000 orders for 1075s and installed 1,800. Nobody can believe it." The U.S. sales force, hampered by a slow summer, made a major push for outright sales in the last part of 1984.

The limousine reached downtown. Hicks got off at Standard Oil of Indiana. It was an old customer from his days as a sales manager. "I can still remember the first contract I signed with them in 1967," he said. "It was a $500,000 order for Xerox equipment. They use much more than that today." He, like other top Xerox managers, still makes calls on large customers. Hicks would catch up with the review later.

The first meeting at Xerox Centre was with a small group of service managers, headed by Alice Neville, who was district manager for technical services in the Chicago loop. The consensus was that Polaris was more reliable and required less service than the 1075. "What's the customer's break point on service response time?" Otto asked. It was averaging three hours in Chicago on high-volume machines from the time the customer made the initial call to Xerox, and it was expected to decrease substantially. "The tech reps must talk to the customer without exception within two hours, even if it's only on the telephone," Neville said. "That takes the heat off. It removes the fear of the unknown."

In addition to the normal inventory carried by each serviceman, the Chicago branch rents rooms in various locations around town to store spare parts. This practice speeds up calls. When a serviceman is out of a certain part, he doesn't have to drive as far to get it. Commonly used parts, such as photoreceptors, are also stored on the customer's site.

Marino said Xerox was trying to be conservative in its volume estimates for usage of Polaris. "We want to focus on UMC," he said. "If the volume estimates are too high that would justify a higher machine cost. It would also increase the need for parts. Going from 90K to 120K on Polaris will cause a small scramble on spares."

The next meeting was with the sales reps who placed Polaris in their accounts. Twenty-three people crowded into a conference room, all anxious to tell the Rochester brass what the sales force needed for Polaris to be successful. About half the sales people were women.

A saleswoman said the law offices in Chicago were jaded against Xerox because of some early reliability problems with the 1075. She had twenty clients with a total of a hundred Kodak machines, twenty-two at one account. Photoreceptors, especially, had failed much more quickly than anticipated. Xerox at this point, however, was on its fifth version of the photoreceptor and had extended its life by a factor of four. A year earlier, the company had been faced with the possibility of curtailing production of the 1075 because of a shortage of photoreceptors. Now they were lasting so long there was an oversupply.

"I know the problems on the 1075 were fixed, but maybe in this case it would be wise to wait three or four months after announcing before we install Polaris into law offices," she said.

"Our philosophy on Polaris is to get it right the first time," Otto said.

Another salesman said his customer had five 1075s but liked Polaris better. It was easier to use. The machine had been installed almost two months and hadn't logged a service call yet.

"What kind of copy volume do you expect from it?" Otto asked.

"Per month: 125,000," the salesman said.

One of the problems with the 1075 launch was that Xerox did everything special during the test phase. The machines were given absolute top priority. The company flew parts back and forth from Rochester, and that speeded up the complaint response time and gave the test customers great service, but it also skewed the test results. The special treatment stopped after the launch. With Polaris, Xerox was trying to replicate normal operating procedures during the test phase.

"You might knock the 1075," another salesman said. "But let's face it, it saved our shirts. We needed it when we did. We had a chance to knock out Kodak equipment and we didn't. Now we have another chance with Polaris."

"The customer perceives Xerox and Kodak as equals in terms of quality," a twenty-three-year veteran said. "Yet Kodak has had good retention on its old 150s. Why? They should be in Xerox's bag because of added features on our machines. It's just good Kodak marketing and service. "Give me good face off pricing, a good seeding strategy, some ability to go after Kodak and IBM, and we have a chance to set us up for the rest of the eighties in high volume."

Another saleswoman said a major concern at her account was response time on low-volume Xerox machines. It was not as fast as on the high-volume machines. "Customers compare service in total, not Xerox high-volume against Kodak high-volume," she said. "Our slow response time in the low end has a halo affect on the high end." She lost an account to Kodak because of poor service response on a mid-volume Xerox 3450, which was making just 20,000 copies a month. Another said she lost a customer to Kodak because of an eight-hour response time on a 1045.

"We're aware of that problem and we're working on it," Otto said. "With the number of service people we have now, however, you and your customers should understand that the response times will be different."

"Is anybody running into the 225 out there?" Otto asked.

"They're putting it out on free ninety-day trials in some accounts," one salesman answered. Several concurred.

"They seem to be countering with the 200 rather than the 225," the twenty-three-year veteran said. "We had a bloody bidding battle at one account. We wanted to replace the population of 150s with 1075s. Kodak bid back with 200s. We just couldn't go to their level so we ended up splitting the business."

"How about the 250?" Otto asked.

"I know an account where they just put it in on nine-month free trial," the salesman said.

"I have a customer who was going to get a 250," another said. "He took the Polaris on test and now has canceled his 250 order."

"What about the paper capacity of Polaris?" Hicks, who had just returned from Standard Oil, asked. "Does anyone complain about that?" Polaris has two paper trays, one holds 1,000 sheets and the second 500. He worried that customers might perceive they were always refilling the paper trays.

"No complaints," the saleswoman with the twenty legal accounts said. "My customers like the ability to pull out the drawers and refill while the machine is still running. They like the machine. The only thing they have to take my word on is reliability."

"One of the things I thought really worked well on the 1075 was the guarantee letter," another said. "That takes the heat off on reliabil-

ity. It said something like, 'If you don't like the machine anytime during the first year Xerox will take it back.' Is there any chance of getting
that on Polaris?''

"I liked that letter, too," Hicks said. "Why not?"

Marino was still worried about security. "Does our competition know
about Polaris?" he asked.

"Two days after it was installed in one of my accounts three people
from Pitney Bowes came to sell supplies," someone answered. "They
hadn't been there in twelve years. The suspicion is they knew."

Marino asked his final question: "Is Polaris right today?"

The general consensus: Yes.

The meeting broke up at 1:00 P.M. The Xerox managers from Rochester split up and made calls on Xerox customers in the loop area. Hicks
visited two law firms, talking to the people in charge of acquiring copying equipment and also the operators of the machines. The first customer had been testing Polaris. The second had several Xerox machines
but was also testing a Kodak 225.

"I understand you have a 225 and I was just wondering what your
impressions were of it? How it compares to our machines?" Hicks asked
the procurement manager.

"I've signed a nondisclosure with Kodak," the manager said.

"Well, I guess that settles that," Hicks said.

They talked about Xerox service and machine reliability. "You take
too long to service the 1045," the manager said.

The afternoon session was with tech reps who were actually servicing Polaris. "This is getting boring," one said. "There are no complaints. The machine likes to run. The more the better."

"It runs so well," another said, "that you actually have to keep reminding yourself to change the little things like fuser oil."

"Polaris is perceived as a more physically attractive machine than
the 1075," a third said. "That may sound funny, but I remember a dirty
4000 that just wouldn't run. We kept getting calls. We'd go out and fix
it. The customer would call again. We put new covers on it so it looked
new. It didn't run any better, but the customer stopped complaining. His
perception was that it was running better."

"I've sat in meetings like this since 1974 and I've never had a meeting like this," Hicks said. "It's hard to fish out something negative."

"This is the first time we may have underestimated volume on a machine," Otto said. "We're always trying to stretch it out. Now it's
stretching us out."

The focus group session involved nine users, all young. In theory, the machine operators didn't know they were testing a Xerox machine. But in reality it doesn't take much to figure out whose machine it is. The choices are limited—Xerox, Kodak, IBM—and the look and style of each company's machines are distinctive. Many of the operators, without prompting, referred to the copier as Polaris. The interviewer told them they were being videotaped and recorded, to help in compiling her research. They were not told about the people on the other side of the mirror.

The Xerox side of the mirror was dark. It was approaching 6:00 P.M. and the people were tired after a long day. There was some concern about catching the 7:30 flight back to Rochester, but when the session started, all eyes were riveted to the show.

"I had experience on the 1075, and this Polaris is a piece of cake," one of the users said.

"I like the smaller size of Polaris," a manager of a central reproduction department at a CPA office said. "We took out the big 9400 [Xerox] machine and I got a brand new desk. I have pictures on the wall now."

One woman said she ran an 18,000-copy job in one night. "And I didn't get no jams," she concluded.

That caused a commotion on the Xerox side.

Hicks patted Marino on the head.

"That a way, Joe," Otto said.

The interviewer asked how the operators would rate Polaris on a scale from 1 to 10. Eight rated it a 10. The ninth a 9.5.

Later, in the car to the airport, McNulty said, "My reaction is one of almost total disbelief. I didn't hear anything negative all day long. We got this list of items from the tech reps, but only about two of them would even raise your eyebrow an eighth of an inch. They are usually a tough group to please." McNulty is the manager of quality assurance for Hicks. He reviews every new machine developed in the United States, Europe, and Japan.

"My main concern now is getting the message of the feature power across to the salesmen and to the customer," Marino said. "We might need more training on just what it can do."

"I think we got a winner here," Otto said.

20

The 10 Series—
Heart of the New Xerox

It's going to be a hard game of catch-up
for the Japanese.

—DALE KREDATUS, Analyst

VEN Wayland Hicks is a little embarrassed to talk about it.
"How many people did you have working on the design of
the 1075?" he was asked.

"Let's just say somewhere between 1,000 and 1,500," the normally
straightforward head of copier development and manufacturing answered. "That was way too many. Today, I could do a similar project
with 300." It also took about seven years for the 1075 to reach the market from the initial stages of concept research. For a similar clean sheet
copier today, the whole process takes less than four years.

The process of eliminating the bureaucracy that stagnated copier
product development began near the end of the 1075 and 1045 projects.
The copier division, as determined by the McKinsey study and guided
by Kearns, was split into four strategic business units (SBUs). Kearns
put the four best people he could find in charge of those units, looking
for a mix of marketing and technical backgrounds. Hicks became head
of the mid-volume business unit. The original idea was for each unit to
develop its own strategy and business plan and then deliver products to
meet its objectives. The units have since lost some of that autonomy
because Xerox has found it impossible to have completely different
strategies in each copier segment, but the basic philosophy remains
the same.

Instead of the cumbersome matrix that had manufacturing and service engineers checking on design engineers, everyone protecting their
own turf, and no one with absolute responsibility to get the product out,

Xerox created, within the business units, what it calls product delivery teams for each new machine. Each team is made as self-sufficient as possible. The emphasis is on multifunction engineers instead of specialists. Xerox is even training engineers in both design and manufacturing disciplines. Each team is located in one place—some critical skills such as electronics hardware and software design still cut across programs—and a chief engineer, the most coveted job in the design community, is put in charge. It's his direct responsibility to develop and deliver the product to the market.

In one stroke, Xerox eliminated the seemingly endless stream of go/no go product reviews by top management that did nothing but waste time and slow the development process. Instead, the chief engineer is given a set of boundary conditions. If he stays within the cost and schedule targets there is no need for a review. No longer is time wasted preparing for a review with your boss and then another with your boss's boss.

"I don't mean this to be disrespectful to myself or the management above me or below me," Hicks says, "but the further away you get from a project the less you know about it and the less you're likely to be able to contribute to it. The amount of time our new system cuts out is absolutely amazing. I mean, Dave Kearns would sit through a program review meeting, and first of all if he would have had Christ sit there and give him counsel, he wouldn't have understood the questions to ask because he was just too far away from it."

A prime example of how the new system works is the 1090. It took just two years to develop and had just 150 people on its product delivery team. It is a derivative of the 1075, even though faster and more sophisticated. The comparison is not strictly one-to-one, but the trend is clear. Xerox is doing products faster, with fewer people, and at less cost than before. Because of that, the manufacturing cost on the 1090, which lists for $85,000, is not much more than the 1075, which lists for $60,000.

The 1090 was available around the United States within two months of the announcement date, the fastest Xerox had ever rolled out a product. The Xerox goal is to get the product technically mature at launch and achieve peak reliability in the first month. Xerox, in fact, was beating its maturity reliability goals on the 1090 with the first machines shipped to customers. In late 1985, the 1090 was receiving the highest customer satisfaction scores of any Xerox machine ever made.

One of the measures of reliability Xerox uses is defects per hundred machine drawings (DPHM). At the end of the production line a certain percentage of machines are inspected—every machine during the customer compliance test phase in the first weeks of build up. Every defect counts, even a fingerprint on a platen. Just before the European announcement of the 1040 in May 1985, Hicks was receiving daily telex reports from Venray on production and defects. The DPHM score was running 50, essentially meaning one-half of a fingerprint per machine—that was a lower score than any previous copier. "Two years ago I would put machines out that I wouldn't today," Hicks said. "In that regard, the old 1048 problem was good experience for us. It helped us get better control of the manufacturing process." With the 1045 and 1075, for instance, Xerox placed just fifty of each machine in each of the first two months of customer availability. It wanted to make sure the machines were right before it got a large number of them in the field. With more confidence in reliability and the rapid launch, Xerox placed more than 2,000 1040s in the first two months of availability.

The 1075 ranks with the 9200, introduced in 1974, as the largest and most costly product development projects Xerox has ever undertaken. The 9200 made xerography, for the first time, a direct competitor with offset printing. Peter McColough says the 9200 took eight years and cost $300 million to develop. If you press him, he will even admit a few million more in development costs. At the time of its introduction, industry analysts placed the development cost at about $500 million. The 1075 was of equal scale, meaning more than $600 million in 1982 dollars. There's the jet fighter comparison Kodak's Mike Murray likes to make.

Despite its high cost and long schedule, the 1075 is the most significant product Xerox has introduced since the 914. It boosted company morale at a critical period during the height of the employment cutbacks—many within the company were actually wondering if Xerox had a future. It put Xerox back on top in terms of technology, and its success in the marketplace, even exceeding the company's most optimistic forecasts, is creating a strong financial base, just as the 914. From its introduction to the end of 1985, we estimate that more than 60,000 1075s (based on reports from vendors who supply parts for the 1075) were placed with customers around the world. Xerox anticipated average monthly copy volume of 37,000 copies from each machine, but is getting closer to 65,000. Some machines are making hundreds of thousands of copies a month. The 1075 now accounts for more than $1 billion in annual revenue.

On September 22, 1982, the news may have been made in New York and Paris, but the big story was in Rochester. After the 10 Series was unveiled that day, some Xerox engineers in Rochester chartered a plane and flew over the town with an illuminated sign saying, "We did it." At the huge Webster plant, trailer trucks were parked at the intersections with twenty-foot signs saying, "Happy Birthday 10 Series."

It had been a long time since Xerox workers had something to cheer about. The day before the 10 Series introduction, Xerox announced its intention to buy Crum and Forster, an insurance company, for $1.6 billion. It was an admission, many observers said, that the prospect for copiers was dim. One Rochester investment firm that had been a long-time Xerox booster sold its entire Xerox holdings, 500,000 shares, because of the Crum and Forster deal.

But the 1075 and the 10 Series proved to everyone inside the company that copiers weren't dead. A few days after the introduction, Dave Kearns said the 1075 and 1045 represented "the most significant product announcements in Xerox history." He was right. In 1983, for the first time in more than a decade, Xerox actually gained market share in copiers. That trend continued in 1984 and 1985. The 1075, because it was primarily designed and built in the United States, quickly became a symbolic rallying point for a company trying to relearn how to compete and beat the Japanese at their own game.

For the first time, with the 10 Series, Xerox designed machines on a multinational basis, involving engineers from the United States, Canada, Europe, and Japan. Previous practice had been to engineer a machine for a particular country and then reengineer it before introducing it to a different country, which tended to slow down its worldwide availability and increase the costs in those other countries when it was introduced.

The 1075, in fact, was the first major Xerox copier product with a significant American component to be manufactured and assembled in the United States and then shipped to Japan, beginning just three months after it was introduced in the United States. And three months after that it was in Europe. By contrast, the 9200 didn't get to Europe until almost a year after it was introduced in the United States, and didn't get to Japan until almost two years later. Fuji Xerox engineers were brought to Webster in 1980 to help facilitate the quick introduction of the 1075 to Japan. Japanese government inspectors were flown to Webster to make sure the machine would conform to Japanese regulations. Special papers used in Japan and Asia were shipped to Webster to use in the testing.

The effort resulted in the 1075 winning a Grand Prize award for industrial design from the Japanese Ministry of International Trade and Industry, the first Xerox machine and the first American-made product to do so.

By the end of 1983, Xerox had placed 16,000 1075s worldwide, about three times as many as some analysts had forecast. IBM was forced to drastically cut the price of its Series III Model 60 copier because it didn't match the 1075 in features. Kodak speeded up the introduction of its Ektaprint 200 and 225 models in order to go head-to-head against the 1075. Kodak also made the first across-the-board price cuts in the history of its earlier Ektaprint models. "The 1075 is a better product than what was out there against us before," admitted Kodak chairman Colby Chandler.

Xerox moved to meet the demand by adding a 1075 manufacturing line in Venray, since moved to Lille, and new 1045 lines at factories in Mexico and India. The Mexico plant alone was projected to make 35,000 1045s between 1983 and 1986, and that was in addition to the huge production at Venray. By the beginning of 1984, back orders on the 1075 and 1045 exceeded the back orders on any other product in the company's history. Xerox was getting orders for fifty, sixty, even a hundred 1075s at a time. An unprecedented feat for a machine that size.

"With the 1045, Xerox is drawing a line that the Japanese aren't going to cross," Dale Kredatus, an industry analyst with Data Decisions, said at the time of its introduction. Several Japanese firms—including Ricoh, Sharp, Panasonic, and Toshiba—were expected to show 1045-level machines at the giant Hanover, West Germany, trade show in April 1983. None showed up, which surprised Xerox and caused some speculation that the Japanese, after seeing the 1045, had retreated to redesign more competitive machines. The first real Japanese competition for the 1045 didn't show up in the United States until 1984, with the Ricoh 6080, and 1985, with the Canon 7550.

"Now the competition is clearly reacting to us," Hicks says.

The doom and gloom that had permeated Xerox in 1981 and 1982 were gone. The enthusiasm of the days of the 914 was returning. Peter McColough said, "Prior to the 10 Series, people were questioning whether the company was going to stay in the forefront of technology. Now Xerox is back on top."

America's and Xerox's big advantage over Japan is technology. This is evident in the 1075 and its sister product, the 1090. The most impressive technological aspect of these machines are their series of microprocessor brains. They work in unison, talking back and forth, to continually monitor copy quality, increase reliability, and control the operations of the machine. If more electric charge is needed on the copy paper, the machine automatically boosts the charge. If more toner is needed, the machine boosts the toner. The controls make sure the 50,000th copy is as good as the first. You can be running a complicated job, like making thirty copies of a ten-page report, and the machine knows where every piece of paper is. The controls, which communicate more than a hundred messages to users through a display screen and printout, help the operator locate a problem and fix it quickly without having to call a service representative. It then continues a job right where it left off.

To pass all this information among the computer chips, scientists at Xerox's Palo Alto Research Center came up with a miniature version of Ethernet, the company's local area network. The mini-Ethernet, with some artificial intelligence software, works like a computer coach that knows what you're trying to do, then makes it easier for you by asking the right questions. PARC also used videotapes of people using the 1075 to help improve the design of the control panel. The microprocessors, developed by Xerox's electronic division in El Segundo, increase the productivity of a highly trained, dedicated user of the machine and at the same time make it easy for a casual, walk-up user to make his single copy.

The 1075 sold in the United States has up to nine microprocessors built into it, including five in the engine, the part of a copier that actually puts the marks on paper. The Japanese version has ten. The extra one is necessary because of the wider variety of paper sizes and types used in Asia. The 1090 also has nine. The microprocessors are much like those in microcomputers. The master microprocessor has a memory of about 64,000 characters. The memory of the entire 1075 configuration exceeds 100,000 characters. Previous Xerox machines weren't so well endowed with electronic smarts. The 8200, also a 70-cpm machine, had just one microprocessor as do the 9400 and 9500.

Other technical breakthroughs for Xerox on the 1075 are the recirculating document handler and the organic photoreceptor, which was under development for sixteen years. Kodak proved that the RDH was possible but Xerox perfected its use, making it possible to mix papers as thin as onion skin with 110-pound card stock. "We're trying to go from armor plate to wet toilet paper," Hal Bogdonoff jokes. Kodak's handler can be used with a much narrower range of papers. Xerox uses a vacuum corrugated feeder, which sucks the bottom sheet in a stack of originals against a vacuum roller. The sheet is then fed in a so-called racetrack configuration around an oval shape. It is stopped for exposure and then continues around to be thrown out on top of the stack. The vacuum system is more reliable, lets you handle a wider range of papers, and is less likely to cause damage to originals. The Xerox RDH can shuffle through a stack of originals, one at a time, one-sided copies or two-sided, to allow the user to make completed sets, eliminating the need for bins and sorters. Xerox engineers sometimes get cocky when they demonstrate the handler's capabilities. They will actually crumple a flimsy carbon, straighten it, and mix it with card stock, regular paper, and a photograph. "You're not supposed to do this," they say as they load the sheets. The machines shuffle through the sheets without a miss.

The organic photoreceptor, also used by Kodak, eliminates the need for a drum and allows a machine to be built in a much more compact area because the paper path has more flexibility. In major metro areas, where office rents can range up to $100 a square foot, machine size is a major consideration. The 1075, about three feet wide and from four feet to eight feet long depending upon finisher options, takes up 25 percent less space than a Xerox 8200.

The photoreceptor provided the one major bit of drama during the entire 1075 launch. The higher-than-expected machine placements and higher-volume usage combined with increased failure rates during the cold, dry winter of 1983–84 had Xerox on the verge of shutting down production. The belts were supposed to last more than 100,000 copies, but they were failing after only 40,000 to 60,000. Hicks and Steenburgh had a pilot line in Webster, designed for only short runs, running twenty-four hours a day to try to keep up with demand. "We almost ran out of belts," Steenburgh says. Engineers redesigned the photoreceptor to make it more tolerant to cold and low humidity. Current versions average more than 200,000 copies between failures.

While it was changing its product delivery system, Xerox continued to improve its manufacturing capability, a process that still continues. "The notion is that to build a 10 Series of copiers you also need a 10 Series line of factories. The latest in technology," says Bob Willard, a strategic planner who heads one of the manufacturing group's horizon teams.

Xerox has taken a flexible, generic approach to automation. The volume production levels of copiers, as even some of the Japanese companies are discovering with their low-volume machines, are not high enough to justify elaborate automation and robotic assembly geared to a single product, as in the auto industry. The theory is to automate materials handling and then have an assembly system that can handle a variety of products in the same facility, thus avoiding the spending of a lot of money to automate each new line—modular design is complemented by modular assembly. Since product lives are getting shorter, automation geared to a specific product can get very expensive.

"In years past, we designed a new production line for each new product," says Mike Martindale, manager of assembly technology. "Now what we do is design a line that can handle a certain cubic size and then we adapt that line to build a particular product of that size. This makes much more sense and is far less expensive."

At one time, copiers were made in several buildings at Webster. Now, all final assembly is consolidated into Building 200, with its million square feet of floor space. More than $40 million has been spent on automation in Building 200 since 1981, mainly in materials handling. Attached to it, Xerox erected an eight-story warehouse with 12,000 storage locations at a cost of $8 million. Fuji Xerox workers at Ebina laugh at the warehouse and wonder why it was needed, but no one at Webster laughs. Xerox estimates it has cut its parts handling expenses by 60 percent, and in the process eliminated the need for a hundred forklifts.

Before the warehouse was built, parts used to be stored at seven different locations throughout Monroe County. "I hate to say it, but in the old days we used to receive a part in Webster, handle it, take it out ten miles, store it three months in a warehouse, pay for the storage, bring it back in, handle it again, store it, bring it to the line, and put it in the machine," says Bob Sternberg, who for four years supervised operations in Building 200 and has since left Xerox for Control Data.

All parts now arrive in one location and are automatically delivered to the high-rise warehouse or assembly lines by overhead shuttle cars, conveyors, and wire-guided vehicles. Xerox names its German-made Robo Carriers after Snow White and the Seven Dwarfs. "When you say Sleepy's down, people can identify with it better," Sternberg says. It once took thirty people to deliver parts, now just two. Vendors package the correct numbers in each case so Xerox doesn't have to manually break down bulk deliveries. Most parts packages have bar codes that are read by laser scanners tied to a computer which instantly determines their destinations and how urgently they are needed.

As much as possible, Xerox tries for Japanese *kanban*, or just-in-time delivery of parts. Xerox trucks make daily runs to vendors within a forty-mile radius of the site, picking up parts for the next day's use.

Xerox is also maximizing productivity in other ways. On some 10 Series machines, for instance, reduction capability is an option for which the customer pays extra. Each machine, however, is built with that capability. If the customer doesn't want it, it isn't activated.

Xerox is training its engineers in design for automated assembly and is already testing robotic assembly of some copier components; however, it has not as yet adopted those fully automated methods for mainline manufacturing. The training takes place in the Automation Institute, a separate classroom/laboratory set up in another building at Webster. The goal is to put all 3,500 engineers in Rochester through the one-week training. The first thing the engineers are told is that by designing for automated assembly they can reduce the number of parts in a copier by 50 percent.

21

PARC—Once a "Diamond in a Cowpile"

It's gotten respectable to work on copiers.
It used to be you didn't talk about that.
                            —TOM MORAN, Xerox's Palo
                            Alto Research Center

G EORGE PAKE, the first and only president of Xerox's Palo Alto
        Research Center, never used to get many long-distance phone
        calls from Xerox Webster. Yet there was one in 1978 he'll
never forget. It came from George White, a vice president of advanced
development who was with the Xerox team designing the 1075 copier.
White thought PARC could help him with a nagging problem: Getting
the computers running the 1075 to talk to one another. White was putting together an eight-man task force of Xerox's brightest technology
experts. So far it included computer chip designers in El Segundo, California, and a copier/duplicator team in Rochester, but that wasn't enough.
"They had crackerjack people at PARC and we needed them," said
White, now at Harvard Business School.

White wanted the 1075 to be the most sophisticated copier ever made.
He wanted it to think, not in a human sense, but in some way utilizing
PARC's research in artificial intelligence. He wanted the 1075 itself to
guide users through the copying process. Most of all, he wanted the new
copier to have an electronics system that wouldn't become obsolete long
before the copier.

In research unrelated to copiers, PARC scientists had come up with
Ethernet, a network of "smart" cables to connect personal computers
with other office equipment. The advantage of Ethernet is that you can
add or subtract equipment without disrupting the network. White thought
a miniature version might solve his problems.

"He had a vision of what Ethernet would simplify," said Pake. He also thought a mini-Ethernet might give Xerox the flexibility to add computer power to the 1075 as technology improved.

Pake put together a committee of top PARC scientists and called it the computer applications working party or CAWP. However, Pake was a little skeptical. Committees usually don't work, he thought, and PARC people weren't thrilled about working on copiers. "In the early days, I can't remember any of the scientists wanting anything to do with copiers, even though they all knew that the copier business was paying everybody's salary," said Pake.

Created in 1970, PARC's mission was long-term research in computer science and electronics. Researchers probed the frontiers of integrated circuitry, artificial intelligence, and laser beams—all things that could make the paperless office a reality. Scientists snickered when you mentioned copiers.

The suit-and-tie crowd in Webster also had a tough time dealing with the laid-back, T-shirt culture at the research center. "We had a room full of bean bags on the floor surrounded by circular blackboards," recalls Gary Starkweather, a longtime PARC scientist. "The guys from back East didn't understand."

The shame was that, throughout the early 1970s, PARC had fifty-eight of the world's top hundred computer scientists under one roof. Alan Kay, a famous PARC alumnus and former Atari chief scientist, said they came because of a "wonderful bribe": Ten years of blank-check financing to pursue any research they wanted. "It was like a dream. There was nothing we couldn't do." But they had trouble getting Xerox decision-makers to take some of their ideas seriously, even one that could have revolutionized the computer industry. What Kay and his colleagues dreamed up, and built into a product called Alto, was arguably the world's first truly personal computer. Years ahead of its time, it featured a pointing device (a mouse), overlapping windows, a black-on-white screen, and graphics capability.

"All those ideas had sort of been floating around," said Pake. "So I told Alan [Kay], 'Go off and build a machine. I don't care if it has to be hauled around in a truck, but build a machine that has the power you want and is the kind of tool you want and then worry about making it portable.' Eighteen months later, we had a prototype."

Sixty Altos went out to Carnegie-Mellon, MIT, and Stanford. Kay wanted to make 10,000 or 20,000 more and get them into universities for further research. But on August 18, 1976—a day Kay says is "engraven in our hearts''—Alto's funding was cut off. Steve Jobs and Steve Wozniak, meanwhile, were down the road building the first Apple in a backyard garage. Had Xerox marketed Alto, all the Basic and CPM machines (such as Commodore and Atari) might never have appeared.

Not all the blame can be pinned on top management, however. Kay and his colleagues "never saw the computer revolution coming," Pake said. "They couldn't visualize a little thing you could buy from IBM for $3,000 being of any use."

Outsiders considered PARC one of the finest basic research centers in the United States, if not the world. It was the model, in 1984, when Bobby Inman, former deputy director of the CIA, was setting up the Microelectronics and Computer Technology Corporation, MCC, the nation's largest corporate research consortium. Yet as far as benefits to Xerox were concerned, said PARC vice president William Spencer, "PARC was a diamond in a cowpile."

Xerox had the same problem with PARC that AT&T had with Bell Laboratories: getting good ideas into the marketplace. Too many things escaped to other companies. PARC technology, for example, wound up in Apple's Lisa and Macintosh computers.

Pake's phone conversation with White began to change all that.

One of the first scientists Pake turned to was Tom Moran, a fast-talking ten-year PARC veteran and an expert on human-computer interaction. Moran remembers the first time he met with the copier people: "They came out here with a cardboard mock-up of the [1075] copier. They were trying to use a separate computer to simulate its final behavior. It was funny because they brought this flow chart . . . I swear it was thirty feet long, it filled the conference table . . . an intricate flow chart of what happens when I push this button. If this, then that. If this, then that. But once there's ten widgets in the machine, the thing just blows up. It was totally the wrong way to look at the problem.''

Moran decided he'd "try to get the copier design people into the twentieth century." But he and PARC colleague Austin Henderson were very careful not to openly criticize. "We played the role game carefully," Moran said. "They were the designers of the machine. We'd say very little about the design. What we tried to do was support their design.''

At first, Moran had been just as skeptical as Pake. He'd always thought his work was much more relevant to the office systems part of Xerox than the copier side. "I mean, that's the way we always thought of ourselves." But a new spirit, which Pake traces back to chief executive

David Kearns, had begun to sweep through the entire company, including PARC. "People began to think of the company as a whole," Pake said.

Moran could see where up to ten computers in the 1075 interacted just like any other group of computers. The issues and the problems were the same. The programming was the same. He realized the 1075 was just as interesting, just as complex as anything he'd worked on before.

The first, and biggest, problem was simplifying the 1075's electronics system. That's where the mini-Ethernet came in. Moran and Henderson used a programming tool called Trillium, based upon artificial intelligence research, to break the underlying electronics into a bunch of different cells or computer groups. Each cell handles different information—what's being copied, how many copies to make, two-sided or not. Their plan was to design the 1075 so that when you hit buttons on the outside, sensors sent information directly to these underlying cells.

"First we tried to get the panel to ask you to describe the job so the computer inside gets the information it needs," Moran said. "Then it puts up a set of questions relevant only to what you're trying to do." The mini-Ethernet would transmit the information, then monitor the state of the machine and relay the information to the user. All this was pretty complex, but Moran didn't want it to seem that way. He wanted people to be able to use the copier without a training lesson.

So with help from anthropologists at the University of California at Berkeley, PARC scientists videotaped a couple dozen people using a 1075 prototype. Some users were taped in pairs so their conversation would reveal what problems they were having. What was amazing, Moran claimed, was that even very intelligent people were having difficulty with what Xerox considered very straightforward tasks. One problem was with instructions written on little flip cards attached to the machine. "They were pretty cryptic," Moran said. For example, one said, "Open the BDA. I was one of the subjects of the experiment. I didn't know what BDA meant so I went looking around the machine. I went to pull this handle and it wanted to pull the other way. Nothing made any sense. It turned out BDA stood for Bound Document A."

Moran knew from his computer research that it's almost impossible to design a machine that anyone could operate without experience or prior instructions. However, if people could ask questions, literally hold a conversation with the machine instead of reading flip cards, their problems might be solved. "Think of it as communication between the designer of the machine, the person who wrote the instructions, and you, the user. It's like we're talking and you misunderstand me. We take a little sidetrack and we solve it. The same thing happens with a copier. That's what makes the machine friendly or comfortable.''

Not only did this vastly improve the user friendliness and diagnostics of the 1075 copier. It also sparked efforts to use PARC's expertise throughout the company. Copier repairmen, for example, soon could be using artificial intelligence training to get a basic understanding of how the electronics system operates in a copier. The Trillium design tool is now being used at a dozen or more Xerox labs.

Pake, wearing a "Team Xerox" button on his lapel, says, "I've seen an enormous improvement. People are beginning to think of the company as a whole company. The researchers here are much more oriented toward the needs of the company. I'm feeling very good about that.''

It used to be that PARC scientists saw products they'd never heard of coming out of Xerox's Office Products Division in Dallas. Or they'd see things at Webster or El Segundo that they definitely could have improved. "Today, we talk directly to the guys working on something,'' said Starkweather, who has a big poster of Chester Carlson outside his office door. "A lot of people are getting their first view of Rochester. You see a lot more PARC people on airplanes now.''

22
Dantotsu—
Best of the Best

I T's a Japanese term made popular by Tony Kobayashi at Fuji Xerox. The copier development group in Webster has adopted it as a guiding motto: Each new Xerox product must contain at least one *dantotsu* feature.

What exactly is *dantotsu*? There are several possible translations: unchallenged, absolutely brilliant, undoubtedly the best, leadership, better than best. In many ways, the best definition is the same as the goal of benchmarking, best of the best.

In addition to *dantotsu*, each new Xerox copier development program follows these principles:

- The needs of the customer come first, then comparisons to the competition and to company benchmarks are made. Prior to commitment to a new product concept, the prospective customer's needs will be validated through market research.
- Leadership products are defined as meeting customer needs for performance at lowest industry cost. A set of features should be selected at a cost below the value assessed by the customer.
- A follow-on product must not have any performance or customer-valued feature deficiencies to the product it is replacing.
- Variant products should have better feature value and performance than the parent product.
- The marketing theme for a new product should be articulated early in the development cycle.
- Commonality across products should be optimized.

Pretty basic stuff. But Xerox is the first to admit that it forgot many of these basics in the 1970s. Getting back to the basics is one of the marks of the New Xerox. "We can compete with anybody," Wayland Hicks says. "It's just three yards and a cloud of dust."

Engineers love to talk about how difficult and frustrating designing a product is. "It takes about seven 'ah shits' before you get it right," one Xerox copier engineer says. Eric Steenburgh compares the process to peeling an onion. "It's an iterative process," he says. "You begin with big, huge problems. Then you tone it down. Now you have medium-size problems. Then you have a million little problems. You have to solve every one of them in order to get the product to where it will perform satisfactorily in the field."

When Hicks took over the mid-volume business unit and was pushing the 1075 to completion, one of his most important tasks was finding the chief engineer who would actually prepare the machine for the marketplace. His biggest fear was rejection by the customer. If the market didn't like the 1075, Xerox had no fallback position. He selected Steenburgh. Some of Hicks's peers thought he made a mistake. Didn't Steenburgh work on the 3300 fiasco? Yes, but he also helped introduce the Memorywriter electronic typewriter, which was a tremendous success—within two years, Xerox replaced IBM as the industry leader.

What Steenburgh, who in 1985 replaced Charlie Christ as head of copier manufacturing, learned from the 3300 failure and the Memorywriter success he carried to the 1075 program. The combined experience on those three projects has become the basis for a new approach to product development, an approach designed to eliminate such $90-million mistakes as Moses and increase the possibility of successfully designing low-end machines to compete against the Japanese.

Xerox divides a new product development into three stages. The project can take from two to five years for a copier, longer for an office systems product. It can cost from a few million dollars for an accessory to hundreds of millions for a clean sheet product. It can involve from 100 to 1,000 people.

STAGE 1

(One to three years, 20 percent of program spending.)

Product Concept and Feasibility

- Establish a product concept; conduct initial market research: What does the customer really want? What are the needs of the market by volume band? What will the market be like when this product is ready?
- Determine how this concept fits into the overall business strategy: Does it fill a hole in the product array? Does it shore up existing business? Is it supposed to attract new business?
- Determine the various product options that can meet this concept.
- Determine what technological breakthroughs have to be made to meet the concept's goals: Can they be made? (One of the big breakthroughs on the 1075, for example, was the organic photoreceptor.)
- Evaluate each option against the competition today and what the competition will be when the product is ready. (This is accomplished through benchmarking.)
- Determine how this product can best use the company's business and technical strengths.
- Scope forecasts such as unit manufacturing cost, return on investment, and other financials.

Product Readiness

- Establish small program teams.
- Set performance goals and architecture of machine.
- Commit to meeting performance, schedule, and cost forecasts.
- Complete subsystem testing.
- Complete appearance proposal.
- Bring on a chief engineer who establishes his product delivery team.

GOOD START

The company and the product delivery team commit to the project.

STAGE 2

(Two to four years, 60 to 80 percent of program spending.)

- Test prototypes, possibly test prototypes or cardboard mock-ups with potential customers to see if machine is still on target.

- Issue drawings and work with vendors to get the best possible design at the lowest cost.
- Get control of the number of changes in the product; lock the technology in.
- Buy parts.
- Start-up manufacturing, first on a pilot line where engineers and manufacturing people work closely together, then shift to mainline.
- Develop service procedures.
- Conduct user tests, both in-house and external—use focus groups with users. Bring in engineers to watch through a one-way mirror and show them videotapes.
- Bring in service representatives and salesmen to get their reaction to the product. Have the engineers listen.
- Make initial machine installations; observe. Continue to collect data on machine failures, paper jams, copy volumes, user satisfaction.
- Rapid launch. The goal is high reliability and high production volumes from month one.

STAGE 3

(Ongoing maintenance, several years.)

- Conduct regular surveys of customers to see how they judge the machine's performance. Xerox calls this survey Customer Satisfaction Measurement System (CSMS). It samples 10 percent of each machine's population each month. These surveys are also sent to customers who have competitors' machines so Xerox can compare.
- Use that information and feedback from tech reps to help optimize field performance.
- Continue variant and accessory programs. The best time to launch a variant product, Hick says, is when the original machine is nearing its sales peak and beginning to level off.
- Manage the asset, milk the cash cow. Best example is the 9000 series.

"I would rather kill five programs in the product development phase than kill one program a year or six months before it goes to market," Hicks says. "That's when it's really tough. You have already pissed away two or three years. You have created a high level of frustration, you have spent an awful lot of money and you get nothing out of it other than grief. And, you normally leave yourself a hole in the marketplace.

What you want to do is catch that in the product feasibility stage when you have only ten or eleven people working on a program. Then, if you have four concepts competing for a niche and you kill three, you still have one that might make it.''

The critical stage is Good Start, the final filter. Some projects or product concepts are terminated early in the feasibility stage. Good Start is where Xerox makes a final determination, before committing huge resources, that a project does indeed fulfill customer requirements and fits with overall business strategy.

The company, while committing to the product itself at Good Start, also wants those working on it to commit. Xerox uses terms such as ''sign up'' and ''get ownership'' to illustrate this commitment. The chief engineer is the key job in the new product delivery system. He is appointed two or three months before Good Start so that he can assemble his own team. Within the Xerox engineering community, chief engineer is the most coveted position.

The 3300 was first introduced in October 1979, two years before Xerox switched to SBUs. It made twenty-three copies a minute and sold for $7,300. Xerox had high expectations. The 3300 was supposed to be an answer to the low-cost Japanese machines, but there were numerous paper jams and copy quality complaints. When Xerox suspended production in April 1980 more than 4,000 machines had already been placed. The company had to make special price concessions on those or replace them. Boxcars full of 3300s sat on the railroad track near the Webster plant. Meanwhile, a crash team was assembled to figure out how to fix the machine. The 3300 was reintroduced in April 1982 at a price of $5,495, but the damage was done. It was never a success. The 3300 was the last Webster-designed machine to reach the market in the low end.

''Xerox is a company where if you are a good guy and you fail, you are usually, not always, given another chance,'' Steenburgh says of his 3300 experience. Some people did lose their jobs because of the product's problems. Steenburgh says if Xerox had held the original 3300 back another three to six months, until all the problems had been discovered, the company could have saved tens of millions of dollars. ''But I don't know how you put a dollar figure on a kick in the face, which it was,'' he says.

The 3300 was an example of not fitting a specific product into an overall business strategy. Xerox violated most of the basic principles it now tries to follow:

- The machine didn't have the right product specifications. It was supposed to be a very low cost, bare-framed machine to go head-to-head against the Japanese. Along the way product planners added a semiautomatic document handler, which added cost and about 20 percent to the design complexity. It also increased failure rates when the machine went to customers.
- Reliability goals weren't tough enough. The customers did not agree with what Xerox considered an acceptable failure or breakdown rate.
- Poor trade-offs were made for cost over quality. The 3300 had to sell at a low price level to go against the Japanese, so Xerox engineers kept pounding at UMC. Hal Bogdonoff remembers demonstrating a 3300 for Dave Kearns just before it was announced. When the machine was switched on, there was a loud noise. "Kearns sort of rocked back on his heels and said, 'What's that,' " Bogdonoff remembers. The engineers had used the cheapest motor available even though by itself it exceeded the noise specifications on the entire machine.
- Xerox priced the product too high. It worried about replacing, or churning, its base of 3100s already in the field, so it priced the 3300 over the 3100. The only problem was that the 3300 didn't work as well, a fact customers were quick to point out.
- The accelerated development program—twenty-seven months for what then normally took four years—got out of control. In their haste to meet the schedule, engineers made parts drawings on envelopes. They would walk parts directly in from the shipping dock. It's good to move fast, but you still have to maintain a certain level of documentation control so that everyone can keep up with design changes. "The 3300 flop scared the hell out of us," says an engineer who later worked on the 1075. "We said, 'Oh, my God, we're not going to do that.' "
- Xerox didn't listen closely enough to its early customers. Some 400 machines had been placed in Atlanta and Miami, and the customers complained about the same problems that later forced the machine to be pulled, but Xerox didn't take the complaints seriously. It was already up to full production and it didn't know what it was building, the problems it was creating.

The entire focus of today's product development process at Xerox is to have a design, testing, and manufacturing system that assures quality with the first machine out the factory door. "There's no sin in stopping the program at the launch date if the product is not right," Steenburgh says. "Where you really run into problems is when you go to a national launch and the product is not right. All the supply pipelines are already filled with spare parts. In a nutshell, we took the 3300 into the market-place before it was ready. When we got the data back from the market-place saying, 'Hey guys, you don't have this one right.' We had to stand up to that and take the product off the market for a while. Luckily for me, I was in a different job by that time."

Xerox went to every customer who owned a 3300 and offered them an alternative. If the customer wanted to keep his 3300, Xerox took price concessions until it fixed the problems and then retrofitted all the ma-chines when it came out with the 3300 II.

The failure of the 3300 taught Steenburgh to pay more attention to the customers and focus more on their early responses. He learned that customer complaints on a few machines could be indicative of major problems. For the Memorywriter and 1075 he did a lot of one-way mir-ror observation of customers actually using the equipment. He also brought in engineers to watch. "There's nothing like a one-way mirror to moti-vate an engineer," he says. "When a customer complains about some-thing, the engineers say, 'Hey, that's my piece of the action they're talking about.' They go right back and fix the problem."

After the 3300, Steenburgh became a vice president for market de-velopment on the Memorywriter. The product was made in Dallas, but he worked out of the sales group at Xerox Square in Rochester. One of the reasons the Memorywriter was such a big success was that it was marketed by the Xerox copier sales force, as opposed to the ill-fated Xerox 820 personal computer, which was sold by the Office Product's Division's own sales force. There was some argument over using copier people to sell typewriters. Some felt Xerox needed a specialized sales force to sell a new product. Copier people wouldn't know how to do it. Besides, it would divert time from copiers and the salesmen wouldn't meet their targets. Steenburgh argued that it was synergistic, the sales-men would actually sell more of both. Xerox put a demonstration chip in the machine for copier salesmen to fall back on if necessary during a customer demonstration. The chip would put the machine through its paces. Steenburgh created an 800 number for salesmen to call from a customer's office to find out the exact delivery date of the machine. The operator knew the production schedule at the plant. Xerox shipped ma-chines straight from the end of the line to the customer. Steenburgh was right. Sales revenues per copier salesman doubled with the addition of the Memorywriter.

"We had been very aggressive in marketing plans for the Memorywriter," Steenburgh says. "If you can't get 20 percent of a marketplace you won't be a big player in it long term. If we were going to sting Big Blue, we wanted to sting them good and hard and get their attention."

Xerox did its own human factors testing on the Memorywriter by bringing in several hundred operators and having them work on machines for periods ranging from four hours to a day. The operators had some suggestions for improvements, but the basic message was: You have it right. Steenburgh wanted to be sure. He hired a market research firm in Dallas and gave it twelve early prototypes, models usually reserved for engineers. The Dallas firm had people come in and use the machines for two weeks at a time.

"We found people at the end of that period saying, 'You don't have it right,' " Steenburgh said. "We said how can this be? What did we do wrong? When our engineers analyzed the data they found we didn't have the touch right on the keyboard. If someone was using the machine for only half a day or so, they couldn't use it to its full capability. Those operators were more forgiving. In their unfamiliarity with the machines, they were more willing to take blame for some problems rather than place it on the machines. If you use the machine for two weeks, however, it's different. You are better able to lay problems correctly on the machine itself. The keys don't feel right. The touch was too light. The operators were making more errors than normal."

Because of the extra research, Xerox made the keyboard vendor stiffen the touch. The new keyboards were again tested with operators and this time they liked the machines. "If we had not done that second piece of market research, we would have gotten thousands and thousands of Memorywriters into the marketplace before we would have found the right feedback and understood the problem," Steenburgh says. "Then we would have really been in trouble."

On another subject, market research told Steenburgh not to do something. He originally wanted to call the Memorywriter the Freedom Machine. He prepared an elaborate presentation, complete with violin music. "It brought tears to my eyes it was so impressive," says Jim Kearney, whose engineering group designed the Memorywriter. What Xerox and Steenburgh discovered, however, was that the word *freedom* was already closely associated with another product in the market: sanitary napkins. "We dropped that idea real quick when we found that out," Steenburgh says.

When he was working on the Memorywriter at Xerox Square, Steenburgh first came in contact with Hicks—both men begin their workdays early. They would meet at 6:30 in the morning and be the only two people on their floor. When Hicks went to Webster to head the mid-volume SBU, he called Steenburgh.

"Wayland said, 'Get your butt out here and set your career straight. You learned from the 3300,' " Steenburgh recalls. "The 1075 was the biggest thing we had going in Xerox. I took a shot at it knowing if it didn't succeed I'd be gone. It was clear. Two times is bad, you know. It would have been all over."

Aware of the extensive new technology in the 1075 and the problems that come with it, and knowing he didn't have enough customer contact on the 3300, Steenburgh started to test the 1075 with customers a year before its launch. He began with three machines in the engineering building at Webster for Xerox people to use. Then, when the engineers' confidence level in the machine improved, Steenburgh put machines outside, one in marketing and one in administration at Xerox Square. Machines were installed at two test sites in Chicago, then twenty. Focus groups were set up and engineers were brought to Chicago. Tech reps, the people who service the machines, were brought in periodically before the launch and a few months after. All the while, Steenburgh and Xerox were listening to what the customers said and making improvements based on those suggestions.

As a last precaution, Steenburgh called Kearns and invited him to tour the 1075 manufacturing line before the product launch. He remembered an embarrassing meeting with employees during the height of the 3300 problems in 1980. A worker stood up and told Kearns that anyone on the production line could have told him the 3300 was not ready to be released.

"I told David, we're not going to have that again," Steenburgh recalls. "If there is anybody out there who is going to tell you something they haven't told me, please come up and find out." Kearns went to Webster and spent half a day wandering around the line talking to production workers. He told the workers how important the project was, how the quality had to be right, and asked them to speak up if they thought something was wrong. When Steenburgh took him to the airport later, Kearns said, "You made me part of this decision so if this one's screwed up we're both to blame."

"I don't think there has been any product that was ever launched that didn't have problems," Steenburgh says. "But this launch had customer sensitivity, it had focus, it was a helluva good training program. Everybody was going to make it work."

23

Getting Lean
and Mean

We've been so busy cleaning up the mess
down on the factory floor, we've forgotten the
mess upstairs.

—DAVID KEARNS

OV. 2, 1981, the front-page headline of the Rochester *Times-
Union* was "Xerox starts widespread firings here." The report was based entirely upon unnamed sources, mostly employees agonizing over their fates. Xerox wasn't talking, but it was
obvious, the time had come to cut the fat out of the copier division.
Xerox employment had swelled to 15,666 in Monroe County, 117,247
worldwide, by the end of 1980. Throughout the 1970s, the business was
growing so fast that nobody worried about hiring. "If you needed someone, you hired him," said Deborah Smith, vice president of personnel
in Xerox's Business Systems Group. "That's how all the layers got
into place."

Most companies blame their blue-collar work force for poor productivity. Xerox knew the problem wasn't with the 4,700 union workers at
the company's Webster manufacturing plant. It was with the people
managing them. "Let's face it," chief executive David Kearns said, "the
poor productivity of white-collar people puts blue-collar people out
of work."

The company had thousands of people just checking things, Smith
said. "Somebody would do something out in the field and they would
send a report into the region. The region had somebody who did nothing
but check over all the reports and consolidate all the materials. Headquarters would check it over, consolidate it some more, then send it up
the line. You had checkers checking checkers. It was ridiculous."

And because Xerox had little outside competition for so long, employees battled each other for recognition and promotions, not market share. "We have been competing against ourselves," said Kearns. "We've got to turn the spirit and vigor of Xerox from an inward thing to an outward thing."

Of course, Xerox had fired people before. More than 2,600 left the Monroe County payrolls in 1975 after the recession. But this time mostly white-collar workers were involved, and management, rather than the economy, was dictating the change. To do more, and faster, Xerox had to get lean and mean. The philosophy was simple: Only those people and positions that directly contributed to profits would survive.

The company's first move, in September 1981, was a voluntary reduction program. Xerox offered severance pay of up to fifteen months' salary to most salaried employees, including 300 of the 600 at the Stamford, Connecticut, headquarters. Worldwide, 250 to 300 volunteers were denied a chance to leave because they were too crucial to Xerox, but thousands (Xerox won't say how many) took the offer, some walking out with six-figure cash settlements. Unfortunately, that wasn't enough, and word spread throughout Xerox that thousands more had to go.

In top-secret meetings, management deliberated over where to make the cuts, and how. "We scrubbed and scrubbed and scrubbed the lists," Smith said. Each organization was given a target. Then lists of people to be fired were drawn up. Those lists were reviewed, first by department and personnel managers, then by vice presidents. Then personnel officers sat down with the senior staff and went through the lists again. Trade-offs were made. Lists of the highest-tenured people were sent to corporate headquarters. "You have no idea how many review processes we went through," Smith said.

Those fired, starting the morning of November 2, were told two things: that Hay Career Consultants was waiting at a local Holiday Inn to help them find new jobs, and to make an appointment with a security guard to clean out their desks—and soon. Many, like forty-two-year-old Dennis Sampson, a twelve-year Xerox veteran with three daughters in college, couldn't believe what was happening to them. "I have no illusions," Sampson said. "We may have to separate the family for a while."

Because Xerox wasn't talking, nobody knew where the firings would stop. Speculation was that 10 to 30 percent of the Monroe County work force would be involved. With thousands of employees looking over their shoulders, hundreds more cleaning out their desks, and security guards flooding the buildings, morale and productivity slipped toward all-time lows. An acidic verse, written and circulated by Xerox workers, captured the moment:

There once was a man named C. Peter
Who thought that he was a world-beater.
But his talents and brain
Sent his firm down the drain
And its stock prices started to teeter.

The shareholders truly were floored
By disasters that Peter had scored.
Before they could shout,
"Throw the bum out!"
He made himself head of the Board.

He said, "Here's my main man, Dave Kearns,
Who understands all my concerns.
I haven't a doubt
That he'll soon bail us out.
We've all seen how quickly he learns."

Dave said, "Those sly Japanese
Have brought our poor firm to its knees.
But now we can't lose
Cause we've got SBUs
And we'll win back our share in a breeze.

Just think of the challenge and fun
As lean and mean we start to run.
We can't be beat
Cause we're fast on our feet,
Treading water 'til OPD's done.

In order to capture new highs,
The company we must resize.
I don't mean we'll fire,
We'll simply dehire—
The work force we'll restrategize!"

As November's about to begin,
They've rented the Holiday Inn.
They'll first redeploy
And then deemploy—
While passing out Kool-Aid and gin.

(There was an editor's note to the last sentence: An "obscure reference to Guiana.")

By the end of 1981, the cuts, voluntary and involuntary, had trimmed the Xerox work force by 2,000 worldwide, 552 in Monroe County alone.

Some departments had been cut in half, others eliminated entirely. Smith's department fell from forty-five to twenty-two.

That was just the beginning. In 1982 and 1983, Xerox employment dropped another 13,923 worldwide. A fifth of the total reduction, or 2,934 jobs, came in Monroe County, where employment dropped 22 percent (15,666 to 12,180) between mid-1981 and January 1984. Most of the reductions were among white-collar, nondirect workers, but more than 700 of the cuts came in the blue-collar manufacturing work force in Webster. In late 1983, Kearns promised employees the job cuts were over, giving everyone a much-needed boost in morale. Notes Hicks, "That was obviously a breath of fresh air. A lot of people in Monroe County had lived under a Damoclesian sword and it caused them to wonder, 'Do I really have a job? Is it really going to be there for a long time? Laying off people is no fun. You go home from work and look at yourself in the mirror and say I don't feel good about what I'm doing.' It's a lot more fun to grow a business than it is taking people out of it."

The company had lost some good people, but the financial benefits were obvious. Long term, Xerox would save up to $600 million a year in salaries. There were also equally important psychological benefits. Top Xerox managers had preached about teamwork and the Japanese threat. The firings, and a subsequent reorganization, drove the message home. "If we had only reduced employment by 5 percent, there would have been no real change," says Charlie Christ. "If we hadn't pushed that hard, it would not have forced us to open our minds."

The severity of the job cuts convinced union leader Tony Costanza that Xerox had to become more competitive. "I'd never thought I'd see Xerox in trouble like they were. It could never happen."

In the seventies, Xerox management had a typically American "Us versus Them" approach to labor. During a 1970 strike, workers surrounded the gate entrance wielding baseball bats. The company called in the state police. The next two years, Webster's productivity was terrible. If an assembly worker ran out of parts, he would fold his arms and sit down. When the foreman told him to get some more, he'd say, "That's not my job." During a later dispute, disgruntled workers sabotaged the conveyor belts to stop an assembly line.

In 1980, two things happened. The company opened up to the union about its problems, convincing hourly workers that their only true job security was to make Xerox more competitive. And management started giving workers a bigger say.

Late that year, Xerox planned to lay off 180 hourly employees to save $3.2 million in production costs for making wire harnesses. Instead of the usual step of threatening a strike, the union helped set up problem-solving teams in all four manufacturing plants.

"We said, 'Give us a chance to compete,' " Costanza recalled. " 'Give us a chance to go in and look at the budget: the cost of electricity; the space that we rent; the overhead cost; our cost; the machinery; the process. Let us look at those things—that was out of their scope at one time.' "

The results, by June 1982, was a $3.7-million cost reduction, eliminating the need for layoffs. It was written into the union contract that before Xerox contracted work to a vendor, a union study team must have the chance to make internal efforts competitive. One team studied energy usage at Webster's Building 200. By replacing inefficient and unnecessary bulbs, they saved the company $250,000.

In 1983, Xerox showed the union exactly what was happening to the company in the world marketplace. Displays and demonstrations of Japanese machines were set up right in the factories so workers could see their competition on company time. It was this sharing of information that helped Xerox convince the union to accept a contract guaranteeing job security, with no wage increase in the first year.

When Xerox planned to build a new $30-million toner plant, a team of workers went to Webster officials and asked for tax breaks. They asked Rochester Gas & Electric for a break on energy costs.

"If we didn't have the process in place, I think there would have been an arbitrary decision," said Larry Pace, a Xerox industrial psychologist. "Power rates are cheaper in Oklahoma City. We have a facility there that's not being used. So therefore it's a no-brainer. Let's move the work to Oklahoma City."

But Webster won, and instead of just sending engineers in to set up the plant, Xerox went to the people who would actually do the work: How should we set this up and make it as efficient as possible?

"When we hired a production worker in the old days, we used to say crudely that we hired his hands and not his head," said John Foley, a vice president of personnel. "Very frankly, what we are finding out is that there is an awful lot in his head."

24
Ryan's Miracle

In my mind, the sales and service organization is one of the real sustainable, competitive advantages we have. Bar none. IBM or anybody else.

—DWIGHT RYAN

D WIGHT RYAN walked over to his Xerox desktop computer, inserted an eight-inch floppy disk and typed his password. "This will take a few moments to tie into Webster," he said, "but I want to show you something."

It was a daily report of Xerox sales in the United States. Ryan heads the American sales and service organization. The report lists the previous day's sales, the total for the month to date, and a projected total for the entire month. It was mid-December 1984.

"Look at those outright sales," he said. "We're going to do $300 million for the month. That was never thought possible before. The best we had ever done was less than half of that."

That total was mainly from copiers and duplicators, but also included Memorywriters, electronic printers, and computers. It did not include leased equipment.

The pressure was on Ryan in the last quarter. After a good first-half, the summer months had been a disaster as far as meeting his placement goals. With the Xerox insurance subsidiary losing money and a huge write-off from the Shugart subsidiary's discontinued disk drive business, if the mainline copier business didn't meet its profit plan, the year would be a total washout. More importantly, the company would not meet its aggressive targets for increasing market share as well as copier profits.

But Ryan was confident. "I'm on profit for October, I'm on profit for November, and I will be on profit for December," he said.

275

Xerox once had a television commercial with a monk looking skyward and saying, "It's a miracle." That's how some view this December for Ryan's sales force. It sold $270 million in copiers and $40 million in typewriters. Ryan exceeded his revenue and profit goals for the year despite the horrible summer months.

When you talk with Xerox workers about who is the most likely candidate to become the next chief executive, three names come quickly: Bill Glavin, Wayland Hicks, and Ryan. Then, they usually add a fourth, Bob Adams, head of the Xerox Systems Group. The further you pursue that question, however, the narrower the list becomes. Glavin and Adams are both in their mid-fifties, about the same age as current chief executive Dave Kearns. That leaves Hicks, early forties, and Ryan, fifty. Their styles are different. Hicks is outgoing, almost flamboyant, smooth in front of a crowd, whether it be journalists and industry analysts or Xerox workers. He likes to be at center stage. Ryan is more reserved, content to stay behind the scenes. He is not smooth in front of people. He talks in company buzzwords and can sometimes be very difficult for an outsider to understand. Both men, however, surround themselves with strong managers and encourage contrary points of view. They also work well together. In the old days, that wasn't always the case between the Xerox copier sales force and the development and manufacturing group. They were almost rivals, clamoring for the attention of top management in Stamford. Today, Hicks regularly gives progress talks to Ryan's people and Ryan does the same for Hicks's people. The message is usually the same: "We can't be successful without you."

Ryan is the main marketeer for Xerox. His group of more than 30,000 sales and service people accounts for more than $6 billion, about half of Xerox's worldwide revenues. He likes to joke about maintaining good relations with his "vendors." Hicks supplies the copiers and Adams supplies the workstations, electronic printers, and other office systems products. They set the strategic tone, but Ryan's group has a lot of autonomy. If he is in danger of not meeting his plan, as he was in the last quarter of 1984, he can take the pricing actions he thinks necessary. "I am a businessman not a philosopher," he says. "Businessmen get things done and philosophers just talk about getting things done."

If you have never been in his office before, the first thing he does is give you a tour. On the twenty-ninth floor of Xerox Tower, it is huge. Joe Wilson had his office on this floor, as did Peter McColough before he moved the corporate headquarters to Stamford. Ryan has a corner location, with windows along two walls. On a clear day he can almost see the manufacturing center in Webster, fifteen miles away. His desk is in a corner, flanked on one side by his computer. There is a couch, two lounge chairs, a low coffee table, and a much larger conference table around which eight people can easily fit. Along another wall are paintings and prints he brought back from England where he had been with Rank Xerox in the late 1970s. Just in front of those is his trophy case: the top sales region award from the West Coast, a plaque from Glavin commemorating when Rank Xerox passed $2 billion in revenue in 1978, a similar award for the systems business in 1976, and a wooden baton, engraved, "From Adams to Ryan, July 1, 1984." That was when he took over marketing responsibility for Adams's products.

"The old thinking at Xerox was that the biggest challenge in the business was to break the back of new business," Ryan says. "Kearns used to think there was a maximum number of new nets you could put through the U.S. sales force in any year. As long as the company felt that way, you drove a lot of strange things. My point was there was no such thing as that kind of a limit if you set yourself up correctly." "New nets" is the Xerox term for net additions to its copier population. Replacing existing Xerox machines maintains the size of the company. New additions grow the company. "I never thought there was a limit," Ryan said. "We just had to make certain we had equipment upside and that we didn't pay for conversion to sale."

Translation: The machines have to be available when the sales force needs them, whether they are excess products built into the plan or they are diverted from Rank Xerox or Latin America. "You can't starve the sales force," Ryan says. The incentives have to be established so that salesmen only receive commissions on new business, not conversions of existing Xerox lease business. In that way, the salesman makes money only if he sells new business.

"We're placing across the board well over 300,000 of new units," Ryan said of 1984. "Well over 100,000 nets just of the basic copiers— new business—and yet people said we had a maximum of 40,000 nets." For the first time Xerox moved more copier units in the United States in 1984 than it did in Rank Xerox, which has focused on smaller machines much longer.

Ryan is a hometown boy. He was born in Syracuse but went to high school in Rochester and enrolled at Cornell with a scholarship from the Rochester newspapers. He earned a master's in business at the University of Rochester and joined Xerox in 1961 after working at Procter & Gamble.

Ryan's year-end 1984 problems actually began in 1982, during the height of the company's employment cutbacks in the United States. "It was a bloodbath in the field. We didn't lay anybody off. They just quit," he says of the disenchanted sales and service force before the roll-out of the 10 Series. Then, in 1983, Xerox pushed outright sale of older equipment the first half of the year and the 10 Series the second half. The large outright sale made his first-half 1984 comparisons difficult. As the 10 Series was introduced, Ryan had to hire and train new servicemen to handle the new machines. There was a hiring constraint in the company but he hired anyway. Costs were high because the new people weren't as efficient as more experienced servicemen. When the summer of 1984 deteriorated, Ryan was forced into cutting prices and pushing a tremendous outright sale in the last four months of the year. "By the time we got to September, we just opened up everything we knew how to do," he says, including lowering the sales price on the 1075 to $36,000 in multiple-machine accounts—normal selling price was about $60,000. Kodak had never before seen such deep discounting from Xerox.

The best way for Xerox to head off Kodak, Ryan says, is to try for the same overall sales/lease mix. Trying to sell a higher percentage of machines than Kodak, which would make Xerox profits better in the short term, would make it tougher to sell against Kodak, and tougher to maintain Xerox profit levels over the long term. He admits some difficulty convincing his boss, Bill Glavin, of his view.

"I do operate with a lot of respect for our competition," Ryan says. "But without fear. You have to be able to match them. And when I say 'them,' one of my complexities of life is that I've got some very different competition. Step over a volume band and it's another machine family and I have a whole new set of people to deal with. So you try to think about how you line yourself up to be most comparative. You're going to be something different against each competitor."

Ryan was sitting at his conference table as he spoke. He had a legal pad in front of him. He used it like a teacher uses a chalkboard to illustrate the important points during a class. He always has note paper handy. At speeches by Dave Kearns, Ryan makes notes on index cards so he can use the same words when he speaks to his own staff.

He was asked if he felt any pressure to make up for the poor performance in the insurance division. "No," he said. Then he wrote "No" on his notepad, underlined it, and pointed to it again.

As the company's chief marketeer, Ryan coordinates the arrival of new products with the phasing out of old products from the lineup. His staff closely monitors the progress of development programs. His group was represented at Venray when Wayland Hicks concluded that the Andes and Somerset programs would probably not meet their target dates.

"The business of business is survival," Ryan says, responding to a question about coping with late products from Hicks. "To the degree that we share responsibility, he has certain things that he can't say, so I take care of them for myself. One of the reasons we get at cross-purposes is that he may not want to admit that a product will slip because he is absolutely trying to drive it to completion on time. It works the other way, too. He might come to me and say, 'Ryan, you don't have a ghost of a chance of making that fourth quarter.' I will say that's absolutely bullshit. Actually, he doesn't do that to me and I don't second guess him up here. The corporate staff in Stamford does that to their heart's content."

Ryan tries to avoid major product launches in the last part of the year. If a program misses it causes big problems because there is no time for a recovery to make the year's forecasts. "You get into some very hard calls at the end of the third quarter," he says. "You can't cut price on the 1075 to 36K on December 1. There's no time for that to have any effect. Your high-volume marketing exec, who personally has his budget tied to the district's budget, is not going to waste time doing something that is not going to be lucrative by December 31."

There was a close call on the 9900 at the end of 1984. For lack of some parts, especially printed circuit boards, the manufacturing group was running behind schedule on producing the machine. Dave Myerscough, Ryan's top manager, threatened to take the 9900 out of his year-end supply and demand case. The sales force, instead, would count on it in 1985. Manufacturing didn't like that possibility, so it chartered planes to pick up parts—line workers put in 22,000 hours of overtime in November and December alone. When the machines were ready for shipping, distribution assigned two drivers to each truck so they could drive cross-country without stopping. By the middle of December, manufacturing had caught up with the demand. As a result, the 9900 added more than $50 million in sold revenues at the end of the year.

Ryan views Xerox products—copiers, typewriters, workstations, electronic printers—as a continuum. The technologies will all eventually merge and all serve close to the same customer base. He thinks the systems business is the future of Xerox and the company will sell a lot more copiers over the next decade under an umbrella that includes systems. Xerox salesmen often lead with the Memorywriter when they make a call, and then work into copiers. This illustrates the strength of the integrated sales force. Half of a salesman's time is spent finding new customers. If, after he has found a prospect, he has more products to sell, he has a better chance of "intersecting" with the customer. "We used to go into one account, say Boeing, in the morning to sell copier/duplicators and, in the afternoon, our laser printing people would go in and tell them to buy a laser machine," says Joe Sanchez, head of the Printing Systems Division. "Then Kodak would climb over both of us to get the account."

The unified sales approach didn't come easy. Xerox went through several sales reorganizations in the late 1970s and early 1980s, including, at one time, splitting its copier force in two. One group generally handled larger accounts and the other smaller. Ryan says that experimenting cost Xerox some lost sales, but now he thinks the company has the right approach. From an accounting standpoint, many noncopier sales come free. With copier prices declining, a salesman who used to sell three copiers a month couldn't make it now if he weren't also selling three Memorywriters a month. "We would not have retained our best copier sales reps if we had not broadened the product line," says Ryan, who thinks Xerox could have a significant personal computer business today if the copier sales force had been given that product to sell as it was given the Memorywriter. "IBM, fortunately for us, abandoned the lower market area, the mid-size customers. For example, where we sell Memorywriters and copiers to a mid-size business through our direct sales force, they won't take an order for their Memorywriter equivalent unless it gets up to almost twenty units. Otherwise you go through some alternate ordering channels. Therefore, we can continue to make up some UMC disadvantage, some feature differentials, through our direct sales force.

"The company has debated over the years on lease versus sold. In my mind, they are all the same. They are all a customer which you convert into profit at a rate that is useful to you, that, hopefully, is driven by the marketplace as opposed to your internal needs."

Xerox used to refer to its lease base as its "annuity" for the future. Now it is trying to build an annuity stream—yearly revenues from supplies, full-service maintenance contracts on sold equipment, and leased machines—that remains relatively constant. In this way, the outright sale of equipment becomes the growth curve of the business. "When you say you're gaining market share, one of the underlying questions is do you have an annuity going from year to year that's greater than what you are giving up?" Ryan says. "That is a real measure of turnaround; all your sales activity for the year builds on top of that. Then you have a very attractive potential growth."

The American sales organization is divided into four groups: Group One, account managers—the top several thousand accounts will overlap directly with office systems and printing systems sales representatives; Group Two, specialists in accounts, both national and large local accounts; Group Three, geographic, dealer-type, walkers; Group Four, mass marketing, direct mail, retail chains, warehouses, computer dealers. The field sales force is estimated at 5,500 people, of which a third are women. About 25 percent of the people are in Group One, 35 percent Group Two, and 40 percent Group Three.

He drew another graph. Through 1989, Ryan sees a growing trend away from direct sales, but he thinks Xerox will make more money by keeping as much of its direct force intact for as long as possible. His view is not universally accepted within Xerox. Some think that strategy will sacrifice market share. "I pay people megabucks in Group One to handle customers like Boeing," Ryan said. "I pay very little to handle people in Group Three. I'm making that force look like a dealer. Why should I pay the dealer the profit? I want the profit."

Despite his view on the direct sales force, Ryan is trying to broaden Xerox distribution through retail chains, direct mail, and other alternative channels as quickly as he can. He feels this is the best way to move low-cost, mass market products such as a hybrid machine that combines the capabilities of a computer printer, facsimile, and copier. Xerox has yet to make much money in sales through alternative channels. "It's a bitch to get those big chains signed up," Ryan says. "It's a bitch to make all those legal agreements—and some of them have a lot of power. So therefore, you negotiate and you negotiate and you negotiate. And sometimes you just end up dealing with a gentleman's handshake because you can't get the contract signed—and that's not just for us by the way, that's for IBM, too."

The ability to make a big sales push is also dependent on the training and support the sales staff receives. The salesmen have to know how to sell the products they receive. Xerox does a good job in this area, so good, in fact, that Xerox copier salesmen are constantly courted by other companies, many of them computer companies such as Wang and DEC. One of the best examples of this rigorous training is a ninety-one-page guide called *Succeeding Against Kodak,* focusing on the Ektaprint 250. It was given to every major account representative but is marked "For Internal Use Only." We were able to obtain a copy from a source outside Xerox.

Many companies use similar devices; Xerox itself has several similar variations. The company issues a short, two- or three-page "knockout" on new competitive products and sends the information to the branch offices within two days of the product's announcement. In addition, selling guides are periodically issued that outline strategies for selling the company's broad line of equipment, offer bonuses to salesmen for replacing IBM or Kodak equipment, offer incentives to encourage customers to take several Xerox machines, and suggest special face-off products—for example, the Xerox 1025 against the Canon NP-155.

The Xerox guide for Kodak is amazingly complete. It was compiled in part through a survey of seventy customers of Ektaprint 250s. It discusses the history of Kodak's plain paper copier business, includes an organizational chart of Kodak's copier division, describes Kodak's strategies and identifies its vulnerabilities, describes each Kodak copier in detail, constructs a face-off between Kodak and Xerox products, describes the 250's productivity, describes Kodak's pricing plans, develops an offensive strategy against Kodak, determines Xerox's vulnerabilities, and establishes a defensive strategy against Kodak.

"Your success against Kodak will depend in part on how well you know the background of the corporation, their marketing strategies, products, pricing, and how they compare to Xerox products and meet customer's needs," the guide states in its introduction.

The booklet contains charts, graphs, photographs, diagrams, and a study guide with multiple choice questions after each section so the Xerox salesman can test himself on what he has read. There is also a section that, in conjunction with a filmstrip, asks the Xerox salesman to describe in his own words how various jobs would be performed on the Ektaprint 250 and then Xerox equipment.

Some items taken directly from the guide, issued in mid-1983, give a better understanding of how thoroughly Xerox prepared its sales force to go against a new threat from Kodak:

- Kodak has approximately 23 percent of the 50,000-plus copies per month volume band in the copier/duplicator market.
- Kodak has approximately 315 copier sales representatives.
- Sales representatives work on 90 percent salary and 10 percent commission.
- The Kodak sales rep is perceived to be concerned about the needs of the account and establishes a high trust level with the account.
- Kodak uses a "seeding" strategy in marketing their products. Their objective is to gain at least one placement in a major, multiple machine account; develop the volume; and finally, close all of the growth business.

- More than the desired 10 percent of EK 250 placements were trades from EK 150s/EK 100s.
- For the marketplace Kodak covers, their sales force is considered small, especially in comparison to Xerox, which has five times as many Account Representatives and High-Volume Marketing Executives.
- While the machine is impressive in the demonstration area, the knowledgeable CRD manager/Commercial Printer quickly sees it as a "plain vanilla," upgraded EK 150, when he or she tries to picture it meeting all of the job requirements the CRD has.
- In the past, Kodak has overcome obstacles through expert merchandising techniques. But the EK 250 may be another story. By understanding Kodak's tactics and identifying their vulnerabilities, you should be better prepared to slow Kodak down in your assignment.
- The most professional way for you to show an account that Xerox should be chosen over Kodak, is to objectively prove that the EK 250 will not do the most important jobs as well as a Xerox unit. [This unit is accompanied by a Job Requirement Sheet that the sales rep is supposed to have his customers complete.]
- You should make your customers aware, in a professional manner, of the physical limitations of two-sided copying on the EK 250. [The 250 can't automatically make two-sided copies of two-sided originals. It also skips frames during certain operations, lowering the rated speed from ninety copies a minute to as few as sixty.]
- Report irregularities of new Kodak offerings [pricing terms or conditions] to the Competitive Hot Line.
- Xerox people have long commented that once a Kodak machine is installed, it is very difficult to "knock out." This is, of course, due to the fact that Kodak offers strong support for customer training and ongoing follow up.
- As you implement your own program against Kodak, remember their strategies include "seeding" and "coexistence." Do not allow the first EK 250 into your accounts.
- Don't talk down (i.e., "knock") Kodak or what the account likes about Kodak. Remember, the account may have been a Xerox user who at one time made a significant business decision to leave Xerox for Kodak.
- Keep calling back. If you cannot knock out the Kodak, coexist with it. Memorywriters, 1035s, 2830s, 1045s, 5600s are just a few things you can offer to handle some of the Kodak customer's business. Make

the establishment your establishment, a Xerox establishment, then systematically and professionally go after 100 percent of the business. Don't stop until you've got it all.

The guide concludes with a worksheet requiring each salesman to hand in to his sales manager a list of all the Kodak installations in his territory, when their contracts expire, their monthly volumes and pricing plans, and a list of the first three accounts the salesman is going to approach.

25

Myerscough—
The Brain Trust

I'm not selling machines, I'm selling
copies. To me, machines are enablers to get
the copy volume because copy volume is the
thing that gets you the revenue. I want to make
it very easy to make copies on my machines.

AT&T and GM are really in the business
of making a profit, not buying copying machines. Give them what they want and everyone is better off.

—DAVE MYERSCOUGH

DAVE MYERSCOUGH has a wide range of contacts during his normal business day. He negotiates directly with the copier and
systems divisions on prices and sales targets for copiers, supplies, Memorywriters, electronic printers, and workstations. He determines how many machines to move through the Xerox direct sales force
and how many through alternate channels. When he sets his strategy, he
tries to think the way his competition does, whether it be the Japanese
and their dealer allies or Kodak. "He's got to be the brain trust of this
organization," Dwight Ryan says of his number two man.

Myerscough, a twenty-year Xerox veteran, will also get right on the
phone with a customer to cut a deal. He is a primary example of how
Xerox has become more entrepreneurial and fast moving in its traditional business. The computer on Myerscough's desk contains data on
every major Xerox customer. While he is on the phone, he can look at
the number of Xerox and competitors' machines a customer has, the copy
volumes on those machines, the contract terms, and when the contracts
run out. He sometimes knows the customer's operation better than the
customer.

The business units set the initial strategic goals in pricing and product volumes and then negotiate with Myerscough. They agree on a profit level, a list price for a product, and a so-called achieved price. (The achieved price, which is lower than list, is the one used in the company's forecasts.) Myerscough can do anything he wants within that price range. If something unexpected happens, such as the Japanese suddenly doubling production, and he feels he has to go below the achieved price, he negotiates again with the business unit on a new range, but most of the decisions have been made in the operating plan and it's just a matter of when to use the pricing incentives. "What I do is try to keep prices as high as I can as long as I can," Myerscough says. "Say I want to put in 100,000 installs. I would like to get 100,000 installs at the highest price level. So I will measure monthly where I believe I am against my supply and demand. At some point in time I know I got to bring that price down to get those machines in—that's an oversimplification, but it's not too much more complicated than that."

Each salesman then has his own price range with much less latitude. In some cases, where a salesman is going against a dealer handling Japanese machines, Myerscough will give some special authority to cut price. "We have a constant hot line here," he says. "We tell our sales reps if you have an issue, or something you need, please call the hot line and we'll give you any information you need. We have books up here on every competitors' machine. We know dealer cost, the UMC on a machine."

In the seventies, you could track Xerox, Kodak, and IBM within ninety days of each other on copier price changes. If Xerox raised prices 5 percent, so did the others. There was no collusion, but each company was well aware of the others. "Now, when Japan Incorporated comes in, you got a whole new ballgame," Myerscough says. "They are really manufacturing companies, not marketing companies. They make their profits coming out of the plant. Their job is to flood the pipe. They really don't care, candidly, how they flood it—within reason. They wouldn't want to destroy the whole price level. But they are less concerned on how they get market share. I don't think they have a long-term viewpoint on that. They want to get share and they'll keep flooding the U.S. marketplace to get that share. Because of that, we've gone from what I would say was a margin-maintenance pricing philosophy—it's not just Xerox but American Industry in general—to a market share philosophy. When you talk on a margin-maintenance basis, the big discussion is your sales volume because you are going to keep your price the same. You say, that's the margin I want, let the installs move it. When you start going to a market share, gross profit discussion, as the Japanese do, you say, 'I'm going to build 100,000 of them so I can get my unit cost down. Now the only thing I don't know is how much money I am going to make on these mothers.' "

The biggest improvement at Xerox in recent years, in Myerscough's opinion, is responding more quickly to customers and changes in the market. "In the seventies, we'd analyze something for six months and by that time you forgot what you wanted to do or the opportunity had gone by," he says. "We have to be much faster today because the market is moving faster." Two of the best examples: tailor-made agreements in preferred account contracts (PACs), and saving 9000 series machines from the scrap heap with new central reproduction department (CRD) pricing.

PAC PRICING

"In this business you can't say, 'let's dribble,' " Myerscough says, characterizing Xerox's all-out effort to win back the loyalty of the largest customers in the United States. During its monopoly years and extending into the early 1980s, Xerox had become inflexible with customers. It set the terms and the customer could take it or leave it. Xerox obviously offered better pricing to its larger customers, but anytime someone asked for unique treatment the answer was always "no". Myerscough thought Xerox should be making special efforts for its major accounts. So beginning in late 1982, the company targeted 200 major accounts for special treatment. It wasn't a secret list; it just went down the *Fortune* 500. Myerscough told the accounts, "I don't think we've been treating you right." Before a salesman was allowed to even attempt to sell a machine he had to make a series of three calls on the customer to find out what Xerox had done wrong before and what the customer really thought of Xerox. In Xerox terminology, the salesman had to find the customer's "hot buttons," those issues that make the customer angry.

"This whole PAC pricing system says let's listen to our customers and really try to find out what they want and then try to decide if they were unusual requests or not," Myerscough says. "Most of the time I find that their requests aren't unreasonable. Now, I might not want to respond to them for some business reasons, but they are not usually unreasonable requests. In major accounts it's not price level as much as terms and conditions. If you're satisfying their needs I think you can be a lot more flexible in terms and conditions on your big accounts."

For example, Myerscough once wrote a contract for 1,000 machines that allowed the customer to return 15 percent, 150, if the company sold a division to another company. "I had eighteen lawyers all over the place asking me if I really wanted to do that," he says. "They were talking about the financial exposure. I said, If someone sold a division and didn't need the machines, why would I make them keep them? Then they would have a bad taste in their mouth. As long as I'm sure of getting all their copies, why would I worry?' "

Another unusual request was from a California company that wanted to install 1,200 machines. Myerscough had to throw two golf carts into the deal. The company was situated in a campus environment and it wanted on-site tech reps to read the meters, repair the machines, and do routine maintenance such as change toner. Because of the company's insurance policies, the tech reps, who were Xerox employees, had to use Xerox carts to make their rounds. "I couldn't do it in my model approach to an account, but it was a reasonable request," Myerscough said. "It was cheap at half the price. In fact, I believe when I added the whole thing up it cost me less in administration, service, and distribution cost than it would have if I had run it through the regular model."

No copier vendor owns an entire major account. "If I ever had one or two the lawyers would get very nervous," Myerscough says. Most customers deal with at least two copier vendors—that provides some insurance against poor performance and helps keep some leverage on each copier supplier. "We coexist with the competition," Myerscough continues. "You're always in a game where you try to keep everything you have and get some of theirs. We try to take the mystique out of it. When I go talk to a customer, I say I want all of your business. If I give you the best box, and I give you the service, and I give you all the flexibility you want, why do you have two or three vendors?"

Along with its PAC pricing and accelerated rate of product introductions, Xerox has also changed its philosophy on how long it will try to keep a leased machine at a customer's site. In the 1960s, it wrote off its rental machines over seven years. Today, that period has been cut to as few as three years. "You can't have an old box with PAC pricing," Myerscough says. "Either I'll give you a very attractive sales price because you need it to use on the shipping dock, or I'm going to give you a 10 Series box. If you are really serious about your major accounts why would you have old machines there?" That approach has cost Xerox some money, but Myerscough would rather take the old machines out than get a false sense of security that the revenue from them would continue. He knows the competition is calling with new machines and he could lose some of those placements if he didn't replace them himself.

"That's the first time anybody has ever gone to an account that way," he says. "The customers really were taken aback. I remember I went up to an account in New England. He said, 'I understand but I don't believe it.' I said, 'Why don't you believe it? I have a little computer on my desk, I know what your machine population is, I know what you've done, and I've forecast out what population I am going to have by 1986 and I don't like the answer. So if I'm upfront now, I will make you a happier customer because I know you are going to be unhappy and I know there are going to be competitive salesmen in here over the next six months saying how much better their machine is, and guess what? They're right.' Half of marketing is simplistic and we make it too complex."

By the time the contracts on the first PAC machines expire, all of those 10 Series machines will be completely depreciated—a situation that will give Xerox more flexibility. It can then offer the customer all new machines, renew the old ones at lower cost, or sell them outright. "But I'm in control," Myerscough says. "I can say to the customer, I've got this new technology. You've got 1,000 machines. You've probably got 600 of them you want to trade in and the other 400 I probably want to give you a better price on. I don't think every department needs to have a Cadillac. You might need some Chevys. Now I'm in control to give you what Chevys you need, what Fords you need, and what Cadillacs you need."

9000 CRD

The 9200 was introduced in 1974. It and other older machines in the 9000 series, such as the 9400 and 9500, have had a long life. In general, they are very productive with dedicated operators, but the newer, more sophisticated 10 Series machines, such as the 1075 and 1090, are competition to the 9000 because they are easier to use, especially in a walk-up environment.

"My style is if I know what is going to happen I'm going to get in front of it and make it happen versus letting it happen," Myerscough says. "So I go through a strategy and say I got 10,000 of the 9000s out there. I think out in the future. I'm not worried about what I'm doing now. So I got to be looking at those 9000s and not get a false sense of security.''

Xerox always pulled some copy volume away from offset printing because of the productivity advantages of the 9000, but it couldn't compete on long runs because offset is a cheaper process. It couldn't get the price down to offset levels when it had a 9000 that had to be depreciated. Now, however, it has this asset that is still good as well as fully depreciated. Myerscough's answer was one price—$1,800 a month—for all the copies a customer could make on a 9000.

''I've done enough work in sales to know that somebody will have to be running twenty-four hours a day to beat me on that price,'' he says. ''All the finance people say, 'Well, geez, you're giving something away.' What am I giving away? It's a fully depreciated machine. I'm getting guaranteed $1,800 a month, plus paper, plus toner, plus other supplies. From my viewpoint, I've just taken a box that has been around ten years and I think I got almost another ten years of life out of it. To me, the 9000 in all-you-can-eat CRD is new technology.''

Xerox installed 2,000 machines on 9000 CRD pricing in 1984 and could have put in 600 more; it just didn't have enough 9500s.

''I think we're doing a lot of things different today because we're taking some risks,'' Myerscough says. ''Four years ago, lawyers and finance people would have had those fully depreciated boxes so tied up it would have taken us four years to get out of it. I looked at that box and I said, 'Wow, that's just revenue, that's $50 to $100 million dollars' worth of revenue a year on a box I was going to scrap.' And your competition can't do it because they don't have any fully depreciated boxes.''

26

The Xerox Mole
Inside Japan

Japanese companies talk more than American.
—TADASHI KOBAYASHI,
Fuji Xerox

ETER MCCOLOUGH calls it invaluable: "A resource we wouldn't
have unless we were on the ground in Japan." David Kearns and
every other top Xerox manager in the United States agrees. Fuji
Xerox is Xerox Corporation's window on Japan. It helps keep Rochester
and Stamford up to speed on what is happening at Canon, Ricoh, and
the rest of the Japanese copier makers, both on specific products and
longer-term corporate strategies.

Tadashi Kobayashi, no relation to President Yotaro Kobayashi, is the
Fuji Xerox manager for competitive analysis. He does a monthly competitive newsletter, which is sent to about sixty Xerox people in the United
States, and also sends special bulletins when necessary. He has been with
Fuji Xerox since 1969 and in his current position since 1976. Before
joining Fuji Xerox, he worked at Oki Electric. He attended college in
the United States and majored in business.

You'd like to be able to tell tales of intrigue and espionage in the
profession of corporate intelligence gathering. As Kobayashi's
American counterpart, Hal Bogdonoff, says, "I dream of a beautiful
blonde at Kodak throwing me down on the sidewak and screaming secrets in my ear." But it is rarely so exciting. Kobayashi, for instance,
focuses his research on twelve rather commonplace areas:

1. Published sources, such as newspapers and government statistics.
2. Research studies by such firms as Dataquest and Yankee Group.
3. Patent analyses.

4. Information from dealers, both Fuji Xerox and competitors.
5. Information from vendors.
6. Information from Fuji Xerox salesmen.
7. Fuji Xerox's own market research.
8. Fairs or shows by individual competitors.
9. The big copier fairs, such as Hanover, West Germany.
10. Analysis of competitive products after they are introduced.
11. Special investigations, such as surprise product developments—very rare.
12. An annual worldwide competitive conference by Xerox Group.

"I really wish you wouldn't use the word *investigation* in relation to my work," Tad Kobayashi says. "It has a bad connotation. Everything I do is completely legal and aboveboard. It's just a matter of taking information from a variety of sources and putting the pieces together into something that might be true."

Most of Kobayashi's information comes from the first category: daily and weekly newspapers, trade publications, and government statistics. All of this information is publicly available, but most of it is written only in Japanese.

"Japanese companies talk more than American," Kobayashi says. "So I think there is much more detail in our press announcements. In America, a fact is a fact; it stands by itself. In Japan, it's fact plus missions, hopes, expectations, these types of things."

The stories about the Canon-Kodak alliance are a good example. Canon announced the alliance in Japan and Kodak announced it in the United States on the same day. In the U.S., the general interest and business newspapers mentioned only the joint development of an unspecified mid-volume copier, possibly more than one. No timetable was mentioned. No additional products were mentioned. The American press got its information from Kodak.

In Japan, however, the press mentioned specific machines, a specific timetable, and a volume expectation. Here is a translation from *Nihon Keizai Shimbun,* September 21, 1984: "The products Canon will supply to Kodak are high-speed copiers NP-9030 and NP-7550. The products will partly incorporate Kodak's specs and be supplied on an OEM basis under the Kodak brand. Canon plans to ship the products within this year and Kodak to market them next spring. Canon hopes to supply a total of 1,000 units a month to Kodak."

Other Japanese newspapers mentioned the possibility of joint collaboration on 8mm video or other products involving a combination of

Canon's optoelectronics and Kodak's chemical technologies. One said Canon was going to market the Kodak Ektaprint 200 in Japan, something Kodak had never done before with any of its copiers. Two newspapers mentioned this alliance as being part of a new strategic challenge by Canon to Xerox's dominance in copiers.

The Japanese newspapers got their information from Canon and its president, Ryuzaburo Kaku.

Kobayashi translates and telexes the information in these stories to the United States and then follows up with further developments. The day he was interviewed at Fuji Xerox headquarters in Tokyo, he was carrying a letter he had sent to the U.S. about Canon and Kodak. "Kodak has fifty engineers at Canon," the letter said. "We think they are working on, but there is no confirmation, the 7550, 9330, and a color copier. We will keep you posted." Kodak, in fact, introduced its own versions of the 7550 and 9330 in March 1985.

Speeches by Japanese executives or seminars by the companies themselves often exhibit the same trait for amplification and putting facts into a larger corporate context. The speeches may not include specific numbers, but they often indicate a new strategic thrust or emphasis.

Patents in Japan are supposed to be opened to public view a year and a half after they are filed. Kobayashi watches these to get some idea of the areas competitors are concentrating their research and what types of products might be coming. The competitors, though, are getting smart. Important information may be hidden in different patents, forcing him to piece together possible combinations. "Some patents might be true and some might just be ideas with no intention of ever getting into a real machine," Kobayashi says. Canon, for instance, filed more than 300 patents in regard to its Personal Copier cartridge system.

"The Canon PC was a surprise," he said. "We couldn't have forecast that machine. Their project was kept completely secret. We had access to some of the patents relating to the PC only two months before it was introduced. Usually, we see the patents at least six months before. Even if we had known those patents, however, I don't believe we could have forecast that machine. They kept a very tight lid on it. Canon is very good at keeping information inside. I have heard rumors that even some of Canon's top management doesn't know about new products until they are ready to be announced."

In the United States, at the other end of Kobayashi's information pipeline, and running a competitive intelligence operation of his own, is Bogdonoff. One wall of Bogdonoff's small office in Webster is stacked shoulder high with patent filings from Japan, sent by Kobayashi.

Bogdonoff can't read Japanese, but he can read the technical diagrams and they get most of his attention. On two other walls of his office are charts with the English names of the top Japanese copier manufacturers and their Japanese equivalents. "It's just like identifying enemy planes during the war through their silhouettes," he says of the Japanese *kanji* characters.

In Japan, as well as in the United States, dealers sometimes handle more than one brand of machine, so they may hear about new products from several different companies. Vendors also deal with a variety of manufacturers. And Fuji Xerox sales and service representatives often run into a customer who has been told about a new machine coming from a competitor. This also happens in the United States. One of the ways Xerox knew about Kodak's imminent entry into plain paper copiers back in the mid-1970s was because Xerox engineers bumped into copier vendors flying into Rochester—and the vendors were not there on Xerox business.

"We don't usually get detailed information from vendors," Kobayashi says, "just trends. A vendor may say, 'Oh, we have just received an order from Canon.' He's not supposed to reveal information, but once you know about the order you can collect related information from other sources to put the puzzle together." This information flow also works in reverse. A vendor tells a competitor about an order from Fuji Xerox. "If we find out that has happened, we warn the vendor and tell him he is in danger of losing our business," Kobayashi says.

From time to time, Fuji Xerox will do its own market research—a nationwide survey, for instance, on machine installations to determine market share statistics for itself and its competitors.

In Japan, various companies hold their own product fairs or shows. Canon, for instance, has a Canon Grand Fair in November or December at which it sometimes shows prototypes of potential products—one product, shown in 1982, was a color-ink jet printer, which is still not available. Also, when a product is announced in Japan, it is customary to show it first to your industry organization. Fuji Xerox, Canon, Ricoh, Minolta, IBM, and Konishiroku are all members of the Japan Business Machines Association. They hold product demonstrations for each other. The big international shows for copiers are the Hanover Fair in West Germany in April, the Business Show in Japan in May, and the National Office Machine Dealers Association (NOMDA) convention in the United States in July.

Competitors aren't allowed to use their own test charts to make test copies on the machines shown at the Japan Business Machines

Association; instead, the demonstrating company hands out copies, but they can at the big shows. Fuji Xerox, as do the other copier makers, has a special chart to help determine copy quality, half-tone reproduction, background, blue reproduction, and toner density, among the machines other capabilities. Fuji Xerox goes from booth to booth and makes test copies from each machine. The competition does the same.

A copy from a particular machine is in many ways like a fingerprint. From a single copy, xerographic experts can determine the type of toner used, the type of fusing method used, even the development method. When Xerox was testing prototypes of the 1075 in-house, all of the tens of millions of test copies were either burned or shredded. Some Xerox researchers are even occasionally called upon to work with the FBI. If the source of a suspect copy can be narrowed to a particular building, Xerox can then determine the particular department or even a specific machine. In 1984, Japanese detectives traced a copy of a terrorist's letter back to a particular Canon copier by tiny tails on the edges of some letters.

"You give me a copy made from any one of the major Japanese machines and 80 percent of the time I can tell you which company it is," Kobayashi says.

Fuji Xerox purchases competitive products when they first appear and tests them. These machines are installed at Ebina where they are broken down to try to determine the manufacturing cost, the type of manufacturing process, the types of materials used, who the vendors are, and how many hours are needed to manufacture it. Tests are also run to determine how the machines perform under different conditions, such as low temperature and humidity.

At the end of the interview, Kobayashi, true to the nature of his job, pressed the authors for some details on what they had discovered during their tours of copier manufacturers in the United States, Europe, and Japan. This is a common trait among Japanese businessmen. They come right out and ask you how their operation compares with the competition. "Is Canon making as many machines as they would like you to think they are?" Kobayashi asked.

We explained to him, as we did the others, that we could not discuss what we considered confidential source information until it was published.

"I think they overestimate their capacity, and they do it by design," he said. "If people think something is number one they may just buy it because of that."

27
Fuji Xerox
Grows Up

The interview was over. Now it was Motohiko Tsuchiya's turn to ask the questions: "Sometimes the people in Rochester are hard to work with when we are working on a product similar to one they are working on," the director of copier development and manufacturing for Fuji Xerox said. "Do you have any suggestions for how we can cooperate better?"

The interviewer took a piece of paper and wrote two numbers: 17,000 and 12,100, with an arrow pointing down, the Xerox employment trend in its hometown. "Some people there think you are costing them as many jobs as the rest of the Japanese competition."

"I know that," Tsuchiya said. "I understand that. That attitude is fine if there were no Canon. But there is. Why don't they want to do what's best for the company?"

THE HISTORY of Fuji Xerox in a sentence: A marketing subsidiary that sold American-made equipment in Japan becomes an expert design and manufacturing company that wants the unhindered ability to sell Japanese-made equipment in the United States and around the world. And this makes Fuji Xerox both a partner and a competitor of Xerox Corporation.

Rank Xerox workers in Europe may speak different languages, but there is no question they pledge their allegiance to the Star-Spangled Banner. Xerox owns 51 percent of Rank Xerox and gets two-thirds of the profits, but Fuji Xerox is a fifty-fifty joint venture between Fuji Film and Rank Xerox. No one in the United States tells Fuji Xerox what to do. Its 15,000 workers still first salute Hi-no-Maru, the Rising Sun of Japan.

This independence, frankly, saved Xerox in the low end of the copier market. Xerox would not have a competitive machine today at 30 cpm or slower if Fuji Xerox had not ignored the desires of Stamford and pressed ahead with developing its own products. On the other hand, this independence has caused the two companies to waste millions of dollars on developing similar products, and has led to frustration on both sides of the Pacific. Some Fuji Xerox workers think their American partner is hindering their growth and the development of their own world markets. Some Xerox workers, especially in the Rochester engineering and manufacturing community, fear Fuji Xerox as much as Canon and Ricoh. The more successful Fuji Xerox is at developing its own products, the greater is the threat that it will take even more work away from the United States.

"I think the relationship between the two companies is excellent," David Kearns says. "It is probably one of the best partnerships that exists between a Japanese and an American company, but it is not without difficulty. There is competition. That problem is never going to go away. One of the strengths of Fuji Xerox is its independence, but it is also tough. It's tough to manage."

"Fuji Xerox is in a unique and difficult position," agrees Jeff Kennard, the Xerox liaison between Tokyo and Stamford. "They're Japanese so they know what has to be done to be successful. But they are also part of Xerox Group so they have to be good corporate citizens."

Fuji Xerox is indeed one of the most successful joint ventures in Japanese business history. In two decades it has grown from a strictly sales organization into a completely self-sufficient high-technology company with annual revenues exceeding $1.5 billion, more than half the size of its Japanese parent, Fuji Photo Film. Net profit exceeds $60 million. More than $1 billion of Fuji Xerox revenues come from the copier business, ranking it just behind Canon and Ricoh and just ahead of Kodak and IBM on a worldwide basis for plain paper copiers. From 1975 to 1985, Fuji Xerox had the best year-over-year compound growth record in the entire Xerox Group; sales and profits both quadrupled in that span. President Yotaro "Tony" Kobayashi has set an even tougher target for the future. He wants revenues and profits to quadruple again by 1990.

In image-conscious Japan, Fuji Xerox is proud of the Xerox name. Atop its headquarters building in Tokyo is a huge neon sign that says "Xerox" not "Fuji Xerox." Fuji Xerox workers are quick to point out that their company has a better reputation, and much more renown, in Japan than Rank Xerox does in Europe. But as the American company began to experience its earnings difficulties in the early 1980s, that image began to fade. Fuji Xerox employees in Tokyo actually felt as if the poor performance of Xerox Corporation was hurting them. The earnings stories were in the Japanese press as soon as they were in the American. Fuji Xerox began to slide in the rankings of the most-admired Japanese companies and began to have some difficulty recruiting new employees. When Xerox sold its headquarters building in Stamford in early 1985 as part of its strategy to increase return on assets, there was particular concern in Tokyo. Japanese companies don't sell assets.

Xerox Corporation has not developed a successful low-end copier since the 3100, which was introduced in 1973. Fuji Xerox has been supplying low-end machines to the rest of the Xerox world since 1977—the same year Fuji Xerox spent $500,000 for a McKinsey & Co. study when some executives at Stamford were actually considering abandoning the low end. McKinsey told Fuji Xerox: "You've got to be there. Change your distribution system and find a way to stay in that market." More recently, Fuji Xerox has moved into the design of mid-volume machines with the 3500 and 5870, which sells in the United States as the 1055, and is helping significantly on the design of the 1075 replacement product.

The basic reason for Fuji Xerox's desire to be independent is best summarized by Yoichi Ogawa, general manager of Fuji Xerox's corporate research labs: "Our market should be protected by ourselves," he says. The problems arise because the feeling is mutual among many Xerox workers in the U.S. What's good for the company as a whole may not be good for particular segments of it. Understanding that dilemma is understanding Fuji Xerox.

An example: From 1980 to the beginning of 1985, Fuji Xerox shipped 800,000 small copiers to the United States and Europe in the form of kits. Fuji Xerox refers to these as "knockdown" or "KD" units. It's almost used as a disparaging term. Fuji Xerox would rather supply completed machines. Instead, half of the kits were assembled in Webster and the other half in Mitcheldean, England. The main reason was to save American and British jobs.

Decisions such as that, made because of labor and community relations half a world away, make Fuji Xerox think its own growth is being stunted. It can operate on its own in Southeast Asia, where it is licensed, but if it wants to sell in the United States or Europe, it still has to go through Xerox channels. Canon is exporting 80 percent of its production; Fuji Xerox only 20 percent, lowest among the Japanese copier makers. Until it can become as export conscious as other Japanese companies, Fuji Xerox won't grow as fast. "We have to develop *dantotsu,* or super-, products so Xerox Corporation will import more Fuji Xerox products,'' says Tadashi Kobayashi, the manager of competitive analysis. "It's a real sore point."

No one understands that dilemma of internal competition better than Bill Glavin. It's his job to coordinate the activities of Fuji Xerox with the rest of Xerox Group. Glavin called a summit meeting between the copier development groups of the two companies in November 1984. Xerox was wasting too much money in duplicative development programs. Xerox Corporation spends about $600 million a year on research and development, $400 million of that on reprographics. Fuji Xerox spends $100 million a year on R & D, $60 million on reprographics.

"That was an important milestone in our future," Glavin says. "We finally turned our partnership into an advantage, not a disadvantage. The first disadvantage has been both of us spending money to develop a product for the same segment of the market. The second disadvantage is that because we don't use one product worldwide, we're not getting the manufacturing volumes we would like."

Glavin and Kobayashi were joined at the summit by Tsuchiya, Wayland Hicks, and their top managers.

"I started the conference off by telling everybody that others are trying to find out how to make deals with the Japanese and here we've been working with somebody for twenty-two years. Why the hell can't we make it work better?'' Glavin said. "I mean Canon and Kodak got together because they didn't have the other guy's products. You couldn't have made a better match; they're not going to have duplicative products. Here we are working with somebody for twenty-two years and we don't manage that."

The duplication of effort began in 1976 when Fuji Xerox initiated the 3500 project. It was a declaration of independence. It came after a series of copiers—code-named SAM, Moses, Mohawk, Elf, Peter Paul & Mary—on which Fuji Xerox was depending were canceled by Rochester. One after another they expired, all the while Fuji Xerox's market share in Japan was declining. Kennard remembers that when Tony Kobayashi was told about the death of Moses, the Fuji Xerox boss was also asked to stop work on the 3500. "Tony refused," Kennard says. "He said, 'As long as I am running this company I can no longer be totally dependent on you for developing products. We are going to have to develop our own.' ''

Glavin remembers the reaction in Rochester: "It was the first big machine they had designed and the engineering community in the U.S.

said, 'Absolutely no way is Fuji Xerox going to do what they say they are going to do. They just can't make it. They don't know how to make machines. It will be a disaster.' So the rest of Xerox Group went down the path of the 1045, a similar machine. If we were to look back now, that would be another decision which we would say was wrong, but at that time it would not have been wrong because Fuji Xerox had never built a machine in that class. It required a tremendous amount of help from the United States, which we gave them. The machine was successful and it was the beginning of a whole family of products. You can find a heritage of the 1055 coming from that 3500. When they started to show what they could do, they sprouted their own wings, so to speak, and started to go off designing their own machines.

"That led us down the path of a lot of duplication of products. They have products we don't have and we have products they don't have, in the same market segment. They do not develop products with new technologies. They take a technology from a product that has already been used and matured in the United States or in Europe and add to it technologies from other machines, but they do not develop their own new technologies. When you do that, you can make a new machine quicker and for less cost. So every time Wayland sits down with them and says let's do this product, they'll come up with one that's better than his because he's trying to put in new technologies. And they say, well, we can do it in two years. Well, he can't. It takes him three years. We kept getting ourselves further and further apart.

"The competition has been healthy; we both have learned a lot. But after our summit conference we now have a number of operating and management principles that say we will no longer diverse ourselves through product families. Anytime Wayland and the Fuji Xerox product planners cannot come up with one common product worldwide, they cannot advance any further without my personal approval.''

A low-volume copier code-named Benkei, which means warrior, is a good example of the manufacturing volumes Glavin referred to. The product, designed and manufactured by Fuji Xerox, was announced in Japan in October 1984 (the 3870) and in the United States in early 1985 (the 1025). Glavin said Fuji Xerox planned to sell 60,000, but because the two companies coordinated the development, they planned to sell 180,000 units worldwide the first twelve months. The 1025, by the way, was the first machine Xerox assembled in China, through its joint venture there. Other Fuji Xerox–Xerox summits on copiers and the systems business have been held regularly since.

The Japanese photographer was almost ready to take the picture. Then he stopped. Something was wrong with the rug in front of the Fuji Xerox board of directors.

"Well, will you look at that," one of the Americans on the board cracked. "He even has to comb . . ."

Tony Kobayashi interrupted. "It's that attention to detail that makes Japan great," he said.

Almost every day in the Japanese newspapers you can read the phrases, "before the war" or "after the war." That's how they measure time. For a Japanese businessman, however, it's "before the oil shock" or "after the oil shock." That's when their world changed. The Fuji Xerox profit chart is typical of many Japanese companies. Since 1966, there have been only two down years for profit, 1970 and 1974. The first was the so-called Nixon shock, when gold-backing was removed from the dollar and it was allowed to float against world currencies. The second was the oil shock. That's when Fuji Xerox and many Japanese companies discovered they could never do business the same way again.

"Before the oil shock, Fuji Xerox enjoyed a monopolistic position in PPC," says Toneo Noda, the managing director for finance and overseas operations. "After the oil shock, even though the world had changed, our thinking was still like a monopoly." Or, as Atsushi Hirai, managing director for quality control, says: "We were spoiled by overconfidence. We had deaf ears to customer complaints. Xerox copiers were excellent in performance, but they were too costly."

The answer for Tony Kobayashi, then a vice president, was a total commitment to quality. He headed the so-called New Xerox movement in 1976, which became the pattern for David Kearns's Leadership Through Quality at Xerox Corporation. "Fuji Xerox through the 1960s and up through 1971–1972 was not only a glamorous company but also hard working," Kobayashi says. "Having come from Fuji Photo Film I knew Fuji Xerox was different. We had a different attitude. But while we were working hard, we were really missing something: the real customer requirements. There had been some feeling among customers that our prices were too high. Could we make it cheaper? Our feeling was that we were offering the best. The best can command the highest price. What's wrong with that?"

After the oil shock, Fuji Xerox tried to raise prices twice in ten months, 9 percent in January 1974 and 10 percent in November 1974. The first time the other Japanese copier companies followed. The second time they didn't. It put an end to the American way of raising prices when costs went up. "The oil shock made our customers much more acutely aware of cost," Kobayashi says. "They turned to less costly alternatives as a short-term solution. To their surprise, and certainly to ours, many of those customers decided to stay with those machines. The quality wasn't that bad. In 1973, 1974, and 1975, the company had been used to high levels of expenses and profits. We came to the conclusion that unless some really drastic and fundamental changes occurred, the company was going to sink very quickly. We really thought it was a question of survival. In the U.S., the dangers were still a couple of years off. People have to feel and face the reality before they change. That was the beginning of our TQC [total quality control]. In a sense, New Xerox movement means continually renewing, almost forever. I think we have come a long way, but our friends have also come a very long way. Very."

Kobayashi is fond of quoting Joe Wilson. Near the beginning of a book Kobayashi published to commemorate the first twenty years of Fuji Xerox is a reprint of Wilson's favorite poem, Robert Frost's "The Road Not Taken." Kobayashi still quotes that poem. "The road not taken is a sense of challenge," he says. "Joe Wilson would say if there is a choice, choose the more challenging. Joe Wilson was the most important, single individual in the Xerox world. He always emphasized the importance of excellence. He had the long term in mind, but he was also very realistic. He was a very tough man to demand the best out of the short term as well. It is that combination of idealism and realism that is the key to TQC today. It is something we had before. It is something we had forgotten."

The similarities in Wilson and Kobayashi go beyond philosophy: Wilson earned a degree at Harvard Business School; Kobayashi was born in London and earned a business degree at Wharton. Wilson was deeply involved in community affairs in Rochester; Kobayashi serves on more than twenty outside commissions and advisory boards. The fathers of both men were leaders of their respective companies—Joseph R. Wilson was president of Haloid Company, Setsutaro Kobayashi was president of Fuji Photo Film and the first president of Fuji Xerox when it was established in 1962. Some Xerox workers, on both sides of the Pacific, even ask: Can Tony Kobayashi ever become CEO of Xerox Corporation? It is used more as a compliment to his ability than as a statement of high probability. A Japanese running an American *Fortune* 500 company? However, it illustrates the high regard people have for Kobayashi and the spirit of Joe Wilson.

Jeff Kennard was in Japan during the year leading up to winning the Deming Prize in 1980. "It was an incredible ordeal," he says. "Wives were writing Tony at home—very un-Japanese—saying 'My children haven't seen their father in two months.' After we won the award, Tony wrote everyone and said, 'Now we have to earn it. The real work and sacrifice is only just beginning.' "

Warriors of Japan have always sacrificed.

For the first ten years of its existence, Fuji Xerox was strictly a marketing organization. It took what Xerox had to offer and did the best it could with the products in the Japanese market. Sometimes it was painfully obvious that these Fuji Xerox machines from America weren't designed with the Japanese in mind. When the Xerox 7000 arrived in Japan, for instance, secretaries had to stand on a box to reach the print button. It had been designed with the taller American secretary in mind. Today, in some offices around Japan, you can still see a small wooden platform nudged up against the 7000.

The machines were manufactured at facilities owned by Fuji Film. Those factories were taken over by Fuji Xerox in April 1971 after long negotiations and strong urging by Peter McColough and Joe Wilson, and it was the first step toward independence. Even before the transfer of the plants, Fuji Film had begun design work on a brand new copier, the 2200. It was based on the Xerox 660, but smaller and had a moving platen. Yoichi Ogawa, currently general manager of corporate research at Fuji Xerox, was in charge of the 2200 project, which began in 1967. With a staff of six, he was able to develop a breadboard prototype within a year. After that it went to Fuji Film's Iwatski plant where thirty engineers worked on it. When it was introduced in 1972, it was the world's smallest PPC.

Toshio Arima, now manager of corporate planning at Fuji Xerox, went to Rochester to convince Xerox to take the 2200. "We laid it out in front of them," he said. "We said a Konishiroku machine is coming, a Ricoh machine is coming. But they didn't believe it. For some internal reasons we didn't understand, they said 'no' to us." So Arima went ahead with plans of his own for the 2200 in Japan. It was the best low-end machine available at the time. Had Xerox taken it, he thinks it could have forestalled the Japanese invasion of the U.S.

One of the reasons the United States didn't take the 2200 was the moving platen. Xerox engineers, reared on such fixed optics machines as the 914, didn't think a moving platen was what customers in the U.S. wanted. The NIH—not invented here—syndrome was hard at work. The engineers in the United States couldn't believe this Japanese company could develop machines as good as theirs.

Glavin thinks the 2200 decision set the tone toward Fuji Xerox for most of the seventies. The machine was the subject of the first copier/duplicator meeting he attended in Rochester. He had just left Xerox Data Systems (the old SDS) and was still living in California. He ran planning and finance in Rochester. After a six-month study, the copier management group made a presentation to Peter McColough on what Xerox ought to do in the low end of the market. Following normal meeting procedure, an overview of the meeting was quickly given, including the top recommendation, take the 2200 from Fuji Xerox. "The answer is unacceptable," Glavin remembers McColough saying. "We are not going to buy a machine from Japan. The meeting was scheduled for three hours but it stopped in five minutes," Glavin said. "The group said, 'Well, if that's the answer, we haven't got the right position here today.' They walked out. The reason I remember the meeting so distinctly was that I walked out of there—I had never been involved with the Xerox management group—and I went to Ray Hay, my boss, and I said, 'Ray, how in the hell could you have a team of guys that are experts working six months on something and the old man just said, look, we aren't going to buy anything from Japan? You mean to tell me that nobody knew that?' "

Others at Xerox also remember that meeting, but McColough doesn't.

Glavin agrees with Arima that Xerox could have stalled the entire Japanese copier invasion of the United States by taking the 2200. Other industry observers make the same argument, but the idea seems unlikely. Savin and Ricoh were well into the development of the 750 by that time, and no one could have stopped Paul Charlap from his appointed duty. Even Glavin's boss, Kearns, disagrees: "I have never bought that thesis."

On the other hand, while the 2200 wouldn't have stopped the Japanese, it may have slowed them down. Rank Xerox proved that with the 2202, which was a speeded up version of the 2200. The U.S. finally took a Fuji Xerox machine in 1979, the 2300. It was so successful that in 1980 700 tons' worth of machines had to be airlifted to the United States, in addition to regular ocean shipments. With the 2300, Fuji Xerox started to regain market share in Japan.

Yuji Okano is a public relations specialist for Fuji Xerox based in Tokyo. He is in his late-thirties. He usually awakes at 6:30 A.M. so he can catch the

7:30 train for the one-and-a-half-hour commute to the office. He doesn't return home until 12:30 the next morning.

"When do you sleep?" he was asked.

"Saturdays," he said.

Okano is married and has two small children.

Quality control was practiced at Fuji Film, which won the Deming Prize in 1956. When Fuji Xerox became a manufacturing company, it instituted its own statistical quality control measures for production under the guidance of Professor Tetsuichi Asaka of the University of Tokyo. This was the beginning of QC circles. Kobayashi's New Xerox movement took those activities companywide, and today there are more than 1,780 active QC circles at Fuji Xerox.

The first goal of the New Xerox movement was to design and build a copier in half the time and at half the cost of previous machines. The Fuji Xerox 3500 accomplished that. Code-named Ace, it was the 914 of Fuji Xerox and showed that they were capable of operating and thriving in the post–oil shock business environment. Teams of Xerox engineers traveled to Japan to study the project and composed long reports that said the 3500 would never meet its cost, schedule, or reliability targets. They were a little right and a lot wrong. Original specifications called for a 60-cpm machine; Ace came in at 40 cpm. The goal was to complete the machine in two years; it took twenty-six months. It also exceeded its cost target somewhat, but only fifty-two people worked on it and the total development cost was only $8 million. "The 3500 was a damn good machine," David Kearns says. "Fuji Xerox learned a great deal doing that."

Kearns first visited Japan and Fuji Xerox in 1975. He has since made the trip more than twenty-five times. His first impression was: "How is Fuji Xerox ever going to be successful? They were basically taking equipment designed in the U.S. and making changes to it for their market. What that did was bring the product to market later and at a higher cost against their competitors over there, who I realized even then had lower costs, though I didn't realize how much lower. I encouraged them to begin to develop some products of their own, which they wanted to do." Kearns, at that time, didn't have responsibility for product development in the U.S., so he wasn't concerned about competition between the two groups. "When I first saw the Ace machine, I applauded," he says. "I really was impressed. There were a number of people at Stamford who thought that was not a good thing to do."

After success with the 3500, Tony Kobayashi challenged the workers at Fuji Xerox to win the Deming Prize. The workers accepted his challenge. People would actually punch out after their shifts and then go back and work another eight hours without punching in again because they didn't want to charge the company for the time. TQC was expanded to vendors and to subsidiary companies. Xerox Corporation is continuing that same strategy today with its vendors around the world.

Product development is now one of Fuji Xerox's strengths. It spends 8.5 percent of revenues on R & D in addition to a 3 percent technology royalty to Xerox Corporation. The key to that strength in copier development lies in the closeness and cooperation between the designers and manufacturing, not in automation. In fact, the Fuji Xerox Ebina plant was one of the last of the Japanese copier facilities to automate its materials handling in mid-1985. During a tour of the facilities in early 1985, Sharp, Canon, and Ricoh were far advanced. For instance, at one station in Ebina, a worker visually inspected the parts packages on a conveyor and decided where to route them. At Canon and Ricoh, and even Webster, that function is performed automatically by a light sensor reading a bar code. Ebina's top priorities are automating parts handling and then moving into automated production. The goal is to complete automation by 1987.

The major advantage at Ebina, however, is that the design engineers are down the hall from the manufacturing floor. If there is a problem, it gets solved quickly. The design community at Ricoh and Canon are offsite from manufacturing. In Europe, mid-volume Xerox copiers are designed at Welwyn Garden City in England and manufactured across the English Channel at Venray. Even in Webster, the designers are located in a different building from manufacturing. "Sometimes even a walk down the hall is too far when you have a problem," says Yoichi Oshima, manager of product planning and program management at Ebina. Shortly after Oshima began his current job he moved his office down the hall to a site just off the main manufacturing floor.

Oshima works for Motohiko Tsuchiya, the Wayland Hicks of Fuji Xerox. Tsuchiya headed the New Xerox movement, reporting directly to Tony Kobayashi. He echoes Kobayashi's philosophy on the never-ending process. "QC training is elementary school," Tsuchiya says. "Many people felt good about winning the Deming Prize, but our work was just beginning."

Kearns's comments recalling when he first talked to Kobayashi about total quality control sound oddly similar. "I did not understand the real meaning," he says. "I almost went back to school. When they talked about total quality control they meant running their company in a very different way. I really didn't understand that then. As I understood more of what they were doing, and as others within the company did, I think that became an important motivator, a real knowledge base for change at Xerox."

The Fuji Xerox product development system is patterned after Xerox Corporation's low-, mid-, and high-volume business units, which were set up in 1981. Fuji Xerox established low-volume and mid-to-high volume units in 1982. In 1983, they were combined under Tsuchiya. For each product, a team is assembled that remains together from concept to launch. Service technicians are brought in during the early stages of a project to test their reactions to new machines. This helps designers better understand the service requirements of a machine. Typical development time for a so-called clean sheet product is two to three years. A derivative product can be pushed out much more quickly. About sixty engineers are involved on a typical project, and about six months before mainline production begins, many key assembly-line workers are used to make prototypes. These workers are shifted back to the mainline and their experience helps the factory reach full production faster. The whole idea is to shift more responsibility to the manufacturing line. "You are manufacturing the machine so you should develop how you want to do it," Tsuchiya tells his production people. "Come to the model shop and develop your concept."

In one hallway near the engineering area is a bulletin board for the employees. In January 1985, it was covered with photographs of the engineers at a year-end party. Funny hats, costumes, and bottles of Kirin beer were everywhere.

"What's the purpose of those photographs?" Oshima was asked.

"Forget 1984," he said. "This is a new year with new challenges."

Fuji Xerox has never had a strike. Ask the question, and managers get a puzzled look on their face. They don't know what a labor dispute is. Fuji Xerox has never had a lawsuit filed against it by employees alleging discrimination, or by customers, competitors, or the government. Oh, there have been some minor disputes involving a traffic accident with a company vehicle. But those have been settled quickly. Fuji Xerox has only eight people on its corporate legal staff, five of them lawyers. In comparison, Xerox Corporation has sixty-eight lawyers in the United States, not including Crum and Forster; another thirty-five outside the country, not counting Japan. Fuji Xerox legal workers aren't even lawyers in the traditional, American sense. They have gone to law school, but they haven't taken a bar exam. They handle contracts, but they don't advise senior management on legal matters, a major part of a corporate lawyer's job in the United States.

Fuji Xerox also doesn't have any female managers. "So far, women haven't stayed long enough to qualify for managerial positions," explains Kazuhiko Ijichi, manager of personnel. "Some females are project leaders, but no managers. We are prepared to promote women in the future. We expect that." At Fuji Xerox, as at many Japanese companies, it is thought that a worker's overall level of ability cannot be accurately assessed until he is well into his thirties.

The Ebina factory, located about thirty miles west of Tokyo next to Atsugi City, the site of Ricoh's main plant, accounts for 60 percent of all Fuji Xerox production. It employs 3,500 people, about 1,100 of those part-time. Full-time workers throughout Fuji Xerox are guaranteed jobs until age fifty-five to sixty. The average wage for production workers is about $12,000 a year, which includes bonuses. (Every Fuji Xerox worker gets an annual bonus; for most, it is equal to about six months' regular pay.) That's 10 percent higher than the average wage at Canon and about 20 percent higher than the average wage at Ricoh's Atsugi plant. While only about 11 percent of the full-time employees are women, they make up the majority of contract workers or part-timers. The plant has seven of its own buses and hires eighteen more to help transport the workers to company-owned dorms or other housing. There are no Xerox dorms in Rochester.

About 400 workers live in bachelor dorms, for which they pay less than $40 a month. "It's a steal," says Kazu Sugiyama, who was product manager for the 1055 and lived in the United States for three years while helping prepare the 1075 for the Japanese market. Another 1,000 workers with families live in contract housing, subsidized by Fuji Xerox. Most Fuji Xerox workers are eligible, after three years with the company, for a company loan with which to buy a home.

At Ebina, all the workers dress in blue uniforms and wear blue hats. In one section of the plant a huge chart lists the names of every worker. Next to each name are colored dots, a different color for each month of the year; each dot represents a suggestion that worker has made. The average worker makes 200 suggestions a year; the highest total is 1,700. Many of the suggestions deal with new tools or alterations in the workers' workstations that will help them be more productive. Most of the suggestions are implemented.

Ebina has 124 main vendors, 57 percent of whom are located within thirty miles of the plant; not one is outside Japan. Typical parts inven-

tory is five working days, which will be reduced to two and a half by
1987. Lead time for production was six months in 1982. Now it is two
months. When a brand new machine model is introduced it starts down
the regular production line at the rate of fifty a day. It will take about a
month or 1,000 machines to reach full production. Because the designers work so closely with manufacturing, there are very few design changes
once mass production begins—an average of twenty per machine and
that's usually within the first month. The company's goal is to solve all
problems during the preproduction stage. If problems occur on the
mainline, a massive effort is needed to correct them. Production capacity at Ebina is much like Venray: about 200 mid-volume console models
a day.

The setting was surreal. The music was Japanese, but it had an odd quality about it, almost as if someone was playing the Star Spangled Banner on a
sitar. The curtain across the stage was embroidered with a large peacock. The
people in the audience were dressed in three-piece suits. Tony Kobayashi
walked onto the stage and said good morning. In unison, the crowd responded. Kobayashi talked about the theme for the day: On the cover of the
program were two pyramids and four camels lumbering across the desert. The
pyramids were built over a long period of time by thousands of people. Camels walk slow but they make steady progress, kind of like the story of the tor-
toise and the hare. Kobayashi talked about the accomplishments of the
company, but at one point said, "I feel like being skeptical." When he finished, two young workers in suits took the stage and acted as cheerleaders to
get the crowd warmed up. On cue, 450 people stood. Tony Kobayashi, other
members of his board of directors, they all sang the QC Circle Song:

> With beaming smiles exchanged
> Friends gather with bright spirits
> Ah, these friends talk about
> New dreams of quality control
> And strive with goals well in mind
> QC Circle filled with light
>
> With morale constantly growing
> The days assume the pure mission
> Ah, these days are beautiful
> Prosperous enterprises bloom as flowers
> They strive for the ideal of tomorrow
> QC Circle filled with aspiration

By communicating well with each other
The path is chosen with proper measure
Ah, that path means happiness
Further growth of Japanese culture
Powerfully and affluently
QC Circle filled with future
Welcome to the Xerox Circle Convention.

Fuji Xerox has been regaining market share, on both a unit and copy volume basis, in Japan, just as Xerox has in both the United States and Europe. Most people in the industry concede that Japan is the toughest copier market in the world. No one releases exact figures for domestic placements or copy volume, but Fuji Xerox calculates that during 1985 it had 50 percent of the copy volume in Japan, while Ricoh had 20 percent and Canon 10 percent. In terms of unit placements, Ricoh led with 35 percent, Canon had 21 percent, and Fuji Xerox 20 percent, up slightly from the year before. The reason for the disparity in shares is the same as in the U.S.: Fuji Xerox is strongest in the larger, higher-volume machines that produce most of the copy volume. That's also where most of the profits are, 80 percent in the case of Fuji Xerox. Ricoh is stronger in the smaller machines, and Canon is stronger in the United States than in Japan.

Fuji Xerox divides Japan into three markets: big cities, medium-level business establishments, and rural areas. It's similar to Xerox Corporation's approach in the United States. Fuji Xerox has five sales channels:

1. Direct sales: 54 branches, 206 locations, 2,500 salesmen.
2. Sales subsidiaries: 29 marketing subsidiaries set up as joint ventures, 51 percent owned by Fuji Xerox—some of these are with Suntory, a major distillery in Japan—with more than 1,500 salesmen.
3. Dealers: Some sell two or three kinds of products, and since in Japan many companies want exclusive dealers, this is a rather unique approach. Fuji Xerox had 500 dealers at the end of 1985 and set a goal of 1,000 by 1988.
4. So-called push channels: Sales agents go out and kick a door and say hello.
5. So-called pull channels: This is storefront business; Fuji Xerox has four stores in Japan on an experimental basis.

Ricoh's direct sales force, by contrast, is limited to national major accounts such as the central government and has more than 4,000 dealers in Japan. Canon uses only dealers, roughly 800 in Japan, for its NP copiers; for its personal copiers, Canon has roughly 3,000 outlets, including stationery, camera, department, and discount stores.

About 30 percent of all Fuji Xerox establishments are concentrated in the Tokyo and Osaka areas. This represents more than 60 percent of the market value of the products sold. "If we want to conquer Japan we must conquer Tokyo and Osaka," says Haruhiko Yoshida, manager of the marketing planning department. In the 350 miles between Tokyo and Osaka are two-thirds of Japan's 120 million people—that equals 75 percent of the country's buying power. Obviously, winning the Tokyo-Osaka market is a must if you want a high market share.

Fuji Xerox is convinced Xerox Corporation will have to adopt a similar aggressive dealer strategy. The problem is not just having a good low-volume, low-cost copier product, but also having a strong distribution network that can move those machines in large numbers and at low cost. "We need the dealers from two viewpoints," Yoshida says. "Market share and profitability. In PPCs the mid- and high-volume areas are almost mature, almost saturated. So if we want to install our product we have to replace Canon and Ricoh. Some customers don't buy a brand, they buy from a particular dealer because he is a friend. We have switched our strategy to forge a better relationship with dealers. If we succeed in our dealer operation it will be good know-how for Xerox Corporation in the future."

One area in which Fuji Xerox had great success was stopping IBM from becoming a major factor in copiers in Japan. The giant computer maker had serious designs on the Japanese copier market shortly after it launched its first plain paper copier in the United States in 1971. Fuji Xerox, however, stopped the attack dead. Today, there are fewer than a hundred IBM copiers in all of Japan. This despite the fact that IBM Japan, at almost $4 billion a year in revenues, is one of Japan's biggest companies. In order to do this, Fuji Xerox identified every IBM trial site or account in Japan. It then got a Xerox machine on the site, even if it had to put it in for free. It also developed a new machine on short-notice, a speeded-up 2400. Fuji Xerox then gave special pricing against IBM. The strategy worked. Today, IBM is no factor in the Japanese copier market.

Fuji Xerox also has operating companies in Korea, Taiwan, Philippines, Indonesia, and Thailand. Those markets, however, account for less than 5 percent of the company's total revenue. A sore point is the fact that in other areas in which Fuji Xerox would normally consider its territory—Singapore, Australia, New Zealand, and China—it has to export through Rank Xerox because that company holds the territorial rights.

At one time, Fuji Xerox products even had to be first shipped to London where they were reshipped to Australia or Singapore. It doesn't happen anymore, but Rank Xerox still attaches its own markup to the products. "Since virtually all of our competitors are Japanese, that markup puts us at a price disadvantage in those areas," Yoshida says.

During a tour of the new Fuji Xerox training center at Tsukahara, near the base of Mount Fuji, we passed a courtyard that had a highly polished metal cone in the middle. "Remember that," Yoshiaki Nagai, a senior technical trainer, said. "I'll explain later." We passed two more courtyards—one had a tree, the other a stone statue. "Remember that," Nagai said after each one. Later he explained: "In Japan, when we do things we think in terms of three things: mind, technique, and body. The stone is our mind, the tree our body, and the cone our technology or technique, always progressing to the top."

In the United States, workers jump from company to company to gain new experiences. In Japan, they move from job to job within the same company. Many of those changes would be considered lateral moves in the United States and not promotions. In Japan, however, they are considered important for training and learning. About 1 percent of Fuji Xerox revenues are spent on education and training. Hirosuke Yoshino, manager of the management development and training department, believes each employee should spend about 5 percent of his or her working time in some educational activity. "Otherwise the company can't expect to improve its employees."

The Tsukahara training center was completed in October 1984 at a cost of $8 million. It has more than 2,000 Xerox office machines on site for use in training service employees. It has two video studios, one two-stories high, that can simulate a small office environment for interpersonal relations training. In 1984, more than 6,000 people were trained at Tsukahara. The shortest stay was two days, the longest fifty-three, for a basic training program required of all new employees.

About twenty Fuji Xerox instructors teach English to 350 employees a year. Anyone who would have contact with Xerox Corporation must learn English. The American parent company does not have a similar program for the Japanese language.

On the floor of the Suzuka Fuji Xerox factory in Suzuka City, near Nagoya, are eleven injection molding machines, making everything from small plastic copier parts to rubber rollers. There isn't a human within fifty feet; the machines run twenty-four hours a day, automatically. The raw materials are automatically supplied and the finished parts are automatically picked up by unmanned dorries. The parts are shipped the same day they are manufactured. Even the dies for the different parts are changed automatically.

Suzuka Fuji Xerox is one of five subsidiary companies of Fuji Xerox. Companies establish subsidiaries to take advantage of a more favorable location or wage situation, a common practice in Japan. The subsidiaries aren't bound by the same labor agreements as the parent company. Suzuka makes parts for copiers as well as printed circuit boards for Toshiba personal computers, parts for home appliances and automobiles, and even a practice putting machine for Matsushita. It has just begun to market its products around the world, including the United States. The plant has thirteen shaft-making machines that are operated the same way as the injection molding machines. They run twenty-four hours a day and only three or four workers are needed each shift. The same computer that controls the delivery of raw materials and the shipment of finished parts also handles customer billing. Most of the suppliers of the raw materials used in the plant are an hour away in Nagoya. Typical inventory levels of raw materials are two to three days and some electronic components can be stocked for up to a month, depending upon shortages in the semiconductor industry.

Each machine in the $20 million plant, which was completed in December 1982, is labeled with its cost and the operator's name. "That's so each worker knows the investment we have in him," says Hiro Matsumoto, managing director of Suzuka Fuji Xerox. The plant won a factory automation prize from the *Japan Economic Journal* (the same prize won by Ricoh's Atsugi plant in 1984) just eleven months after it opened. Because it is so advanced, the plant is popular for tours. In its first two years of operation, more than 200 Xerox Corporation personnel went through Suzuka and more than 4,000 Japanese customers. "We are very glad to have many visitors because after a while they will be our customers," Matsumoto says. "If a prospect comes to our plant, there is a 95 percent chance he will do business with Suzuka. He will be that impressed."

In 1984, Xerox Corporation bought 1 percent—$500,000—of Suzuka's production. In 1985, that was doubled to $1 million. Matsushita buys some parts from Suzuka that eventually wind up in copier components it supplies to Canon and Ricoh, but Canon and Ricoh have not yet contacted Suzuka directly. "We wish they would," says president Chuji Kurihara. "We'll sell to anybody."

It was 1978. Jim O'Neill, then in charge of copier development and manufacturing for Xerox, was in Japan to review a proposed laser printer based on the 3500. O'Neill, who previously had worked at Ford, had a reputation for asking questions that could always be answered by numbers.

"How many people worked on this project?" he asked the five young Fuji Xerox engineers making the presentation.

"We did," they said.

"How long did it take you?" O'Neill asked.

"Six months," they said.

"I'm not even going to ask you my third question," O'Neill said. "The cost is insignificant."

Kearns doesn't discount the complaints Fuji Xerox has about being stifled, about not being able to sell enough of its products around the world, but he says Wayland Hicks and Bob Adams have similar discussions with Rank Xerox and Dwight Ryan. Everybody wants the marketing groups to take more of their product.

"Fuji Xerox has been good for Xerox," Kearns says. "We make good money [about a third of Fuji Xerox profits go to the United States]. We have gotten good products from them. I do think we have to be careful inside the company not to build up Fuji Xerox bigger and better than it is. There are a lot of things they do better in Webster than they do at Fuji Xerox. And there are things they are still doing better at Fuji Xerox than we are. But I tell you, we're gaining on them. And we're going to catch them. I hear statements from the Japanese, even Fuji Xerox, today that sound like Americans twenty years ago. You talk about Singapore or Korea and they say, 'No, they don't have the quality, they don't have the infrastructure, they don't have the trade experience, they don't have the education.' It's kind of interesting."

28

David Kearns—
Echoes of Joe Wilson

In the long run, our customers are going to determine whether we have a job or whether we do not. Their attitude toward us is going to be the factor determining our success. Every Xerox person must resolve that his most important duty is to our customers.

—JOE WILSON

ONE DAY each month, David Kearns answers phone calls from Xerox customers. If he is in a meeting when a customer calls, he leaves and takes the call. Complaints are handled immediately. This isn't just for large customers. Kearns listens to those with only a single Xerox machine. The telephone duty rotates among the top twenty Xerox officers and managers at Stamford headquarters. Kearns has adopted Joe Wilson's twenty-year-old statement as the motto for today's Xerox Corporation.

"A commitment to quality must be our most basic value," Kearns says. "And when I speak of quality I mean giving our customers what they want and what they expect."

Quality and the customer: Many Americans companies today are trying to get back to those basics. No one, however, is doing it with the same vigor as Xerox. All 100,000 Xerox employees around the world will have gone through up to forty-eight hours of formal training in quality by 1987. Kearns is determined that his legacy to the company, when he leaves in 1990, will be quality. He has stated publicly that he wants Xerox to be recognized as one of the premier quality companies in the world.

"We hear these wonderful tales of the good old days when Joe Wilson had the capacity to build this sense of teamwork," says George

Pake, the founder and still president of Xerox's Palo Alto Research Center. "It's probably too early in David Kearns's career to make that kind of comparison, but David certainly is building a teamwork spirit in the company and I greatly enjoy seeing it."

More than any other individual, Kearns, in his quest for quality, is responsible for the changes that have occurred and continue to occur at Xerox.

- Kearns was among the first at Xerox to truly recognize the significance of Fuji Xerox, how it was coping with its own problems and how it could be a more valuable asset for the company as a whole. An American company can never operate in exactly the same way as a Japanese company, but it can borrow and adapt some techniques.
- He recognized the need to completely alter Xerox's product development system. The old method was stagnating. Products were getting lost in the bureaucracy and Xerox people were fighting among each other rather than against outside competitors.
- He recognized the need to shrink overhead and increase productivity.
- He adopted the practice of competitive benchmarking companywide as a way to measure and challenge Xerox performance. Benchmarking remains an important element of his quality strategy.
- He saw the importance, later than he should have, of unifying the Xerox sales force and using the contacts the company already had in offices around the world through its copiers to also sell new technologies and systems equipment.
- Most importantly, he recognized the necessity of getting his people to believe in the changes that were occurring.

Xerox has regularly coined fancy names for new programs or company efforts to help the company perform better: Overhead Value Analysis; Business Effectiveness. Deadening names, really. The reaction from the employees was just as deadening. They derisively called them the "Flavor of the Month." They knew they would hear a lot of talk about the program for a while, but then it would fade away, just like all the rest. Nothing really changed.

Xerox still hasn't gotten away from the names. It's quality effort, for example, is called Leadership Through Quality. But a funny thing has been happening since the effort was begun in 1983 with the Kearns pronouncement: "This may very well be the most significant strategy that Xerox has ever embarked on.'' People are taking it seriously—even those who scoffed at it when it began are changing. They can see their bosses and the brass in Stamford doing exactly what they preach: Pay more attention to the customer. They are seeing the new attitude reaping benefits in the marketplace through increased market share. They are seeing how the new attitude has resulted in accelerated product development. The engineers are listening to their customers—Xerox servicemen and salesmen as well as users—and making changes in response to what they are hearing. Even former newspaper guys, who can be among the most cynical people around, in the Xerox public relations department admit this effort is something different.

Frankly, Xerox workers in the United States would laugh at Kearns if he asked them to sing Fuji Xerox's Quality Circle song. But in effect, he has them doing something very similar. Everyone in the company, from the PR staff to the secretaries at Stamford headquarters asks: Who is my customer and am I meeting his or her needs?

Kearns was once asked why anybody should take his new program seriously? What was different about it from all of those programs that preceded it? His reply was uncharacteristically testy: "We understand now that it never ends," he said. "Before we thought that after we reached a certain point, improved a certain bit, fine, we could stop. But it's a whole different way. Our competitors will continue to get better and so will we. It's like in sports, you have to win a new pennant every single year. We're in a worldwide competitive battle. Next year will be tougher than the year before and it will continue to go like that."

In many ways, Dave Kearns is indeed another Joe Wilson. In fact, there was rejoicing in some company quarters when he was named chief executive in 1982. A hometown boy was running Xerox again, all would be well. Kearns, like Wilson, grew up in Rochester. He attended the University of Rochester as an undergraduate and today is chairman of the school's board of trustees, a position once held by Wilson. Kearns's father, Wilfrid Kearns, was a prominent Rochester businessman, as was Joe Wilson's father. David Kearns joined Xerox in 1971 after seventeen years at IBM, where he was a vice president in the data processing division, the training ground for IBM's top management. Bill Glavin, also from IBM, encouraged Kearns to switch companies. Glavin thought either one of them could wind up running Xerox. When Kearns and Glavin were moving up at Xerox in the 1970s, IBM watched closely. Some top IBM management meetings had a single topic: Who was doing better at

Xerox? The Ford guys or the IBM guys? IBM likes to see its alumni succeed. It's a vote of confidence for its own management training and selection process.

Kearns is still fond of IBM and his days there. He tells about how he once gave a demonstration to a group that included Tom Watson— Mr. Watson, Kearns says. "I was quite a bit further down in the organization than I am now. So I got a little nervous during the presentation. I was pouring a glass of water when Mr. Watson asked a question. I turned to him, answered 'yes,' and poured the water all over the floor." Once, when talking about one of his daughters, who had just announced plans to marry a Xerox salesman, he reflected on the different policies at IBM and Xerox toward hiring children of executives. IBM encourages it, Xerox doesn't allow it. "It's interesting when you think of it," Kearns said. "Tom Watson, Jr., was at IBM because of his father. Joe Wilson was really at Haloid because of his father. They both came to different conclusions about kids in the business."

Kearns first worked with IBM as a salesman back in Rochester. One of his first accounts was a struggling company called Haloid. That was 1955. "I never made much money on that account," Kearns says, laughing. "But the guy that took my place sure did."

The biggest impression you get of David T. Kearns, whether it's the first meeting or after a long period of study, is that he is . . . well, very human. Peter McColough talks about the quiet types at Xerox. Kearns fits that description. He raised rabbits as a kid and sold them to University of Rochester researchers. Later, when he attended the U of R, his grades were average, many Cs. He washed out of navy pilot training because of air sickness, but now has a private pilot's license. He drives his own car—a Chrysler—to work, no limo, and runs regularly, even once competing in the New York City Marathon.

Kearns's office is filled with photographs of his family. They are on the wall behind his desk, on his desk, on his stand-up reading and writing desk—and on a coffee table in the reception area off to the side of his desk. He has six children. Family is important to Kearns, just as it was to Wilson; he can talk with great passion about restoring Xerox's dominance and beating the Japanese and the next moment mention that he has to be home for parent's night at his son's school. "Or else I will be in trouble," he says. No matter where he is or what business is pressing, he tries to be home for dinner. That is family time.

He was going on a weekend camping trip one day in 1977 to the Adirondacks with his family and some friends when McColough informed him that Archie McCardell was moving to International Harvester and that he wanted Kearns to be the next Xerox president. Kearns still went camping, at McColough's urging.

Kearns likes being the boss at Xerox, but has made it clear that in 1990, when he is sixty, he wants to do something different. His highest pay at Xerox was $709,000 in 1981, the best year for Xerox earnings and the year before he became CEO. In 1982 and 1983, his compensation declined along with the company's performance, and in 1984 it started increasing again. He owns about 20,000 shares of Xerox stock, a fact of which he doesn't hesitate to remind complaining shareholders at annual meetings, and has options on about another 140,000 shares. His fortune is tied to the company just as the other shareholders. He is a member of the boards of directors at Time Incorporated, Chase Manhattan Bank, N.A., and Chase Manhattan Corporation.

He was once asked if he thought he was underpaid. He quickly acknowledged that he makes less than other chief executives of companies in the office equipment industry and of companies similar in size to Xerox. And he mentioned the salary declines, then he added: "But, of course, the answer is 'no.' For a young man from Upstate New York I never expected to ever make this much money. And of course, my mother is extraordinarily happy."

Kearns lets his top managers have a lot of autonomy, but he also keeps reminding them that he is watching. A story once appeared in one of the Rochester newspapers quoting a customer critical of the treatment he received from Xerox and praising the treatment from Kodak. Kearns sent a clipping to Dwight Ryan with the note: "How did this happen?"

His greatest satisfaction at the company seems to come through seeing his people do well. He talks about calling Joe Marino to congratulate the chief engineer after the launch of the 1090. "Those guys are terrific," Kearns says. "It's one of those things where you love to see a guy like Marino win." When Dwight Ryan's sales group broke all records for outright copier sales in the last quarter of 1984, Kearns said: "I think the most fun I have had in the business was talking to that group. I really had a good time."

Xerox employees love to hear him speak, mainly because of his enthusiasm. It's contagious. He speaks only from notes, which frustrates his speech writers and makes company lawyers nervous, but he is good on the run. At the 1985 annual meeting in Rochester, a shareholder named Myron Jacobs asked about Xerox bonuses to executives. Kearns called Mr. Jacobs by his first name and told the other shareholders how he had made his first IBM sale to Jacobs. "I can't believe that after twenty-five years the chairman still remembered my name and my company,"

Jacobs said to the gathering. "A salesman never forgets his first sale," Kearns said.

Kearns may have had trouble understanding the concept of quality when he first talked to Tony Kobayashi of Fuji Xerox, but he understands it today and constantly talks about it in his speeches, both to Xerox and outside audiences. A common example:

"I've never quite understood why it's taken American business so long to grasp the importance of quality. Maybe it's because most people wrongly assume that quality is an intangible that cannot be measured. In fact, quality can be precisely measured by the oldest and most respected of measurements in business: Profit. The reason for that is very simple. You might think it costs more to make a better product because it takes more time and energy. But, in the end, the costs of making that product better are actually lower because you don't have to go back and fix the defects. In other words, the cost of quality is more than offset by the gains of doing it right the first time."

Kearns and Xerox extend that concern beyond the manufacturing line. The focus on quality also means quality management. The company doesn't have to make up for poor decisions. Fred Henderson, a corporate vice president who oversees the Leadership Through Quality effort (Xerox thinks so much of the term that it won't allow it to be abbreviated in company publications or even company communications, official, or unofficial), says 85 to 90 percent of a company's quality problems are a result of senior management. No effort to improve quality will be successful without their full support.

The costs of Xerox's formal quality training are enormous. Kearns and his group of top managers personally went through six and a half days of training. The minimum amount of time is about forty hours. The training centers on group effectiveness and lays out a step-by-step process by which to determine what the customer's needs are and how they can be met. "We focus a lot on how to make meetings more effective because that's where a lot of work can get done," Henderson says. "The process takes the bureaucracy out. It balances the strong personalities that used to dominate. It forces them to be just one person and not a bully. It gets the good ideas out on the table and gets the decisions closer to the facts."

For a training video on quality, Xerox rented a diner in Richfield, Connecticut, from midnight to 6:00 A.M., and had people play the roles of cook, waiter, receptionist, and hungry diner. "It's a simplistic example," Henderson says, "but it really does show all the relationships and how people interact."

By the end of 1984, 4,000 top managers had been trained in Leadership Through Quality. By the end of 1985, 13,000 Xerox managers and more than 30,000 individual workers were trained. There were about 250 people certified as trainers. Xerox won't say what it is spending on Leadership Through Quality, but just in terms of salaries alone, the number is huge. Based on an average salary of about $38,000, the cost for the trainers is more than $9 million a year. The value of the time for all 100,000 employees over three years is more than $70 million. This is in addition to the $125 million Xerox estimates that it spends every year to retrain about 40 percent of its employees to manufacture, sell, and service new products. The payoff, however, is also large. Xerox thinks the cost of poor quality can equal up to 20 percent of a company's annual sales—more than $2 billion a year for Xerox. Through its Leadership Through Quality effort, Xerox thinks it can grow to $30 billion in annual revenues by 1992.

Xerox defines quality as conformance to customer requirements. It's basically the same definition Phil Crosby created in his book, *Quality Is Free*. Henderson and several other Xerox officers, in fact, attended Crosby's school while they were formulating their own strategy. "We have consciously never called this a program," Henderson says. "Programs have start dates and stop dates and come in binders." Henderson says Crosby helped focus Xerox on manufacturing, Fuji Xerox helped focus on the customer. Henderson and his group then spent most of their time applying what worked in manufacturing to other functions in the business, such as secretaries, payroll, personnel, and telephone operators.

Ask any Xerox employee in the world today about quality and you will get the same answer: Quality is not goodness or luxury but providing what the customer wants. It doesn't make sense to give the customer a Cadillac, at Cadillac prices, if all he wants is a Chevy. Quality is not inspected into products, but built in. The term "customer" is also broadly defined. Customers can be external or internal. "We ask a sales rep what he really needs to do his job better, a fifty-page full-color brochure or a two-page checklist," says Deborah Smith, a vice president for personnel under Dwight Ryan. "Do you really need that 300-page report I send you every month? No, then I won't do it."

The strategy is set for the long term, a concept foreign to Xerox during the supergrowth years of the 1960s and early seventies when ninety days was considered long term. The company and its people were moving fast. If a manager didn't get a promotion or new job at least once every two years he would think his career had topped out. Henderson is a good example of the mobility during those years. He joined the company in 1966 as a sales trainee in Atlanta. In 1970, he moved to Rochester. In 1971, he became the branch manager in Wilmington, Delaware. In 1973, he became the branch manager in Washington, D.C. In 1974, he moved to California and became the operations manager for seven branches. In 1976, back to Rochester as national service manager. In 1977, back to the West Coast as western regional manager. In 1979, he moved to Stamford as a vice president in marketing.

"Xerox has been what's referred to as a fast-track company," Kearns said in a 1982 interview, as he was formulating his quality strategy. "People expected very fast promotions. I think a lot of the satisfaction came from thinking about the next job or the promotion rather than the job they had. From a management standpoint, what we need to do is create an environment in which satisfaction comes from the job you have. Not that people shouldn't be ambitious and looking for new jobs, but people are going to be in jobs longer than they were. Therefore, they really have to get satisfaction out of that job, not just say, "Well, I'll put up with this for the next two years because I know I'm going to get another job after that.""

When Kearns became chief executive, some industry observers admitted he was a nice guy, but that was exactly what the company didn't need. Xerox needed somebody who was hard. A strong leader. They wondered if he would be tough enough to make the tough decisions that were necessary.

Kearns still doesn't come across as tough, but he is proving to be exactly what Xerox needed. He has made the tough decisions. But more importantly, he has been a pioneer in American industry in recognizing and coping with the Japanese manufacturing challenge, rather than just complaining about it and pleading for protection.

As Shelby Carter, the former top salesman at Xerox, says, "You can tell the pioneers because all the arrows are in their backs."

Attitude. State of mind. That's what is important, David T. Kearns was saying.

"President Reagan keeps talking about the country being better off," he said. "The attitude is almost more important than the reality. It's the same at Xerox." It was the end of a long interview in his office. Kearns was tired, but he was getting into sacred territory. "We really are better,'' Kearns said of Xerox. ''It's very important for our people to know that and understand that. But at the same time, we have to be much better.''

He went over to his stand-up reading desk and brought back a lapel button that said: ''Be Better.''

''I have this little thing that I write on my notes,'' he said. '' 'DTK. BB.' Be Better. I'm always writing myself little notes when I'm going into a meeting. 'Behave yourself Kearns. Don't get upset.' This whole thing about the New Xerox, our new attitude, is that we're damn good, but we got to be better. And it will always be that way. We have to get ourselves in that mode so that we don't get to a certain level and say, 'Now it's the good old days again. We don't have to keep improving.' The good old days when Mr. Wilson and Peter were running the company are gone. They had a whole different set of issues. They didn't have the Japanese and they didn't have any money. They couldn't fund the business. They didn't have any marketing organization. Be Better. That's the kind of thought process we have to get into. We are good and we have to understand that we are good and that we have to be much better than we are. Not a little bit better but a lot better.'' His voice dropped to whisper. ''Because the Japanese are.

''The big difference between Americans and Japanese, and Hicks has heard me say it so many times that he is getting sick and tired of it, is expectation levels. Their expectation levels are tremendous. And where we sometimes question whether our competitors can do it, they absolutely believe their competitors will do it, so they reset their goals a little bit higher. So if General Motors sinks a billion dollars, or two billion or eight billion into their new car program, you can bet the Japanese have a Saturn plan of their own that's grander and better and faster than the one GM is doing. That's just the way they think. The Japanese businessman today honestly believes he can have the largest economy in the world.

''I'm still learning. Everytime I come back from Japan, I say I come back invigorated and scared to death. That's the way it should be. We can never stop improving.''

Postscript:
The Best of the Best Revisited

When the boys at the Xerox skunkworks in East Rochester scoped out a personal copier to compete against Canon, they gave it the code name Nothing. "We figured that even if we had a manufacturing cost of zero, the machine would still have a selling price that would not be competitive going through our delivery system," says John Webb, who likes to call himself and others in the skunkworks the "radical fringe of the big house." They pressed ahead. In sixteen months, a group of a dozen engineers spent $1.5 million, less than one-tenth the typical development cost, creating a prototype with a projected UMC of $220. Good, but still not good enough—the project was killed in mid-1985. Another Xerox design failure in the low end from the United States. This time, however, a funny thing happened. The Nothing team continued working. Their design for the machine's paper handling system was so good that it was adopted on a machine being created at Fuji Xerox. A small victory, certainly, but it was more than any Xerox American design team had ever done before in that market segment.

I F there's one certainty about the copier industry—and all of American industry—it's that the business of doing business isn't going to get any easier, especially in manufacturing. The easy way out would be for American companies to shift all of their production offshore, to the least costly venue, or for the American government to institute protectionist trade barriers. Those, however, are only short-term solutions. They are an admission that American companies can't be competitive and will never be competitive. Over the long haul, such measures endanger the American economy as well as the world's. Xerox has determined that to continue to be a world-class company, to reach its goal of

$30 billion to $35 billion in sales by 1992, it has to be a strong manufacturing and design company everywhere it operates in the world. There is no alternative. It has to be competitive everywhere. Certainly, some sites will be able to do some types of projects better than others, but Xerox can't abandon any of those functions completely at any location. Dave Kearns still dreams about being able to design and manufacture a low-end copier in the United States for the Japanese market. Xerox hasn't been able to accomplish that yet, but it hasn't given up trying. Indeed, in 1984, Xerox became one of the United States's top fifty exporters for the first time. The copier king ranked forty-fourth, with exports of $414 million, according to *Fortune* magazine. How does a company survive in this brave new business environment where constantly accelerating technological advances are unleashed on a world that is becoming more and more a single marketplace? There are some lessons to be learned from Xerox and the copier industry. No revelations. The lessons have been talked about many times before. But as Don Shula, coach of the Miami Dolphins, teaches, a team can't get enough of the basics. Whether your team competes in football or business, the main lesson is the same: If you can block and tackle better than the other guy, you are going to win.

Remember How You Got There in The First Place.

For Xerox, it was a combination of great technology and great marketing that made the 914 a supersuccess. That one-two punch was forgotten for a while, but the company has regained it. "The world of information systems is so bloody competitive that you have to have two things to even be remotely successful," says Xerox's Bob Adams, whose fast-growing systems group should equal the company's copier division in sales in 1990. "You need a world-class product at the time you announce it. And you need a world-class delivery system to deliver it. Neither one of those by itself is sufficient."

Concentrate on What You Do Best.

Despite all the talk about the totally electronic office of the future, the basis for future automation for the next several years will still be the copying machine, whether it uses a conventional light lens or a laser in an electronic printer. Xerox is in a better position than anyone to capitalize on that because it is the best company in the world at putting marks on paper. Unlike the computer companies going after the same business, Xerox says its entré to the office systems market is *output*. To paraphrase analyst Amy Wohl: There is about as much chance of the paperless office becoming a reality as the paperless toilet.

Know Your Competition.

Xerox, for the longest time, didn't really understand the Japanese. Now it probably knows more about them than any other American company. And more importantly, Xerox is determined to keep learning more about all of its competitors through benchmarking.

If You Got It Flaunt It.

America's great strengths are dynamic individuals and creativity. Unleash your engineers, marketeers, and managers. Don't stifle them.

Develop a Sense of Urgency.

If you wait until tomorrow, the Japanese or some other competitor will beat you to the punch.

Streamline.

Large groups only dilute individual responsibility and slow down product development.

Strive to be the Best of the Best.

Sounds corny, but why play if you're not interested in winning. *Dantotsu* should be the motto of *all* companies.

Remember the Final Judge: the Customer.

Don't get arrogant. Do your market research ahead of time and no matter how convincing the results seem, keep monitoring and checking. Don't quit sampling once the product hits the market. Follow it.

Protect the Heartland at All Costs.

It's inevitable that some competitor will find a niche, but don't let him move uncontested into the area where you make all your money. That's why Wayland Hicks stressed putting up the brick wall in the midrange with the 1045 family and why he pushed the 1075, 1090, and 9900 to counter Kodak.

If You Have a Problem, Face Up to It.

Don't blame it on a poor economy or try to hide behind cries for protectionism. Many problems in companies are well known, however, that doesn't mean the solutions are simple—they can be extremely difficult. But if you never face them or have the determination to solve them, you never will.

Understand that Business Is a Global Game.

The Japanese are learning this lesson very quickly. One day in mid-1985, a story appeared in the *Financial Times* saying the EEC would investigate the Japanese copier companies for dumping in Europe. The next day the *Financial Times* carried another story saying Canon was shifting more and more of its production for European markets to its factories in Germany and France. Canon knew what was coming and did a superb job gearing up its own public relations/lobbying effort to counteract it. The company also plans to be making copiers in the United States by 1987 at a plant it is building in Newport News, Virginia Xerox, of course, has been fostering its internationalization since the days of Joe Wilson.

Admit You Can't Do It All by Yourself.

In 1985, Xerox licensed the Landa process for high speed copying from Savin at a cost of more than $20 million. It was the largest licensing agreement for Xerox since Chester Carlson. In the mid-1970s, if anyone at Stamford had suggested licensing a competitor's technology, he probably would have been laughed out of corporate headquarters. Today, Xerox technicians are working at Benny Landa's labs in Israel and some of Landa's people are at Xerox labs in Webster. It's the best evidence yet that the not-invented-here syndrome is dead at Xerox.

A large cartoon on the wall in Bill Sullivan's office shows him dressed in a Superman outfit, smoking a pipe, holding a giant grenade, and pounding on a door marked: "Xerox Upper Brass." The date is April 13, 1976, four days after Kodak introduced its revolutionary recirculating document handler for its Ektaprint copier. Sullivan's group today draws such special assignments as custom-designing the more than 1,500 Xerox copiers on U.S. Navy ships. The 1025 that goes on submarines, for instance, is literally cut in half so it can fit down the hatch. The cartoon refers to the time Sullivan burst into a high-level meeting and lobbed a fake grenade, pin pulled, into the middle of the group. Momentary terror. "Gentlemen," Sullivan said, "there are a couple of different reactions you can have. You can sit and think it is a dud. Or, you can act as if it's real and respond." No one has to throw any dummy grenades today to make the point. The threats to Xerox, and all of American industry, are real. But there should be no terror. American companies, as Xerox has shown, can meet and beat the challenge.

Glossary

THE XEROX FAMILY

Fuji Xerox Company, Limited   A fifty-fifty partnership created in 1962 between Rank Xerox and Fuji Photo Film of Japan. The profits are split evenly. Eventually, about one-third of Fuji Xerox profits go to Xerox Corporation, plus research and development royalties. Fuji Xerox is an independent company. It coordinates projects with Xerox Corporation. Its territory is Japan, Singapore, Hong Kong, Korea, Philippines, and Taiwan. Fuji Xerox revenues are not consolidated into Xerox Corporation results.

Rank Xerox Limited   A partnership created in 1956 between Haloid and The Rank Organisation Limited of the United Kingdom. Originally it was a fifty-fifty partnership and Rank Xerox had marketing rights to the world, except North America. Xerox bought the majority 1 percent in 1969 and took over the Latin American operations. Two-thirds of Rank Xerox profits go to Xerox Corporation. Rank Xerox revenues are consolidated into Xerox Corporation financial results.

Xerox Corporation   Originally the Haloid Company, which was founded in 1906. Became Haloid Xerox, Inc., in 1958 and Xerox Corporation in 1961.

THE XEROX PROCESS

Fusing   After the image has been transferred to a piece of copy paper, heat and pressure are usually applied to embed the toner in the paper. In the early days of xerography, a chemical vapor was used to accomplish the same task. A few years after the Xerox 914 became the rage, Xerox customers, including the state of California, were discovering that the toner was falling off the paper of old copies. They were upset because they were filing these copies for posterity. Xerox had a special group work on a so-called assured fusing method. Toner doesn't usually fall off the paper anymore.

Development   The 914 used so-called cascading development, the toner cascaded over the charged silicon drum. Canon introduced jumping development with its 200-J, the toner particles actually jumped across a void rather than coming in direct contact with the drum. Many machines today use magnetic brush development, the toner is held by a magnet and then deposited on the photoreceptor. After development and transfer, soft brushes and magnets, are used to clean the photoreceptor.

Photoreceptor/Photoconductor This is the xerographic equivalent of film in a camera. A photoreceptor, coated with an electrically charged photoconductor, is exposed to the image from the original and, after development, it transfers that image to the copy. Some machines today have drum-style photoreceptors and others have organic belts. Light sensitivity is very important, just as in film. Light blue is a particularly difficult color to reproduce. The very first automatic plain paper copiers, the Xerox 914 and 813, could copy light blue very well, but they were relatively slow machines, making less than ten copies a minute. The Xerox 2400, on the other hand, which made forty copies a minute, couldn't reproduce light blue well. The original 9200, introduced in 1974, which made 120 copies a minute, couldn't either. Xerox had made a trade-off. The company knew how to increase the speed of the machine, but didn't know how to make a photoconductor that could cope at that speed with the high light sensitivity required to photocopy light blue. Today, it is still an issue, but most manufacturers can do both. Selenium was the early photoconductive material used on the drums. It is still used on many older Xerox machines. Some Japanese machines use cadmium sulphide. Canon is pioneering amorphous silicon. Kodak and Xerox are using organic photoreceptors, organic light-sensitive substances on a filmlike base.

Toner This is the xerographic equivalent of ink. After the photoconductor has been exposed, toner, which is usually a fine powder but can also be a liquid, is introduced. Because of electrical charges, the toner is attracted to the dark areas of the image. Dry toners usually consist of a plastic material with some carbon black added. The type of plastic can vary widely. Xerox uses a hard, brittle plastic and therefore has adapted a manufacturing process that breaks the plastic up into smaller and smaller pieces by literally throwing it against a wall. Kodak toner, on the other hand, is more resilient—it bounces. Many of today's machines use dual component toner, the actual toner is carried to the copy by carrier particles. Others are monocomponent development, the toner particle itself is attracted to the copy. Liquid toners are used by some Japanese manufacturers.

Xerography This is the process for making plain paper copies that was invented by Chester F. Carlson, who called his original discovery electrophotography. An Ohio State professor coined the term "xerography," from the Greek words for "dry" and "writing," when the process was being perfected at the Battelle Development Corporation, a subsidiary of the Battelle Memorial Institute in Columbus. The basic process hasn't changed much since the early days of commercialization, when copies were developed much like a photographic print. Even the fancy electronic printers sold today by Xerox, Canon, IBM, Apple, and Hewlett-Packard, among others, use the same basic process of charging, exposure, development, transfer, fusing, and cleaning. The new machines, however, use a laser instead of a light lens.

INDUSTRY TERMINOLOGY

Clean sheet A copier, or any product, developed from scratch. The 1075 was a clean sheet product.

CRD Central reproduction department. This is the copy center in a company, usually manned by highly trained personnel.

Dantotsu Tony Kobayashi first used this term in reference to the type of products Fuji Xerox must develop: superproducts, best of the best, better than best, absolutely brilliant. The term has been adopted in the United States.

Engine The actual guts of a copier, or laser printer, that put the marks on a piece of paper.

Operating company Xerox terminology for sales company. In the United States, it's BSG, Business Systems Group. The operating companies negotiate with the product suppliers—Wayland Hicks in copier products and Bob Adams in systems products—on supply and price.

PPC Plain paper copier, as opposed to CPC, coated paper copier.

RDH Recirculating document handler. Put a stack of originals in an RDH and the device automatically shuffles through them to make exposures. This greatly increases the productivity of copiers. Xerox had the first patents on these devices, but Kodak was the company that perfected the technology in 1976. This is one of the major technological differences between Japanese and American machines today, although the Japanese, with Canon leading the way, are catching up to American sophistication in document handling.

SADH Semiautomatic document handler. Requires interaction between operator and machine.

Variant A new product that is developed from an existing product. The 1090 copier is a variant of the 1075.

Walk-up This is a copier anybody in the office can use; no dedicated operator. It is in a hallway, a corner of the room, anywhere a large number of people have convenient access.

Xerox copier generations 914 and 2400 are examples of first generation, basically mechanical devices; 4000 and 9200 are second generation, electromechanical; 10 series is third, all-electronic controls. Xerox also refers to a second-and-a-half generation. These were the 8200 and 5600, which were really stopgap products, rushed to market to combat Kodak.

Index

About the Authors

Gary Jacobson, former Executive Editor of the *Times-Union*, covered Xerox activities for four years. He now works as a free-lance writer in Dallas.

John Hillkirk, technology writer and columnist at *USA Today*, has covered the copier and computer industries for several years. He is a former editor of the *Times-Union* in Rochester, the headquarters of the Xerox Corporation.